Dimitrios Meletis, Christa Dürscheid
Writing Systems and Their Use

Trends in Linguistics Studies and Monographs

Volume 369

Dimitrios Meletis, Christa Dürscheid

Writing Systems and Their Use

An Overview of Grapholinguistics

Die Druckvorstufe dieser Publikation wurde vom Schweizerischen Nationalfonds zur Förderung der wissenschaftlichen Forschung unterstützt.

Despite careful production of our books, sometimes mistakes happen. We regret that the original version of Chapter 6 'Writing system typology' is in need of correction. Please note that changes were introduced on pages 226 and 229.

ISBN 978-3-11-163176-9
e-ISBN (PDF) 978-3-11-075783-5
e-ISBN (EPUB) 978-3-11-075789-7
ISSN 1861-4302
DOI https://doi.org/10.1515/9783110757835

Library of Congress Control Number: 2022931908

Bibliographic information published by the Deutsche Nationalbibliothek
The Deutsche Nationalbibliothek lists this publication in the Deutsche Nationalbibliografie; detailed bibliographic data are available on the Internet at http://dnb.dnb.de.

This volume is text- and page-identical with the hardback published in 2022.
The book is published open access at www.degruyter.com.

Typesetting: Integra Software Services Pvt. Ltd.

www.degruyter.com

Preface

We begin our preface in an unusual way, as each of us writes a few words separately. Doing this is motivated by the genesis of the present book, which also explains why Christa Dürscheid commences with her notes (although she is the second author) followed by remarks from Dimitrios Meletis (who is the first author).

"There is [. . .] no linguistic work that synoptically presents writing-related aspects of the language system. This is the gap that this textbook aims to fill." This quote – translated into English – stems from my book on grapholinguistics (*Einführung in die Schriftlinguistik*, in short referred to as *Schriftlinguistik*), which appeared in its first edition 20 years ago now. In fact, these two sentences open its preface. I place them also at the beginning of this preface for the following reason: Although my introductory book was frequently used in teaching and also widely received by the research community, the response was mostly limited to the German-speaking world. My wish was to change this, to make *Schriftlinguistik* (both the discipline and the book) known beyond the German-language area – which has now been achieved by the publication of the present book. However, it would be wrong to assume that this monograph is merely an adaptation of the German-language introduction (even if this had been the original intention); rather, Dimitrios and I have reviewed and re-handled the broad field of grapholinguistics. Thus, our book does not centre on German, as *Schriftlinguistik* did; also, it is not a textbook but a work that presents its own theoretical approaches and is addressed to peers. Nevertheless, it is fair to say that the 2002 book on grapholinguistics is the model for this monograph, and select parts of it have found their way into two of the following chapters. It will become evident, however, that the present book goes far beyond that – which is mainly thanks to the co-authorship with Dimitrios Meletis. With that, I pass the word on to him.

The subject of writing had already fascinated me before, but it was during my studies when I picked up Christa Dürscheid's *Einführung in die Schriftlinguistik* that I discovered an entire field devoted to it. This field would soon become my primary topic of interest – and research. Most captivating for me were aspects that turned out to be research gaps pointing to relevant desiderata. For example, since an important facet of my interest in writing concerns typography, one of my first own academic ventures led to the question of how the visual appearance of writing had been treated in linguistic research. A later and much bigger project was motivated by my background in general linguistics and my focus on comparative and typological perspectives. It centres around a question that is easily posed but highly complex: What do the world's writing systems have in common? In the course of addressing this question, I attended international conferences on

https://doi.org/10.1515/9783110757835-202

writing and had the privilege to meet many scholars working in different disciplines and on diverse writing systems. When I presented my own research there – which is infused with ideas from German grapholinguistics but, as mentioned, applies this foundation to broader questions – I also observed that there was an interest in this rich tradition of studying writing that was, alas, linguistically inaccessible to many. Furthermore, I felt there was a need for a more unified framework and vocabulary that facilitates research and exchange and became determined to contribute to this goal. Meanwhile, at an important point in my career, I approached Christa and gained her as a mentor. This has shaped my research in many ways. Among the things we have in common are hopes and visions for the field of grapholinguistics, which eventually translated into the idea of reworking Christa's book together. However, our plans for an adaptation gradually turned into something new, resulting in a book that benefited from the coalescence of our two different perspectives (and generations). *Schriftlinguistik* enlightened me – I hope this new work will do the same for our readership.

At last, we both want to thank Cristina Stanley and Florian Koller for their help with the book's comprehensive bibliography. We also wish to express our gratitude to the University of Zurich, where we found the working conditions needed to write a book such as this. Finally, we would like to extend our thanks to the Swiss National Science Foundation, which generously supported the publication. And with that, there's only one thing left to say: that we wish the book the resonance that grapholinguistics deserves.

Zurich, January 2022
Dimitrios Meletis and Christa Dürscheid

Contents

1 Introduction

At the outset of this chapter, the relevance of writing in our society will be highlighted. This is followed by Section 1.1, which addresses the status of writing in contemporary linguistics and the emergence of *grapholinguistics* as the discipline devoted to it. Then, in Section 1.2, the reasons of why the study of writing was not always an accepted branch of linguistics are traced. Finally, after this historical sketch, the content and structure of this book will be presented (Section 1.3).

Writing is a cultural technology that has changed humankind by shaping the way we think and the way we communicate. The role it plays in our everyday lives in most modern societies is so vital that it is almost impossible to overstate its relevance. Indeed, when trying to imagine what one's days would look like without writing, one will likely soon realise that in literate communities, life without literacy appears almost unthinkable. As a mode of communication fundamentally different from speech, writing fulfils numerous functions. Many of these have developed only in the recent past, which led to a noticeable increase of contexts in which writing is used. Due to digitalisation, for example, writing has become a very convenient and easy way of communicating. As its use in messenger services and social media shows, it is strikingly flexible with respect to degrees of formality and registers. At the same time, it is also a deeply personal and social matter as individuals and even entire cultures use it to convey their identities – be it through the choice of a specific script (such as the Roman script), the appearance of one's handwriting in different contexts (e.g., on a shopping list vs. in a handwritten letter to a friend), the use of a specific typeface when designing a document, or the decision to obey or disobey orthographic norms, to mention only a few examples. These underline that virtually every conscious and also unconscious choice made in writing is a form of social action.

It is precisely for this reason that many people perceive writing as a skill intimately tied to themselves, so much so that it could be argued that in literate communities, writing is regarded as a common good. It is to be expected, then, that matters concerning writing potentially result in heated debates. Take as examples discussions surrounding spelling reforms, the abolishment of cursive handwriting in early literacy instruction, or the question of whether certain emojis count as written words and lead to a decay of writing. Against this background, it is undeniable that writing has ceased to stand in the shadow of speech. It is obviously no longer the conservative technique reserved for scribes of the elite that it had been in ancient societies. Instead, it is now firmly established as an integral part of many lives. As such, it has also gained relevance as a subject of research, leading to the necessity and emergence of a field devoted to it.

https://doi.org/10.1515/9783110757835-001

1.1 The emergence of grapholinguistics

In linguistics, over the course of the last decades, the investigation of writing has gradually increased in popularity (cf. the next section for an illustration of how it had previously been neglected). This ultimately resulted in the emergence of an interdisciplinary field referred to as *grapholinguistics*. Grapholinguistics, as defined by Martin Neef (2015: 711), is "the linguistic sub discipline dealing with the scientific study of all aspects of written language". The discipline's designation is a translation of German *Schriftlinguistik*, a term that had first appeared in an edited volume by German linguists Dieter Nerius and Gerhard Augst (1988) and has since become firmly established in the German-language research area, which, as will become evident below, has produced much of the central linguistic research on writing. The English equivalent *grapholinguistics*, which forms part of this book's subtitle, while not without its critics, is also gaining traction, as both a book series and a conference series have recently been named after it, to name just two examples.[1]

In a well-known German dictionary of linguistics (Glück and Rödel 2016), grapholinguistics is defined as a "label for efforts of gaining consistent descriptions and analyses of the written form of language and of developing them to a general theory of writing as a constitutive part of a general theory of language" (Glück 2016d: 596, our translation). It is notable that this effort is inherently interdisciplinary: given that writing is a complex phenomenon, it cannot be comprehensively studied by means of linguistic theories, models, and methods alone, which is why grapholinguistics integrates research from various disciplines (including psychology, cognitive science, history, pedagogy, sociology, and information design) to gain a more complete picture of writing. In short, grapholinguistics is the interdisciplinary field focused on the study of all aspects of writing.

The German term *Schriftlinguistik* is noticeably more widespread than its English equivalent *grapholinguistics*. This asymmetry reflects the fact that – at this point in time – the field is much more established in the German-language area. In fact, specifically in Germany, writing has been treated as a valuable subject of linguistics since roughly the second half of the 20th century. Simultaneously, some of the central – and first – linguistic works on writing, among them David Diringer's *The alphabet* (first published in 1948) and Ignace J. Gelb's *A study of writing* (1952, here cited in its second edition of 1963), were published in English. And indeed, to this day, the most relevant monographic works that

1 The book series *Grapholinguistics and Its Applications* is published by Fluxus Éditions (Brest). A complementary series of biennial conferences is titled *Grapholinguistics in the 21st Century*; its first iteration was held in 2018 in Brest, France, and the second one in 2020, virtually (due to the Covid-19 pandemic).

cover writing are written in English (take Coulmas 1989; Sproat 2000; Daniels 2018 as examples). The same is the case for the most important edited volume covering the world's writing systems (Daniels and Bright 1996), an encyclopaedia of writing systems (Coulmas 1996a), and an extensive bibliography (Ehlich, Coulmas, and Graefen 1996). Why, then, has the German-language research community arguably been so instrumental in the development of grapholinguistics?

Firstly, as mentioned above, in the German-language area, unlike in the Anglo-American linguistic culture, writing was not a niche topic attended to by few select scholars but had been widely accepted as a linguistic subject since at least the 1980s – so much so that at that time, in then-separated Germany, two influential research groups were founded that devoted themselves to the subject: the *Forschungsgruppe Orthographie* (established in 1974) and the *Studiengruppe Geschriebene Sprache* (started in 1981). Obviously, by that time, a paradigm shift had occurred, as German linguists no longer felt the need to justify their interest in writing (cf. Günther 1990b). A turning point was reached with the publication of an extensive handbook titled *Schrift und Schriftlichkeit/Writing and its use* (Günther and Ludwig 1994/1996). In two volumes, it includes over 140 chapters written in either German or English and covers a vast spectrum of facets of writing. Notably, it also brought together a remarkable number of scholars interested in the field, including non-German scholars. Then, in 2002, a second publication appeared in German that proved constitutive of the discipline. Not only was it the first textbook on the topic but also the first work that was explicitly termed 'grapholinguistic': *Einführung in die Schriftlinguistik* ('Introduction to Grapholinguistics'). It solidified grapholinguistics' status as a full-fledged linguistic subdiscipline and is now available in its fifth edition (Dürscheid 2016a).

With respect to the study of writing, the second major difference between the Anglo-American and German[2] research traditions is that in the latter, writing is commonly approached in a more abstract and theoretical matter, whereas works from Anglo-American linguists commonly focus, to a large degree, on the individual description of different writing systems. This also coincides with a synchronic orientation in German grapholinguistics vs. a focus on diachrony in the Anglo-American tradition. Books such as Rogers (2005), Sampson (2015), and Daniels (2018), but also the individual contributions in Daniels and Bright's (1996) edited volume describe in detail many of the world's writing systems. However, they rarely touch upon general theoretical aspects of writing as a complex phe-

2 To clarify: when we speak of the 'German' research tradition, what we mean is not necessarily research published in German but grapholinguistic research carried out in German-language countries (especially Germany) – in the context of which, notably, scholars have also published (if only few) studies in English.

nomenon, which is characteristic of the German grapholinguistic tradition. For example, German grapholinguistics has always been interested in how writing systems *can be* described instead of 'only' describing them. In other words, it addresses, at a metalevel, the methods and categories required for a further productive analysis of writing. At the same time, however, it admittedly sacrifices a universalist perspective as theoretical findings and proposals are based mostly on alphabets – and even more specifically, predominantly on the German writing system. It is also notable that most of German grapholinguistic research was exclusively published in German and is thus, alas, not readily accessible to an international readership.[3] For this reason, much of it has remained unknown outside of the German-language realm.

This book rests upon the view that a combination of both research traditions appears most promising: careful descriptions of diverse writing systems can inform theoretical work, which is hitherto based on single (in most cases alphabetic) systems. As a result, the assumption of models and units of writing as well as a general theory of writing can be refined. Thus, the following chapters are devoted to different aspects of writing, introducing and elucidating core concepts of grapholinguistics by means of examples from several writing systems. This way, the sheer diversity of the world's writing systems becomes an asset as it allows to exemplify central ideas and concepts of writing on the grounds of a large and diverse data basis. Simply put, the present book aims at gaining an integrative understanding of the complex phenomenon that is writing. At this point it must also be noted that while we strive to give as broad an overview of the contemporary situation of grapholinguistics as possible, given the breadth of diverse treatments that the topic of writing has received, the theoretical and methodological approaches we include in this book can only amount to a non-exhaustive selection. This is also reinforced by our presentation of the topic and field being subject-driven rather than oriented towards specific theoretical paradigms. Importantly, the fact that not all theories could be considered is not meant to lessen the importance of those that we do not explicitly mention.

To conclude this brief introduction to grapholinguistics, we shift the focus onto the present and, even more importantly, the future by examining the current state of the field. When it comes to central publication outlets, it is important to mention the academic journal devoted solely to writing, *Written Language & Literacy* (since 1998).[4] Like journals from other writing-related disciplines (such as

---

3 Note that much of the literature cited in this book stems from this German grapholinguistic tradition. When we cite passages from these works, the quotes represent our own translations.

4 From 2009 to 2020, there was a second journal solely devoted to writing, *Writing Systems Research*.

the psychological *Reading and Writing* or the interdisciplinary *Visible Language*), it offers a way of disseminating disciplinarily heterogeneous research on writing. Additionally, several conferences are devoted to the topic, the most important of which is a series of international workshops organised by the *Association of Written Language and Literacy*. Publications which will likely become central to the field keep appearing, such as Peter T. Daniels' (2018) book *An exploration of writing*, a culmination of his scholarship from almost three decades, or *The Routledge handbook of the English writing system* (Cook and Ryan 2016), which – precisely in line with grapholinguistics' interdisciplinary nature – combines a treatment of theoretical, historical, pedagogical, sociolinguistic, and psycholinguistic aspects of the English writing system. Another noteworthy project is a dictionary of grapholinguistics edited by Martin Neef, Said Sahel, and Rüdiger Weingarten; it has been in the works since 2012 as part of the series *Dictionaries of Linguistics and Communication Science*. It is a promising sign that a dictionary on grapholinguistics stands in line with other dictionaries for well-established fields such as morphology and syntax.

These positive developments stand in stark contrast with how writing was treated in linguistics before the second half of the 20th century. Since remnants of the view that contributed to this depreciative treatment of writing are still palpable today, the next section will outline the thinking behind the earlier disregard of writing as an object of linguistic study.

1.2 Views on writing in the history of linguistics

As evident from the previous section, grapholinguistics has developed only recently.[5] Before that, writing had been largely neglected as an object of research by linguistics and many other disciplines. One of the reasons for this is a view referred to as *logocentrism* (from Greek *lógos* 'word, saying, speech, discourse, thought'). This term was coined by French philosopher Jacques Derrida in *Of grammatology* (originally published in French as *De la grammatologie*), his famous plea for the importance of writing. There, he argues that only speech was ever recognised as a valuable object of scientific study while writing never played a role. This is precisely due to the mentioned logocentric mindset, which is characterised as follows:

5 This section as well as few designated parts in the following chapter are partially based on Dürscheid (2016a: Chapters 0 and 1).

> The distinction between speech and writing here is essential: logocentrism views thought as something essential that is mediated for the purposes of discourse, first through speech, and then later through writing. Speech is thus the original signifier of meaning, while writing is merely a signifier of a signifier [. . .]. Logocentric thought privileges speech for this characteristic as well as its interiority – 'thinking to oneself' is typically thought of as internally 'hearing oneself speak' rather than 'reading one's own writing.' (Harrison n. d.)[6]

In his book, Derrida identifies and illustrates logocentric thinking in several central philosophical texts. One of the most important critics of writing he mentions is Plato. In Plato's *Phaedrus*, Socrates reports on the Egyptian god Ammon, whose fellow deity Theuth is considered the inventor of writing in Greek mythology. In this context, Socrates takes the opportunity to scrutinise Theuth's 'invention'; three of his points of criticism shall be discussed below. Note that these passages (Phaedrus 274c–278b, reproduced here in their English translation by Robin Waterfield) are commonly used to characterise Plato as a critic of writing:

1) Writing, Socrates claims, allows for easy recollection but prevents people from using their memory:

> It will atrophy people's memories. Trust in writing will make them remember things by relying on marks made by others, from outside themselves, not on their own inner resources, and so writing will make the things they have learnt disappear from their minds.
> (Phaedrus 275a, cited from Waterfield 2002: 69)

2) The written text, Socrates continues, cannot give answers to the questions readers might have. Like a picture, the text does not speak:

> Yes, because there's something odd about writing, Phaedrus, which makes it exactly like painting. The offspring of painting stand there as if alive, but if you ask them a question they maintain an aloof silence. It's the same with written words: you might think they were speaking as if they had some intelligence, but if you want an explanation of any of the things they're saying and you ask them about it, they just go on and on for ever giving the same single piece of information. (Phaedrus 275d, cited from Waterfield 2002: 70)

3) Finally, the writer, Socrates points out, has no control over the text. What has been written has detached itself from the writer, has become independent, and is available for use and abuse by anyone:

> Once any account has been written down, you find it all over the place, hobnobbing with completely inappropriate people no less than with those who understand it, and completely failing to know who it should and shouldn't talk to.
> (Phaedrus 275e, cited from Waterfield 2002: 70)

6 The definition is taken from the website of *The Chicago School of Media Theory*, cf. https://lucian.uchicago.edu/blogs/mediatheory/keywords/logocentrism/ (accessed September 12th, 2021).

At this point, it is necessary to raise the question of whether Socrates actually warns against writing and not instead against the abuse of writing. Does it not apply to all media – including writing – that it is not the medium itself that is 'good' or 'bad' but the purposes for which it is employed by users? Hans-Georg Gadamer emphasises this line of argument in his interpretation of *Phaedrus*:

> It is hardly plausible that the invention as such was to be characterised by Plato as a doubtful merit. There is no mention of whether the stern rebuke that the wise Egyptian king administered to the inventor was meant as a rejection of the invention – of which every Plato reader knew that it had already long prevailed. Rather, it is clear that only the abuse and the temptation that lies in the written transcription of speeches and thoughts is rejected by the Egyptian king. [. . .] Writing is rather accepted as a consolation and a remedy for the forgetfulness of old age and, in a broader sense, as a means of remembrance for those who know – and know how to think. (Gadamer 1998: 15, our translation)

In this vein, Plato's criticism of writing can actually be interpreted more positively – not as a blanket warning against writing but as a suggestion of how to use it meaningfully. In any case, it is beyond question that Plato's criticism of writing applies only to the level of the individual and not to that of entire societies, which can pass on their legacy to future generations with the help of writing.

In his historical reconstruction of logocentrism, Derrida goes on to quote philosopher Jean-Jacques Rousseau, who discarded writing as a "supplement to speech" (quoted after Derrida 1997: 7). Specifically, Rousseau holds that speech represents thinking directly while writing is "nothing but a mediated representation of thought" (quoted after Derrida 1997: 144). This very view was also the one prevalent in linguistics. Let us give an example: in his central work *Principles of the history of language*, Neogrammarian Hermann Paul argues that "[n]ot merely is writing not language, but it is in no way an equivalent for it" (Paul 1891: 434). One reason he states is that every letter, every character "will still remain the sign, not for a single articulate sound, but for a series of infinitely numerous ones" (Paul 1891: 434), meaning the correspondence between signs of writing and sounds is by no means direct or exclusive. Paul partially attributes this observation that writing inadequately depicts speech to the situation that "almost every nation, instead of creating an alphabet independently to suit the demands of its own language, has adapted the alphabet of a foreign language, as best it might, to its own" (Paul 1891: 437). Paul's well-known conclusion is that the relation between writing and language is about the same "as that of a rough sketch to a picture worked out with the utmost care in colour" (Paul 1891: 438).

It is worth noting that German scholar Helmut Glück, who presents Paul's point of view in detail, correctly points out that Paul's "theoretical verdict on 'writing' contrasts remarkably with the fact that 'writing' is given its own and unchallenged rights in practical grammar work" (Glück 1987: 80, our translation). And, after all, Paul also acknowledges that the development of supraregional standard varieties of languages is closely linked to writing (⟶ Section 5.5.3.1). Against this background, according to Glück, portraying Paul exclusively as a critic of writing is unjustified, although with his strong theoretical claims about writing, Paul himself certainly contributed to this assessment.

In the 20th century, a critical stance on writing was maintained by Ferdinand de Saussure. Like Paul before him, Saussure holds that spoken and written words relate to each other like face and photograph – the latter merely represents the former. In an overview of the position writing assumed as a research topic in linguistics, Klaus Heller and Dieter Nerius (2007: 57, our translation) poignantly summarise Saussure's line of arguing: "Not ideas but sounds are expressed by graphic 'signs', language can also exist without writing, and the natural primacy of the spoken word is highlighted by the fact that one learns to speak before one learns to write" (⟶ Section 2.3.1). Notably, in his influential *Cours de linguistique générale*,[7] Saussure does concede that writing can develop its own idiosyncratic systematics. These, however, amount to nothing more than a "tyranny of letters" (Saussure 1916: 37 [31][8]), and the sole object of linguistics remains the spoken word, the *mot parlé*, resulting in a disregard of the written word, the *mot écrit*:

> Language and writing are two distinct systems of signs; the second exists for the sole purpose of representing the first. The linguistic object is not both the written and the spoken form of words; the spoken forms alone constitute the object. (Saussure 1916: 28 [23–24])

Saussure's criticism of writing is echoed by the linguistic strand of American structuralism, one of whose most important representatives is Leonard Bloomfield.[9] Bloomfield's (1933: 21) verdict that writing is "merely a way of recording language by means of visible marks" is widely cited to argue that American structuralism did not accept writing as an object of linguistic study. Note, however, that Glück (1987: 68) cautions against considering Bloomfield's well-known statement as indicative of the paradigm's stance as a whole, since other structuralists actually dealt intensively with questions of, for example, learning to read and write as well as with introducing literacy to unwritten languages. Thus, Glück

7 In this book, following general practice, quotes are cited with Saussure's name although Saussure himself did not authorise the text (cf. Ágel and Kehrein 2002: 4). See also Jäger (2018) on the myth of the *Cours* and a critical examination of the role it played in the history of linguistics.

8 The page numbers in square brackets indicate the corresponding pages in Wade Baskin's (1959) English translation of the *Cours*.

9 According to Ágel (2003), the linguistic paradigm of generativism also carries on the tradition of Saussure's *mot parlé* (cf. also Davidson 2019).

(1987: 74, our translation) criticises the common practice of attacking Bloomfield and others – including the above-mentioned Paul – "as narrow-minded advocates of the dependence hypothesis, which they are not" (⟶ Section 2.3.1 for the dependence hypothesis).

Similarly, our criticism of the logocentric view in linguistics must be relativised; even though the assumption of a primacy of speech had long been dominant, several linguists already opposed this view as early as the 19th century. Heller and Nerius (2007) mention Polish-Russian linguist Jan Baudouin de Courtenay and the German linguist Georg von der Gabelentz as examples. Both objected to the contempt of treating writing as an object of study that was prevalent at the time. Von der Gabelentz' view can be characterised as follows:

> For him, the written and the spoken language are of equal importance, they stand side by side and are equal as two complementary 'languages' of a linguistic community: 'Images of sound and writing', he notes (von der Gabelentz 1891; 1969, 135), 'are gathered in two parallel inventories, and the optical language is just as real, is just as much a living language as the acoustic'. (Heller and Nerius 2007: 57, our translation)

In the first half of the 20th century, it was Czech linguist Josef Vachek who, in his important work on the problems of written language, maintained that writing should be regarded as an independent and fully functional form of language and shall therefore be studied separately from spoken language. In this vein, Heller and Nerius (2007: 60, our translation) underline that Vachek "succeeds in explaining the specifics of spoken language on the one hand and written language on the other on a uniform theoretical basis by taking their different functions in communication as a starting point". This is particularly evident in Vachek's following assessment:

> The presence of the two language norms in [cultivated linguistic communities] cannot be reasonably denied. [. . .] from the synchronistic viewpoint de Saussure's distinction of the spoken norm as historically primary as opposed to the written norm as historically secondary is for their functional evaluation beside the point. Both norms are simply linguistic realities and each of the two [. . .] has its specific function. (Vachek 1989: 108)[10]

Notably, not only Vachek but also other scholars of writing who were members of the *Prague School*, an influential linguistic circle that had been founded in 1927, opposed the dogmatic view of the primacy of speech over writing. In sum, however, the view that speech was the central object of linguistic study dominated scientific discourses up until the 20th century, with just few linguists opposing it. It was only

10 This quote is originally from Vachek's (1939) paper "On the problem of written language"; it was reprinted in Vachek (1989), a collection of his works on writing, from which it is cited here.

in the second half of that century that a change in thinking set in. At that point, several linguists turned to the subject of writing out of theoretical interest.

Arguments in favour of the relative autonomy of writing as a phenomenon and a subject of research were first concisely presented in Florian Coulmas' (1981) German book *Über Schrift* ('On writing'). In it, he emphasises that writing exhibits qualities of its own that elevate it beyond a mere depiction of speech (cf. Coulmas 1981: 42). The exact considerations used to argue for the so-called autonomy hypothesis are presented in detail in → Section 2.3.2.

In a historical sketch of the treatment of writing in linguistics, a striking peculiarity cannot be left unmentioned: despite the widespread view that the sole object of linguistic study ought to be speech, the majority of linguistic studies has always been based on written data and thus relied on writing. This situation has been given various names, among them *scripticism* (cf. Harris 1980; Ágel 2003) or *written language bias* (cf. Linell 2005). These terms underline that descriptive linguistic categories – such as *phoneme, word, sentence* – were related to or even based in writing, and grammatical analyses were carried out with and on written material.[11] This is also noted by well-known German scholar Otto Behaghel in the introduction to one of his speeches on written and spoken German:

> When in the last centuries one spoke of the German language, when prestigious societies devoted themselves to the German language, when places of learning and dictionaries of the German language were created, it was the noble, dignified, strictly measured language of writing, of the book, which one had in mind, the language of those who were much admired and moved on the heights of literature. (Behaghel 1927: 11, our translation)

Regretfully, Behaghel (1927: 12) observes, written German was simultaneously depreciated by being branded as *Tintendeutsch* (literally 'ink German') given that during this period, dialects – i.e., different varieties of spoken language – had emerged as "the object of penetrating scientific research" (Behaghel 1927: 11–12, our translation). Indeed, the study of dialects represented the first turn towards the spoken word in the course of the 19th century. Ironically, dialect research was also carried out by means of the written modality since at that time, due to the limitations of technology, specifically the recording of speech, only written texts and data could serve as a basis for research. This situation is indeed characteristic of the entire history of linguistics far into the 20th century, as observed by Günther:

> It is typical of the linguistic researcher in our century that on the one hand he is convinced that speech alone is his object of investigation and that on the other hand his analyses are generally based on written or transcribed material. (Günther 1988: 14, our translation)

11 Against this background, it is only fitting that the term 'grammar' is based on the Greek noun for 'letter' (*grámma*); cf. also the adjective *grammatikós* 'knowing one's letters'.

Ágel (2003: 10, our translation) also addresses this contradiction: he holds that on the one hand, linguistics is explicitly logocentric, while on the other, it is implicitly affected by scripticism, which results in the *mot écrit* becoming "the actual protagonist of grammatical descriptions". Notably, Ágel (2003: 10, our translation) also advocates an important distinction between scripticism and so-called *writing-relatedness* (from German *Schriftbezogenheit*). While the former is characterised as the "contradiction between logocentrically intended theory and its unintended writing-related realisation", writing-relatedness describes the neutral situation in which research is based on writing and/or focuses on writing explicitly and intentionally. This, of course, applies to all grapholinguistic research.

In a nutshell, whoever absolutises speech as the primary or even sole object of linguistic study and simultaneously uses writing and written data as the only measure of grammatical description must accept the accusation of scripticism. We, of course, argue that both speech and writing should be treated as subjects of linguistic research in their own right, and the present book reflects this stance.

1.3 Overview of this book

This book is intended to give an overview of the different facets of grapholinguistics. The basis for this is a presentation of the structure of writing systems and the tools needed to study it. To provide it, we will propose definitions of the core concepts of writing, examples being *grapheme* or *allography*. It is paramount to underline that these will not be built on the basis of a single type of writing system. Instead, examples throughout the following chapters will address a variety of diverse systems including Chinese, English, Japanese, Arabic, Thai, German, and Korean. The result is a comparative framework in which different writing systems are not merely juxtaposed but analysed in relation to one another.

Furthermore, as the book's title highlights, the structure of writing shall not be studied in complete separation from its use. Instead, we aim to highlight the complex connections between structure and use. Specifically, the final sections of each chapter will introduce additional perspectives, most of which centre on use-related aspects of writing. In these sections, important issues will be exemplarily discussed to weave psycholinguistic, sociolinguistic, and other usage-based questions into the book and expand the theoretical and methodological horizon by emphasising the interdisciplinarity of grapholinguistics. For example, in → Chapter 4, *Graphematics*, the most important graphematic units and concepts will first be presented from a structural point of view before a psycholinguistic perspective is opened up at the end of the chapter to examine whether the established descriptive concepts and units are also psychologically real, i.e., play a role in actual reading and writing processes.

As for the content of the individual chapters, in ⟶ Chapter 2, a definition of writing is provided, after which the intricacies of modelling the relationship between speech, writing, and sign language as different modalities of language are characterised. In this context, several typical features of speech and writing are addressed, which simultaneously reveal crucial differences and similarities between them. Then, the above-mentioned opposing views on the relationship between speech and writing are discussed: the dependence hypothesis, claiming that writing is derivative of speech, and the autonomy hypothesis, arguing that an investigation of writing must proceed with the underlying assumption that writing, as its own system, exhibits idiosyncratic features that can only be captured when writing is analysed independently of speech. The next part of the chapter introduces the conceptual level of spoken vs. written communication and illustrates that, for example, while academic talks are spoken, i.e., produced orally, they actually display linguistic features of prototypical written communication (such as syntactic complexity). The chapter's final section adopts anthropological perspectives to deal with practices of orality and literacy and the problematics of studying them.

The following three chapters are devoted to the core subdisciplines of a structural grapholinguistics. Chapter 3 focuses on graphetics, the study of the visual form and appearance of writing as well as its physical (e.g., haptic) features, and addresses its description and its functions. In the first and theoretical part, models examining the visual aspects of writing will be presented. The second part then deals with applied graphetic questions by focusing on two concrete manifestations of writing, typography and handwriting. The use-oriented perspective that is opened up at the end of this chapter is that of emergent literacy research; examples will show how – and which – graphetic features are first acquired by children who learn to read and write.

Chapter 4 then deals with the linguistic functions of writing – in other words, how the previously introduced graphetic units of writing are used to convey linguistic information. It begins with a definition of graphematics and proceeds with a thorough description of its goals and methods. A large portion of the chapter is dedicated to graphematic units, the basic and most central of which is the grapheme. Other units that have been discussed in the literature – such as graphematic features, the graphematic syllable, and the graphematic word – will also be exemplified. Furthermore, the functions of punctuation will be addressed, and the chapter will deal with remaining issues central to the linguistic treatment of writing systems: allography, graphematic variation, and graphotactics.

The usage-oriented perspective introduced at the end of the chapter is that of psycholinguistic research on processes of reading. The important question discussed here is whether the descriptive graphematic units formerly presented are psychologically real, i.e., play a role in recognition processes.

As the last of the three structural chapters, ⟶ Chapter 5 devotes itself to orthography, defined here as the standardisation of writing. Accordingly, it will treat important prescriptive aspects of writing and focus on the regulation of writing systems by external authorities as well as the codification of orthographic rules in rulebooks and dictionaries. The first part of the chapter will show that, synchronically, orthographies are optional parts of writing systems, and outline their characteristic features. Different types of orthographic rules will be presented and, given that aspects such as capitalisation and grapheme-phoneme correspondences are not of universal relevance, a dedicated subchapter will address how orthographic regulation manifests itself in diverse writing systems. What, for example, is orthographically regulated in the writing systems of Chinese or Arabic? The final part of the chapter will adopt a sociolinguistic perspective. Sociolinguistics is arguably integral to an investigation of orthography since literacy practices are forms of 'social action'. A number of topics will be discussed in this context: the choice of an orthographic standard for a given language, the development of an orthography for an unwritten language, the potential social meaning of deviations from the orthographic norm (including their functions as well as attitudes and associated sanctions), and orthography reforms and the discourses surrounding them.

Chapter 6 is devoted to a presentation and discussion of different types of writing systems. All the major phonographic types (i.e., alphabets, abjads, abugidas, and syllabaries) as well as the morphographic type of writing system will be characterised by means of representative examples. An issue closely associated with the typology of writing systems is the existence of universals, which is why a section will address potential universals of writing and how they can be discovered as well as what they may reveal about the general nature of writing. The history of writing, which is tightly linked to both typology and the study of universals, is the additional perspective incorporated into the chapter. Core diachronic developments will be presented to shed light on how different types of writing systems have come into existence and illustrate how the typology and history of writing systems interact.

Finally, ⟶ Chapter 7 will provide both a conclusion by highlighting the interconnectedness of the perspectives discussed throughout the book and a brief outlook.

2 Language, speech, and writing

In this chapter, we will first define what writing is and then present an in-depth analysis of the relation between speech and writing (Section 2.1). After that, the central features of both speech and writing as well as the main differences and similarities of these two modalities will be discussed (Section 2.2). The following section (Section 2.3) is devoted to two opposing views that conceptualise writing as either dependent on or autonomous with respect to speech. Section 2.4 then introduces models that highlight differences between the linguistic resources as well as means of expression commonly used in speech and those used in writing. Finally, an anthropological perspective is opened up (Section 2.5) to first discuss the concepts of orality and literacy according to the autonomous model of literacy, after which they are critically evaluated in light of the so-called ideological model.

2.1 Speech and writing as modalities of language

Any analysis of writing and written language must be preceded by a definition of writing. Inherent in such a definition is the question of how writing is related to speech. This is an important issue given that in the history of linguistics, writing was long discarded as an object of research precisely because it was regarded as derivative of speech (⟶ Section 1.2). The considerations in this section are based on definitions of writing by two well-known linguists dealing with writing: Coulmas (1996a: 555) defines writing as "a system of recording language by means of visible or tactile marks which relate in a systematic way to units of speech", and Neef (2015: 708) conceptualises writing as a notational system for language. These two definitions already address important points in the investigation of how speech and writing relate to one another. We highlight four of them in particular:

(1) Writing represents language, not ideas.

Firstly, it is important to establish that writing is a notational system. The word 'notation' derives from Latin *nota* 'mark' (through *notare* and finally *notatio*) and designates the act of representing a system using a set of graphic marks. There exist different notational systems, among them well-known mathematical notation (which most know from formulas such as $c^2 = a^2 + b^2$) or the notational system for transcribing music. As yet another notational system, writing differs from the mentioned systems in that it represents language. For example, in English, the written word <cat> stands for the lexeme *cat* which has as its meaning something along the lines of 'a small domesticated carnivorous mammal with soft fur, a short snout, and retractable claws'. Crucially, the lexeme *cat* is a unit of language. This means that the written sequence <cat> does not refer directly to the concept

https://doi.org/10.1515/9783110757835-002

of 'cat' or even a real cat, but merely to the word *cat*, which, in turn, has as its meaning the concept 'cat' and can be used to refer to a cat that exists in the real world.

This definition of writing is nowadays agreed on by most scholars of writing, and it is the one we adhere to in this book. It is commonly referred to as the narrow definition of writing as it accepts as writing only *glottography*, which literally means 'language writing' as it derives from Ancient Greek *glōtta* (a variant of *glōssa* 'tongue, language') and *gráphō* 'scratch, draw, also: write' (cf. Dürscheid 2016a: 100–103). By contrast, following the broad definition of writing, *semasiography* (from Ancient Greek *sēmasíā* 'designation, meaning') is also treated as writing. Semasiographic signs refer directly to ideas and meaning without making a detour through language, examples being street signs, cave paintings, or emojis. When writers add a smiling emoji at the end of their text message, for example, readers usually do not read it as a sign of writing that stands for the word *smiling* or *happy* but rather interpret the intended communicative meaning in the context of the entire message and communication situation (cf. Dürscheid and Meletis 2019). Thus, unlike glottographic signs, semasiographic signs cannot be read, i.e., encoded directly – they can only be interpreted.

(2) Speech and language are different phenomena.

In his definition of writing, Coulmas mentions both language and speech as distinct phenomena. He first underlines that writing, with its marks, represents language. Secondly, he points out that these language-representing marks of writing systematically relate to speech. This is important to note, as 'speech' is often mistakenly treated as a synonym of 'language'. Speech, however, is only one possible modality of language, which is itself an abstract system. This is a distinction that proves essential for understanding the relationship between speech and writing.

Similarly, in his grapholinguistic approach, Neef (2015: 709) argues that a "specific writing system is never an entity of its own existence but something that is related to a specific language system and that in this sense is dependent on it". To name an example, the English writing system is dependent on the English language. 'Language', in this context, is to be understood as a system that is abstract and consists of linguistic units at various levels: these include not only sounds but also words, sentences, etc. Thus, claims such as "[s]ince writing represents language, it must represent the sounds of speech" (Daniels 2009: 36) are reductive as writing is not simply "visible speech" (which is the title of one of the most important books on writing, cf. DeFrancis 1989). It is graphic language – i.e., visible and/or tactile, cf. (4) – instead. To see this, it suffices to consider the Chinese writing system, in which written units directly correspond with morphemes, not sounds.

To sum up, lexemes such as the above-mentioned *cat* are units of language that can be realised either in writing, as in <cat>, or in speech, as in [k^{h}æt] (which, in this form, is of course also only a transcription of speech). Accordingly, on the one hand, both speech and writing relate to the same units of language. On the other hand, they also relate to and interact with each other. This relation will be discussed in (3) and, in more detail, in ⟶ Section 2.3 below.

(3) Speech and writing are two modalities of the same language system.
If speech is not equated with language and language is treated as an abstract system consisting of subsystems such as morphology, syntax, etc., then the next step is to treat speech and writing as two distinct modalities.[12] In general, language can be materialised in three different modalities: the spoken modality, the signed modality, and the written modality. A given language system, however, can never be materialised by all three, but instead only by either (a) the spoken modality alone (in oral cultures ⟶ Section 2.5), (b) a combination of the spoken and written modalities (in literate cultures), or, in the case of sign languages, (c) the signed modality alone (but see below for ways of transcribing sign language).

In their model of language, Ulrike Domahs and Beatrice Primus (2015) consider all three modalities and note that each of them is characterised by a systematic hierarchy of units. Specifically, since the modalities share structural features in their organisation, Domahs and Primus assume a modality-indifferent 'phonology'[13] which Brentari (2002: 35) defines generally as the "level of grammatical analysis where primitive structural units without meaning are combined to create an infinite number of meaningful utterances". Accordingly, here, 'phonology' is not interpreted in its traditional sense in which it is concerned (only) with the spoken modality. Instead, this broad approach attempts to capture the fact that in each modality (i.e., spoken, written, and signed), a combination of lower level-units creates units of a higher level: in writing, for example, combining the basic units <c>, <a>, and <t> results in the word <cat>. Notably, only after the three modalities have been analysed independently should correspondences and interrelations between them be studied. Their relationship and hierarchy are modelled as in Figure 1, in which English and American Sign Language (ASL) serve as examples of languages that are spoken/written and signed, respectively. As illus-

12 Note that 'modality' is an ambiguous term in linguistics. In the semiotic meaning in which it is used here, it denotes a particular way in which information (in this case language) is encoded.
13 This proposal of a modality-indifferent phonology is much older in sign language research, going back to Stokoe (1960). He had already argued that sign languages exhibit sub-lexical structures that are systematically organised (cf. also Sandler and Lillo-Martin 2006).

trated, writing is not located at the same level as speech: it will be shown below (⟶ Section 2.3.1) that there exist languages that are spoken but not written; by contrast, there are no languages that are only written but not spoken. Thus, writing occurs only in those languages that also have a spoken modality – it is always coupled with speech.

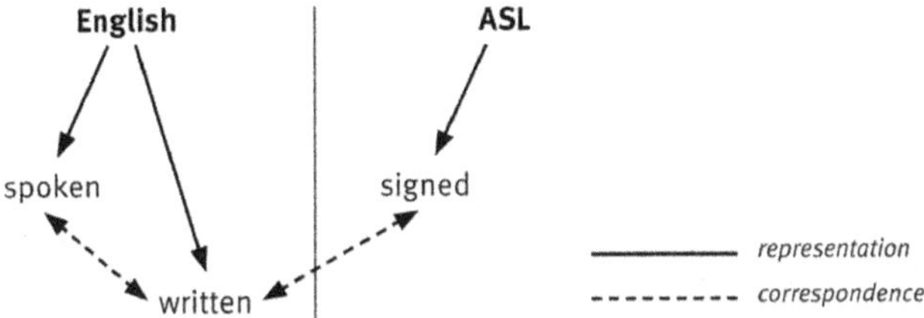

Figure 1: Relationship between the three modalities (spoken, signed, written) of language.

Turning to the relationship between the signed and written modalities, it is important to note that while there exist ways of transcribing sign languages directly (such as SignWriting[14]), these transcription tools are not 'used' in everyday life in the same way writing systems are used in/for spoken languages in literate cultures. Thus, as language systems, sign languages technically only exhibit one modality (signed) and are unwritten. This, of course, does not mean that L1 users of a sign language (in this case ASL) are necessarily illiterate, as indicated by the arrow between 'signed' and 'written' in Figure 1. What is special about their literacy, though, as highlighted by the vertical division line, is that they are literate in a *second* language, the surrounding spoken language. Accordingly, users of ASL who read and write English are bilingual, with ASL being their first and English their second language. Notably, at the same time, they are also bimodal, with signing as their first and writing as their second modality (cf. Morford et al. 2011). To sum up, the signed and written modalities belong to different language systems, and thus English literacy acquisition for Deaf L1 signers of ASL is indirect (via the spoken modality).

(4) Writing is not only visual but also tactile.

As Coulmas (1996a: 555) points out, written marks are visual *or* tactile. However, it can be argued that writing is simultaneously visual *and* tactile but that one of these

14 SignWriting is a system invented in 1974 by Valerie Sutton, an American developer of movement notation. It "uses visual symbols to represent the handshapes, movements, and facial expressions of signed languages" (http://www.signwriting.org, accessed April 14th, 2021).

channels is always dominant. For example, braille writing is primarily tactile, but the marks are also visual (although this is not how braille is perceived by people who use it). Both the visuality and the tactility of writing originate from the fact that it is graphic, a word that, as stated above, derives from Ancient Greek *grâphō*, 'scratch, carve'. This means that writing is always produced with instruments (such as pens) on a material surface (such as paper), which is why the result is both visual and tactile.[15] Notably, most analyses of writing are visuocentric – this book being no exception. However, the tactility of writing should be acknowledged and kept in mind, especially in the analysis of the materiality of writing (⟶ Chapter 3).

2.2 Differences between speech/speaking and writing

This section is dedicated to the differences between speech and writing as two distinct modalities of language as well as the differences between speaking and writing as the two processes through which they are called into existence.[16] While consensus in works focusing on writing is that there are profound differences between speech/speaking and writing,[17] it is notable that many authors consider in their discussion of distinct traits only prototypical examples of speaking and writing. In terms of speaking, these are usually instances of face-to-face communication. A non-prototypical example, on the other hand, would be a telephone conversation, which lacks eye contact as an important feature of prototypical spoken communication. Messages left on answering machines also do not count as face-to-face communication as neither eye contact nor the possibility of direct intervention for the listener are given. As these considerations already show, features of speech are investigated predominantly through the lens of production, i.e., the act of speaking, as well as its concrete use in specific communicative situations.

By contrast, writing is often viewed from a more static perspective, as a product, with the linguistically elaborated text being regarded the prototypical written utterance. Specific examples include literary texts and newspaper articles. Notably, non-prototypical written utterances such as brief notes, greeting cards, or even text written on a blackboard are usually neglected in investigations

15 The tactility of written documents is, of course, most often relegated to the background. Yet, for example, when brushing over a page covered with printed text, the written marks can sometimes also be felt haptically.
16 Parts of this as well as the following two sections are based on Dürscheid (2016a: Chapter 1).
17 Note the unfortunate ambiguity of the term 'writing' in English, which refers to both the modality as a whole and the process involved in producing written utterances.

of writing. The latter, for example, is regarded atypical because of how it is produced and perceived: readers can directly witness how the text is being written on the blackboard, i.e., production and reception occur simultaneously. Unlike speaking, writing is not usually characterised by such synchronicity; instead, the reception of written utterances commonly occurs only after they have been (completely) produced. This applies even to 'more synchronous' forms of writing such as chat communication: while chat messages can be read by recipients immediately after having been produced and sent by authors, they can usually not be read during the writing process itself, although there do theoretically exist chat programs that allow participants to watch the text while it is being produced; however, these are seldom used.

In the following, we will list differences between the two modalities by addressing prototypical features of speaking and writing as processes as well as spoken and written utterances as the resulting products. Note that the transition from production to product is rather fluid, which means most features concern both, making their assignment to one of them a matter of degree. Furthermore, neither the processes nor their products are homogeneous (or autonomous, see below) objects of investigation as they are always embedded in specific communicative practices. This, in turn, may be associated with certain linguistic resources and strategies and will be discussed in ⟶ Section 2.4. In any case, a blanket comparison of speaking/speech and processes and products of writing faces the risk of neglecting the diversity of said communicative practices:

> We do not speak and write per se, but all speaking and writing happens in and is part of *communicative practices*. We speak in the context of afternoon tea, a business meeting, arranging a doctor's appointment via telephone, a speech, a theatre role, etc.; we write a letter, an essay, a protocol, a shopping list.
>
> (Fiehler 2000: 97, our translation, emphasis in original)

In other words, spoken and written communication are no clear-cut categories. They rather manifest themselves "in copies of concrete practices" (Fiehler 2000: 100, our translation), which has also emerged as the core tenet in anthropological research on literacy (⟶ Section 2.5.2). Thus, the ensuing comparison is of heuristic nature and is intended to merely illustrate fundamental differences. Therefore, initially, prototypical features are presented; only in the next step will borderline cases that do not fit straightforwardly into this comparative framework be discussed. Note that the comparison is based on contemporary conditions of spoken and written communication. This is important to emphasise since in the Middle Ages, for example, different conditions applied to speaking, writing, and reading.

Central differences that concern mainly production, i.e., the acts of speaking and writing, include:

1. Shared vs. distinct communication situations: Speech is bound to both a specific time and space. In writing, writers and readers are not bound to a shared perceptual space and communication situation.

As announced above, this feature captures only the prototypical form of speaking that occurs face-to-face. By contrast, other forms of direct interaction between speakers and listeners such as telephone calls as well as video conferences enable the transmission of speech without requiring that interlocutors both be present at the same location. Speech is, therefore, not necessarily bound to space. For messages left on answering machines or, nowadays, spoken messages sent through applications such as WhatsApp, speech is also not bound to time and synchronicity (cf. the next feature). Inversely, there are also types of writing that require writers and readers to be in the same room such as when course instructors use visual aids (e.g., a blackboard, an overhead projector, PowerPoint slides) that consist of or include written material. Crucially, this production-oriented feature is associated with the degree of explicitness and decontextualisation of the language used in types of spoken and written discourse (cf. Kay 1977; Olson 1977 and ⟶ Section 2.4).

2. Synchronicity vs. asynchronicity: Communication is synchronous in speech and asynchronous in writing. Production and reception of written texts occur consecutively and readers – unlike listeners – cannot directly intervene in the production process.

Like the preceding distinction, the dichotomy synchronous/asynchronous is valid only under certain conditions. Notably, with the advent of new communication technologies, its importance has gradually faded: for example, chat communication, unlike conventional written communication, is quasi-synchronous even when considering minor technical delays that occasionally occur. However, participants of prototypical chat communication can only intervene in the communication process *after* their chat partners have already sent their contributions and these appear on the screen. In other words, direct simultaneous interaction is (commonly) not possible. Listeners in prototypical spoken communication, on the other hand, can directly intervene by interrupting their conversation partners at any time.

3. Independence of vs. dependence on tools: Speaking is not bound to any tools. Writing, by contrast, requires tools: a writing instrument and a writing surface.

Writers need both a writing instrument and a writing surface, whereas speakers do not require any tools or materials. Note that the latter statement is only true when our physical articulators – lips, teeth, tongue, etc. – are not conceived of as 'speaking tools'. There is, of course, a striking difference between such 'speaking tools' and tools used for writing: while speech is made possible by the body's own articulation apparatus, writing instruments are usually external (save for special cases such as writing directly with one's fingers, as is done in air writing, writing in the sand, writing on someone's back, etc.). Thus, physicality is a feature constitutive of speech. This applies even to non-face-to-face communication such as telephone calls, where speakers' voices may appear detached from the body but are, in fact, still bound to it. In writing, by comparison, external tools "push" themselves "between the writer and the produced utterance so that the reader can no longer experience it physically in the same way the oral utterance is experienced" (Günther 1988: 12, our translation).

Turning to the product, Günther (1983: 34) emphasises that written texts retain few features that can be identified with their writers because writing separates itself materially from writers, while speech – produced directly with one's voice – is closely associated with speakers' identities. Accordingly, writers often become invisible behind the text, rendering it to a large degree materially depersonalised, whereas in speech, speakers always remain audible as individuals. This, of course, applies to varying degrees to different forms of writing: handwritten texts, for example, do retain a certain degree of physicality that is missing from typographic texts. Yet, while typefaces do lack any direct physicality, they can still be associated with writers (their personalities, their aesthetic preferences, maybe even their social, political, . . . backgrounds) due to their sociosemiotic indexical potential (⟶ Section 3.3).

The necessity of using tools is also one of the reasons why the processes of speaking and writing differ in their speed of execution. Chafe (1982) claims that the average speed of speaking in English is 180 words per minute and that writing is more than ten times slower than that. The exact ratio is not of relevance here as it is incontestable that speaking is faster than writing. This, paired with the permanence of writing (cf. Feature 5), affects the organisation of written utterances.

The size of inventories of (possible) material units is another crucial difference that is related to the use of respective 'tools': in speech, the physical capacities and restrictions of human articulators limit the number of possible sounds that can be produced (cf. the International Phonetic Alphabet, especially blank white cells for possible but unattested sounds and grey cells for physiologically impossible sounds). There are no comparable productional restrictions in writing (cf. Günther 1993a: 33): in handwriting, our hands do not limit possible shapes – at least not ones we can cognitively imagine – and in typography, the makeup of shapes appears even more unrestricted as they are not directly produced with our hands. This is likely one of the reasons for the visual diversity of the world's scripts. Note that restrictions on shapes might still be imposed by cognition and perception given that highly complex shapes are more difficult to store in memory and to process visually. In this vein, Watt (1999) offers an interesting thought experiment by positing that extra-terrestrial shapes[18] would look different from human shapes precisely because the latter are restrained by the limits of human eyes, hands, the brain, as well as the writing materials used.

4. Dialogicity vs. monologicity: Speech is dialogical, writing is monologic.

The assignment of the attributes dialogical and monologic to speaking and writing, respectively, is not absolute. In fact, there are types of spoken communication that are monologic in their basic structure, examples being sermons, lectures, and speeches given before parliament. In these cases, mutual communication with or direct feedback from recipients are uncommon. Vice versa, types of written communication can certainly be of a dialogical nature. In text linguistics, for example, letter writing is regarded as a type of dialogical communication (cf. Vater 2001: 167). However, this assessment is only reasonable if the communication constituted by sending and receiving letters is analysed more globally and from an interactional perspective (cf. Häcki Buhofer 1985: 108). If, on the other hand, the isolated acts of writing and sending a single letter are considered, letter writing does appear rather monologic given that the addressee, unlike in spoken communication, has no possibility of intervening during the production of the text. Also, unlike in chat communication, there is a – sometimes significant – temporal delay before the addressee can respond. As for the features characteristic of the product, letters, unlike, for example, legal texts, are often organised in ways that convey to addresses that senders expect a response. This goes to show that, depending on the communicative practice in question, writing can also be regarded as dialogical.

5. Transience vs. permanence: Spoken utterances are transient, written utterances permanent. Written material can be archived and can always be retrieved in the same form, which does not apply to spoken utterances (cf. Martinet 1962: 112–113).

Due to the differences in data transmission, it is indeed the case that spoken utterances are fleeting – meaning as soon as they have been uttered, they are already 'gone' again – whereas written texts continue to exist. However, from the perspective of the product, nowadays, this dichotomy applies only to a limited

18 Regarding this question, the writing system designed by Jessica Coon (Associate Professor in the Department of Linguistics at McGill University) for the science fiction film *Arrival* (2016, directed by Denis Villeneuve) is noteworthy (cf. Nawar 2020: 52). In the film, it is used by aliens who land on the Earth and is characterised by a high degree of complexity. Notably, it is not related to the language the aliens 'speak' but rather constitutes its own language system. This also distinguishes it from a human writing system, which is always based on a spoken (or signed) language (⟶ Section 2.1).

extent given that spoken utterances can be preserved, e.g., in the form of audio recordings made on smartphones, tape recorders, answering machines, or in the form of video that additionally captures the visual channel. Note, however, that even these recorded spoken utterances are always "fleeting in their respective reproduction" (Günther 1983: 32, our translation). The main difference between unrecorded speech and such utterances is thus that the latter are repeatable and retrievable again and again, which creates a form of 'transient permanence' (or 'permanent transience'). And not only in the context of modern recording techniques is the distinction between transience and permanence not as fundamental as it is generally assumed to be: in many contexts, what is originally transient is often made permanent when spoken utterances are written down (e.g., in court), and vice versa, written texts become fleeting when read out loud (e.g., during the news, sermons, political speeches).

As mentioned above, given that the act of writing is much slower than speaking and the produced written utterances are visually permanent, writing is both surveyable and (re)organisable (cf. Akinnaso 1982: 114). This means that writers can rethink and reorganise their thoughts and expressions before and after they have written them down. As Goody (1977: 157) puts it, "words are laid out clinically on the page" and are "capable of being struck out, re-ordered, substituted, pored over, reflected upon". These possibilities are not afforded in the same way in speaking. Notably, whether reorganisation can be carried out easily and conveniently in practice depends also on the writing instruments used. In handwriting, writers can strike out words, which can give off a 'messy' impression to potential addressees and 'wastes' space on the writing surface, or they can use additional tools such as whiteout. By contrast, in digital writing, written utterances are present – in real-time – only on the screen in the form of electronic pixels and can be modified (corrected, rewritten, reformatted, deleted, etc.) again and again. Only when a text is printed does it become available as a permanent material product.

This is closely related to another difference between speech and writing that is determined by their (lack of) permanence: speech is prototypically unplannable and unplanned while writing is plannable and planned (cf. Akinnaso 1982: 114–115; Ochs 1979). In writing, processes such as the above-mentioned (re)organisation happen deliberately, which makes writing – or more specifically the process of text composition involved in writing – a much more conscious act than speaking.

Relevant differences that mainly concern the product, i.e., spoken or written utterances, include:

6. Multimodal (acoustic, visual) means of expression vs. monomodal (graphic) means of expression: Speech is used in combination with other acoustic and visual means of expression that carry information, examples being prosodic features, facial expressions, and gestures. These are not available in writing, which, in turn, exhibits its idiosyncratic graphic means of expression such as bold print that have no direct equivalent in speech (cf. Akinnaso 1982: 112).

In writing, given the visual/tactile channels of data transmission, acoustic, gestural, and certain visual means of expression available in speech cannot be used. There are ways of 'compensating' for this, i.e., achieving similar communicative effects, for example by using (iterated) punctuation (*You coming???*), all caps to highlight the information structure of an utterance (*What would YOU like to do?)*, or repetition of letters to add emphasis (*It's so saaaaad!*). Certain punctuation marks such as <, ; .> can indicate pauses, others highlight illocutionary force: <.> marks statements, <?> questions, and <!> exclamations (cf. Akinnaso 1985: 105). Notably, while these examples suggest there might be correlations, the mentioned resources of writing do not have effects that are directly equivalent to means of expression used in speech such as intonation or facial expressions. But even in speech, it is not always possible to make use of the entire repertoire of these features: take non-face-to-face communication on the phone, where only speakers' voices can transmit information while body-related means of expression transmitted through the visual channel such as facial expressions and gestures are unavailable.

Note that inversely, as implied, writing also exhibits resources that speech is lacking. Examples include graphic means used to, among other things, subdivide statements and provide additional information such as paragraphs, spaces, and indentations, but also features used to show emphasis, e.g., uppercase writing, bold face, italics, or underlining (⟶ Chapter 3 and Akinnaso 1985: 105).

7. Extension in time vs. space: Speech is a sound continuum that extends in time. Writing is made up of discrete units that extend in space.

Speech and writing differ crucially in that the former is perceived by the ears and the latter by the eyes. Thus, in writing, according to Köller (1988: 157, our translation), there is "a transposition of language from the level of time to the level of space".[19] Köller calls this the 'spatialisation' of language, which has far-reaching consequences for the analysis of writing and its comparison with speech. While speech represents a sound continuum that cannot easily be broken down into segmental units, writing is a sequence of visual segments that are arranged spatially. Paul already drew attention to this fact when observing that language and writing relate to each other like line and number:

19 From the perspective of production, time of course plays a role also in writing, especially in situations in which communication occurs synchronously such as when instructors produce text on a blackboard that is read by students in real time.

> We have seen [. . .] the importance of the continuity as well in the series of possible speech-sounds as in the series of sounds consecutively spoken, for a proper view of the phonetic side of language. But an alphabet, however perfect it may be, lacks continuity in both these respects. Language and writing bear the same relation to each other as line and number.
> (Paul 1891: 434)

Günther (1988: 17) argues that this distinction requires a treatment of speech and writing as two independent objects of investigation. Specifically, continuous elements cannot be described with the same methods as discrete segments, and units that extend in time cannot be readily compared with those that extend in space. Depending on the writing system, the segmental units of writing (i.e., the 'numbers', as Paul calls them) can be of varying complexity and can be arranged differently in space (cf. as an example the representation of vowels in abjads and abugidas in ⟶ Section 6.2.3). Nevertheless, written units are always positioned spatially on a two-dimensional surface. It follows, according to Fiehler (2009: 1172, our translation), that "all units are present simultaneously in written communication, which thus [. . .] takes on the character of a completed product". This does not apply to time-bound speech. Speaking, therefore, always appears as an ongoing process instead of as a finished product since, if an utterance is 'finished', it will already have faded due to the transience of speech (cf. Feature 5).

In sum, there are crucial differences between speech and writing that are based on their modality-specific features. The constitutive differences between them can be condensed as follows: (a) speech is body-bound and does not require any tools. By contrast, writing is not bound to the body and does require tools. Also, (b) speech extends in time, as opposed to writing, which extends in space. In the interest of a precise description of writing, a detailed discussion of these differences proves indispensable. However, in a next step, it is vital to complement the juxtaposition of the two modalities with an independent fine-grained analysis of writing. Only this combination of steps can do justice the interdependence of speech and writing, which as evidenced exhibit not only differences but also common features.

2.3 Dependence vs. autonomy

As mentioned at the outset of this chapter, the question of how to model the relationship between speech and writing is of great relevance to grapholinguistics. In this section, now, two opposing views regarding this very question will be discussed: the dependence and the autonomy hypotheses. Dedicated subsections set out the arguments put forward for the dependence of writing on speech on the one hand and writing's relative autonomy on the other. Notably, there is also a third, mediating position, the so-called interdependence hypothesis (cf. Glück 2016b: 301–302). We will not deal with it in detail as it essentially represents a more moderate version of the autonomy hypothesis (cf. Neef and Primus 2001: 354). What the autonomy and interdependence hypotheses have in common is the assumption that speech and writing are "methodologically differentiated and theoretically elementary categories of language description and analysis" (Glück 2016b: 302, our translation). The crucial difference between them is that the interdependence hypothesis still assumes a relative functional and methodological dominance of speech over writing that is rejected by proponents of the autonomy hypothesis.

2.3.1 Dependence hypothesis

The central points underlying the argument that writing is dependent on speech are discussed below.

Linguistic argument: Writing is nothing more than a visualisation of language, i.e., sound translated into written signs.

This point is closely associated with the work of Paul (1891) and Saussure (1916). More recently, it has also been advocated in one of the standard references on generative phonology (Chomsky and Halle 1968). Its basis is the assumption that the grapheme level is subordinate to the phoneme level. The concept of grapheme as well as its relation to linguistic units such as phonemes will be treated in detail in ⟶ Chapter 4; at this point, it suffices to say that according to this argument, graphemes (for the time being, 'letters, characters') merely depict phonemes. In other words, graphemes are not considered autonomous units of investigation. According to this view, the graphemes <g> and <c> in English <gap> and <cap>, for example, only function to represent the phonemes /g/ and /k/. Correspondence rules determine how phonemes can be converted into graphemes as well as how irregular cases can be dealt with.

Developmental-psychological argument*:* Writing is acquired after speaking or signing both phylogenetically and ontogenetically.

It is undisputed that in the history of humankind, speaking and signing precede writing. Günther notes:

> The earliest direct predecessors of writing [. . .] date back to the XI millennium BC at most. At this point in time, social forms of organisation in which tools, etc. were used had long existed. These are, according to general consensus, not conceivable without (spoken) language.
>
> (Günther 1983: 17, our translation)

To this day, there exist cultures without writing while there are no cultures without either spoken or sign language. Coulmas addresses the difference between them:

> Even today, many languages are still without writing, and from a systematic point of view, writing can be considered a historical coincidence. The lack of writing is a cultural or social phenomenon; the absence of (spoken) language, however, is a pathological one.
>
> (Coulmas 1981: 109, our translation)

German linguist Utz Maas (1992) argues that it is more accurate to speak of a *socio-genetic* rather than a phylogenetic origin of writing given that it has not emerged naturally but rather developed gradually as a sociocultural technique. Likewise, it is undisputed that in the development of individuals, the acquisition of speech or sign language precedes learning to read and write; also, speaking and signing are acquired naturally, whereas literacy must be learned through instruction. However, there are notable exceptions that are often neglected: 1) For Deaf children, literacy acquisition in a second, spoken language (such as English) does not happen on the basis of speech. It is indirect as L1 users of sign languages acquire the written modality of a spoken language they have no or very restricted access to (⟶ Section 2.1). However, evidence shows that literacy acquisition is 'easier' for them when they have fully acquired their first language (such as ASL), suggesting that the successful acquisition of writing hinges on the prior mastering of either spoken or sign language (cf. Petitto et al. 2016). 2) The acquisition of a nowadays dead and thus unspoken language such as Latin is possible only because learners have acquired the spoken (and written) modality of their first language. Needless to say, these dead languages were also once spoken, otherwise they would not have a written modality that has outlasted the spoken one.

Logical argument: There are spoken languages that are unwritten. By contrast, writing can only exist in languages that are also spoken.

Many of the around 7000 existing languages of the world have no written form and are thus only spoken, such as many of the indigenous languages of Africa. Furthermore, all sign languages are only signed (with the exception of transcription systems, see above). Thus, while speech and signing are conceivable without writing, writing is not conceivable without them. This, of course, is directly related to the phylogenetic and ontogenetic subordinacy of writing addressed by the developmental-psychological argument above.

Functional argument: Speech is used on far more occasions than writing.

To this day, speech is used on many more occasions than writing. It could therefore be argued that it has functional priority. However, certain possibilities afforded by writing such as the compilation of lists have no equivalent in speech (cf. Reißig 2015). And arguably, nowadays, everyday life cannot simply be regarded as the undisputed domain of speaking as many situations can be handled just as well or even exclusively by means of writing (even more so in the digital age). As Lyons ([1981] 1992: 22) already pointed out, writing serves as a helpful tool in situations in which speaking is inconvenient or impossible. In general, it can be concluded that there are communicative purposes for which speech is more suited and others for which writing is the fitting choice – and some might of course be equally well fulfilled by both.

2.3.2 Autonomy hypothesis

Proponents of the autonomy hypothesis argue that writing should be regarded as an object of research in its own right, thus advocating a clear theoretical and methodological separation of speech and writing. Their main arguments are presented in the following.

Structural argument: Writing consists of discrete units while speech represents a continuum.

It is unsurprising that the central distinction between segmentality and continuity already mentioned in ⟶ Section 2.2 is used to argue for the autonomy of writing. Günther (1988: 17, our translation), for example, stresses that it is precisely this difference that requires the analysis of speech and writing to be carried out separately, as "one cannot describe continuous elements with the same methods as discrete segments". Yet, ironically, it is proponents of the autonomy hypothesis who define the basic descriptive unit of writing, the grapheme, by analogy with the phoneme (cf. the analogical conception of the grapheme in ⟶ Section 4.2.1).

Psychological argument: The processes of reading and writing do not necessarily function with recourse to speech.

Advanced readers can grasp written words holistically. Users of the English writing system, for example, when writing or reading, do not encode or decode written words letter by letter; thus, they do not necessarily take a detour through speech. Instead, both processes can unfold in a rather direct way, unmediated by speech (cf. the models of word recognition in ⟶ Section 4.7.1). In other words, we commonly do not read by pronouncing words out loud; neither do we write by reciting words out loud in advance. Thus, "[t]he written word is independent of whether or how it is pronounced" (Günther 1983: 25, our translation). However, there are notable exceptions to this. Before becoming trained readers of segmental phonographic writing systems, i.e., during the process of literacy acquisition when they are not yet closely familiar with many written words, children commonly rely on speech (or more specifically, grapheme-phoneme correspondences) both in reading and writing as they often *do* read and write letter by letter. And even advanced readers still decode words which are unfamiliar to them one letter at a time. This, of course, is only useful for 'regular' words, i.e., words whose pronunciation does not deviate in any way from grapheme-phoneme correspondences.

Note that the independence of reading and writing from speech becomes even clearer in morphographic writing (⟶ Section 6.3) such as Chinese or one component of Japanese, which lack a direct relationship between written units and their spoken correspondences. There, written units refer directly to morphemes, i.e., to linguistic meaning, which means reading and writing do not require a detour through speech.

Linguistic argument: Writing affords the possibility of distancing oneself from the object of investigation (for example, language). It makes linguistic structures accessible to analysis at a metalevel.

Written texts are commonly semantically autonomous, which means they are understandable for readers in and of themselves, i.e., without further information. This affects their reception, as Köller observes:

> Since communication in written language is semiotically reduced to the optical channel and given the sensual blandness of graphic signs, our attention is automatically focused on the cognitive content of linguistic utterances or on the representational function of language. Overall, this makes our attitude towards language and its content more abstract and distanced. (Köller 1988: 157, our translation)

Thus, writing allows reaching a linguistic metalevel by turning language into an object of analysis that can be investigated systematically. Importantly, this is not to say that metalinguistic awareness and discourse are not possible in speech. It just highlights that the possibility of making language visually permanent through writing it down facilitates metalinguistic activity in crucial ways.

Cultural argument: Writing prevents cultures from forgetting, it assumes a "documentary function" (Köller 1988: 157, our translation).

Content encoded in writing can be accessed over and over again, which is one reason it has been argued that all knowledge is dependent on written tradition and that writing represents "the central element of knowledge transfer" (Fiehler 2009: 1173, our translation; but cf. ⟶ Section 2.5 below for oral knowledge transfer). This feature of writing has also been criticised for supposedly contributing to a decay of human memory capacity (an argument going back to Plato, cf. ⟶ Section 1.2). At the same time, at the collective level, it preserves a society's cultural assets for future generations – instead of individual memory, it is 'cultural memory' (cf. Assmann 2018). Although he is considered one of the central critics of writing, Paul (1891: 433–434), too, acknowledges this as a great achievement of writing:

> The advantages possessed by written over spoken matter with regard to effective operation are sufficiently obvious. By its means the narrow circle to which the influence of the individual is otherwise confined may spread till it embraces the entire linguistic community; by its means that narrow circle may extend itself beyond the generation then living, and exert an immediate influence on all that follow. (Paul 1891: 433–444)

Material argument: Writing exhibits characteristics that have effects on both language and speech.

Erfurt (1996: 1397–1398) lists interesting examples from French that illustrate writing's impact on language, one of them being that final consonants in modern French are spoken only because they have been preserved in writing (cf. *avec, chic, août, neuf*, etc.). Further examples that writing affects language come from word formation: acronyms such as *NATO* are constructed from the initial letters of abbreviated words and are then themselves pronounced as words. More often, as in initialisms, letter names are strung together *(CIA* /ˌsiːaɪˈeɪ/, *FBI* /ˈɛf.biː.aɪ/) and the resulting words are spoken by pronouncing each letter individually. The example of *EU* (European Union), which is spoken /ˌiːˈjuː/, not /ˌjuːˈjuː/, which would be the first sounds of the respective words, shows that it is initial letters rather than initial sounds that are used to form abbreviations.

Another interesting phenomenon worth mentioning concerns the visual iconicity of letter shapes, which can influence the names of objects visually similar to them. Examples are *D-track, S-bend, T-shirt, U-turn, V-neck, V8 engine,* and *Y-connection* (cf. Coulmas 1981: 120; Brekle 1981: 197).

Finally, consider (written) 'words' such as *er* and *hm*. They serve to express paraverbal information in writing. If they are utilised as nouns by language users (e.g., in the sentence *Because of their many ers and hms it was difficult to follow.*), these paraverbal written 'words' are taken as tools to describe a communicative situation. Thus, "[b]y being written, these units, which are actually not words, acquire word-like character" (Coulmas 1981: 120, our translation). And as these written paraverbal utterances (cf. also *hehe, haha, erm*) take on the character of words, they become part of the language system and are thus also available in speech, for example when a speaker "says [hiːhi]" instead of actually laughing (Coulmas 1981: 121, our translation).

In conclusion, it must be noted that the arguments put forward for and against the dependence of writing on speech are not contradictory. From a historical perspective, it cannot be denied that writing came secondary to speaking. However, when writing is analysed synchronically and independently, this subordination loses much of its relevance. Ultimately, the position taken in the discussion about the relationship between speech and writing depends on one's perspective and respective goals. Since in this book, we are interested in the study of writing in its own right, we lean towards the autonomous position.

2.4 Linguistic resources in spoken and written communication

2.4.1 Interaction between modality and linguistic resources

In this section, we will investigate the interaction between the features of speech and writing as distinct modalities (as discussed in ⟶ Section 2.2) on the one hand and the linguistic resources used in various forms of spoken and written communication on the other. Reconsider decontextualisation and explicitness as examples. As Günther (1983: 33, our translation) notes, "it is characteristic of written communication that the reader is not present during the writing process and that the writer is not present during the reading process". In this sense, written texts are utterances that are part of 'stretched' communication situations. The absence of respective communication partners and thus the lack of a shared context makes necessary more explicit expression in writing. Consequently, writers cannot freely use, for example, deictic expressions to refer to the place or time at which they are writing since readers will not be able to retrieve the meaning of words such as *here* and *now* when no further context is provided. In other words, written texts are largely independent and detached from their producers (cf. one of Plato's critiques of writing ⟶ Section 1.2). For this reason, texts must include all the information necessary to be comprehended on their own by addressees, i.e., writers must conceive them in ways that make them understandable despite the fact that they are detached from the context in which they were produced (cf. Ehlich 1981). This, of course, affects the use of linguistic resources in writing. In speech, above-mentioned expressions such as *here*, *there*, *that one* can be readily used by speakers to refer to places, objects, etc. that exist in the shared perceptual space of speakers and listeners. Furthermore, listeners can use pronouns to directly react to any of the speakers' preceding utterances (cf. *I don't understand this!*); these pronouns acquire their meaning only from the situational context. By contrast, in written communication, such references must be contextualised explicitly, as in the example *In your last letter, you wrote* [. . .]. *I don't understand that*$_{[anaphoric]}$. Here, the anaphoric element *that* refers to the textual space created by the writer and not the reader's perceptual space (cf. Ehlich 1981).

Another aspect revealing that modality-specific features and linguistic resources interact is that spoken utterances are frequently characterised by ungrammatical sentence structure, dialectisms, colloquial expressions, ellipses, self-corrections, discourse particles, etc. – features which are notably absent from most (formal) written texts. Of course, these features also do not occur in all spoken forms of expression but are rather bound to the degree of formality of specific forms of communication (see below). For example, scientific talks or sermons, because they are of a more formal nature, are usually characterised precisely by the lack of these features. On the other hand, certain written texts such as notes that were jotted down quickly, comments and messages in social media or messenger services, and greeting cards addressed to close friends may well exhibit these features characteristic of prototypical spoken communication.

In her interesting but little-received study on informal writing in everyday situations, Häcki Buhofer (1985) shows that written texts can exhibit linguistic features commonly attributed to spoken communication. She argues that features usually assumed to be characteristic of writing are based on narrow analyses of literary texts, i.e., a specific and formal genre of writing. It is for this literary bias in analysing writing that written communication is generally considered to be more explicit, more formal, and more elaborate than spoken communication. Associated with this is also the assumption that writing is more difficult and that, by comparison with spoken utterances, written texts "contain a surplus of linguistic achievement" (Häcki Buhofer 1985: 74, our translation). According to Häcki Buhofer (1985: 322, our translation), this is an inaccurate simplification: "One does not conclude from the difficulty of giving a speech that everyday speech is difficult. Nor does one have to conclude from the difficulty of writing an essay the difficulty of everyday writing". As this discussion underlines, there appears to be no fixed correlation between the choice of certain linguistic means of expression and the modality of language used (spoken or written). In the following, we will discuss this observation more systematically.

Most of the differences between writing and speech that were addressed in ⟶ Section 2.2 arise because data in the two modalities is transmitted through different channels: writing is visual and tactile while speech is primarily acoustic and accompanied by gestural and visual components (such as facial expressions). This leads to different material features, both dynamic (i.e., concerning production and perception) and static (i.e., concerning the resulting product, written and spoken utterances). As implied above, it is these material features that are assumed to favour or facilitate (but not determine) the use of certain grammatical, lexical, etc. resources at the linguistic level. That speech is mostly produced synchronously and quickly (in comparison to writing, where writers commonly have more time and write for an absent audience), for example, is claimed to be associated with fragmented or ungrammatical sentences.

2.4.2 Koch and Oesterreicher's model

An attempt to account for the association between modality and linguistic means of expression comes from Peter Koch and Wulf Oesterreicher, scholars well-known in the German-language research area. In their paper "Language of immediacy – language of distance: Orality and literacy from the perspective of language theory and linguistic history" (the translated version of their original and widely received German 1985 paper), they point out that the terms 'spoken' and 'written' are ambiguous, leading them to propose a more fine-grained approach. Firstly, in line with what was established above, they observe that 'spoken' and 'written' can refer to how an utterance is materialised. In this respect, Koch and Oesterreicher (2012: 443, emphasis in original) speak of "the *phonic* and the *graphic* code as the two forms of realization of linguistic utterances" and term this the dimension of medium[20] (or medial dimension). Secondly, 'spoken' and 'written' can also refer to the communicative strategies and linguistic resources that are used in communication, which was the second aspect mentioned above. According to Koch and Oesterreicher, now, every time language users produce an utterance, they choose such forms of expression that are either based mostly on linguistic resources characteristic of speech ('spoken') or those characteristic of writing ('written'). This is captured by the dimension of conception (or conceptual dimension).

What makes this medial/conceptual distinction not only valuable but indispensable is that any given utterance can be classified as conceptually (rather) spoken[21] or conceptually (rather) written regardless of whether it is medially

20 Koch and Oesterreicher's use of the word 'medium' may be misleading as it is unrelated to the technical meaning of the word that understands a medium to be an object on which information is, for instance, stored, transmitted, or received, such as a telephone or a computer.

21 We adopt the English terminology proposed by Koch and Oesterreicher (2012) in the official English translation of their German paper (Koch and Oesterreicher 1985) but want to note that we deem the use of '(conceptually) spoken' for the conceptual dimension problematic as it is semantically associated with the medial dimension from which Koch and Oesterreicher actually seek to distinguish the conceptual dimension. A terminological alternative – and more accurate translation of German *mündlich* – would be to speak of 'conceptually oral'. Cf. also Biber and Finegan (1989: 493): "It is possible to characterize particular genres as relatively literate or oral, where 'literate' refers to language produced in situations that are typical for writing, and 'oral' refers to language produced in situations typical of speaking" (cf. also below).

spoken or written, i.e., realised in the phonic or graphic code. To give an example: usually, a greeting card addressed to a close friend – which is clearly medially written – is conceptually spoken, whereas a scientific lecture – which is medially spoken – is commonly conceptually written. Such cross-combinations of the medial and conceptual dimensions are deemed particularly interesting for research. Notably, while the medial dimension is absolute in that an utterance can exist only in either of the two modalities[22] (but cf. Heyd 2021), the parenthesised use of 'rather' above implies that the conceptual dimension represents a continuum with numerous intermediate stages (cf. Koch and Oesterreicher 2012: 444).

Figure 2 shows how different forms of communication can be classified within Koch and Oesterreicher's approach. While the vertical axis reflects the absolute dichotomy of graphic vs. phonic, the horizontal axis reveals where various types of discourse are positioned on the conceptual continuum between spoken and written. Note that these positions of forms of communication are only approximate and may change depending on their specific features. For example, a private letter may also be positioned closer to the pole of conceptually written communication when it exhibits certain linguistic properties (see below). Inversely, it is possible that instances of phonic forms of communication that are usually classified as conceptually spoken (e.g., telephone conversations and interviews) display only few features characteristic of conceptually spoken communication.

A further feature of Koch and Oesterreicher's (2012: 445–451) model is that they assign the attributes 'immediacy' and 'distance' to the poles of conceptually spoken and conceptually written communication, respectively. These terms are intended to refer to the situational conditions in which the two types of communication usually occur. They include the spatiotemporal proximity of communication partners, their familiarity or unfamiliarity with each other, the degree of privacy or publicity of communication, and spontaneity; they are listed in Table 1.

In her critical discussion of the model, Hennig (2000: 116) points out that the forms of communication characterised by the communicative conditions listed under 'language of immediacy' are most likely to occur in everyday communication (e.g., personal conversations in one's family or among friends).[23] However, considering certain forms of communication such as telephone conversations (in general), consultations, discussions on talk shows, etc., it becomes apparent that the conditions of communication proposed by Koch and Oesterreicher prove insufficient. The parameter 'private (non-public)/public', for example,

22 As was mentioned in previous sections, with sign language, there exists a third modality of language that is neither spoken nor written.

23 For a recent discussion and modification of the model, see Werner (2021).

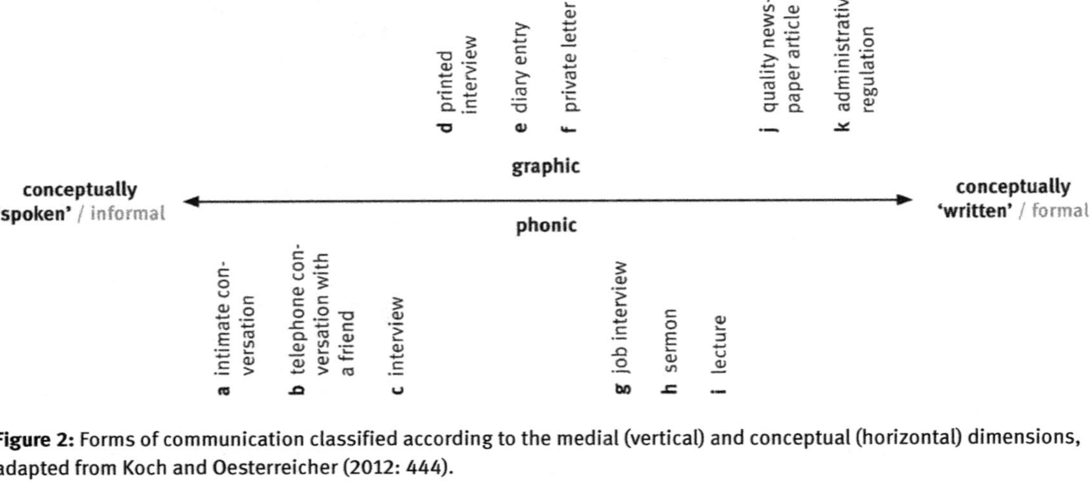

Figure 2: Forms of communication classified according to the medial (vertical) and conceptual (horizontal) dimensions, adapted from Koch and Oesterreicher (2012: 444).

Table 1: Conditions of communication (Koch and Oesterreicher 2012: 450).

language of immediacy	language of distance
dialogue	monologue
familiarity of partners	unfamiliarity of partners
face-to-face interaction	spatiotemporal separation
free development of topics	fixation of topics
non-public	public
spontaneity	reflection
'involvement'	'detachment'
context embeddedness	contextual dissociation
expressivity	'objectivity'
affective speech	

cannot cover consultations as they are not exactly private but at the same time also not public in the sense of being accessible to everyone (cf. Hennig 2000: 117). Phone calls are not face-to-face communication, yet they are not characterised by spatiotemporal distance as only spatial distance applies.

On closer examination, thus, the assumption of a correlation between conceptually spoken/immediacy on the one hand and conceptually written/distance on the other is untenable. Another contemporary example that highlights this is communication on the social network Twitter: users on Twitter employ forms of expression that in many cases can be classified as conceptually spoken, and they do this despite (mostly) not knowing each other and the fact that their communication is public. It is likely that the anonymity afforded by Twitter invites communication following the maxim 'write as you speak'. Analysed within Koch and Oesterreicher's framework, the communicative conditions 'dialogue', 'spontaneity' and 'free development of topics' apply to Twitter communication, whereas 'face-to-face interaction', 'familiarity of partners', 'privacy', and 'context embeddedness' do not apply. Interlocutors share a virtual space but are not present at the same location and thus cannot deictically refer to a non-virtual shared perceptual space. Nor is Twitter communication embedded in a synchronous setting as, unlike in prototypical speech, addressees are presented only with the finished (written) utterance that was posted by other users while the production process itself is/was not perceivable to them.

These considerations regarding Koch and Oesterreicher's approach raise the question of how features associated with the poles of conceptually spoken vs. written communication can be adequately captured if not through typical conditions of communication. One possibility are linguistic resources and communicative strategies themselves: for example, utterances that are conceptually spoken are usually linguistically less elaborated, which is to say that they are less formal than conceptually written utterances (cf. Akinnaso's approach below). In this vein, Koch and Oesterreicher (2012: 450) collect important linguistic resources and communicative strategies under the heading of 'verbalisation strategies' (cf. Table 2). Notably, this approach remains solely descriptive as it does not explain *why* these features are used in medially spoken vs. written communication (cf. Akinnaso 1982: 116 and below).

Table 2: Verbalisation strategies.

pole of conceptually spoken communication	pole of conceptually written communication
process orientation	'reification'
tentativeness	finality
less/lower:	*higher/more:*
density of information	
compactness	
integration	
complexity	
elaboration	
planning	

These verbalisation strategies, in turn, are characterised by specific means of expression. For example, an utterance is regarded linguistically less elaborated when it consists of shortened sentences and exhibits grammatical errors and anacolutha. Such an utterance is then usually interpreted as being positioned closer to the pole of conceptually spoken communication. At the lexical level, the use of interjections, word repetitions, fused words, colloquial expressions, conversational particles, etc. is common for conceptually spoken utterances. Conceptually written texts, now, can either be defined *ex negativo* by the absence of these features or on the basis of specific features characteristic of conceptually written communication, which include participle clauses (e.g., *Entering the room, she initiated a conversation.*), nominalisations (e.g., *his insistence on an answer*), and hypotactic constructions (e.g., *He is dismissed because he is sick.* instead of *He is dismissed, he is sick.*) (cf. Akinnaso 1982: 99–111 for a thorough discussion of lexical, semantic, and syntactic features found in spoken and written communication).

2.4.3 Alternative approaches and open questions

We now turn to two approaches similar to Koch and Oesterreicher's: that of F. Niyi Akinnaso and that of Douglas Biber. On the one hand, what Akinnaso subsumes under the term 'modality' corresponds neatly with Koch and Oesterreicher's medial dimension and our conception in ⟶ Section 2.1. On the other hand, for Akinnaso, the linguistic resources captured by their conceptual dimension are based on the degree of formality characteristic of communicative situations (cf., for example, Akinnaso 1985). His two 'dimensions', thus, are modality and formality. Koch and Oesterreicher (1994: 587) also emphasise that the medial and conceptual dimensions are independent of each other, but their terminological choice – referring to linguistic resources and strategies as 'conceptually spoken' and 'conceptually written' – does highlight a certain correlation between them. By contrast, Akinnaso's terms underline that linguistic resources are independent of modality but, by relying on formality, put emphasis on a different determining factor for the diverse linguistic resources used in various forms of communication (such as lectures, phone calls, letters, or WhatsApp messages).

In fact, Akinnaso scrutinises the assumption of a correlation between linguistic resources or strategies typical of certain forms of communication and the fact that they are commonly used in spoken vs. written communication. He argues that it is based on the fact that comparisons of speech and writing have hitherto focused mostly on contrasting formal written discourse with informal spoken discourse (cf. Akinnaso 1985: 329), i.e., data differing not only in their modality but also significantly in their degree of formality. Such comparisons result from misleading assumptions such as "that 'literacy' is superior to 'orality'" and "that formal writing is more complex than any form of speech" (Akinnaso 1985: 330; cf. also ⟶ Section 2.5.1). Referring to his own research on (especially ritual) oral communication (cf. Akinnaso 1982, 1983) as well as on sociolinguist Deborah Tannen's (1982) work on written communication, Akinnaso claims that when subject (i.e., the person speaking/writing), topic, communicative task, and level of formality are kept constant, one can "achieve similar linguistic structuring in both spoken and written" communication (Akinnaso 1985: 331). The bottom line of his approach, which is similar to the one arrived at by Koch and Oesterreicher, is that linguistic features assumed to correlate with the spoken and written modalities "grow out of either/both the genres chosen or/and the requirements of a specific level of formality rather than out of modality-specific constraints *per se*" (Akinnaso 1985: 330, emphasis in original).

Douglas Biber (1988) has provided another important study on the differences between linguistic resources used in (both) speech and writing. In his corpus-based statistical approach, he establishes six 'dimensions' (cf. Table 3) that partially overlap with the conditions of communication as well as verbalisation strategies proposed by Koch and Oesterreicher (see above) and are used to differentiate between genres (what we have called 'forms of communication') typical of spoken and written communication.

Table 3: Dimensions allowing a differentiation between oral and literate genres (= forms of communication), based on Biber (1988: 115).

dimension	description
(1) **informational vs. involved production**	discourse with interactional, affective, involved purposes, associated with strict real-time production and comprehension constraints vs. discourse with highly informational purposes, carefully crafted and highly edited
(2) **narrative vs. non-narrative concerns**	discourse with primary narrative purposes vs. discourse with non-narrative purposes (expository, descriptive, or other)
(3) **explicit vs. situation-dependent reference**	discourse that identifies references fully and explicitly through relativisation vs. discourse that relies on nonspecific deictics and reference to an external situation for identification purposes
(4) **overt expression of persuasion**	features on this dimension are associated with speakers' expression of their own points of view or with argumentative styles intended to persuade addressees
(5) **abstract vs. non-abstract information**	texts with a highly abstract and technical information focus vs. texts with non-abstract focuses
(6) **on-line informational elaboration**	informational discourse produced under highly constrained conditions in which information is presented in a relatively loose, fragmented manner vs. other types of discourse, whether informational discourse that is highly integrated or discourse that is not informational

As Biber (1988: 160–161) notes, speech and writing are "relatively well-distinguished among Dimensions 1, 3, and 5", although even with respect to these dimensions, there is considerable overlap. Thus, genres of spoken communication tend to be involved, are situation-dependent, and non-abstract, while genres of written communication are characterised by informational production, explicit reference, and abstract information. Overall, Biber's approach is largely compatible with Koch and Oesterreicher's distinction between conceptually spoken and written communication. Terminologically, his use of the term 'oral' to refer to language produced in situations typical of speaking and 'literate' to designate language produced in situations typical of writing appears more appropriate than Koch and Oesterreicher's suggested terms (cf. Biber 1988: 161). The gist of both conceptions is that they associate specific linguistic resources and forms of communication/genres in which they are used with modality.

Several open questions regarding the medial dimension/modality and the conceptual dimension (or, per Akinnaso, formality) shall not be left unmentioned at the end of this section:

1. Some utterances cannot as a whole be assigned to one of the two poles as only individual passages in them can be straightforwardly assigned to conceptually spoken/written communication or informality/formality (cf. Dürscheid 2006). Take scientific lectures, which Koch and Oesterreicher assign to the pole of conceptually written communication without further discussion despite the fact that lectures are organised differently than texts intended for silent reading. When planning a lecture, writers (who, at a later point in time, are in most cases also the presenters) often intentionally include features uncharacteristic of conceptually written communication precisely because the text is ultimately intended for oral presentation. By means of prosodic features (such as volume), for example, speakers can put emphasis on elements that can only be hinted at in the written version (e.g., with underlining). This is part of a strategy called staged or enacted orality, which can concern both the medial and conceptual dimensions. With respect to the medial dimension, enactment occurs every time written texts are presented orally (e.g., in radio or television broadcasts as well as in the theatre, in scientific lectures, or sermons).

Note that in the context of staged orality it is irrelevant whether it is obvious that a written text serves as the basis of such spoken communication or whether speakers attempt to 'conceal' it – as is arguably the case when newsreaders read from a teleprompter (cf. Burger and Luginbühl 2014). In both cases it is a matter of transfer from one modality to the other and only the degrees of enactment differ. Burger and Luginbühl (2014: 189, our translation) call these utterances "secondarily spoken texts" (from German *sekundär gesprochene Texte*). If, by contrast, attempts are made to imitate the spontaneity and dialogic nature of spoken communication through the use of certain linguistic resources, then enactment concerns (also) the conceptual dimension. This is occasionally used as a stylistic device in literary texts (e.g., to mark inner monologues) and is also characteristic of imitated dialogues in foreign language textbooks and newspaper texts (following the maxim 'Write how people speak'). Inversely, features of conceptually written communication can also be used in speech. This is referred to as staged or enacted literacy and captures how speakers may intentionally use syntactic structures and lexical expressions that are commonly associated with conceptually written/formal communication (e.g., *furthermore*, *however*, *by no means*). While such expressions can be used ironically, they can also be used to render spoken utterances stylistically more elegant and linguistically more elaborated (e.g., during scientific discussions or job interviews). Notably, enacted literacy occurs more sporadically than enacted orality because spoken utterances are not usually thoroughly planned before they are uttered and speakers – unlike writers – do not have the opportunity to refine their formulations (cf. Feature 5 in ⟶ Section 2.2).

2. A point closely related to the first one is that the development of information and communication technology has led to new forms of and platforms for communication not included in the frameworks of Koch and Oesterreicher, Biber, or Akinnaso (e.g., video chat, WhatsApp, Facebook). In order to do justice these 'new' kinds of data and consider the specific characteristics of online communication, a distinction between digital and non-digital forms of written communication becomes necessary (cf. Heyd 2021). It is relevant on the grounds that, as is repeatedly emphasised in media research, the mode of transmission has a significant influence on a text's linguistic features (cf. McLuhan's 1964 well-known phrase 'the medium is the message').

At this point, we have still not arrived at a definite answer of why the medial and conceptual dimensions often correlate. A likely contributing factor is the normativity inherent in many forms of (Western) literacy instruction and thus literacy acquisition. As Akinnaso (1982: 111) notes: "All along in the process of acquiring writing skills, the learner is taught to pay particular attention to the choice of words and their arrangement, appealing to such notions as 'grammaticality,' 'correctness,' and 'proper organization'". And while he does also mention "modality-specific pragmatic constraints" (Akinnaso 1982: 199), his later focus, as mentioned above, is on formality, as he argues that the linguistic resources used in various forms of communication are influenced mainly by the formality of the communicative situations in which they (supposedly) commonly occur. However, that there are many interesting examples that do not fit into this mould of prototypicality and make necessary a fine-grained analysis has been evidenced by several examples given above.

Finally, while the question of whether or not linguistic features are associated with the spoken or written modalities cannot be settled here, it is noteworthy to remark on the motivation that underlies the assumption of such associations. As Akinnaso puts it, "researchers have been looking at spoken and written language as 'autonomous' objects" (Akinnaso 1985: 352) that are viewed as "separate, discontinuous entities, thus making it difficult, if not impossible, to look for anything other than differences" (Akinnaso 1985: 324; cf. ⟶ Section 2.5.1 for the discontinuity hypothesis). Most detrimental, however, has been the neglect of focusing on "how particular forms of language are motivated and perpetuated by the functions they perform" (Akinnaso 1985: 352). If we return to the conception introduced above (⟶ Section 2.1), it is one and the same abstract language system that is materialised in the modalities of speech and writing. Language users exploit the system's resources depending on pragmatic factors such as their intended communicative purpose and the circumstances of the communicative situation they find themselves in. And while the linguistic features characterising the resulting utterances may and will certainly differ depending on whether they are (medially) spoken or written, the pragmatic factors are arguably more decisive. In a nutshell, both conceptual 'writtenness/spokenness' and formality/informality of utterances depend on – as Akinnaso puts it – the functions these utterances are intended to perform.

2.5 Perspectives from anthropology

While the preceding sections have focused on a linguistic view of the relationship between speech and writing and the concepts associated with them, in this section, the perspective is shifted to anthropology through an exemplary discussion of the concepts (or rather: heterogeneous, broad fields) of 'literacy' and 'orality' as well as how they are related. These terms are indeed most closely tied to the discipline of anthropology, where, in the 1960s and 1970s, pertinent research on literacy gained traction. During that time, several influential books and articles were published, among them *The Gutenberg galaxy* by Marshall McLuhan (1962), *Preface to Plato* by Eric Havelock (1963), "The consequences of literacy", a widely cited paper by Jack Goody and Ian Watt (1963), *The savage mind* by Claude Lévi-Strauss (1966), and, notably, Goody's *The domestication of the savage mind* (1977), whose title is an obvious reference to Lévi-Strauss (cf. Chandler 1994).

What these works have in common is their (at times implicit) assumption of a so-called 'Great Divide' between different types of cultures: literate cultures on the one hand and oral cultures on the other. Aside from *Great Divide theory*, this view is also referred to as *discontinuity hypothesis* since it conceives of literacy and orality as utterly divergent phenomena. Myriad binaries are claimed to correlate with this absolute dichotomy, binaries that are instrumentalised to describe different kinds of society. They include primitive (cf. 'savage' in the mentioned book titles) vs. civilised, pre-logical vs. logical, and traditional vs. modern, a selection that should already highlight problems inherent in such a view. Summarised succinctly, a dichotomy based on such binaries represents a form of othering (cf. Besnier 2000: 143) exercised to support "claims regarding 'Western' superiority" (Street 1995: 154). It is absolutely vital – both from an anthropological perspective and in the context of an interdisciplinary and cross-linguistic grapholinguistics – to strive for a more fine-grained picture of practices of orality and literacy that captures their relationship with several factors of social, cultural, political, historical, technological, and ideological nature, among others. That being said, we have already introduced the core of a second important distinction: that between autonomous[24] models of literacy (and orality), in which literacy is interpreted mostly as a homogeneous set of skills (= reading and writing) independent of the sociocultural context, and an ideological conception of literacy, which indeed conceives of literacy as closely interacting with the above-mentioned factors. In essence, the ideological conception holds that a given literacy practice is inseparably embedded in and influenced by the specific context in (and purpose for) which it is used.

A work in which the assumption of a 'Great Divide' is most palpable is Walter Ong's book *Orality and literacy. The technologizing of the word* (first published in 1982, cited here in its 30th anniversary edition from 2012), which "has dominated the approach to literacy, not only in academic circles, but also in more powerful domains" (Street 1995: 153), feeding policy debates and propagating the significance of literacy in the media (cf. Street and Lefstein 2007: 97). Because of the clarity with which its (at times grandiose) claims are formulated, it will be the focus of the following section, serving as a representative of both 'Great Divide' theories and autonomous conceptions of literacy. After that, the opposing ideological conception of literacy will be presented.

2.5.1 Autonomous conception of literacy and 'Great Divide' theories

Before turning to Ong, it is necessary to comment on research that has greatly influenced him, especially anthropologist Jack Goody's work.[25] In essence, Goody investigated the attributes that others (among them Lévi-Strauss) had described as characteristic of primitive and advanced cultures under the lens of "changes in the mode of communication, especially in the introduction of various forms of writing" (Gee 2007: 72). By examining societies from ancient Greek culture to non-literate and semi-literate societies of today, Goody sought to show that changes in ways of thought and cultural organisation are bound to literacy. Put simply, he claimed that it is literacy that *domesticated* the *savage mind*, cf. the respective titles of his and Lévi-Strauss' books above. In other words, Goody viewed literacy

24 Note that autonomous conceptions of literacy are unrelated to the autonomy hypothesis as presented in ⟶ Section 2.3.2.

25 Part of this section is also adapted from Dürscheid (2016a: Chapter 1).

as a 'technology of intellect' (cf. Collins 1995: 76). His work is highly representative of the autonomous conception as literacy is regarded as one homogeneous phenomenon that separates cultures that are literate from those that are not, creating the aforementioned 'Great Divide'. This view has been given various additional labels in the literature, among them 'literacy thesis' (cf. Bartlett et al. 2011: 155; cf. also Halverson 1982 for a rebuttal with a focus on Goody's work) or 'literacy myth' (cf. Graff 1986: 62), and it enjoyed popularity especially in American and Canadian scholarship (cf. Collins 1995: 77). Crucially, the 'Great Divide' between literacy and orality carries with it an implicit ethnocentrism, as 'literacy' is defined on the basis of Western literacy, which serves as an allegedly superior background against which not only illiteracy (or 'orality', see below) but also other types of literacy (e.g., in China or India) are devalorised (cf. Collins 1995: 78).

Several beliefs can be condensed from Goody's work as well as the works mentioned above. Olson (1994) identifies six as central, which represent the very core of 'Great Divide' theories: (1) writing is the transcription of speech; (2) writing is superior to speech; (3) the alphabetic type of writing systems is technologically superior to all other types; (4) literacy is an organ of social progress; (5) literacy is an instrument of cultural and scientific development; (6) literacy is an instrument of cognitive development.

While (1) was addressed in ⟶ Section 2.1 and (3) will be discussed in the context of Eurocentric teleologies proposed in writing system typology (⟶ Section 6.5), (2) merits further attention since it contradicts the widely held linguistic view that speech is superior (also in the sense of 'more important to investigate') than writing. Indeed, it appears anthropology was influenced by scripticism (⟶ Section 1.2) in having the "implicit conviction" that "written texts [. . .] were somehow the most proper subject of study" (Finnegan 1990: 131). Unlike in linguistics, however, this implicit conviction eventually manifested itself in the more global, explicit, and, most importantly, accepted view that literacy was superior to orality, which was reflected by anthropology's tendency to focus on literacy. The same – save for explicit awareness – occurred in linguistics as methodology was catered to writing, which served as a data basis for vital findings, while linguists' proclaimed view, however, remained that speech was superior to writing. Olson's points (3) to (6) can be treated as an inseparable package and the core of the 'literacy thesis' as they propagate that literacy revolutionises the cultures that develop it. Crucially, this view "oversimplifies orality and totalises the effects of literacy" (Yagelski n. d.) in a "technologically deterministic fashion" (Finnegan 1990: 143). These convictions also fundamentally shape Walter Ong's work, to which we now turn.

In his research, Ong ([1982] 2012: 3) aims to elucidate "the differences in 'mentality' between oral and writing cultures". This means he is less concerned with the historical transition from orality to literacy and the associated changes in social, political, and economic structures and instead focuses on different ways of thinking that are predominant in what he calls oral vs. literate cultures. "[A] literate person", Ong notes (2012: 12, emphasis in original), "cannot fully *recover* a sense of what the word is to purely oral people". Accordingly, in his study, Ong attempts to provide readers with an impression of how profoundly he believes literacy shapes our thoughts and actions. In his account, literate cultures (or 'high-technology' cultures) are characterised by the widespread knowledge of literacy and the use of writing, whereas oral cultures (or 'verbomotor' cultures) are those that have no knowledge of literacy; they include both those that existed before the initial development of writing but also those that to this day remain untouched by the development of writing.[26] This assessment already implies that for Ong, literacy and orality are, firstly, distinct phenomena that form an absolute dichotomy, secondly, autonomous in that they are not conceived of as embedded in and influenced by social, political, ideological, historical, etc. factors, and, thirdly, in and of themselves homogeneous as there is only 'one' literacy and 'one' orality that can be captured by these umbrella terms. Problematically, Ong's understanding of literacy (for orality see below) is rather biased and microscopic as what he "is claiming for 'literate society' appears to be the particular conventions, beliefs and practices of certain subcultures, most notably the western, academic subculture of which he himself is a part" (Street 1995: 156).

For Ong, like for other scholars adhering to an autonomous conception, literacy is the ability to read and write. Accordingly, at the level of the individual, a literate person is understood as someone who has acquired these skills and, at the collective level, a literate culture is one in which a majority of members have mastered these skills. There are various degrees of this collective literacy, one of them being *preliteracy* (also referred to as *protoliteracy* or *oligoliteracy*, cf. Goody and Watt 1963: 313): preliterate societies are predominantly illiterate, but a small proportion of the population is literate and uses writing for specific purposes. Such societies differ from literate ones mainly in the social functions that written communication assumes: in preliterate cultures, literacy is rudimentary and limited to only few peripheral functions, while in literate cultures, literacy is crucial for the very functioning of society, as their members communicate with

---

26 Note that the percentage of cultures that to this day have no knowledge of literacy is small. As Haarmann (1991: 19, our translation) notes: "In multilingual areas, many of those whose first language is not written also participate in the use of writing, provided that their second language is a written language (e.g., bilingual Kurds in Turkey who read and write Turkish). Only a comparatively small part of the world population remains without access to modern written culture (e.g., indigenous peoples in the Amazon Basin)" (cf. also Street 1995: 155).

each other not just as speakers and listeners but also as writers and readers – in legislation, administration, education, but also in production and trade, to name only some contexts (cf. Glück 2016c: 595). Preliteracy must be distinguished from illiteracy, the "state of complete lack of literacy, the complete absence of familiarity with written communication" (Glück 1987: 182, our translation). Notably, the use of terms such as 'preliteracy' and 'illiteracy' is problematic because they reflect a view in which orality (the phenomenon that is developmentally and chronologically primary) is interpreted from the perspective of literacy, the secondary phenomenon. The reason for this is that literacy is the state 'we' in literate societies are familiar with and accustomed to (cf. Ong 2012: 13; Koch and Oesterreicher 2012: 458). It is also a highly reductive, *ex negativo* approach since the fact that 'oral cultures' (a problematic generalisation in itself, see below) lack literacy is not what characterises them.

As for literacy, Ong (2012: 2) notes that it "began with writing [in the sense of handwriting, DM/CD] but, at a later stage of course, also involves print". In addition to manuscripts (from Latin *manus* 'hand' and *scribere* 'to write'), originally meaning only handwritten texts, and 'typescripts', i.e., typewritten texts, a third relevant type of texts has emerged in what could be called 'compuscripts', which include all texts written with a computer or, more generally, an electronic device (cf. Ludwig 2007). Such compuscripts are created using a (real or virtual) keyboard and are also, in a sense, typographic. However, unless they are printed out and become a permanent analogue text, they are visible only on the screen. Their characters are 'dematerialised', consisting only of electronic pixels rather than colour pigments on paper (or a different writing surface). As elaborated above (cf. Feature 5 in ⟶ Section 2.2), this means that already produced text can be modified rather effortlessly. Entire paragraphs can be moved (or deleted) freely and the text as a whole can easily take on new shapes. This (re)organisability and plannable nature of writing is claimed to contribute to the way humans cognitively process writing.

As for its influence on communication, in most autonomous conceptions of writing, literacy is claimed to have affected not only the medial dimension but also the conceptual dimension: as Günther (1993b: 89, our translation) argues, "the cornerstone of 'pure' conceptual orality is available to highly literate people only in exceptional situations (when cursing, in areas occupied by home supporters at a championship game, etc.)". Accordingly, the main assumption is that literate people use language mainly through the 'lens of literacy', so much so that Ong famously claims that "writing restructures consciousness" (cf. the title of Chapter 4 in Ong 2012). The claim that writing changes our view of language and that literacy has observable cognitive effects is suggested by, among others, the following examples:

1. Although this is not (always) true, literate people using phonographic writing systems often believe they pronounce words precisely the way they spell them. This becomes obvious in the way adults correct children's spelling errors: for example, adults commonly believe that a child who spells German *Rad* 'wheel' orthographically incorrect as *<Rat> would surely have to hear that a [d] is spoken at the end of the word (example taken from Günther 1981: 62). However, in German, obstruents are in fact devoiced in syllable-final position, so what is uttered at the end of *Rad* is indeed [t], meaning the child who wrote <Rat> heard it correctly. Likewise, it is believed that children learning to read and write in English 'must know that the word *better* contains the two consonant letters <t> since they also pronounce these letters when speaking the word out loud'. Assumptions such as these fall prey to several fallacies, the first of which lies in the assumption that since writing is constituted by individual segments, speech must also consist of segments when in fact, it is an acoustic continuum (⟶ Section 2.2). The second misconception is intimately related to the first and concerns the belief that since segments of writing can be classified unambiguously, 'segments' of speech can also be classified unambiguously. And the third fallacy: that what is spelled with <d>, <b>, <tt>, etc. in writing must be spoken as /d/, /b/ or /tt/ in speech. This is based on the implicit assumption that letters merely represent sounds (which is in line with the dependence hypothesis ⟶ Section 2.3.1), and that there are transparent and regular grapheme-phoneme correspondences.

2. Our conceptions of segments of sound (= phonemes), words, and sentences are highly influenced by or even based on/in writing. For example, users of writing systems that exhibit blank spaces between words commonly define 'word' to be precisely the unit enclosed by spaces before and after it (which even the scientific definition of the graphematic word is based on, cf. Fuhrhop 2008 and ⟶ Section 4.3.2). Furthermore, for alphabets, we understand a sentence to be a linguistic unit that is separated from the preceding and following sentences by a capital letter at its beginning and one of several punctuation marks (full stop, question mark, exclamation mark) at its end (cf. Schmidt 2016). There exist several views aiming to explain this dependence of linguistic concepts on writing: a more moderate view, held by, among others, David R. Olson (2002, 2016), claims that through literacy, language users become aware of their hitherto implicit knowledge about (their) language. In other words, literacy provides access to a linguistic metalevel by making explicit (and, crucially, visualising, i.e., permanently and visibly externalising) knowledge about language – that it consists of sounds, words, etc. In this vein, phonological awareness, broadly defined as the awareness of the different (segmental) sounds of one's language, which is often

claimed to be a vital prerequisite of literacy acquisition, is assumed to actually be a result or by-product of learning to read and write.

Another, less widespread view is more extreme in that it does not (only) hold that literacy makes users aware of units of language such as sounds, words, and sentences, but instead proposes that literacy constitutes, i.e., 'graphically and cognitively creates', those units in the first place. This way, "literacy re-constructs an alterior, re-formatted language that is made in the image of those graphical structures: the grapheme, the discrete word and the sentence" (Davidson 2019: 135). Proponents of this view argue that it is the segmentality of writing that not only facilitates but makes possible (or even inevitable)[27] thinking about the acoustic continuum of speech as consisting of segments, and that consequently, these sound segments are but epiphenomena (cf. Faber 1992; cf. also Morais 2021). Notably, just because these categories employed by literate language users to conceptualise language are created (or, according to the more moderate view, made conceivable) by writing does not mean that they do not become cognitively real once they have been established. In other words, while these categories may be 'fictions', they are "ideal fictions" in the sense of "internalised forms of technology" (Davidson 2019: 143) proving so plausible that diachronically, they have prevailed as categories we use to think about and make sense of language.

This view represents a form of graphic relativity according to which we introject "our language on lines laid down by an orthography: a case of making the inside (i.e., internal, cognitive representations) more like the outside, i.e., the external, public representations realized by a writing system" (Davidson 2019: 138). If this were true, it would mean that cognitive representations vary in users who have acquired and use distinct writing systems that differ significantly in the way they function (e.g., English and Chinese). And indeed, to empirically support his view, Davidson relies heavily on examples from Chinese, which uses a non-segmental morphographic writing system in which neither phonemes nor words are represented by visually or functionally salient units (⟶ Section 6.3). His specific examples include the fact that Chinese phonological theory developed differently than Western segmental phonology precisely because phonemes cannot be extracted from Chinese writing; furthermore, the literate Chinese think about language more in 'hanzi' (i.e., graphemes corresponding with morphemes) rather than words. Additionally, he mentions general cognitive differ-

---

27 A relevant question, here, is whether there would be any need to think of sound as consisting of segments or incentive to conceptualise it in such a way if it were not for segmental alphabetic writing.

ences between literate and illiterate or preliterate language users: the latter, for example, "do not show any awareness of [words]" (Davidson 2019: 140), and their "interpretations of sentences are fuzzier, often mistaken and determined more by pragmatics and less by syntax" (Davidson 2019: 146). In sum, the question of metalinguistic awareness and cognitive concepts is at the core of an assumed literacy/orality dichotomy.

Notably, claiming these specific linguistic concepts are at least crucially influenced by literacy does not mean that there can be no oral metalinguistic awareness. Indeed, Collins (1995: 79) emphasises that "[s]erious attempts to explore extant oral traditions suggest that nonliterate peoples can not only have richly developed philosophies of language but also systematic awareness of language as form, richly developed metalinguistic discourse".

3. Linguistic normativity is another aspect that is claimed to be affected by literacy. For example, the linguistic structure of written communication often serves as a prescriptive benchmark for spoken communication. At the syntactic level, this is reflected in teachers and parents telling children to speak in 'complete sentences'. The linguistic norm that we strive to conform to is thus based on the means of expressions that are typical of (conceptually) written communication. Interestingly, even grammarians adhere to norms based in writing. This is evident when sentences that are completely appropriate pragmatically, such as the utterance *To school.* as an answer to the question *Where are you going?* are characterised as elliptical. Obviously, the informatively and syntactically complete but partially redundant *I am going to school.* serves as the measure, although communicatively, nothing is 'missing' from the elliptical version, which is completely comprehensible in the given situational context. Of course, syntactic and pragmatic perspectives lead to different assessments here, but this example serves as further support for a writing-based understanding of 'sentence' (cf. the preceding point) which is, of course, more central to syntax than to pragmatics.

Arguably at least as important as their views on literacy is the way proponents of an autonomous conception treat its 'counterpart' orality. Again, Ong's views will serve as a more or less representative example. A problem with his treatment of orality that applies also to other scholars must be mentioned right away. Street (1995: 155) boils it down: "not only does [Ong] know little about the rich variety of different cultures that he aggregates together as 'oral', but according to his own argument he cannot ever know about them, since he himself is from a literate culture". As is evident from this, scholars' unfamiliarity with 'true orality' leads to what Ruth Finnegan (1990: 141) calls a "gross over-simplification" as the myriad facets of oral practices are squeezed into the corset of a hollow umbrella term such as 'orality'. Like 'literacy', the term 'orality' gives the false impression of a homogeneous phenomenon. Finnegan goes on to argue that

> writers have sometimes taken the term 'oral tradition' to be an undifferentiated and clearcut *thing* (as if with the same characteristics everywhere), 'oral society' as a meaningful and comprehensive characterisation of a single type of society, and the many differing modes of thought or thinking throughout the variegated riches of so many human cultures as summed up in the supposedly meaningful 'oral mentality'. [. . .] These simple-sounding terms are used as if they could really encapsulate in a single concept all the diverse ways (and we know from historical and anthropological research that they are diverse) in which human cultures and individuals outside a certain Western literature elite tradition have formulated and created and transmitted their insights and imagination.
> (Finnegan 1990: 141, emphasis in original)

That being premised, Ong distinguishes between two types of orality (primary and secondary), where primary orality corresponds to what was termed 'illiteracy' above:

> [. . .] I style the orality of a culture totally untouched by any knowledge of writing or print, 'primary orality'. It is 'primary' by contrast with the 'secondary orality' of present-day high-technology culture, in which a new orality is sustained by telephone, radio, television, and other electronic devices that depend for their existence and functioning on writing and print. (Ong 2012: 11)

As mentioned above, it is one of Ong's main goals to demonstrate just how difficult or even impossible it is for a literate person to think 'in the shoes' of a culture that has not been exposed to writing. To do so, Ong addresses readers directly:

> Try to imagine a culture where no one has ever 'looked up' anything. In a primary oral culture, the expression 'to look up something' is an empty phrase: it would have no conceivable meaning. Without writing, words as such have no visual presence, even when the objects they represent are visual. They are sounds. You might 'call' them back – 'recall' them. But there is nowhere to 'look' for them. (Ong 2012: 31)

A sound, however, Ong (2012: 32) continues, "exists only when it is going out of existence. It is not simply perishable but essentially evanescent, and it is sensed as evanescent". We will not go into detail here about the strategies 'oral cultures' develop to preserve in memory what they cannot write down in order to pass it on to succeeding generations. Methods that are often mentioned in the literature include formulaic repetition, the use of fixed expressions, and the rhythmising of speech (cf. Ong 2012: 57–67; Koch and Oesterreicher 2012: 457). A prominent example is the vast oral tradition of Indian culture with its enormous masses of texts (folktales, ballads, chants, prose, verses, etc.) that have been handed down orally.

To turn to Ong's central and most controversial claims, now, what does he hold are the relevant differences between ways of thought in oral vs. literate cultures? Oral thinking, according to him, is "situational rather than abstract" (Ong 2012: 49), whereas writing affords the possibility to make abstractions, to distance oneself from a given communication situation. To support this view, Ong reports on the research of psychologist Aleksandr Lurija, who, in the 1930s, had conducted field studies with both illiterate and moderately literate people (cf. Lurija 1976). Participants were asked, for example, to give names to geometric figures. They did so by naming them after objects (e.g., *moon, house, ball*) but not abstract concepts (e.g., *circle, square*). Ong cites Lurija to underline the supposed lack of a need for abstraction:

> 'Try to explain to me what a tree is.' 'Why should I? Everyone knows what a tree is, they don't need me telling them', replied one illiterate peasant, aged 22 [cited from Lurija 1976: 86, DM/CD]. Why define, when a real-life setting is infinitely more satisfactory than a definition? Basically, the peasant was right. There is no way to refute the world of primary orality. All you can do is walk away from it into literacy. (Ong 2012: 53)

It is paramount to underline that Ong does at points relativise differences by arguing that oral thinking should not be measured against the thinking of literate cultures (without, however, dropping his view of an absolute dichotomy between literacy vs. orality). This is evident in his critical comments on Lurija's approach:

> [. . .] an oral culture simply does not deal in such items as geometrical figures, abstract categorization, formally logical reasoning processes, definitions, or even comprehensive descriptions, or articulated self-analysis, all of which derive not simply from thought itself but from text-formed thought. Luria's [sic] questions are schoolroom questions associated with the use of texts, and indeed closely resemble or are identical with standard intelligence test questions got up by literates. They are legitimate, but they come from a world the oral respondent does not share. (Ong 2012: 54–55)

By mentioning 'schoolroom questions', Ong is up to something, which is spelled out by Gee (2007: 77), who observes that in Lurija's research, it is "unclear whether the results were caused by 'the ability to write and/or read' ('literacy' in the traditional sense) or by schooling, or even the new social institutions to which the Russian revolution exposed" Lurija's literate subjects. We will return to the question of how schooling is responsible for several of the effects attributed to literacy in the next section.

If the distinction between conceptually spoken (or informal) and conceptually written (or formal) (⟶ Section 2.4) is included in a rough and global comparison between literacy and orality, it can be argued that the use of linguistic strategies associated with conceptually spoken/informal communication is characteristic of oral cultures. Scheerer (1993) provides as an example the comparison of paratactic sentence structures in the history of creation (e.g., many *and*-constructions) and any paragraph in Kant's syntactically complex *Critique of pure reason*. Yet, while the "commonplace of literacy research that speech is additive rather than subordinating" (Ágel 2003: 20, our translation) may be justified to a large degree, it must be emphasised that there also exist oral forms of expression that can be classified as conceptually written/formal communication or – to phrase it more appropriately – elaborated spoken communication. Koch and Oesterreicher (1985: 29–30, 1994: 593) mention as examples proverbs, incantations and magic formulas, riddles, sagas, and heroic songs (cf. also Akinnaso 1983 on ritual oral communication).

To also characterise briefly the second type of orality described by Ong, it must be said that secondary orality, in contrast to primary orality, is associated with mass media. It exists only on the basis of literacy and owes its existence to technologies that allow the worldwide distribution of news via speech (radio, television, telephone, computer). Crucially, secondary orality connects a much larger group of people than primary orality ever could. In this context, Ong (2012: 134) notes that "[r]adio and television have brought major political figures as public speakers to a larger public than was ever possible before modern electronic developments". However, when considering more recent technological developments such as the internet as well as the online (and mobile) communication they make possible, secondary orality appears to have reached a pivotal turning point, maybe even a tertiary orality (cf. Heyd 2021). On the internet, communication takes place also in the modality of writing (e.g., via text chat, email, in social media). Communication via phone nowadays also proceeds not only in the form of phone calls but additionally via SMS (which, however, are used increasingly seldom) and currently widespread messenger apps such as WhatsApp, Facebook Messenger, and WeChat (in China), and apps such as TikTok and Instagram rely heavily on multimodality. Notably, voice messaging is gaining popularity in these initially text-based applications. Furthermore, as ongoing research deals with how speech recognition programs can convert what is spoken into writing – technologies involved in language assistants such as Siri or Alexa (cf. Brommer and Dürscheid 2021) – much of written communication may in the future be based on speech, further complicating the complex relationship between the two forms of communication.

2.5.2 Ideological conception of literacy

One of the major problems with an autonomous conception of literacy as well as 'Great Divide' theories is the difficulty of allocating with certainty any effects to literacy – or *just* literacy, that is. As Finnegan (1990: 144, emphasis in original) writes, "it is almost impossible to established [sic] that it was just *literacy* that was the cause (almost always it was only one factor in an extremely complex situation)" of both cognitive and societal effects that 'Great Divide' theorists attribute to it. A factor that was mentioned above as another possible influence is schooling; it emerged as central in psychologists Sylvia Scribner and Michael Cole's research, which was laid out in their influential *The psychology of literacy* (1981) and contributed significantly to a paradigm shift in the treatment of literacy.

In a nutshell, Scribner and Cole set out to examine literacy among the Vai in Liberia. The situation there lent itself to an investigation of graphic relativity and the cognitive effects of (specific types of) literacy as there are different types of literacy among the Vai: English alphabetic literacy acquired through formal schooling, literacy in the indigenous syllabographic Vai writing system that is acquired outside of a school setting and "with no connection with Western-style schooling" (Gee 2007: 77), as well as literacy in Arabic. These different types of literacy are not functionally equivalent but rather used for different purposes: English for government and education, "Vai literacy [. . .] primarily for keeping records and for letters", and Arabic literacy "for reading, writing, and memorizing the Koran" (Gee 2007: 77). Furthermore, knowledge of these literacies is not equally spread: some Vai are literate in one of these types of literacy, others in two or all three of them and, crucially, there are also those who are not literate at all. This special situation, in combination with the fact that only one of the types (English literacy) is tied to formal schooling, allowed disentangling the effects of literacy and schooling. The hypothesis was that if literacy is responsible for certain cognitive effects, then all literate Vai regardless of the type of literacy they had acquired should be affected by them, whereas if schooling was responsible, there should be differences between the various groups. In essence, the latter was the case, and "it is now widely acknowledged" that "the institutions of modern schooling often seem to produce the consequences attributed to literacy" (Collins 1995: 80).

However, it must imperatively be added that it would be reductionist to claim schooling is generally the cause for higher-order cognitive skills. Instead, it is associated with specific skills, as the Vai who were literate in alphabetic English performed better at what Scribner and Cole (1981: 242–243) termed 'talking-about tasks', i.e., they were superior when it came to verbal exposition and retained these skills regardless of how long they had been out of school. By contrast, although the subjects literate in English also performed better on other tasks (among them categorisation and abstract reasoning), this advantage was transient as it was dependent on how recently subjects had been schooled. Another relevant finding reported by Scribner and Cole was that the different types of literacy gave rise to diverse skills; being literate in syllabographic Vai helped with the segmentation of syllables, for example. In sum, their approach can be described as a 'practice account of literacy' as it emphasises that a given "type of literacy enhances quite specific skills that are practiced in carrying out that literacy" (Gee 2007: 79).

Although it was not what they had originally set out to do, with their study of Vai literacy (or rather literacies), Scribner and Cole provided a "compelling rejoinder to Ong's theories" (Yagelski n. d.) and to 'Great Divide' theories in general. This firmly shifted the focus of literacy research away from the autonomous conception and paved the way for an alternative view: the ideological conception. Brian V. Street, who was instrumental in the development of this new view, captures its essence by claiming that the effects other authors – most prominently Ong – had ascribed to literacy "are in fact those of the social context and the specific culture in which the literacy being described is located" (Street 1995: 157). In addition, the ideological conception of literacy has at its core various assumptions that negate those of the autonomous conception: (1) it understands literacy not as a "decontextualized 'ability' to write or read" (Gee 2007: 80); (2) it sees 'literacy' as the sum of heterogeneous literacy practices, which is why it speaks of plural 'literacies' rather than a single literacy (cf. Street 1984: 8); (3) these literacies are shaped by institutional circumstances and power relations (cf. Collins 1995: 80) and understood "in terms of concrete social practices" and "the ideologies in which [they] are embedded" (Gee 2007: 80), which lends the conception its name; (4) methodologically, the study of literacies should be particularistic and ethnographic (cf. Besnier 2000: 141).

Although the conception's focus is certainly on literacy, these listed assumptions also have important consequences on the views of a literacy-orality dichotomy. Thus, what applies to literacy also applies to orality; as highlighted by Finnegan's quote above, both are not homogeneous phenomena but "disappear into a myriad of social practices and concomitant values and world views" (Gee 2007: 80). Furthermore, as was already discussed in the context of the 'conceptual dimension' in the preceding section, oral and literate practices do not constitute an absolute dichotomy but rather a continuum (cf. Akinnaso 1985: 331) characterised by a "fluidity of interaction and considerable overlap" (Bartlett et al. 2011: 156). To distinguish it from the discontinuity assumed by 'Great Divide' theories, this view is sometimes also referred to as *continuity hypothesis*.

Eventually, an entire new paradigm developed in the so-called *New Literacy Studies* (NLS) which are founded on social constructivism as they – as outlined above – interpret literacies as social practice and action. While with their advent, anthropology became (or rather remained) pivotal in the study of literacy practices (cf. Bartlett et al. 2011: 165), another discipline grew increasingly devoted to them: sociolinguistics (cf. ⟶ Section 5.5 for sociolinguistic perspectives on writing). And indeed, the boundaries between anthropological and sociolinguistic research are often blurred, highlighting the tight interrelations and great similarities between different disciplines interested in the study of writing and literacy and thus the attractiveness of a comprehensive and interdisciplinary grapholinguistics. Fittingly, the combination of the first, structurally oriented sections of this chapter, which focused on a linguistic description of modalities, and the final, anthropological section once more underlines that the isolated study of the system and its structure is – at least if the goal is a theory of writing – incomplete when its use and its effects (both psycholinguistic/cognitive and sociocultural) are neglected.

3 Graphetics

At the outset of this chapter, the field of graphetics and its three subdisciplines – productional graphetics, descriptive graphetics, and perceptual graphetics – as well as the distinction between signal and symbol graphetics are described (Section 3.1). Next, core structural questions of graphetics are addressed (Section 3.2). In this context, a definition of scripts as visual inventories is provided and the basic units of graphetics – the concrete graph and the abstract basic shape – are introduced. Furthermore, important aspects of the visual organisation of writing as well as several attempts at segmenting basic shapes into constituent parts are discussed. The following section (Section 3.3) is then devoted to handwriting and typography, the two central ways in which writing is materialised, and addresses the most important concepts and questions in their analysis. Finally, Section 3.4 opens up the perspective of emergent literacy research by exemplarily investigating the graphetic features children pick up on in the first stages of literacy acquisition.

3.1 Foundations of graphetics

3.1.1 Definition and scope

In order to be visible – and to even exist – writing must have a material substance.[28] This substance is at the centre of graphetics, the field that will be explored in this chapter. Conceptually, two readings of 'graphetics' need to be distinguished: on the one hand, it is the (1) material subsystem of a writing system, consisting of all its graphic resources. On the other hand, it is the (2) eponymous grapholinguistic field that describes and studies said subsystem.

Graphetic aspects of writing are arguably among the subjects most neglected in linguistic research. Notably, at a time when the material substance of the spoken modality of language was already studied by phonetics, the "study of written or printed shapes [had] hardly been developed at all", David Crystal and Derek Davy noted in the late 1970s (Crystal and Davy 1979: 16). The reason for this marginalisation – aside from a general neglect of writing as an object of research (cf. ⟶ Section 1.2) – is simple: for a long time, the consensus in linguistics was that the appearance of written utterances does not affect their linguistic function – in a broad sense, their 'meaning'. This view was held, most prominently, by Saussure (1916: 143) and is captured aptly by German Egyptologist and cultural scientist Jan Assmann:

28 As mentioned before, writing can also be haptic/tactile as in the case of braille. In the following, we will focus exclusively on the visual form of writing.

https://doi.org/10.1515/9783110757835-003

> An 'R' can be chiselled in stone, written on paper, engraved in bark, printed in Fraktur, Bodoni, Garamond or Helvetica, without affecting its meaning, its reference to the phoneme [r] [sic] in the least. The only decisive factor is its distinctiveness: [. . .] everything else belongs to the 'materiality' of the sign, which is indispensable to make the meaning appear at all, but whose specificity does not contribute anything to the meaning itself.
>
> (Assmann 1988: 144, our translation)

As a consequence, the visual materiality indispensable to extract linguistic meaning from writing becomes 'invisible' to us. This situation has been compared to looking out of a window to see what is behind it without actively noticing the window itself (cf. Krämer 1998: 74; Warde [1932] 1991: 111–113). In other words, when reading, we commonly decode the meaning of written texts while discarding their appearance (cf. Strätling and Witte 2006: 7). With this having been the commonplace (but, as argued below, short-sighted) view in linguistics for a significant period of time, it is unsurprising that questions concerning the materiality of writing were long relegated to the background. Only in the second half of the 20th century did the idea of a 'graphetics' emerge in the context of the fruitful engagement with issues of writing and written language in German structuralist grapholinguistics (→ Section 1.1). Specifically, German linguist Hans Peter Althaus is commonly credited with establishing graphetics as a subdiscipline of linguistics by means of devoting a prominent handbook article to it, which was originally published in 1973 (cf. Günther 1993a: 34; Glück 2016a: 253). The following, widely cited definition stems from the second edition of 1980:

> The objects of graphetics as a subdiscipline of linguistics are the conditions and material elements that constitute visual linguistic communication. These are, in particular, the different ways of putting something into writing, scripts, typefaces, and variants of writing something, as well as individual and social differentiations, historical developments, and calligraphic and typographic norms. (Althaus [1973] 1980: 138, our translation)

Several of the materiality-oriented issues that Althaus mentions as well as the designation of the subdiscipline itself imply that graphetics deals exclusively with the etic level of writing, i.e., with its concrete realisation – as opposed to graphematics, which is devoted to the emic level of writing and emic units, defined as "invariant form[s] obtained from the reduction of a class of variant forms to a limited number of abstract units" (Nöth 1990: 183). This view is based partially on the assumption that the relationship between graphetics and graphematics is analogous to the relationship between phonetics and phonology (cf. Brekle 1994a: 171; Coulmas 1996a: 177; Crystal 2008: 220). The core task of graphetics is, thus, claimed to be the analysis of "the shapes of the graphic signs used, e.g., in handwriting or printing, rather than their systematic relations" (Hartmann and James 1998: 65), or, more generally, "[t]he study of the physical properties of written signs" (Coulmas 1996a: 177).

While graphematics commonly excludes an investigation of the specific visual properties of writing, graphetics studies precisely "various features, especially differences between [different persons', DM/CD] handwritings, different typefaces, and also between handwriting and print" (Fuhrhop and Peters 2013: 182, our translation), to name only a few aspects. However, the belief that graphetics is concerned solely with the etic level and is completely parallel to phonetics is inaccurate since graphetics is, in fact, also interested in emic units and functions (see below).

In a nutshell, linguists were not interested in graphetic issues since these were typically believed to focus only on non-distinctive features of writing. However, this is only true when distinctiveness is interpreted in a narrow sense, i.e., as the ability to differentiate meaning at the denotative level. As Assmann observed, an 'R' always evokes a graphematic relationship with the phoneme /r/. Yet, unlike claimed by him, whether it is printed in Times New Roman or Comic Sans or written by hand *does* make a difference as it has the potential to contribute to the communicative meaning of the written utterance, or its linguistic meaning in a broader sense, in quite significant ways. This part of the overall meaning contributed by graphetics is commonly referred to as connotative and is often claimed to be secondary. However, writing relies heavily on its visual substance, and the importance and hierarchy of the denotative vs. connotative components of meaning need to be evaluated individually for each instance of writing that is produced and perceived in a specific context. Sometimes, indeed, meaning is distinguished exclusively by graphetic means: consider the two sentences <*She* did not tell me.> vs. <She did *not* tell me.> in which the italicisation of different words distinguishes two different readings of an otherwise identical sentence (cf. also Crystal 1997).

This implies that unlike phonetics, graphetics also considers functional aspects, specifically the functions assumed by the visual substance of writing. In her definition of graphetics, French linguist Nina Catach, who is known as the founder of the research group *L'histoire et la structure de l'orthographe* (HESO) and for her sophisticated analyses of writing, underlines this broader scope of graphetics by contrasting it with phonetics:

> [. . .] phonetics is a science of the individual, while graphetics studies concrete realisations and conditions not only at the individual but also at the social and industrial level of writing, which is both a technique and an institution. (Catach 2001: 75, our translation)

The observation that phonetics studies substance at the individual level while graphetics is also invested in material questions at the social level is paramount;

it highlights that written materiality is more interindividual than spoken materiality. Consider, for example, that every speaking person has their own distinct voice. While this might certainly be true also for handwriting, different people's handwriting can be more readily compared to uncover commonalities and differences given the relative permanence of writing. Furthermore, following the invention of print and especially its digitalisation, the social aspects of how writing 'looks' have only risen in relevance as relatively stable visual appearances of writing (in the form of well-known typefaces) have gradually become associated with different social meanings. Crucially, the development of typefaces (of which nowadays, there exist thousands) that users can choose from has greatly increased the visual variety in the typographic manifestation of writing. This, in turn, has rendered choices highly significant: which typeface a person or a group (or an institution) chooses for the design of their texts potentially conveys significant information about them, the context, etc. (⟶ Section 3.3.2.6).

To sum up, graphetic research underlines the visual aspect of a semiotic approach to writing. Thus, graphetics is not merely a surplus or an auxiliary discipline to graphematics but rather a full-fledged grapholinguistic subdiscipline of its own. This is emphasised by the fact that it studies aspects falling outside the scope of graphematics. For instance, Schroeder (1981: 133) lists social, political, and religious questions as pertinent to graphetics and provides as an example the politically motivated prohibition of Arabic script and the switch to Roman script in Turkey in 1928 (⟶ Chapter 7). In this specific situation, the visual appearance of the two scripts and their symbolic meaning were significant (and arguably much more important than any graphematic concerns). Issues like this lie beyond the boundaries of what is studied by graphematics but are central to graphetics – and grapholinguistics as a whole.

The remarks so far show that aside from structural description, graphetics is concerned with materiality-oriented sociolinguistic questions as well. Yet another and equally important perspective is psycholinguistic in nature given that visual aspects greatly affect our processing of writing. While this proves significant for psychological models of reading and writing, these actually often neglect the visual appearance of texts. And it is not only psychologists but also designers, and specifically typographers, who should take this aspect of graphetics into account. Günther (1990a, 1993a) explains this as follows:

> Since if the legibility of a typeface is to be a criterion for the typographer, one must know what the reader is doing: what encourages him, what hinders him, what he wants. This concerns the features of the signal and the characteristics of the reader – and the results of such research should determine the typographer's work.
>
> (Günther 1990a: 98, our translation)

The list of interdisciplinary perspectives adopted by graphetics is not restricted to the sociolinguistic and psycholinguistic ones. Indeed, it represents a field collecting questions regarding the materiality of writing that stem from various kinds of disciplines, including, for instance, cognitive science, art history, philosophy, pedagogy, design, and semiotics. Unsurprisingly, thus, graphetic research also incorporates methods from different disciplines (⟶ Section 3.1.2).

Finally, it must be underlined that as the study of the materiality of writing, graphetics is detached from specific languages (cf. Fuhrhop and Peters 2013: 182). Thus, as opposed to the largely language-specific phenomena studied in graphematics,[29] graphetic questions are of a broader, sometimes even universal nature. For example, when investigating the appearance of the Roman script (cf. ⟶ Section 3.2.1 for a definition of *script*), findings concern not only a single language given the fact that Roman script is used by the writing systems of many languages. Of course, certain aspects related to graphetics can also be language-specific, for instance when a given script is indeed only used for one writing system. However, graphetic questions are more often dependent on other variables, among them culture, time period, or region. Examples discussed in the following sections will illustrate this.

3.1.2 Types of methods in graphetics

The different methods employed in graphetic research can be categorised into two major types based on an analogous distinction made in phonetics:

> The processes of speech that can be represented by instrumental phonetics are not only logically contingent but also very different in their external form. In one case, speech signals are derived, i.e., time functions are represented, in the other case notational symbols are written on paper. While in the first case, we are dealing with a material system whose geometry changes in time and whose temporal changes can be represented on a data carrier, in the second case, we are dealing with contents of consciousness whose categories can only be represented by means of symbolic language. We want to record this terminologically as the difference between a signal phonetics oriented towards the natural sciences and a symbol phonetics oriented towards the humanities.
>
> (Tillmann and Günther 1986: 201, our translation)

29 As will become evident in ⟶ Chapter 4, this language-specificity pertains only to graphematics as a subsystem of writing systems, since every writing system has its own and distinct grapheme inventory, its own graphematic regularities, etc. By contrast, graphematics as a grapholinguistic subfield is more universal given that its questions and concepts – like the *grapheme* – are asked and defined in a broad, cross-(grapho)linguistic manner.

This distinction gives rise to the two types of *symbol graphetics* and *signal graphetics* (cf. Günther 1990a, 1993a). The difference between them can be illustrated by their treatment of various instantiations or repetitions of the same type of unit. Take, for instance, A, A, and A as graphs of |A| (cf. below for the definition of *graph*): symbol graphetically, what is relevant is that these graphs belong to the same category, i.e., are related to each other as they are variants of one abstract unit (⟶ Section 4.6.2 on graphetic allography). Signal graphetically, by contrast, they are regarded as unique optical and physical events that merely resemble each other with respect to some aspects. Accordingly, symbol graphetics belongs to the humanities whereas signal graphetics is associated largely with the natural sciences. Fields that are invested in symbol graphetics are typography (as a profession, not as a materialisation of writing as discussed in ⟶ Section 3.3.2.5), palaeography and epigraphy, sociolinguistics, and, crucially, descriptive (grapho-) linguistics, to name only a few. By contrast, disciplines such as psychology, neurophysiology, medicine, and physics produce signal graphetic research. Günther (1993a) calls researchers involved in symbol graphetics 'eye grapheticians' (by analogy with 'ear phoneticians') as they utilise their eyes to describe and classify symbols, whereas researchers carrying out signal graphetic work are 'instrumental grapheticians' due to their use of instruments and scientific measurements.

3.1.3 Subdisciplines of graphetics

Like phonetics, graphetics is divided into three subdisciplines: productional, descriptive, and perceptual graphetics. As the name implies, *productional graphetics* deals with all aspects concerning production. From a signal graphetic perspective, this includes cognitive and motoric processes involved in writing in all its various modes, mainly handwriting and typing. From a symbol graphetic perspective, the issues addressed feature, for example, a person's (both conscious and unconscious) choices of given visual resources when designing a text as well as the question of what these choices convey about, among other things, the person and the context (⟶ Section 3.3.2.5).

Once a text has been produced, its materiality can be studied by *descriptive graphetics*. This subdiscipline focuses on structural graphetic aspects, which are, given the structuralist paradigm in which (grapho)linguistics has largely been embedded, considered to be the most 'traditionally' linguistic part of graphetic research. In fact, these structural questions also served as a driving force behind the proposal of a graphetics in the first place (cf. Althaus 1980). Here, various methods of description are used to characterise graphetic features that are significant denotatively and connotatively. In its methods, descriptive graphetics is largely symbol graphetic, although the appearance of writing as a physical signal can of course also be analysed. Note that from this perspective, working with written data constitutes a somewhat odd endeavour: written shapes are both linguistic and metalinguistic objects, i.e., they are being described[30] but can simultaneously be interpreted as their own description (cf. Meletis 2020a: 225), as is evidenced by the second part of the word 'de*scription*' that derives from Latin *scribere* 'to write'. The same cannot be claimed for acoustic linguistic data, which can only be described by being transferred into another form. This can be achieved through spectrograms or via transcription systems such as the IPA. Written data, by contrast, do not need to be transcribed – they are already written. Of course, things do get more complicated as descriptive graphetics strives to abstract common features from the units of scripts (such as the Roman script) or even to establish universal features. In this context, the governing material feature of writing comes to the forefront: its spatiality (cf. Harris 2005). It will be covered in detail below.

As the third subdiscipline, *perceptual graphetics* deals with all questions pertaining to (unconscious) perception, recognition, categorisation, as well as the conscious reception of material properties of writing. As the counterpart to productional graphetics, it is interested in how written units are physiologically and cognitively processed by the eyes and the brain (and, for haptic aspects, the hands).[31] Of utmost importance in perceptual graphetics are sociolinguistic questions, which include but are not limited to: which inferences or ascriptions do we make about a person based on the appearance of their (hand)writing or the typeface they choose? In other words, what is the sociosemiotic potential of the materiality of writing? These and related questions will be addressed in → Section 3.3, where the concrete materialisations of writing come to the forefront. Since it is commonly assumed in grapholinguistics that perception is primary to production (cf. Primus 2006: 10; Watt 1988),[32] perceptual graphetics is arguably the most prominent graphetic subdiscipline. This is reflected in the fact that in most graphetic research, a perceptual perspective is adopted.

---

30 Descriptive graphetics is always simultaneously perceptual graphetics (and might even be regarded as a subfield of it) since the analyst describing graphetic data is doing so through perception.

31 Crucially, at this point, the signal and symbol graphetic perspectives merge: when investigating the central question of how a written unit can be identified as a realisation of an abstract category, we are concerned both with the processing of this unique signal and with its identity as a symbol, i.e., an instance of a category.

32 Consider that as writers, we are simultaneously readers since we (commonly) perceive/read the emerging text while we are writing it. By contrast, when we are reading, we do not necessarily write at the same time (but cf. → Section 3.3.2.3).

3.2 Descriptive graphetics

This section is devoted to core structural questions studied by descriptive graphetics. All of them are related to the basic unit of graphetics, which is why we will first address how it can be discovered by abstracting from the concrete materialisation of writing. Next, the focus will be shifted onto the question of how graphetic units are arranged in space on a given writing surface. Finally, the issue of segmentation is dealt with: is there a method of segmenting graphetic units in order to arrive at a – possibly universal – inventory of elementary building blocks (lines, curves, dots, etc.) or even abstract distinctive visual features (such as [straight], [curved], etc.)?

3.2.1 Graphetic units

When analysing the materiality of written utterances, what we are confronted with are sequences of graphs. *Graphs* are specific realisations of graphemes and the central data in graphetics. Each graph, even if it looks similar or identical to other graphs (especially in the context of the same text realised in the same handwriting or font), constitutes a unique physical event. For example, the two graphs that materialise the grapheme <e> in the word <even> on this printed/displayed page are unique and distinct at the etic level, even though to our eyes, they appear exactly the same because they are printed in the same font and printed graphs are commonly perceived as having a stable visual identity. The uniqueness is, by comparison, much more noticeable in handwriting, where graphs materialising the same unit often differ more perceptibly. This example can also clearly illustrate the distinction between the two methodological strands of graphetics (see above): signal graphetically, if measured exactly, no two graphs are identical; symbol graphetically, by contrast, due to their visual similarity, with our eyes (and brains), we identify these distinct graphs as being instances of the same category (they are graphetic allographs ⟶ Section 4.6.2). In other words, there must exist templates we use to match every graph with in order to arrive at its categorial identity. These templates are descriptively conceived of as so-called *basic shapes* and represent the central units of graphetics.

A thought experiment helps to illustrate the concept of basic shapes: if ten people were to write graphs that instantiate the lowercase grapheme <e> directly on top of each other using pencils, the part that is invariant (i.e., that portion of the graphs that is visible most strongly since it was written multiple times on top of each other) is the visual 'skeleton' or 'spine' shared by all graphs, the above-mentioned template they are matched with. This template is the basic shape (cf. Meletis 2020a: 39–41; Rezec 2009). Unlike graphs, which are concrete and thus etic, it is conceived of as an emic unit because it represents an abstraction. Specifically, it is a bundle of visual features that include the number of elements comprising a basic shape as well as spatial and topological information, i.e., information on how these elements are arranged in space and how they are spatially related to one another (i.e., if and how they are connected). The basic shape |e|, for example, consists of the curve |c| and a relatively small horizontal stroke |-|. Additionally, topology is highly relevant in order to know where and how these elements connect and thus to distinguish between basic shapes (cf. Stjernfelt 1993: 306): |T| and |L|, for instance, consist of the same two elements but differ in the position of both the horizontal and the vertical strokes within the segmental space (see below) and in how they are connected.[33] Crucially, even as emic units, basic shapes are graphetic and thus purely concerned with form; linguistic function is not of relevance in describing them. Yet, which units we identify as distinct basic shapes as opposed to variants of the same basic shape within a script *is* determined top-down by graphematic knowledge (see below).

A core question of graphetic research concerns visual variability: how can it be explained that readers can effortlessly categorise graphs from different people's handwriting or from tens of thousands of distinct typefaces as instances of the same basic shapes? The answer is relatively straightforward: as long as the above-mentioned vital information stored in a basic shape is stable, other aspects can vary. This gives typeface designers and every person writing by hand the freedom to create a distinct visual character for their typeface/handwriting. Following this, for every basic shape, a descriptive so-called *graphetic solution space*[34] can be assumed, which is largely determined by the basic shape's core visual features and includes all possible graphs that we identify as variants of it (cf. Meletis 2020d). Crucially, now, as implied above, the boundaries of these graphetic solution spaces are determined by graphematics, specifically by what users of a writing system identify as distinct basic shapes because they have distinctive graphematic values. This sounds vague but should become clearer with an example.

33 As is evident from the examples, following common practice in German grapholinguistics, we will enclose graphetic units in vertical strokes: | |. This distinguishes them from graphematic and orthographic units which are enclosed in angle brackets: < >.

34 The term is coined by analogy with Neef's *graphematic solution space* (cf. → Section 4.1).

With respect to the spatial relation between its two strokes, the graphetic solution space for |T| in the English writing system (which uses Roman script) is arguably larger than in the Greek writing system (using Greek script). This is because in the latter, there also exists the visually similar basic shape |Γ|. Thus, in Greek script, the position of the strokes relative to one another is more significant than in Roman script, where the freedom for variation with respect to this spatial relation is larger. Of course, this distinction is relevant only because the shapes |T| and |Γ| are two units of Greek script that have, historically, developed separately and are (still) used to instantiate different graphemes (⟶ Section 4.2 for a definition of *grapheme*).[35] In other words, it is top-down graphematic knowledge that tells users what to perceive as distinct visual units, which, in turn, determines the degree of possible visual variation. In a similar vein, it also determines what even is a basic shape in a script and what may, by contrast, only be a scribble or a semasiographic sign (such as the heart symbol ♥).

In a nutshell, graphs must sufficiently match the visual information stored in the basic shape they materialise, meaning they cannot too closely resemble other basic shapes within the same script that assume different graphematic functions. However, it is also paramount to note that our example concerns the isolated recognition of individual basic shapes: in 'normal' contexts, readers are commonly not confronted with single basic shapes (unless they are undergoing an eye exam) but rather with sequences of them in the form of meaningful graphematic words. In this case, the recognition of an entire word may precede the recognition of its constituent units, so even if one graph in the word is unrecognisable and cannot conclusively be associated with a basic shape and, in turn, a grapheme, readers will still likely be able identify it because the context provides necessary top-down information (⟶ Section 4.7.1).

A set of basic shapes that is used for a given writing system is called *script*. Scripts are highly conventionalised and often the result of long historical developments[36] (an obvious example being, again, Roman script). Notably, scripts are not necessarily associated with particular writing systems. Consider, for example, the fact that Roman script is used for hundreds of writing systems ranging from European ones such as English, German, Italian, Finnish, or Swedish, to those

---

35 Cf. also the study by Boudelaa, Perea, and Carreiras (2020) for a method of measuring the visual similarity of basic shapes relevant for the concept of a graphetic solution space, there exemplified by an analysis of the basic shapes of Arabic script.

36 Often, but not always: there are also younger, invented scripts such as Cherokee or Cree, which were both introduced in the 19th century.

of Turkic and Polynesian languages, to name only a few. These languages have distinct writing systems even though they share the same script (sometimes with modifications and/or additions such as |ß| in German or |å| in Swedish). Weingarten (2011) captures this by modelling writing systems as ordered pairs of languages and scripts[37]: the English writing system, for example, pairs the English language with Roman script, the Finnish writing system combines Finnish with Roman script. Thus, while these writing systems are visually very similar given that they share the same script, this is not to be mistaken for linguistic similarity as the same basic shapes might have altogether distinct graphematic values in different writing systems. Furthermore, their graphotactic regularities (⟶ Section 4.5), which include rules of combination of units, may also differ across systems.

3.2.2 Spatial organisation of the writing surface

One of the core features of writing that distinguishes it from speech is that it extends in space rather than in time. Its governing principle, thus, is spatiality (cf. Harris 2005), which renders the analysis of the spatial arrangement of elements on the writing surface a central task of graphetics. The main question here concerns the different levels of organisation and the units and phenomena that are relevant to them. In this context, pioneering work comes from German linguist Ursula Bredel, who, in her analysis of the German system of punctuation (⟶ Section 4.4), especially with respect to rules of how marks may be combined, developed a hierarchy of spatial levels (cf. Figure 3).

The spaces in this hierarchy can be distinguished by the different types of blank or empty spaces that are located between them. This is captured by the *empty space criterion* (cf. Meletis 2015: 114–118). For example, the blank space between graphemes is usually smaller than the blank space between words – at least in writing systems that exhibit spaces between words (⟶ Section 4.3.2). The *segmental space* is the smallest space in this spatial hierarchy. It is by default occupied by basic shapes or – at the graphematic level – the graphemes they instantiate. Segmental spaces are concatenated either horizontally or vertically depending on the direction of writing prevalent in a given writing system. Sequences of segmental spaces constitute the *linear space*, which, in its full extension, is what we know as the line. If these lines are combined (necessarily in the dimension different from the one in which segmental spaces are combined),

37 In accordance with this, Justeson (1976: 59) had already defined writing systems as "language-script pairs".

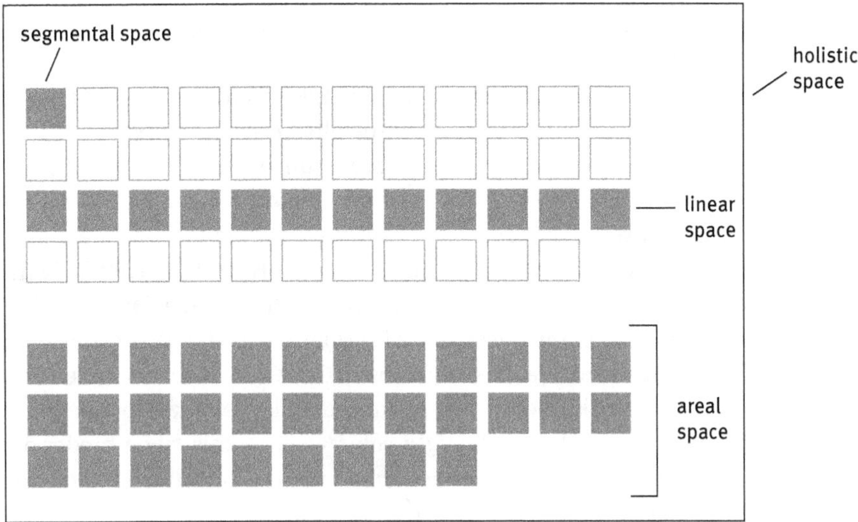

Figure 3: Spatial organisation of the writing surface.

they constitute the *areal space*. This space is occupied by elements such as paragraphs or columns (cf. Bredel 2011: 19). Finally, a fourth level can be added, the so-called *holistic space* (cf. Meletis 2015: 115), resulting from the combination of two or more areal spaces, often with additional non-textual material such as figures or photographs. The entirety of the page you are currently reading is a holistic space, and it is characterised by a layout that can be described graphetically with the help of precisely the spatial analysis outlined here.

In his characterisation of typography, Hartmut Stöckl (2004, 2005) proposes four subdimensions for classifying typographic elements at various levels: microtypography, mesotypography, macrotypography, and paratypography (cf. also ⟶ Section 3.3.2.5). Given that graphetics deals not only with typographic but with all graphic issues (including matters of handwriting), Stöckl's terms can be broadened by replacing *-typography* with *-graphetics*. The first three levels correlate quite neatly with the four spaces mentioned above: *micrographetics* addresses questions that concern the segmental space, i.e., individual basic shapes and the concrete graphs materialising them, *mesographetics* deals with combinations of basic shapes that extend in the linear space, and *macrographetics* is devoted to both areal and, at a global level, holistic spaces and the visual resources available for designing and arranging the appearance of written utterances at this level. By comparison, the fourth level, *paragraphetics*, is not concerned with the two-dimensional organisation of units that appear on the writing surface but with the physical properties of (writing on) the surface itself. Aspects at this level include the thickness, transparency/opacity of paper, or – in case the surface is a screen – resolution, brightness, etc.

An interesting addition to the spatial analysis sketched above is provided by Reißig (2015), who assumes three different so-called *column spaces* by drawing two vertical division lines on a page. These spaces are relevant for distinguishing the *list mode* that is characteristic of lists from the *text mode*, i.e., the default mode for running texts. In horizontal sinistrograde writing systems (i.e., those with a left-to-right direction of writing), list items prototypically occupy only the first, leftmost column space, sometimes also part of the middle column space. This relative occupation of the linear space is visually salient in that readers can usually distinguish lists from texts solely through the length of list items, i.e., how much of the linear space is filled with text. Indeed, if list items lack bullet points or numbers and extend well into the right column space, this might hinder our ability to recognise them as list items as it blurs the visual distinction between lists and running texts.

Note that while much of what has been established above about the division of the writing surface into spaces is of tendentially universal nature, the internal organisation of the linear and especially segmental spaces differs significantly based on the script in question. This makes it necessary to explicate that we will look specifically at Roman script, which has been treated most elaborately in grapholinguistics, and mention other scripts only briefly. When two vertical division lines are drawn in Roman script, the linear space is divided into three vertical subspaces, constituting the three-space schema of the line (cf. Domahs and Primus 2015: 133) illustrated in Figure 4. The lower of these division lines on which basic shapes 'stand' is the *base line*. Above the higher division line we find the *high space*. It is occupied by the upper part of all uppercase basic shapes, diacritics (e.g., the accent in |á|), as well as ascenders of lowercase basic shapes, cf. the upper part of the vertical stroke in |d|. Between the two division lines, the *central space*[38] is located. Of all the spaces, it is the most important one given that most of the visually salient information in basic shapes necessary for recognition is condensed here. Finally, the *low space* is located under the base line. It is occupied by descenders as in |y| or diacritics as in |ç|.

As already mentioned, this three-space schema is specific to Roman script. It may be partially applicable to other scripts such as the Greek, Cyrillic, Armenian, and Georgian scripts (which are all used alphabetically), but it is by no means

38 In another conception, the central space is additionally divided by a line in its middle, resulting in a total of four vertical spaces and what is referred to as the *four-space schema* (cf. Althaus 1980). Since a further division of the central space does not prove as relevant as the other divisions of the linear space, we adhere to the three-space schema.

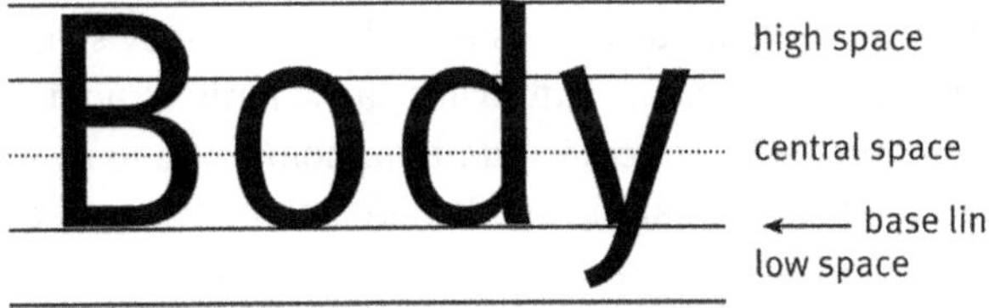

Figure 4: Three-space schema.

universal. Different subdivisions can be observed, for example, in Han'gŭl, the script used in the Korean writing system, or in Chinese script. Chinese graphemes often consist of subcomponents (cf. → Section 4.2.3), and depending on their quantity, the partition of the segmental space may vary. The same is the case for Japanese kanji, where radicals (i.e., semantic components) can appear in various positions inside the segmental space (cf. Figure 5). Unlike in Roman script, thus, there is no unified subdivision across the entire linear space given that segmental spaces occupied by Japanese kanji have their own internal organisation.

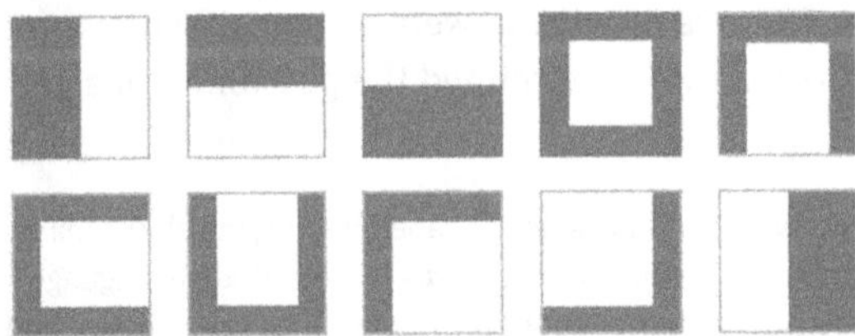

Figure 5: Possible positions of radicals inside the segmental space in Japanese kanji (coloured in grey).

3.2.3 Segmentation of basic shapes

While the preceding section was devoted to the spatial arrangement of written material, this section deals with the internal structure and composition of the written material itself. Interestingly, despite the overall neglect of graphetic issues, a specific question was pondered fairly often: how can basic written units (from whichever script they stem) be segmented into a limited number of smaller building blocks? A closely related issue is how such a segmentation may result in a set of formative elements (such as lines and curves) or even distinctive features of said elements (such as [straight] or [curved]) that can describe an entire script or may even be universal and thus applicable to all scripts.

The reason for the popularity of this question is arguably that many scholars were guided by methods developed in structuralism, particularly structural phonology. As a result, grapholinguistic concepts and terminology are to some degree an "expression of an attempt to share in the benefits of what has been achieved with considerable success in phonology" (Ehlich 2007: 728, our translation). Consequently, then, given the rather fruitful proposal of phonological distinctive features, it was only a matter of time that "the process of continuous minimisation" in which "ever smaller elements of complex phenomena can be identified" (Kohrt 1985: 429, our translation) eventually also reached grapholinguistics. This, ultimately, gave rise to the question of whether the basic units of writing might in fact be graphe(ma)tically complex, which grew popular in the 1970s (cf., for example, Brekle 1971: 57) and was subsequently investigated from various perspectives and with different underlying epistemological interests (cf. Meletis 2015: 50–79 for an overview). In this vein, as Kohrt (1985: 444–445) notes, it is unsurprising that different analyses led to (sometimes remarkably) varying results.

At this point, it is worth repeating that just like phonological distinctive features, the smallest distinctive features of writing were at times assumed (or claimed) to be universal. David Crystal even entertained the possibility of a graphetic equivalent to the IPA:

> But why should there not be an International Graphetic Alphabet, identifying all the marks the human hand can make[39] that are capable of playing a contrastive role in some language – the array of straight lines of varying length and orientation, curves, dots, thicknesses, and so on, which when combined result in written letters, syllables, and logograms?
>
> (Crystal 1997: 23)

Notably, not all scholars of writing agree that the search for formative elements or distinctive features – which are two different things (see below) – is a worthy endeavour. For example, Rezec (2009: 71–81) criticises these efforts, arguing that in order to be of linguistic value, the decomposition of basic shapes into formative elements would need to be governed by rules, or, looked at from the opposite perspective: a set of formative elements coupled with a limited number of rules of composition should result in the basic shapes of a script. The composition suggested in previous analyses, Rezec notes, lacks such systematicity. His main criticism boils down to the fact that the assumption of a small number of formative elements does not actually afford the theoretical benefit of economy – which, however, is precisely the designated driving force behind most attempts of dis-

---

39 Note that this is unfeasible since there are no (obvious) limitations to the shapes that we can produce with our hands (⟶ Section 2.2).

covering formative elements in the first place (cf. Rezec 2009: 81). In the following, only a small selection of these attempts will be mentioned. Before doing so, we need to elaborate on a distinction introduced above: there exist two strands in the search for subsegmental elements. The first one looks for actual visual segments of basic shapes, i.e., straight lines, curves, dots, which we call *elementary forms*. The second one investigates visual features of either entire basic shapes or said elementary forms, e.g., [±long], [±straight], [±curved], etc., which we call *distinctive features*.

The first approach to segmentation was developed by Althaus; he proposed it in his above-mentioned handbook article on graphetics. As illustrated in Figure 6, he identifies twelve elementary forms and seven varyingly sized portions of the segmental/linear space based on its division into four vertical subspaces (see above). Althaus assigns these two inventories identifying numbers, which is how he can provide a descriptive formula for every basic shape. |L|, for example, has the formula $1^6 \longleftarrow 4^3$, which means that the elementary form number 1, |I|, is located in space number 6 and is positioned to the left (hence the arrow facing the left) of elementary form 4, |_|, which is located in space 3. Notably, Althaus' analysis has been criticised, especially with respect to its unclear purpose, which he himself does not elaborate on (cf. Buchmann 2015: 24).[40] Althaus' analysis also underlines that approaches centring on actual visual segments are not as economic as possible: elementary forms 1, 2, and 3, for example, all represent straight strokes and only vary in their orientation.

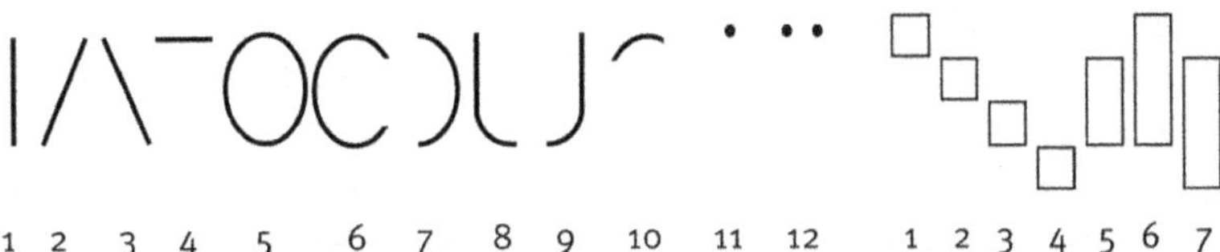

Figure 6: Sets of elementary forms and subspaces of the linear space, from Althaus (1980: 140).

Another approach that remains influential in grapholinguistics is the *hasta+coda-principle* formulated by Brekle (1994a). It holds that lowercase basic shapes of Roman script have an internal structure consisting of a *hasta* (Latin for 'speer'), which is in most cases a straight line that extends over two subspaces of the three-space schema (e.g., the vertical stroke in |d|) and a *coda* (Latin for 'tail') that attaches to the hasta such as the |c| in |d|. This identification of hasta and coda

40 Analyses similar to the one proposed by Althaus can be found in Garbe (1985) and Scharnhorst (1988).

is important for two reasons: first, it is central to Brekle's hypothesis of 'minusculisation' that aims to explain how the lowercase basic shapes of Roman script developed out of the historically primary uppercase shapes. What was decisive in this development is the structure of the original uppercase basic shapes (or majuscules), specifically whether they had a free hasta. A free hasta is defined as that portion of the hasta that is *not* enclosed by a coda, e.g., the upper part of the hasta in |L| or the lower part of the hasta in |P|. The lowercase basic shapes (or minuscules) that developed out of these majuscules, now, feature an ascender or descender depending on where the coda is positioned in the corresponding majuscules. Since in |P|, the coda is in the high space, |p| developed a free hasta in the low space (= descender), while |L|, with its coda on the base line, developed an ascender: |l| (cf. Brekle 1994a: 194 for details). The second reason that Brekle's analysis remains important is that it has been adopted in models of other grapholinguists such as Primus (2004, 2006), Fuhrhop, and Buchmann (Fuhrhop and Buchmann 2009), whose approaches will be addressed in more detail in the course of ⟶ Chapter 4.

An attempt at description/segmentation that actually deals with distinctive features rather than elementary forms is the elaborate and highly complex analysis proposed by W. C. Watt (cf. Watt 1975, 1980, 1981, 1988, 2002, 2012, 2015). It focuses on those uppercase basic shapes of Roman script that are in use in the English writing system. Watt attempts to formulate two 'grammars' in the sense of 'sets of rules': a *kinemic grammar* in which basic shapes are described according to features relevant in (handwritten) production, and a *phanemic grammar* focusing on features relevant in perception. Figure 7 shows the elementary forms of |K| with their respective distinctive kinemic features as an example. Since they are meant to model the actual handwritten production process, they are interpreted dynamically, i.e., as capturing movements rather than the static visual shapes they produce: [FLLG] (falling) evaluates whether an elementary form is written from top to bottom, [PROG] (progressive) evaluates whether it is produced in the direction of writing (in this case from left to right), [TRCE] (trace), interestingly, reveals whether an elementary form is actually written or whether it is just a hand movement made in the air that is necessary to put down the writing instrument at another location on the surface, [FULL] provides information on the relative length of elementary forms (the vertical stroke in |L| is [+FULL], the horizontal one [–FULL]), and [CLWS] (clockwise) is only relevant for curved segments and states whether they are produced clockwise or counter-clockwise. The features Watt assumes for the phanemic grammar are different (cf. Watt 1981), and only in a later publication (cf. Watt 1988) does he try to reconcile the two grammars. Notably, his promising analysis, to this date, likely due to its complexity, remains little-received.

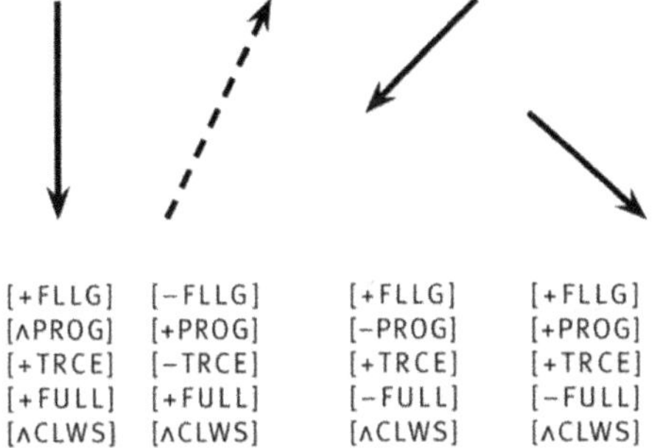

Figure 7: Kinemic features of the majuscule |K|, taken from Watt (1980: 42).

A final attempt worth mentioning is made by quantitative linguist Gabriel Altmann (2004); his goal is to arrive at a method of quantifying the complexity of basic shapes. Three sets of elementary forms are assumed – types of dots, straight lines, and curved lines – and three types of connections (which were identified as being constitutive of basic shapes above) – continuous contacts, crisp contacts, and crossings (cf. Figure 8). The types of elementary forms as well as the types of contacts are assigned numeric values based on their assumed complexity. Notably, these values are arrived at symbol graphetically, i.e., based on what 'eye grapheticians' (in this case Altmann) assume to be perceptually complex. If the values of all elementary forms that a basic shape consists of as well as the nature of their contacts are added up, the result is a numeric value that is obviously higher for more 'complex' basic shapes than less complex ones. Interestingly, Altmann does not restrict this analysis to Roman script but claims it to be universal. This is relevant since even if some of the above-mentioned analyses prove applicable to other scripts, they were explicitly developed on the basis of Roman script. In general (although it is difficult to assess this), for other scripts, the question of elementary forms does not appear to be as heatedly debated. For the Chinese script, for example, it seems rather settled, with the traditional consensus being that all basic shapes are made up of a limited number of types of strokes (cf. Coulmas 1996a: 480).

In any case, the search for a universal set of elementary forms or even distinctive features – in the vein of Crystal's above-mentioned proposal of an International Graphetic Alphabet – is, much like graphetics in general, still in its infancy. Crucially, even though such analyses do exist across disciplines (including psychology, information science, etc.), they have not been noticed by and integrated into a graphetic or generally grapholinguistic framework.

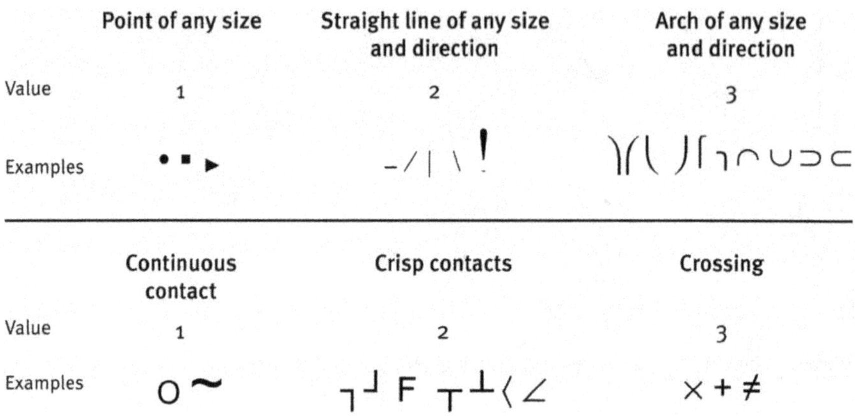

	Point of any size	Straight line of any size and direction	Arch of any size and direction
Value	1	2	3
Examples	• ▪ ▸	- / | \ !	) ((\ ) ∫ ⌐ ∩ ∪ ⊃ ⊂

	Continuous contact	Crisp contacts	Crossing
Value	1	2	3
Examples	O ~	┐ ┘ F ┬ ⊥ ⟨ ∠	× + ≠

Figure 8: Numerical values for visual segments and contacts, taken from Altmann (2004: 69).

3.3 Materialisation(s) of writing

3.3.1 The study of abstract vs. concrete materiality

While the descriptive and theoretical questions concerning the materiality of writing introduced in the preceding sections are located at the graphetic level as they centre on visuality and spatiality, they are abstract in that they are independent of the concrete substantiation of writing. Indeed, that graphs can be categorised as instantiations of respective abstract basic shapes is true regardless of whether they are handwritten or printed, and the spatiality of writing is a constitutive feature of all texts regardless of how they were conceived. In this section, we now turn from this abstract materiality of writing to its concrete materialisations. Its focus will be on two main types in which writing is nowadays produced: handwriting (or chirography, from Greek *cheír* 'hand') and typography. Both can be analysed under a dynamic, process-oriented lens that examines the processes of handwriting and typing as well as our (physiological and cognitive) perception of handwritten vs. printed texts, and a more static, product-oriented lens that highlights these texts and their material properties. Note that the coexistence of these two perspectives renders the terms 'handwriting' and partially[41] also 'typography', like 'writing' itself, ambiguous (see also below).

41 'Typography' arguably invites a product-oriented reading, whereas the associated processes of producing typographic utterances can be referred to as typing, designing, etc., depending on which aspect of typographic practice is in focus.

Until rather recently, neither handwriting nor typography were phenomena of particular interest to linguistics as the concrete materialisation of language was not believed to affect linguistic structure or meaning per se (⟶ Section 3.1.1). Interestingly, despite this, in the context of grapholinguistics, certain graphematic concepts do hinge on material, i.e., visual features: in the assumption of the graphematic syllable (⟶ Section 4.3.1), for example, ascenders and descenders of basic shapes as well as other visual features play crucial roles. And yet, the graphematic syllable is based on a gross abstraction of concrete visual materiality – it represents an analysis of what certain scholars believe to be a neutral 'default' typeface such as, for example, Arial. The goal behind opting for such a 'neutral' typeface is obviously to arrive at the largest possible applicability of the concept by striving for abstractness, a somewhat paradoxical 'dematerialised materiality' – which, by the way, also applies to the concept of 'basic shape' and the attempts at segmentation that were introduced above. Such a procedure, however, erases the significant visual variation constituted by individual handwriting or different typefaces and with it, among other things, any social meaning that such variation carries. This is also the source of the seeming contradiction underlying 'abstract graphetic' units: while they are indeed material because they store visuospatial information, they can at best only be (proto)*types* as they are incapable of subsuming all of their actual instantiations (or *tokens*). In a nutshell, to echo what was claimed above: whether a basic shape or a graphematic syllable is produced in typography or handwriting[42] should not be relevant to the concept – which does not mean it is not relevant at all.

That graphetics – at least in the way it was originally proposed – claims to focus on materiality even though it simultaneously deemphasises actual material richness and variation has been criticised by, among others, sociolinguists (cf. Spitzmüller 2016a). A similar practice also exists in many psycholinguistic studies of writing, whose findings are formulated broadly even though the data that is being tested experimentally is actually very specific instances of writing (e.g., certain words printed in Arial) that cannot be claimed to be representative of all writing. As touched upon above, the materiality of writing is often expected to be 'invisible' so that it does not stand between us as readers and the linguistic content that writing carries – and in a majority of cases, it becomes invisible indeed in that it does not draw attention to itself (cf. the window pane metaphor described above). But when the actual focus of graphetic research is the description of visual features or the processing of said features, materiality

---

42 Cf. Reinken (2018) for an exemplary study of how the graphematic syllable, which had been proposed on the basis of typed text, manifests itself in handwriting – especially in signatures.

cannot be invisible or buried under abstractions. Therefore, graphetics can and must achieve both of the outlined tasks simultaneously: it must study abstractions and generalisations that capture the underlying (idealised) 'structure' and systematics of scripts and their basic shapes, and it must also investigate the actual concrete materiality of writing that is highly relevant sociolinguistically and psycholinguistically.

3.3.2 Handwriting and typography

As the two central materialisations of writing, handwriting and typography are often seen in opposition, as two choices that could not be more distinct from each other. There are indeed several obvious differences, one of them being that physiological and cognitive processes involved in the production (and perception) of handwritten vs. typed texts differ considerably. Also, these two kinds of writing are – depending on the literate culture in question – frequently used in different domains to fulfil a variety of communicative purposes, often resulting in them being ascribed different statuses, nowadays mostly with typography being the more frequently and broadly used choice (cf. Böhm and Gätje 2014: 8). This recent dominance of type has given rise to beliefs such as "handwriting is dying a slow death"[43] which dominate the central discourses on handwriting and will be addressed in the following sections.

When 'handwriting' and 'typography' are seen as different modes of production, they constitute a somewhat absolute dichotomy depending on how *hand*writing is defined.[44] Here, we follow Karavanidou, who defines it as

> a unimanual and idiosyncratic visuomotor activity that involves recalling spelling from memory and translating thought into an autonomous graphic mark by gripping a writing tool and moving it on a surface [. . .] that provides friction [. . .] and natural sound as cognitive feedback, and where the writer must plan ahead spacial requirements, such as linearity, spacing and velocity of the text. (Karavanidou 2017: 155)

43 https://www.pri.org/stories/2016-09-14/handwriting-dying-slow-death (accessed September 22nd, 2021).

44 In typing, we also use and move our hands. However, production is indirect in that it is mediated by the keys we press or screens we touch, as the movements of our hands in reaching the different (analog or virtual) keys do not affect the shape of the resulting printed graphs, which is determined by the script we use and the choice of typeface instead (see below). Although in prototypical handwriting, we also depend on a mediating writing instrument (such as a pen) to produce actual graphic traces, it is still manual movements that directly create the resulting graphic traces and, thus, shapes. In any case, independent of the specific mode of production, writing is always a physical act (cf. Zepter 2014).

As the default[45] activity that produces typographic utterances, typing on a keyboard, by contrast, is "a bimanual, standardized and repetitive activity that invokes a mental schema of the letter coordinates on the keyboard to press the key" (Karavanidou 2017: 155).

By contrast, from a product-oriented perspective, despite differences in their development, use, and the discourses and ideologies associated with them, it is important to keep in mind that handwriting and typography merely represent two ends of a continuum. In other words, when their mode of production is disregarded and they are merely interpreted as categories characterised by their typical visual appearance, the lines between them are blurred. This is evident in typefaces emulating the appearance of handwriting, which are growing increasingly popular, but also handwriting (or hand lettering) that mimics typography (cf. Figure 9 below for examples). Notably, their convergence under a product-oriented perspective means that much of what can be claimed for one also applies to the other – especially with respect to their sociosemiotic potential and the way they are used to 'make meaning' (see below).

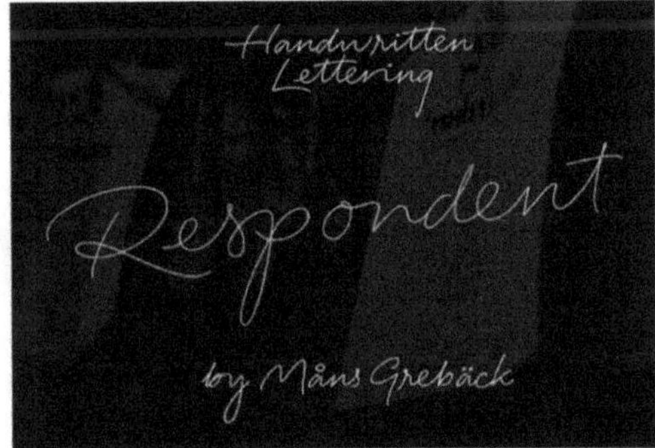

Figure 9: Script typeface 'Respondent' designed by Måns Grebäck (cf. https://www.dafont.com/respondent.font, accessed September 22nd, 2021), and hand lettering that resembles the typeface used in the corporate design of restaurant 'Peti Pari' in Vienna, Austria.

3.3.2.1 The study of handwriting and its use

Handwriting has been – if anything – a marginal issue in (grapho)linguistics (but see Gredig 2021). By contrast, in most literate societies, handwriting still forms an important part of people's lives. This is reflected, among other things, in lively dis-

45 Touching a part of a screen on which virtual keys are presented by means of pixels is also a method of producing (digital) typographic utterances.

courses surrounding the topic, which are expressed in the media but also in public spaces (such as discussion forums on the internet) and concern core domains of everyday life such as primary education. Notably, these discourses are also characterised by recurring culturally pessimistic takes focusing on an alleged 'decay' of handwriting, which is often seen as a 'forgotten language skill' (cf. Medwell and Wray 2008 and below). The discrepancy between handwriting as a subject largely neglected by linguistics and handwriting as a relevant part of language users' actual lives and communicative practices echoes a divide between science and 'everyday life' – a divide that can also be witnessed with respect to other grapholinguistic issues.[46] While not everything that is of interest to science must automatically be of relevance in everyday life, the opposite cannot be stated in such general terms: arguably, whenever a topic assumes a certain status in people's lives, it warrants some kind of scientific study. And indeed, several aspects of handwriting are being studied by various disciplines. A prominent example is the physical conditions that underlie handwriting as well as the various (e.g., physiological and cognitive) effects it is claimed to exert on its users. Likewise, the above-mentioned discourses surrounding handwriting and its associated and debated cultural (in)significance as a part of scribal practices are important objects of study in discourse and cultural studies as well as – to some degree – text linguistics (cf. Gredig 2021: 12–18). Embedding these and other questions of handwriting into a larger framework that can account for their interdisciplinarity is thus a central desideratum. In the following, we will present several aspects central to the study of handwriting. First, we will introduce current discourses on handwriting before we turn to the cognitive effects that are frequently associated with it and finally address the important role handwriting plays in the expression of identity. To start with, however, an important remark on the distinction between handwriting as a process and as a product is necessary.

In the introduction to their edited volume on handwriting, Böhm and Gätje highlight the multifaceted nature of handwriting research; according to them, it

> [. . .] deals, among other things, with the psychomotoric, media-technical, and, of course, pragmatic factors influencing the handwriting process (the manual gesture), with manuscripts and their character as traces of the handwriting process, with the acquisition and development of handwriting in the institution of school and outside of it, with questions

46 Graphematics, for example, is the theoretical reconstruction of a writing system's linguistic functions. These are not tangible for users of the system, who instead rely on rules acquired through literacy instruction, which are in turn captured by orthography. Users, thus, are only directly confronted with orthography, which serves as a writing system's surface representation (→ Chapter 5).

> about the practices and functions of handwriting in the context of media-technical innovations, or with the historically contingent social perception and assessment of handwriting.
> (Böhm and Gätje 2014: 7, our translation)

This list reflects the above-introduced division of issues that concern handwriting as a process and those that are interested in handwritten artefacts. However, a neat separation between the two is not always possible: the mentioned social perception and assessment of handwriting, for example, arguably concern both the process of handwriting as a cultural technique and the resulting handwritten texts. In any case, as the remarks above imply, given the assumption that (abstract linguistic) structure remains unaffected by concrete materiality, it is the aspect of *use* rather than structure that we find at the centre of a grapholinguistic investigation of handwriting. This is why the two perspectives of psycholinguistics (for aspects of processing) and sociolinguistics (for aspects of communication) come to the forefront. The former examines primarily the physiological and cognitive processes involved in writing by hand but also the ones relevant in perceiving handwritten utterances. Here, the fact that people's handwriting is utterly individual, i.e., practically differs in appearance for every person (even if in some cases only in details), results in a remarkable degree of visual variation that poses challenges to the human perceptual system.[47] On the other hand, the sociolinguistic perspective deals with specific practices and products of handwriting (such as letter writing and letters) and the attitudes, beliefs, and ideologies associated with them. Interestingly, the sociolinguistic perspective in certain ways subsumes the psycholinguistic questions just mentioned since the lively discourses on handwriting include, for example, debates on fine motor activity and the cognitive benefits handwriting is assumed to have, especially when compared to typing. Most of what was just mentioned is reflected in contemporary discourses on handwriting, to which we now turn.

3.3.2.2 Current discourses on handwriting

Swiss linguist Andi Gredig identifies four topic areas in German-language discourses on handwriting, many of which can also be found in the discourses of other literate communities: (a) 'digital' handwriting (e.g., handwriting on screens using fingers or technological tools such as special pens but also more generally the status handwriting assumes in the digital realm), (b) handwriting and

47 Note that this is not the case for reading printed typographic texts – even if those, too, nowadays feature a myriad of typefaces that display variation and influence readability to various degrees (see below). Of course, also (grapho)motorically, handwriting consists of a more complex bundle of processes than typing as it requires fine motor skills.

its instruction in school, (c) the personal and sentimental 'value' of handwriting as a reflection of individuality, (d) and handwriting as authenticating proof of identity (cf. Gredig 2021). He also provides a discussion of central topoi found in the discourses and assigns them to five heuristic categories: (1) handwriting as an 'endangered' practice; (2) the survival or 'comeback' of handwriting; (3) the benefits of handwriting for motor skills and cognitive processes; (4) the permanence of handwriting and its perception as a trace of the writing process and writers' emotions; and the (5) aesthetics of handwriting as well as its association with individuality and personality. Both mentioned topic areas and topoi shape the following treatment of handwriting.

One issue of relevance in topic area (a), digital handwriting, is the use of digital tools that allow writing by hand on devices such as smartphones and tablets. These include touchscreens as surfaces but also special styli (plural of 'stylus') as writing tools. When these means are used to write by hand, traditionally analogue handwriting is transferred to the digital realm. And while the digital remains a rather marginal domain for handwriting, it is noteworthy for a slight but remarkable reversal of dynamics: first, following the invention of the printing press and further developments such as the spread of personal computers, it was typing and typography that drastically encroached on handwriting and the domains in which it is/was used. Given the rather recent possibility of writing by hand using digital technology, now, handwriting has at least minimally (re-)entered some of the established domains of typography (for an analysis of 'post-digital' handwriting, cf. Wickberg 2020). This is relevant, for example, for digital notetaking, with taking notes in general being one of the scribal practices believed to remain predominantly handwritten (cf. Krämer 2014 and below). What is negotiated in discourses on digital handwriting is that it combines the advantages of handwriting (e.g., cognitive ones) with the possibilities of technology, which include large data storage capabilities and high and transportable availability (through cloud services that allow accessing data from everywhere), as well as a search function making it possible to find given strings of handwritten text. An additional noteworthy aspect is the fact that no paper is needed, rendering digital handwriting – at least in this regard – an environment-friendly alternative. It must, of course, be noted that it still differs in significant ways from analogue handwriting, largely with respect to the writing surface and its interaction with the writing tool (i.e., the hand and/or a pen). Studies have found, for example, that properties of the surface such as the haptic (proprioceptive) feedback it provides (or fails to provide) to writers is crucial in digital handwriting processes (cf. Guilbert, Alamargot, and Morin 2019; Gerth et al. 2016).

When it comes to the product, digital technology and handwriting merge in typefaces that imitate the visual character of handwriting and are known as *script typefaces* (cf. Böhm and Gätje 2014: 11). The emergence of mimicked handwriting through the availability of such 'handwritten' typefaces can be seen as a 'democratisation' not of handwriting *per se* but of aesthetically pleasing handwriting (cf. Heilmann 2014) given that such typefaces afford any person regardless of their own handwriting skills the possibility to use 'fake'[48] handwriting in the design of their texts. Importantly, this may result in more favourable receptions on behalf of addressees than if producers had typed these texts in 'normal' print typefaces or actually handwritten them with their own – possibly aesthetically less pleasing – handwriting. Another related and rather marginal but noteworthy topic subsumed by the heading of 'digital handwriting' has attracted commercial interest: dedicated robots producing text that visually imitates handwriting. These robots either use pre-existing script typefaces or can be fed sample texts written in a person's actual handwriting that they then imitate with the help of a machine learning algorithm.[49] A business model has emerged around such robots as they are used by clients to produce 'handwritten' messages such as greeting or holiday cards. Ironically, users of such services want their cards to appear more 'personal' through the illusion of handwriting, although this can backfire when addressees realise the texts they have been sent were not actually handwritten (see below).

Against the background of script typefaces and handwriting robots, the question arises of whether the resulting 'handwritten' utterances are actually – consciously or unconsciously – perceived and accepted as digital alternatives to 'real' handwriting by addressees given that they lack a constitutive feature: the impossibility of identical repetition (cf. Gredig 2021: 89). In traditional, analogue handwriting, concrete produced graphs that instantiate the same basic shape never look entirely identical (⟶ Section 4.6.2 for graphetic allography). While typographic or robotic handwriting can simulate the general visual character of handwriting, this prototypical visual variation is superseded by the constancy associated with type.[50]

---

48 Of course, it is in general only 'fake' when handwriting is defined by how it is produced and not when the criteria are visual, in which case this kind of mimicked handwriting would also just be 'handwriting'. In reality, 'handwriting' is often understood as being a combination of those two aspects. Notably, it is 'fake' in a different sense, i.e., with respect to not having been produced by hand by the person using it.

49 Cf. https://www.bbc.com/news/av/technology-48133753 (accessed September 15th, 2021).

50 Some robot handwriting services intentionally add smudges or ink blots to their cards or program some imprecisions so that robots, for example, vary pen pressure or the size and spacing of graphs in order for results to appear more authentically handwritten (cf. https://www.washingtonpost.com/business/2019/12/21/art-imperfection-people-are-turning-robots-write-their-handwritten-cards/, accessed September 15th, 2021).

Another relevant topic area in the pertinent discourses is (b) handwriting in school, with a focus on the style of handwriting that is part of instruction. Here, two major questions are being conflated: whether the instruction of handwriting in general should remain part of curricula, and which type of handwriting is preferable. This can either be cursive, i.e., "linked and typically slanted letters", or manuscript, i.e., "individual unlinked or ball and stick letters" resembling print (Schwellnus, Cameron, and Carnahan 2012: 248). The motivation behind these related questions is how children, in the course of literacy acquisition, can easily and efficiently learn how to write (and – although this is a secondary priority in this discussion – read). The first question is obviously a more extreme version that emphasises the opposition of the processes of handwriting vs. typing. However, the abolition of handwriting in favour of typing is not actually being seriously considered anywhere; the belief that it was results from (partially deliberate?) misinformation spread by the media. Specifically, in early 2015, there was a media outcry when it was widely reported that Finland would be replacing handwriting in school with typing on keyboards when it was actually only planning to phase out the instruction of cursive handwriting (cf. Gredig 2021: 97–100). 'Misinterpretation' is not an entirely accurate description of this situation given that many outlets *did* report correctly on the changes in Finnish education in their articles – just not in their headlines. What Gredig traces for German-language media also applies to English media, e.g., *The Guardian*, which titled "Signing off: Finnish schools phase out handwriting classes" only to then specify in the article's standfirst: "Joined-up writing lessons dropped in favour of keyboard skills, in recognition of changing methods of communication".[51] The exaggeration of the Finnish educational changes and the public debate it evoked in many countries fed perfectly into one of the dominant topoi in the discourses on handwriting: that handwriting is 'dying' (see below).

Notably, the actual change that caught the media's and public's attention – the phasing out of cursive handwriting in favour of manuscript handwriting or non-joined up 'block letters' – is not a phenomenon restricted to Finland. For example, also in Germany and Switzerland, non-cursive types of handwriting styles, so-called basic scripts (in Germany *Grundschrift* and in Switzerland *Basisschrift*) were being heatedly discussed and/or introduced around the same time news of Finland's decision broke.[52] A central motivation behind replacing connected cursive handwriting with handwriting based on unjoined letters is

51 https://www.theguardian.com/world/2015/jul/31/finnish-schools-phase-out-handwriting-classes-keyboard-skills-finland (accessed September 15th, 2021).

52 Cf. https://www.goethe.de/en/spr/spr/20732745.html (accessed September 15th, 2021), an article by the German Goethe-Institut.

the physiological facilitation of the fine motor activity children are expected to master. Furthermore, it represents a reduction of cognitive burden, as children had previously been required to master *both* cursive and unjoined manuscript writing at different stages of their education.[53] Nevertheless, the abolishment of cursive handwriting and the reasoning behind it were met with much criticism and cultural pessimism. Together with the partial digitalisation of handwriting and the dominance of typing in most domains of everyday life, they contribute to the above-mentioned topos of the death of handwriting. A simple Google search for related articles in online media yields many results that underline how strongly this topos has been taken up – ostentatiously, most articles even propagate it in their title (cf. Table 4).

Table 4: Headlines including the topos of the 'death of handwriting' (all links accessed September 22nd, 2021).

Headline
The Death of Handwriting, *The Guardian* (14 Feb 2006), Stuart Jeffries, https://www.theguardian.com/artanddesign/2006/feb/14/art
Mourning the Death of Handwriting, *TIME* (3 Aug 2009), Claire Suddath, http://content.time.com/time/subscriber/article/0,33009,1912419,00.html
Write or Wrong: The Death of Handwriting? *VOA News* (29 October 2009), Nancy Steinbach, https://learningenglish.voanews.com/a/a-23-2009-10-29-voa2-83142932/113450.html
The Death of Handwriting, *Toronto Star* (10 Dec 2009), Andrea Gordon, https://www.thestar.com/life/parent/2009/12/10/the_death_of_handwriting.html
The Death of Handwriting, *Philadelphia Magazine* (21 Jun 2011), Sandy Hingston, https://www.phillymag.com/news/2011/06/21/the-death-of-handwriting/
What are We Losing with the Death of Handwriting? *The Sydney Morning Herald* (3 Feb 2016), William McKeith, https://www.smh.com.au/opinion/what-will-we-lose-with-the-death-of-handwriting-20160203-gmk9uh.html
We're Seeing the Slow Death of Handwriting, *The Takeaway* (8 Sep 2016), John Asante/Adriana Balsamo-Gallina, https://www.wnycstudios.org/podcasts/takeaway/segments/scrawling-history-and-eventual-death-handwriting
Is Handwriting Dead? Hardly. We Need it More Than Ever, *Cornerstone* (12 Feb 2019), Aleka Thrash, https://www.cornerstone.edu/blog-post/is-handwriting-gone-hardly-we-need-it-more-than-ever/
The Slow Death of Handwriting, *The Tribune India* (6 Mar 2020), Kamaljeet Kaur SR, https://www.tribuneindia.com/news/musings/the-slow-death-of-handwriting-51527

53 It is noteworthy that in the US, cursive handwriting appears to enjoy a certain 'comeback' (cf. another aspect discussed in Gredig 2021: 130–131) as it has been introduced to the curricula of several states only in the recent past and is now taught in over twenty states (cf. https://my-cursive.com/the-14-states-that-require-cursive-writing-state-by-state/, accessed September 15th, 2021). For a general review of the literature on cursive vs. manuscript and the arguments for and against them, cf. Schwellnus, Cameron, and Carnahan (2012).

Interestingly, this topos is not only reproduced in the media but also – to some degree – in research on handwriting. For example, in their study on the effects of frequent computer use on basic motor skills that is even titled "The death of handwriting", Sülzenbrück et al. write:

> Future researchers should investigate the influence of modern technologies on human abilities to raise awareness of the potential losses that come along with new technologies and the associated impact on individuals and society. The resulting culturally mediated loss of basic human skills may lead to an increasing dependency on new technologies, which in turn could further deteriorate human skills and potentially also influence human abilities. However, researchers planning to investigate individuals who prefer handwriting to typing should hurry – this endangered species may soon become extinct.
>
> (Sülzenbrück et al. 2011: 250)

Especially the last sentence echoes directly the worries propagated in the media, and additionally emphasises that the death of handwriting could occur sooner rather than later. However, Steve Graham, an authority in handwriting research, disagrees: according to him, "[h]andwriting is alive and healthy" (Graham 2018: 1367). He underlines not only the simple fact that "[p]en, pencil, and paper are very affordable, transportable, and usable", which is especially relevant in regions of the world that are not (yet) as technologised and thus affected by digitalisation, but also mentions the above-mentioned "digital devices that allow writers to handwrite [. . .] their messages" (Graham 2018: 1368), highlighting how handwriting – partially – finds new 'life' in the digital realm. Furthermore, some domains or scribal practices are expected to remain handwritten, thus preventing the 'death' of handwriting. Among them are signing personally, what Krämer (2014: 24) calls 'authenticating identification', as well as the (quick) taking of fleeting and cursory notes in which writers are not concerned with correctness (cf. Böhm and Gätje 2014: 15) and often make use of the spatial possibilities afforded by the two-dimensional writing surface (by drawing mind maps, etc.). And indeed, the cultural pessimism prevalent in discourses is counterbalanced by contrary topoi underlining that handwriting survives or is experiencing a comeback (cf. Gredig 2021: 129–131).

3.3.2.3 Handwriting and cognition

While the focus thus far has been on how handwriting is produced, the assumed primacy of perception over production makes legibility a central aspect in the comparison between typed and handwritten texts. In this respect, type is generally believed to be easier to read because of its visual constancy (see above). Although, like in handwriting, typographic graphs – whether printed on paper or manifested digitally by pixels on a screen – which instantiate the same basic shape are physically unique concrete manifestations, they look identical to the human eye (save for paragraphetic variation due to, for example, damaged screens or printing ink that is running dry). Perceptually, thus, when reading type, less effort is required to match the visual input with the cognitive templates stored for respective basic shapes. This, notably, to some degree also applies to manuscript handwriting. Here, graphs may not appear identical but are still characterised by greater visual constancy given that they are not connected with preceding and following graphs (connectedness being one of the causes for the high variability of graphs in cursive handwriting). Interestingly, variation also appears to have advantages as evidence suggests that the visual variability of graphs produced by children in their own handwriting as well as the variability they perceive in the handwriting of others is actually cognitively beneficial for them: the visual variability of the input provided by concrete graphs leads to a stronger overall representation of the categories or templates they are assigned to in the perceptual system, i.e., in a descriptive sense, of basic shapes (cf. Li and James 2016). Thus, variation attunes visual categorial perception. Further studies such as the one by Longcamp, Zerbato-Poudou, and Velay (2005) provide additional evidence for the assumption that handwriting leads to more robust mental representations of basic shapes that help in their recognition. This also underlines a facet of why perception is considered primary (see above). When we write by hand, we usually receive immediate visual feedback, i.e., we read what we are writing while writing it. The same is not the case vice versa, although studies suggest that perception is also embodied as the reading of handwritten text activates brain regions responsible for movements involved in handwriting (cf. Longcamp, Hlushchuk, and Hari 2011; cf. also Mangen and Velay 2010: 394).

A rather recent phenomenon that concerns the relationship between handwriting, cognitive processes, and digital media is so-called *character amnesia*[54] (in Chinese, the term referring to it is 提笔忘字 *tí bǐ wàng zì*, literally translated as 'pick up pen forget character'), which mostly affects users of morphographic writing systems (nowadays, these are Chinese and Japanese ⟶ Section 6.3). It designates a situation in which users can read certain characters but are not able to write them by hand (cf. Hillburger 2016; Almog 2019).[55] Character amnesia highlights the complex interaction between the structure and the use of a writing system. One relevant factor contributing to it is the remarkable number of graph-

54 It is assumed that this term was coined by sinologist Victor H. Mair in a 2010 blogpost, cf. https://languagelog.ldc.upenn.edu/nll/?p=2473 (accessed September 15th, 2021).

55 A similar situation exists in writing systems using Roman script, where most users identify |g| (or *looptail g*) as a basic shape instantiating the grapheme <g> but are not able to write it by hand when prompted to, instead writing only |g| (*opentail g*) (cf. Wong et al. 2018).

emes resulting from the morphographic nature of the Chinese and (part of the) Japanese writing systems. Specifically, since there is of course a large number of morphemes in these respective languages, and graphemes relate to morphemes, the set of graphemes that needs to be mastered to use the system fluently is extensive, with graphemes numbering in the thousands. The other important factor is the way in which these systems are nowadays predominantly used in everyday life in what are highly technologised literate cultures: through phonetic input methods. For (varieties of) Chinese, this means that users most often type Romanised alphabetic transcriptions[56] of words when writing digitally. For example, they type *shi* and are then presented the characters corresponding with morphemes that are pronounced *shi*. Because of the large degree of homophony in Chinese, for almost every syllable that is typed, several possible characters will appear on the screen, and it is crucial to note that users can successfully recognise the character they had in mind even when due to character amnesia, they would not be able to write it by hand. This dissociation between the ability to recognise a character and the incapability of writing it by hand underlines that cognitively, reading and writing, or more specifically visual templates and graphomotor plans, are separated.

Until recently, there existed little empirical evidence for character amnesia, a situation that has changed with a first large-scale metastudy by Huang et al. (2021). They used the Chinese handwriting database amassed by Wang et al. (2020) in which participants (university students) had handwritten 200 characters pulled randomly from a set of 1600 characters. Analysing the characters that were produced incorrectly, Huang et al. showed that character amnesia occurred for about 42 % of characters and in 6 % of the time. Crucially, they also identified relevant variables contributing to character amnesia, which are mostly character-based (as opposed to user-based):

> People experience more amnesia for characters that are less frequent, embedded in a less-familiar word, acquired later in life, with more strokes, less regular in spelling, or less imageable in their meaning. Among these, character frequency, context word familiarity and age of acquisition are the most influential predictors. (Huang et al. 2021: abstract)

A limitation of this study that must be mentioned is that it focuses almost exclusively on the structure of the system (with the exception of considering the age at which users acquired characters) and thus does not factor in the participants'

---

56 Notably, for smartphones, tablets, and other devices with a touchscreen, there is also a handwritten input method as one can write the character on the screen using one's finger (or a stylus). Provided the character was produced correctly and accurately, it will be recognised and appear typographically.

sociopragmatic communicative practices. While Huang et al. (2021: sec. 5, para. 11) do note that the results are restricted to "university students, who are likely to be relatively good at handwriting", this is merely an assumption about their general skills and not informative regarding how (and if) handwriting plays a role in their lives and literacy practices (e.g., how often they use it, for which purposes, what they think of it, etc.).

As a phenomenon somewhat inverse to character amnesia, handwriting can also serve as an aid in recognising characters. In Japanese, for example, "[i]ndividuals who are presented with unfamiliar kanji will often try to decipher them by tracing them in the air" (Jones and Aoki 1988: 310–311; cf. also Mangen and Velay 2010: 395). What is additionally noteworthy about this is that Chinese hanzi and Japanese kanji are produced in a certain fixed stroke order. While this order is originally based on natural handwriting movements, it has developed into an orthographic 'rule' that is now an integral part of literacy instruction (cf. Zhang 2014). This adherence to a fixed order means that in air (hand)writing, the same (or very similar) movements are involved as in actual handwriting on a writing surface; it thus also activates pertinent brain regions and this can help in recognising a character. This situation can loosely be compared to not being able to recall one's PIN except for when it is actually physically entered on a number pad (or the process of entering it is simulated).

A central aspect in the discourses on handwriting that is evoked – if not supported – by the findings reported above is that writing by hand is claimed to have cognitive benefits, particularly for recognition and memory. The former was illustrated by the development of character amnesia as a pathological state and the strategy of air writing to recognise characters but is generally underlined in neuroscientific research, in which it is stressed that "handwriting is important for the early recruitment in letter processing of brain regions known to underlie successful reading" (James and Engelhardt 2012: 32). On the other hand, that handwriting can aid general memory, i.e., memory of the content that was written by hand (rather than just the memory of basic shapes) is suggested by studies such as Frangou et al.'s (2018). In this study, Finnish students were dictated texts that they had to either write by hand, by typing on the keys of a keyboard, or by touching virtual keys on a virtual keyboard displayed on a touchscreen. The results showed that recollection of the texts was better for students who had handwritten them – both thirty minutes after the task and one week later.

While this study was carried out with dictated texts, i.e., did not require students to produce their own text and therefore focused only on the physical aspects of the writing process and their potential benefits for memory, Mueller and Oppenheimer (2014) showed that the quality of freely produced texts also differs in handwriting vs. typing. Specifically, their study indicated that notes taken by hand during lectures are more beneficial for memory and learning than typed notes. One reason for this is the relative slowness of handwriting (at least when compared to typing), which necessitates writers to process what they hear more thoroughly and put it in their own words. Notetaking using laptops, by contrast, is shallower as laptop note takers tend "to transcribe lectures verbatim rather than processing information and reframing it in their own words", which proves "detrimental to learning" (Mueller and Oppenheimer 2014: 1159).[57] This represents one reason why notetaking is a practice for which handwriting is expected to retain its relevance (see above).

Due to its sheer breadth, the research on cognitive effects of handwriting cannot be exhaustively covered within the scope of this book. For a thorough description of motoric, cognitive, and linguistic aspects of both typing and handwriting processes, cf. Nottbusch (2008). However, the exemplary studies mentioned here explain – and in part justify – the focus on cognition as well as why it is instrumentalised to devalue typing in several strands of the discourses on handwriting.

3.3.2.4 Handwriting and identity

While the public's beliefs about possible beneficial cognitive effects of writing by hand are one of the reasons handwriting is ascribed great value, another central reason is its social importance. Although this societal relevance is, of course, highly culture-specific,[58] it is safe to claim that handwriting is generally held in high esteem as cultural heritage worthy of preservation. This is related to the fact that handwriting is frequently used for purposes that are expected or perceived to have a 'personal' character, e.g., letter writing. Because of the physicality of

57 Of course, taking notes in one's own words with a keyboard on a laptop may just be as beneficial for memory as writing them by hand, as the differences observed in the study were not primarily related to the different modes of production but to the affordances and the prototypical behaviour associated with them.

58 A practice (or bundle of practices) that must be mentioned with respect to the cultural significance of handwriting but cannot be thoroughly treated in the scope of this section is calligraphy, an art form that centres on the aesthetic aspects of handwriting or hand lettering with a pen, brush, or other writing instrument. Several cultures (understood here in a broad sense) such as the Chinese (cf. Yen 2005) and Arabic (cf. Safadi 1978) not only have rich calligraphic traditions that reach far back into the past but value and practice calligraphy to this day. Meanwhile, in Western cultures, the practice of hand lettering (which, notably, often involves styles that resemble type rather than cursive handwriting) has emerged as a trend in the recent past (cf. Gredig 2021: 116–118). Scheffler (1994) gives an overview of calligraphy, while Shepherd (2011) provides a more instructive glimpse into the calligraphic traditions and styles of many cultures.

handwriting (⟶ Section 2.2), writers give something of themselves when writing texts by hand. That way, handwriting represents a way of inscribing the self (cf. Wajda 1999), which – especially in a largely digitalised world – can be interpreted as an act of intimacy (cf. Wickberg 2020) and has become a metaphor for individuality (cf. Böhm and Gätje 2014: 14) charged with cultural ascriptions of singularity, authenticity, and distinctiveness that render it auratic (cf. Neef 2008: 335; for the English translation of Sonja Neef's seminal book on handwriting, see Neef 2011).[59] Vachek highlighted this aspect of handwriting and compared it to the individuality of speaking:

> Any and every written or spoken utterance reflects the individuality of the utterer not only by its contents but also by what may be called its material form, that is to say by the utterer's personal habits of handwriting or pronunciation respectively. This means, practically, that every speaker has his or her own peculiar timbre of voice, a peculiar rhythm and velocity of speech by which he or she differs from all other speakers. Similarly every writing person has his or her peculiar slant of script, a peculiar way of joining the characters of script to one another, a peculiar ratio of large and smaller characters of script, etc. [. . .] which, again, distinguish him or her from all other writing persons. (Vachek 1989: 10)

This individuality is, in many cultures, associated with showing one's identity and lends spoken or written utterances a personal touch. As Sirat (1994: 425) notes, even in otherwise fully typed letters, "a few handwritten words and of course, a handwritten signature show the sender's personal interest and politeness". It is for precisely this reason that the above-mentioned script typefaces and handwriting robots have gained popularity: people use them to convey the personal interest ascribed to writing by hand, but they seemingly do not want to put in the actual effort of handwriting themselves and/or are curious and wish to make use of new technical possibilities afforded by increasing digitalisation. Yet, the perception of these 'fake' types of handwriting on behalf of addresses is by no means always positive. For example, Karavanidou (2017: 157) argues that "even with personalized fonts, the individuality of the human mark is lost". Mangen and Velay (2010: 391) explain this by making explicit the paradox of "digital attempts at reproducing the trace of the tangible", the actual outcome of which is "to even further detach the embodied relation to the inscribing efforts – the writing – from the displayed outcome, thereby adding yet another layer of phenomenological disembodiment". In other words: when typing instead of hand-

59 What must be mentioned in this context is *graphology*, the analysis of handwriting with the goal of identifying writers' psychological personality traits – in other words, parts of their identities. Graphology is largely considered pseudoscientific as there is no scientific evidence to support it (cf. Driver et al. 1996). Here, we are merely addressing the general feature of individuality that is ascribed to the practice of handwriting and handwritten texts.

writing, using typefaces that make the text actually look like typed text is apparently more authentic since that way, the method of writing and its appearance are congruous. Indeed, using technology to fake authenticity does not always work. When, for example, addressees realise that greeting cards they received were (hand)written not by the senders but by a robot, this 'phenomenological disembodiment' cannot only lead to irritation and a perception of inauthenticity but even feelings of deception and betrayal[60] – likely the complete opposite of what senders had intended to achieve or evoke.

The question of what handwriting elicits in addressees or what writers intend to convey by writing a card by hand (or trying to simulate handwriting with a robot) rather than typing it serves as a fitting transition to paramount sociosemiotic questions. With respect to handwriting, these questions, broadly put, deal with the meaning that is ascribed to it (including its appearance). As will be argued below, the sociosemiotic potential is smaller for handwriting than for typography given that producers of typographic texts can easily switch between a myriad of typefaces and typographic resources that are associated with different facets of meaning, whereas it is not as easy to switch styles when handwriting. This will be one of the core issues discussed in the following sections.

3.3.2.5 Typography: Definition, description, and functions

'Typography' is a polysemous term, making necessary a distinction of its different readings at the outset of this section: it designates (1) the technical procedure (= technical reading, cf. Brekle 1994b), (2) the process of designing a printed[61] work (= production-based reading), (3) the resulting design of this printed work itself (= product-based reading), and (4) the profession of designing printed works (= professional reading) (cf. Spitzmüller 2016a: 214). In the following, we will focus on the production- and product-based readings and thus understand typography to be "the arrangement and detailing of text (combined with images and space) according to a premeditated plan, originally for printing on paper (as in books and newspapers), and now also for screen display" (Unger 2018: 229). The endeavour of analysing this process and the products created by it can broadly be referred to as *typography research* and forms part of a larger graphetic and grapholinguistic enterprise. Notably, typography, like handwriting (and writing

60 Cf. https://www.washingtonpost.com/business/2019/12/21/art-imperfection-people-are-turning-robots-write-their-handwritten-cards/ (accessed September 15th, 2021).

61 Nowadays, the meaning of 'printed' is broader as typography is not limited to the production of texts that are actually printed (out) but also encompasses digital texts in which 'print' is constituted by electronic pixels on a screen (cf. Spitzmüller 2016a: 215).

as a whole), can be analysed under both a structural perspective, i.e., as a 'system' characterised by structures, properties, regularities, etc., and the lens of usage, which raises again, among others, sociolinguistic and psycholinguistic questions. While sociolinguistics deals with the social meaning of typography in communication, psycholinguistics predominantly focuses on the role typography plays in recognition and reading processes. These usage-related questions will be addressed in the following, but first, the different structural levels of typographic design and their analysis will be presented.

As for the organisation of typographic properties into different categories, a common distinction in typographic practice is the one between *microtypography* and *macrotypography*. Microtypography concerns "the small-scale aspects of typography, the detailing of text, such as managing wordspaces and interlinear space, the use of punctuation marks" and other aspects, whereas macrotypography comprises "the larger scale aspects of typography, coinciding with layout", i.e., "[a]rranging textual elements such as parts of a main text and footnotes or captions in relation to other elements, mostly images and space" (Unger 2018: 223). A third crucial aspect of typography and arguably the one that stands at the very beginning of any typographic work is type design, i.e., the design and creation of typefaces, which, however, some treat as a part of microtypography (cf. Willberg and Forssman 2013: 9–10; Walker 2001: 18). As mentioned, this division into two (or three) domains stems from professional typographic practice of which both the planning of a global outline and fine adjustments are integral parts (cf. Stöckl 2004: 23). In the context of a linguistic analysis of the functions typography potentially fulfils, Stöckl (2005) proposes a more fine-grained distinction of four typographic levels.[62] Specifically, he modifies the traditional twofold division by adding the dimensions of *mesotypography* and *paratypography*:

> [. . .] the typographic sign system can be broken down into four domains or dimensions of typographic work which represent typographic or textual units of varying size: (i) 'microtypography' refers to fonts and individual letters; (ii) 'mesotypography' concerns the configuration of typographic signs in lines and text blocks; (iii) 'macrotypography' deals with the graphic structure of the overall document; and (iv) 'paratypography' is devoted to typographic media, i.e. surface materials and instruments for producing typographic signs.
> (Stöckl 2005: 209)

Table 5 gives an overview of these four typographic domains as it lists both 'building blocks', i.e., types of typographic resources, and 'properties', i.e., specific manifestations of these resources that are relevant at each of these four levels.

62 This distinction was adapted for a general framework of a graphetic spatial analysis of the writing surface in → Section 3.2.2 (cf. also Meletis 2020a: 38–54).

Table 5: Domains of typography, taken from Stöckl (2005: 210).

Domains of typographic work	Typographic building blocks	Typographic properties
MICROTYPOGRAPHY relates to the design of fonts and individual graphic signs	– typeface – type size – type style – colour of type	– Garamond, Verdana, etc. – point size – 'graph', 'style', 'mode' – black vs. inverted or coloured, etc.
MESOTYPOGRAPHY relates to the configuration of graphic signs in lines and text blocks	– letter fit – word spacing – line spacing (leading) – amount of print on page – alignment of type (type composition) – position/direction of lines – mixing of fonts	– standard, spaced, reduced, etc. – narrow, wide, etc. – double spacing, single spacing – signs/print per page – left-/right-aligned/centred – horizontal, vertical, diagonal, circular, etc. – hand lettering plus type
MACROTYPOGRAPHY relates to the graphic structure of the overall document	– indentations and paragraphing – caps and initials – typographic emphasis – ornamentation devices – assembling text and graphics (image)	– size of text blocks, distance between blocks – ornamented/coloured – underlined, italics, etc. – headline hierarchies, enumerations, tables, charts, indices, footnotes, marginalia, etc. – image-caption-relations, figurative letters, 'typopictoriality'
PARATYPOGRAPHY relates to materials, instruments and techniques of graphic sign-making	– material quality of medium (paper quality) – practices of signing	– thickness, format, surface, etc. – graphing, characting, composing, moulding

What is most remarkable about Stöckl's proposal is the addition of a paratypographic level that equals the inclusion of the third dimension in what is usually a two-dimensional analysis of writing. This dimension considers the properties of the writing surface as well as the writing tools and the different techniques of 'graphic sign-making', i.e., ways in which the writing surface is inscribed. Thus, in this dimension, the appearance of writing is relegated to the background and its actual substantial qualities come to the forefront, e.g., how ink (for instance its colour, chemical composition) and the paper on which it is printed (for instance its thickness, transparency/opacity) interact to manifest the graphs that we perceive. Yet, these aspects cannot be separated from the concrete appearance of writing, which is – at least in part – a product of the writing surface, tools, and what Stöckl (referring to Stötzner 2003) calls different 'practices of signing' (cf. also Wehde 2000: 64–66). In other words, paratypography is a core aspect in the transition from abstract basic shapes to material graphs.

While the outlined approach offers a descriptive systematisation of typographic resources, we now turn to their functions. Antos (2001: 60–61) lists five: (1) an *aesthetic function*, in essence the goal of designing texts in a 'beautiful' way, (2) an *epistemic function*, i.e., that typographic elements are used to visualise the structural hierarchy in/of texts (e.g., with headings, footnotes, etc.), (3) a *motivational function*, attracting and maintaining readers' attention and guiding the reading process, (4) a *synoptic function*, linking text and non-textual material (such as figures) with each other on a 'page',[63] and a (5) *recontextualising function* that allows embedding elements such as quotes from poems or other kinds of texts (including films, etc.) in completely different contexts, e.g., on bumper stickers, t-shirts, or shampoo bottles. Spitzmüller (2016a: 224–225, cf. also Spitzmüller 2013: 209–234) adds even more functions such as (6) the *connotative function* that allows evoking certain associations (like 'modern' or 'old-fashioned', which are sometimes associated with sans-serif and serif typefaces, respectively), (7) the *expressive function*, i.e., that typography can be used to convey the producers'/designers' attitudes or their membership to certain (social) groups, (8) the *indicating* (or *indexical*) function that makes it possible to hint at the context (including the time and place) in which a text originated or also a text's genre, and (9) the *emulative function* assumed by typographic elements that 'imitate' not only certain phenomena found in other modalities, an example of which is shouting, which can be expressed with large font sizes and/or bold print (in addition to all caps, which is, however, a graphematic feature ⟶ Section 4.6.3), but also other types of writing such as handwriting, which is emulated by script typefaces (see previous section). Notably, neither is this list exhaustive, nor are these different functions 'hard' and mutually exclusive categories; indeed, in most cases, typographic elements – intentionally or unintentionally – fulfil more than one of these functions. Yet, it is noteworthy that for a sociolinguistic perspective, the

63 Note that in this day and age, largely due to digitalisation, 'page' has become a vague concept. An analogue printed paper page in a book, magazine, etc. is thus only the default manifestation of a page. From a perceptual perspective, everything that is perceived holistically in a single glance can be conceived of as a 'page' in a broad sense. This includes the portion of a website or document that is currently displayed on the screen of a computer, phone, etc. – which is not stable but can rather be changed dynamically through scrolling – or a PowerPoint slide that is being projected on a wall (cf. Meletis 2015: 142–143). It is important to keep in mind that typography functions in all of these contexts and on all of those 'pages'.

connotative, expressive, indicating, and emulative functions are central, whereas under a psycholinguistic lens, the epistemic, motivational, and partially also synoptic functions come to the forefront. These two perspectives will now be discussed in turn.

3.3.2.6 The sociosemiotic potentials of handwriting and typography

To introduce sociolinguistic questions pertaining to typographic resources, a comparison between the conditions of handwriting and typography proves illuminating. Since handwriting is individual for every literate person, it is characterised by a large degree of visual variability. This variability, however, is relevant mostly interindividually and intertextually, i.e., across individuals and texts. Thus, that a person's handwriting may change over the course of their lifespan or that they may be able to handwrite in different styles at a given point in time is only of marginal interest in an analysis of the functions visual variation performs. Furthermore, in handwriting, resources are rather limited: text may be underlined or written in all caps or with a pen of a different colour, but there is arguably nothing straightforwardly comparable to bold print or italics or changing the typeface within a text.[64] This underlines that in typography, we are confronted with much more variation – or variation at various levels: given that myriad distinct choices are available to almost every person designing texts on a personal computer (or another device), visual variation is also found intraindividually and even intratextually. Simply put, for typography, a single person may use, for example, different typefaces and/or a range of diverse typographic resources in a single text. By comparison, when writing by hand, a single person commonly uses the same handwriting (*their* handwriting) not only within a single text but across all texts handwritten by them.[65] This difference in degrees and scopes of variation between the two materialisations results in a greater sociosemiotic potential for typography.

Thus, the relevant differences between handwriting and typing are not limited to the obvious questions of what is older vs. what developed more recently

---

64 However, while the possibilities may be fewer in handwriting, handwriting itself is not dependent on a computer (or other electronic device), software, or even power supply, making it much more accessible. And, concerning the graphic resources available, limits are only imposed by writers' abilities and the tools available to them but not by (digital) technology (cf. Dürscheid 2020: 34).

65 Note that within the bounds of possibility and depending on the levels of handwritten competence, people can adapt their handwriting to suit a given communicative purpose. For example, a person's handwriting on a letter of condolence may differ from their handwriting on a shopping list (see also below for 'visual politeness').

and they can likewise not be reduced to modes of production, i.e., writing by hand vs. typing. As mentioned, handwriting is a somatic process, i.e., intimately bound to individuals and their bodies. This arguably renders the process-oriented perspective more important for studying handwriting than a product-oriented perspective. Furthermore, if the materiality of a written text is considered in an analysis (e.g., in a comprehensive text linguistic study), depending on the genre and several other factors, it is statistically likely the text in question will be typographic rather than handwritten in nature. This renders the product-oriented perspective more important for typography than for handwriting (and vice versa, typography more central to the product-oriented perspective than handwriting). The situation is of course different for diachronically oriented research given that prior to the invention of the printing press, texts were by default handwritten.[66] Yet, even in diachronic research that has a linguistic focus – rather than a palaeographic or epigraphic one, to name examples – materiality is often disregarded.

Another interesting aspect that concerns the main semiotic difference between typography and handwriting is the latter's established individuality. With respect to handwriting, in order to convey their individuality, i.e., make themselves visible as writing individuals, users merely need to (decide to) write by hand. By contrast, lay users and designers of typographic texts typically do not design their own typefaces but rather choose from the many that are nowadays available. In this respect, it is not only the appearance of the typeface producers choose that reveals something about themselves (their personality, etc.) to potential addressees but rather the fact that they chose it. Analysing this very choice allows making assumptions about users' preferences, tastes, and typographic knowledge[67] (or typographic competence, cf. Wehde 2000: 75), which is shaped, among other factors, by their socialisation, the time and place in which they are currently living, their educational and professional background, and their culture. In a nutshell: for handwriting, which

---

66 Here, 'handwriting' is understood in a broader sense as it also includes other modes of production that all involve the hand and a rather direct mediation of a writing tool. The field of material culture studies has illuminated several materials and 'practices of signing'. The former include stone, plaster, clay, metal, papyrus, leather, parchment, paper, wax, wood, and human skin, while examples of the latter are chiselling, carving, moulding, sealing, stamping, embossing, weaving in, and stitching on (cf. Meier, Ott, and Sauer 2015). As mediators between materials and practices of signing, writing instruments are, of course, also of great relevance.

67 Not all typographic 'choices' are sociosemiotically indexical in the same way. For example, users often leave the default settings of their word processing program (such as the widely used Microsoft Word) unchanged, thus using the typeface that is pre-set (whether Times New Roman, Calibri, or a different one). Note, however, that even this choice or better 'non-choice' of a different typeface reveals something about writers' attitudes such as the relevance they (do not) ascribe to typography.

nowadays is a 'marked' choice for special purposes and domains of written communication in many literate cultures, the *sole fact* that a person chooses to write by hand as well as the resulting handwritten text prove sociosemiotically relevant (e.g., with respect to certain aspects of the communicative situation such as the purpose of the text, the time and place it was conceived, the relationship between the sender and the addressee), whereas the appearance of handwriting *per se* is not sociosemiotically relevant. On the other hand, for typography, the decision of using typography over handwriting is not as relevant in and of itself (given that it has evolved as the 'unmarked' choice) – instead, the actual design choices (e.g., which typeface is used, how text is arranged) become sociosemiotically charged.

To sum up: typographic variation is always meaningful in some way by fulfilling one or multiple of the functions introduced in the previous section (cf. also Spitzmüller 2015). To achieve this, however, typographic elements are dependent on a co(n)text. For example, the highlighting function (as part of the epistemic function) carried out by several words in a text being printed in bold is successful only when the bold print is perceived in contrast with its surrounding non-bold 'default' text (cf. Spitzmüller 2016a: 223; Meletis 2015: 149–150). While such surrounding text represents the context in a narrow sense (in some conceptions, it is referred to as 'cotext'), context in a broader sense also plays a crucial role in the semiotic functioning of typography: typographic resources such as the typeface *Comic Sans* (see below) may, for example, have acquired special context-dependent meaning because they are used by a given group of people at a given time and for given purposes – thus fulfilling connotative or indicating functions. The possibility of choosing from a large set of pre-existing alternatives leads to another crucial feature of typography: with their choice of typefaces (as well as other typographic elements or arrangements), users can consciously or unconsciously associate themselves with certain groups and signal this membership to others. In other words, typography can visually connect people and build or reinforce groups and thereby fulfils an expressive function. Such an association is not as easily achievable in handwriting,[68] where writers may attempt to imitate different styles – as has become a popular trend in the form of hand lettering – but, when using their 'own' handwriting, usually reveal much less (and also rather different aspects) than do the many variants available in typography. Handwriting may indeed indicate the time and region in which a person lives/lived (based on, for example, the handwriting styles that were part of the education of that time and/

68 There are exceptions to this. Whether one uses cursive or manuscript handwriting, for example, can be an indicator of one's views on certain issues and thus signal group membership (e.g., being a proponent or opponent of the instruction of cursive handwriting in school).

or region), but it arguably does not allow for more fine-grained ascriptions that are often possible in the analysis of typography (e.g., that the producer of a text is a fan of heavy metal, cf. Androutsopoulos 2004).

Notably, the specific appearance of handwriting (especially its legibility) can be telling in other respects: as readers, we often infer from it how much time and effort writers have put into their writing, which in communicative genres such as letter writing also serves as a sign of the degree of respect writers hold for addressees,[69] but also provides information on aspects such as writers' age (young, adult, old), their physical state during the writing process, e.g., whether they were tired, drunk, sick, etc. (cf. Parush et al. 1998; Aşıcıoğlu and Turan 2003; Caligiuri and Mohammed 2012), and even their intelligence (cf. Donzelli and Powell Budgen 2019).[70] Many of these factors, especially the physical ones, do not become 'visible' in typography – at least not at the graphetic level.[71]

The association of typefaces with certain variables such as genres or styles occurs either consciously or unconsciously and by lay users, experts (i.e., typographers), and scholars analysing typographic texts. Thus, depending on the degree of their typographic knowledge, users may or may not be aware of the fact that when using a given typeface, they associate themselves with a group of people using the same typeface, a genre characterised by the use of that typeface, etc. In his large-scale treatment of (typo)graphic variation, Spitzmüller (2013: 229–234) identifies three broad social functions: (1) variation can serve to create

---

69 An interesting study in this respect is Schreiber (subm.), aptly titled 'Visual politeness', which traces how in pre-modern Japanese letter writing, the degree of cursivisation of handwriting indicated degrees of respect and social hierarchies: if a person wrote to someone from a socially lower class, handwriting would be more cursive than if they wrote to someone who was regarded equal or placed higher in the social hierarchy.

70 Donzelli and Powell Budgen's (2019) study in a fascinating way combines typography and handwriting as it centres on the metapragmatics surrounding the parodying function of *Tiny Hand*, a typeface based on Donald Trump's handwriting that is meant to allude to his (lack of) intelligence. For a mention of the childlike appearance of Trump's handwriting and a browser plugin that allowed displaying his tweets in a script typeface resembling children's handwriting, cf. Gredig (2021: 90–91).

71 As for respect for addressees, the use of inappropriate typefaces could be regarded as impolite (see also below). Regarding the age and physical state of writers, in typed text, the material appearance of typographic texts is relegated to the background and graphematic and orthographic features such as incorrect spelling are used to infer (or better ascribe) certain characteristics to writers. While in handwriting, the shape of graphs and other properties of the visual appearance can 'suffer', mistakes in typing affect a different level: "if a key is pressed in error, a spelling error will occur but the visual shape of the letter is preserved in perfect condition" (Mangen and Velay 2010: 397). This corresponds with a shift from graphetics to graphematics/orthography.

(social) patterns and signal genres and thus also influence the reception of texts on behalf of readers; (2) it can be used to express attitudes and values (subsumed under the term of *graphic ideologies*), negotiate them, as well as ascribe them; and, as mentioned, (3) it can be instrumentalised by writers/designers to position themselves socially with respect to other (groups of) people. The functions underline that typography (much like orthography ⟶ Chapter 5) is a form of (visual) social action. They also show that typographic knowledge is central not only in production but also in perception: as readers are confronted with typographic products, they often (implicitly) make assumptions about the designers of these products – their background, their knowledge – and the contexts in which these products originated, among other things. These assumptions – whether they are accurate or not – are revelatory with respect to the typographic knowledge held by people who make them, knowledge that is not equally distributed among members of a literate community (cf. Spitzmüller 2016b and below). In short, typography in complex ways visually reflects certain facets of its users – both writers/producers and readers/recipients – which is how it rightfully takes centre stage in the synchronic sociolinguistic study of the materiality of writing.

3.3.2.7 Typographic variation and meaning: three examples

The starting point of any typographic analysis is, of course, the appearance of written utterances. Indeed, recipients do not necessarily always make assumptions about producers as the product can often very well stand on its own and be received and judged as such. Above, it was mentioned that typography can be associated with genres, which requires users to integrate the typographic resources they perceive into a larger picture. However, it is also paramount to note that the concrete typography of a text can contribute to its meaning also at a local, i.e., much more immediate and specific level. Consider Figure 10, in which the same sentence – "You'll always be mine . . . " – receives either a 'romantic' or a 'dangerous' reading depending on the look of the typeface[72] used. Of course, this appearance also invites inferences about the sender and their relationship to the addressee, etc., but above all it underlines the general meaning-making potential of typography. In such instances in which typographic choices contribute vital components to the overall meaning of an utterance that would otherwise not be conveyed, it is debatable whether speaking of a merely connotative function is justified (⟶ Section 3.1.1); in any case, it is not secondary.

72 Even if they look like handwriting, these examples are rather instances of typefaces that merely emulate handwriting (see above).

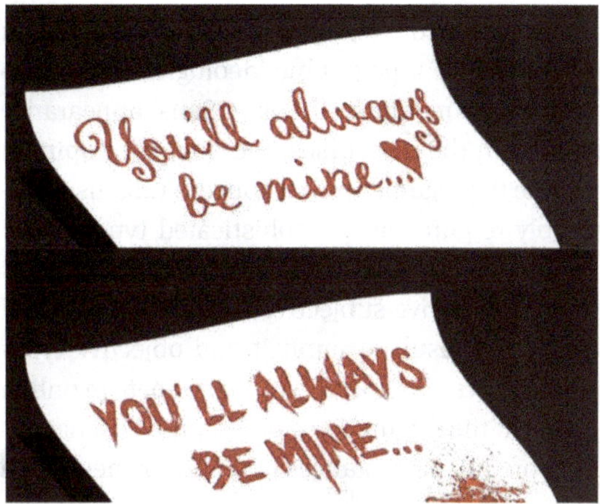

Figure 10: Different meanings of the same sentence constituted by the choice of typeface, adapted from https://starecat.com/content/wp-content/uploads/fonts-matter-youll-always-be-mine-written-in-two-fonts.jpg (accessed September 15th, 2021).

Two more examples shall make the core aspects in the sociolinguistic and sociosemiotic study of typography more concrete. The first concerns the vivid online discourses surrounding the typeface Comic Sans. Starting as a satirical movement propagating a ban of the typeface in the late 1990s, the aversion to Comic Sans gradually developed a momentum of its own so that today, many people do not appear to know the origin of the 'Everybody hates Comic Sans' memes that have grown popular on the internet. In an analysis of pertinent metapragmatic online discourses (cf. Meletis 2020c), two main reasons can be identified as contributing to the dislike of the typeface: the primary argument and the one most participants in the discourses agree on is that Comic Sans is overused. Released in the 1990s as one of the first pre-installed typefaces on personal computers among typefaces that were more neutral and 'serious', it was the go-to choice for users who wanted a typeface with a more 'playful' character. It is the resulting overuse that also led to uses in inappropriate contexts, which is the second reason underlying the dislike of the typeface. Comic Sans, due to its design (see below), is connotated with childishness and may thus be perceived as suitable for purposes such as invitations to children's birthday parties but not for engravings on gravestones or professors' PowerPoint presentations, many participants in the online discourses argue (cf. also Murphy 2017). This underlines that typefaces – or, from a pragmatic perspective, writers' typographic choices – become tightly associated with certain expectations of literacy (or scribal) practices, contexts of use, and genres.

The evaluation of 'appropriateness,' of course, again depends crucially on one's typographic knowledge and subjective typographic ideologies (for appropriateness, cf. also Spitzmüller 2016b). As mentioned, Comic Sans' appearance (cf. Figure 11) is also being negotiated in the discourses, the dominant opinion being that it is poorly designed. Unlike the arguments that concern (mis)use, criticism of typographic design arguably requires more sophisticated typographic knowledge – at least if the evaluation of a typeface as being 'poorly designed' is objectively justified and not merely an intuitive subjective view. However, such subjective sensitivities could also be the result of implicit and objective typographic knowledge. Notably, type designers, as experts, also participate in online discourses on typography and represent the driving force of design-based negotiations; however, they often adopt more nuanced stances and thereby neutralise the emotional tone displayed by lay users.

ABCDEFGHIJKLMNO
PQRSTUVWXYZÀÅÉ
abcdefghijklmnopqr
stuvwxyzàåéîõøü&12
34567890($£€.,!?)

Figure 11: Comic Sans.

Another phenomenon worth mentioning is so-called *typographic mimicry*. It was already introduced above in the context of script typefaces that mimic the visual character of (cursive) handwriting; thus, the emulative function of typography is foregrounded. But not only handwriting, also different scripts can be mimicked by typefaces, which is the core of cultural typographic mimicry (cf. Meletis 2021b). In this practice, typefaces of the 'source' script (such as Roman script in most Western cultures) are designed in ways that emulate the visual features of a different script, the 'target' script (such as Chinese script, Arabic script, etc.).[73] That way, these typefaces visually resemble a 'foreign' script and, crucially, are intended to refer indexically to the 'culture' (understood in a very broad sense)

73 Note that all types of combinations are possible: Chinese typefaces can be made to resemble Arabic script, Japanese (kana) typefaces can imitate Thai script, etc.

this script is associated with, thus performing (more or less successfully) the indicating function of typography. Figure 12 illustrates this. As there are no official lists of visual features characteristic of scripts, the features that are exploited by type designers in their design of such typefaces are often chosen based on intuitive analyses. This subjective procedure invites the perception that typographic mimicry is based on visual stereotypes, and it has accordingly been referred to as 'stereotypography' (cf. Giampietro 2004).

What becomes evident in the analysis of how cultural typographic mimicry is employed is that it is commonly not addressed at people literate in the actual target scripts: typefaces emulating Chinese script, for example, are not meant for readers and writers of Chinese but precisely for people who cannot read actual Chinese. The fact that such typographic mimicry, then, represents Roman script with 'a Chinese touch' evokes (or is rather intended to evoke) specific cultural associations that are instrumentalised predominantly in commercial contexts. Packages of food or restaurant signs, for example, are typical domains in which cultural typographic mimicry is used. Like in the Comic Sans example discussed above, an investigation of online discourses surrounding this phenomenon proves fruitful in condensing users' knowledge and attitudes. In the case of typographic mimicry, major strands also focus on the quality of design of mimicking typefaces, which is largely perceived as poor, as well as on the contexts in which it is practiced – and by whom. An interesting facet of this discussion concerns the question of whether it constitutes cultural appropriation (or even racism) when people who are themselves not members of the indexed cultures engage in cultural typographic mimicry, especially when the typefaces in question are poorly designed.[74] This question is made even more complex by the fact that it is frequently indeed 'in-group' members, i.e., members of the culture these typefaces intend to evoke, who use typographic mimicry to index 'themselves' and their culture to foreigners, e.g., in the form of the mentioned restaurant signs.

In sum, with the heated debates they invite, the discourses surrounding both Comic Sans and cultural typographic mimicry display a large degree of (self-)prescriptivism manifested by the negotiation of who is allowed to carry out certain typographic practices and who is not – and when, where, how, etc. Notably, both examples also show clearly that typography can quickly become an emotional topic. This is unsurprising given that there is no neutral typography (cf. Willberg and Forssman 2010: 72). No matter how 'neutral' we perceive a typeface – such

74 In this context, the (lack of) quality of mimicking typefaces (by contrast with high-quality 'normal' typefaces of Roman script) is interpreted as a reflection of Eurocentric dichotomies such as 'civilised' vs. 'savage' that are themselves associated with a highly problematic perception of an alleged Western superiority.

Figure 12: Restaurant sign with the name ('Cafe Spice') printed in a typeface of Roman script that mimics Devanāgarī.

as Arial or Helvetica – to be, this neutrality is but another ascribed attribute that actually negates the neutrality of these typefaces. Indeed, if we begin thinking about them and evaluating them, typefaces start to mean something to us – and this meaning is transferred to their users, contexts in which they are used, etc. No typeface is neutral because no use of the typeface will ever be neutral.

3.3.2.8 Typography, readability, and legibility

Psycholinguistics offers another major usage-based perspective for studying typography. At its centre, we find questions of legibility and readability (two distinct concepts, see below). Accordingly, a great number of studies have investigated the effects several typographic variables exert on perception, i.e., recognition and reading. Among some of the microtypographic and mesotypographic variables that were the subjects of studies (focused on the Roman script) are the x-height of typefaces, their pitch (i.e., the space between letters), word spacing, line width, alignment, font size, stroke width, and serifs (cf. Filek 2013: 95–179). At the macrotypographic level, variables such as the spatial arrangement of text and non-text on the surface – simply put, questions of layout – are of relevance. Lastly, paratypographic factors influencing specific reading situations such as the transparency of paper and the incidence of light can affect legibility and readability. However, they are seldom at the centre of psycholinguistic research.

As pointed out, *legibility* and *readability* are different concepts. As Lund (1999: 15–20) reconstructs, they have a complicated history, and even in recent times, they are "far from straightforward and agreed upon" (Lund 1999: 20). 'Legibility' was the first of them to be widely used in pertinent research, and it is concerned with the above-mentioned "effect of different typographical arrangements on the reader's ability to carry out the reading task most easily, comfortably, and effectively" (Katzen 1977: 8). This definition, however, was also applied to 'readability' by some scholars starting in the 1930s, and several authors even used the two terms interchangeably (cf. Lund 1999: 16; Wendt 2000: 18). A differentiation is suggested by Anne R. König:

> Readability refers to the comprehensibility of characters from different language families and the content components of texts used for comprehension and entertainment; legibility, on the other hand, refers to the decipherability of handwritten and [. . .] printed documents. (König 2004: 18, our translation)

In other words, readability is a more global concept that subsumes aspects concerning the language (its style, etc.) in which a text is written, whereas legibility in a narrower sense involves exclusively questions of the appearance of writing. This, notably, in the grapholinguistic framework proposed here, corresponds with the distinction between graphematics and graphetics: readability is invested in linguistic aspects of writing (graphematics) and their influence on reading, whereas legibility is concerned with material aspects (graphetics). As graphematics subsumes graphetics, readability also subsumes legibility. In other words, a text can only be readable if it is legible in the first place. But, vice versa, a text being legible does not automatically make it readable as well, since for this to be the case, factors such as choice of words, syntactic complexity, etc. also play crucial roles.

In an especially broad understanding of 'readability', König (2004) suggests that it is not only aspects of the object that is perceived (e.g., a printed text) but also properties of the situation in which perception takes place that determine overall readability. While the former include typographic factors (or chirographic factors, as handwritten texts can also be assessed with respect to readability) and thus issues of legibility as well as linguistic factors such as orthographic correctness, style, and information structure, the latter incorporate (1) cultural factors, (2) the reading situation, and (3) the individual reader. Among these, cultural factors are significantly affected by (typo)graphic knowledge and subsume, for example, the judgment of and attitudes associated with certain typefaces in a given culture but also generally the typographic standards and customs as well as orthographic norms. The reading situation, on the other hand, is constituted by the properties of the place at which perception or reading takes place, i.e., the immediate surroundings (including the above-mentioned light but also aspects such as noise level),[75] and the physical interaction between texts and readers, i.e., readers' posture, the spatial distance between them and the text, and the

75 These factors interact intricately with the individual reader, as each reader has a different tolerance limit for various nuisance factors, examples of which are fatigue, indisposition, bad light conditions, diversion due to noise or movement (e.g., when someone is reading while riding the bus or being on an airplane) (cf. Bosshard 1996: 11).

angle at which seeing and in turn reading takes place. Finally, the many aspects that pertain to the individual reader include but are not limited to eyesight, reading experience, motivation, interest, linguistic knowledge, intelligence, and the intended reading strategy (e.g., reading closely, skimming, cf. Waller 1987). Notably, both cultural factors and factors concerning the individual reader constitute a bridge between the psycholinguistic and sociolinguistic dimensions of typography. Not only (largely socially conditioned) typographic knowledge affects readability but also the connotations evoked in readers by typographic variables such as entire typefaces or the presence vs. absence of serifs.

Due to the lack of space, in this section, we cannot focus on the effect different (mostly micro)typographic variables such as x-height exert on perception (for overviews cf. Lund 1999; Filek 2013, and for the influence of specific fonts on reading processes ⟶ Section 4.7). However, a further comment must be made about abstract vs. concrete graphetic research. In ⟶ Section 3.2.3, the segmentation of basic shapes into elementary forms was introduced as one of the core topics of graphetics. The structural approaches of segmentation mentioned there are abstract since they are interested in how basic shapes in general can be described and segmented rather than graphs of a specific font[76] such as 12 pt. italic Arial.[77] They are thus focused on the invariable formal features of shapes that are characterised by constancy despite the variation constituted by the concrete visual materialisations of writing. By contrast, psycholinguistic research examining the physiological and/or cognitive effects of diverse typographic variables is most often concrete in that it focuses precisely on *variables* – different fonts and their graphs that can have or lack serifs, can be characterised by varying x-heights, stroke widths, etc.[78] Thus, simply put, structure-oriented graphetic research deals with scripts – as sets of basic shapes – and their properties (see the perspective of emergent literacy below for some of them), whereas

---

76 For the difference between *typeface* and *font*, see Murphy (2017: 68): "The term 'font' is more widely used than typeface in colloquial discourse, largely due to its endemic presence in consumer word-processing software, but there is a historical difference between the two terms: in traditional typesetting the word 'font' refers to a complete set of letters and other characters in one typeface, one style (bold, italic, etc.), one weight (the thickness of its lines), and one size". Thus, for example, while *Calibri* is a typeface, 10 pt italic Calibri is one specific font of that typeface.

77 As was noted above, this is a severe limitation of these studies as they, in fact, must still work with a specific materialisation (i.e., a given font), which renders findings restricted rather than universally applicable.

78 It is, however, also interested in generalisations. For example, if a specific x-height is found to be beneficial in a specific study, this will often be claimed in general terms (as opposed to being only valid for the font that was used in the experiment).

chirographic or typographic psycholinguistic research deals with features of specific instances of handwriting or fonts that consist of materialised graphs.[79]

There exist numerous overviews of the methodology of psycholinguistic typography research (cf. the respective sections in Tinker 1963; Wendt 2000; Bosshard 1996; Zachrisson 1965; Lund 1999); especially the summary given by Filek (2013: 72–75) serves as a starting point for the following brief presentation of methods. A first and central group of methods pertains to the physiological preconditions and includes the measurement of perception thresholds. Here, subjects are presented stimuli (in most cases single letters) and the brightness of the presentation is adjusted or the distance between stimuli and readers is decreased until correct recognition takes place (in at least half of the trials). Another variable that can be tested is the duration of presentation, which is gradually increased until subjects recognise stimuli. Less often, threshold experiments of this kind have also been conducted with variables such as sharpness and (reading/viewing) angle (cf. Filek 2013: 73). Aspects that are relevant not only prior to but especially during or after reading that have also been studied in this context concern the physical condition of individuals. For example, the number of blinks – with the conclusion: the more blinking, the 'worse' the readability – as well as fatigue were measured, a concept that itself must first be operationalised (cf. Wendt 2000: 21). With the help of measuring the blink rate, analysing eye movements, as well as asking participants to subjectively evaluate their condition following an experiment, researchers hoped to obtain statements about the level of fatigue. In this context, Filek (2013: 75) notes that such studies regarding fatigue often did not produce valuable results. By contrast, in more recent studies, the "cognitive effort required to process information via the recording of brain activity" is measured and treated as an indicator of fatigue during reading (Filek 2013: 75, our translation).

In addition to analysing the recognisability of characters – which makes up only one part of readability – reading performance is also relevant. In this regard, reading speed as well as reading comprehension have been considered as metrics. The former is studied by providing subjects with a certain amount of text and measuring how much time they require to read it or, vice versa, by determining how much text subjects have read in a previously specified amount of time. As one of the most commonly used variables, however, reading speed is plagued by allowing many *a posteriori* interpretations as the duration needed to read a

79 Technically, they consist of classes of graphs or 'graph classes' that are positioned between the abstract basic shape and the concrete graph. Graph classes such as '10 pt bold Times New Roman |a|' are abstract but contain more specific visual information than the basic shape alone (which itself is indifferent to typeface or style of handwriting), marking their membership to a given inventory, i.e., a person's handwriting or a specific font (cf. Meletis 2020b).

text depends on both the object of reception (i.e., the text) and the reception situation (see above). Gaining control over all influencing factors proves to be one of the biggest challenges readability research must face. The above-mentioned reading comprehension can be tested in various ways, through surveys and tests following or even during experiments; for example, subjects can be instructed to identify out-of-context elements in the text while reading it. In this case, too, the results cannot be clearly interpreted since what is tested is merely that something was understood – not *why* and *how*.

In his epistemological overview of typographic readability research, Lund (1999: 23–33) addresses the above-mentioned methods as well as the criticisms that have been voiced against them. He organises the methodology by dividing methods roughly into three categories: (1) experimental performance studies subsume not only most of the psychological methods, i.e., measuring the reading speed or the blink rate and recording eye movements, but also all studies focusing on perception thresholds. In addition, Lund mentions the search task as a method; it consists of subjects being instructed to search for a specific item in a text, with the duration it takes them to find it being timed. The second category is formed by (2) subjective preference studies that centre on surveying subjects' attitudes and feelings towards different types of stimuli. Finally, (3) typeface typology studies "with regard to method differ widely" (Lund 1999: 32) and thus constitute a heterogeneous group. They are mostly descriptive studies in which characters are analysed in terms of their form and structure and are subsequently compared with each other (hence 'typological'). In other words, this third group focuses on the subbranch of descriptive graphetics while the first two are – as would be expected from readability research – part of perceptual graphetics.

Another important question that concerns readability is how certain mesotypographic and macrotypographic elements can guide the reading process and aid reading comprehension, thus fulfilling a synoptic function (see above). Over thirty years ago, Auberlen outlined the steps necessary to study this function; to some degree, they have remained desiderata up until this day:

> First, embedding work on macrotypographic markings in the theoretical framework of text-reader interaction, with particular attention to models of text processing and the results of experimental reading research. Second, the methodological development of the inventory, modes of use, and impact aspects of macrotypographic markings. And third, the testing of possible effects through a variety of experimental designs to control for design-dependent outcome tendencies. (Auberlen 1990: 107, our translation)

By singling out text-reader interaction, it is made clear that the effect meso- and macrotypographic elements exert on reading processes is a central concern of, among others, text reception research, text linguistics, specialised language and terminology research, and didactics (cf. Spitzmüller 2016a: 226). There exist many proposals of how the functions of such elements can be systematised. The first worth mentioning here comes from Robert Waller, who has extensively studied typography. According to him, typography can serve (1) *delineation*, i.e., "methods indicating the beginning and end of text segments", (2) *interpolation*, "the insertion or juxtaposition of a short segment into a longer one", (3) *serialisation*, "the organization of segments into clear structures, sets, or series", and (4) *stylisation*, "the indication of a mode of discourse differing in voice or genre from the main body of text" (Waller 1980: 241). Jörg Hagemann arrives at similar conclusions; he claims that the consistent use of certain typographic elements (e.g., italics) can promote global text comprehension on behalf of the reader both intra- and intertextually. Designers can thus employ typographic means to provide readers with "implicit reading instructions" (Hagemann 2003: 102, our translation) and "establish a categorical level formation in the overall propositional context [. . .] through equally emphasised expressions" (Hagemann 2003: 107, our translation).

Furthermore, a central function of macrotypography is to constitute so-called *typographic dispositifs* (cf. Wehde 2000). They are based on the fact that specific macrotypographic arrangements are tightly associated with specific genres: recipes or front pages of newspapers, for example, have such recognisable layouts that they are classified by perceivers as such even if the linguistic content is not read. In other words, typographic dispositifs make it possible to just glance at a text and – based on one's typographic knowledge (see above) – know what type of text it is. Notably, what can function as a typographic dispositif is not only culture-specific but also determined by several other factors (period, region, familiarity with a genre etc.). What these remarks underline is how not only at the microtypographic but also at the meso- and macrolevels, typography gains a pragmatic dimension. This raises the following questions: how do authors/designers want their texts to be understood, how do they use typographic means to achieve that, and how is the text ultimately interpreted by readers? In sum, typography, as one – nowadays dominant – way of materialising written language, is a powerful instrument when its influence on the reception of texts is exploited.

3.3.2.9 Multicultural and intercultural typography

At the end of this presentation of typography, it is important to note that it was implicitly focused on what can be termed 'Latin typography'[80] and thus only

80 For the differences between the designations 'Roman script' and 'Latin script', which are often considered synonyms, cf. Daniels (2018: 28–31). Due to its use in the typographic literature,

on one – the dominant – part of actual typographic practice (and, in extension, research). This hierarchy is observed by AbiFarès (2019: 13), who writes: "The dominance of Latin script is felt [. . .] acutely in type design practices, to the point where the world of typefaces is divided into two main categories: Latin and (all the other) non-Latin scripts". Firstly, this dominance manifests itself in the quantity of available resources, as "there is still an enormous gap between the Latin and non-Latin worlds in terms of the quantity and variety of available fonts" (Bil'ak 2019: 11). One reason for this is that up until recently (and to some degree this is still true today), it proved more difficult to create typefaces for 'non-Latin' scripts. Secondly, issues of dominance are also negotiated in terms of 'visual coexistence' (cf. the title of Baur and Felsing's 2020 volume), i.e., the question of how typefaces of different scripts can coexist in an increasingly globalised and multilingual (and, thus, multiscriptual) world. Wittner lists some of the relevant and sociopolitically charged facets regarding this:

> Are they [different scripts, DM/CD] treated with equal importance? Does one express visual dominance over the other? Are they clearly separated? Or do the different languages interact with each other, therefore expressing intercultural communication rather than separation? (Wittner 2019: 7)

The coexistence of different scripts has created new challenges for type designers, one of which is "designing font families that can accommodate most written scripts and sometimes bring various writing systems together under one unifying visual language" (AbiFarès 2019: 13). A project noteworthy in this respect is Google's *Noto* font family, "which aims to support all languages with a harmonious look and feel".[81] Notably, visually unifying different scripts once again raises delicate questions of dominance, and in the design of typefaces for non-Latin scripts, two opposing strategies have emerged:

> On one hand, designers are 'modernising' scripts by minimising shapes and reducing forms, which some criticise as merely mimicking Latin type.[82] Latinisation has been, and still is, a highly controversial and much discussed topic – which is why, on the other hand, technological developments are utilised to make scripts more calligraphic, traditional and livelier by incorporating, for instance, countless ligatures. (Wittner 2019: 7)

in this part of the section, we also use 'Latin typography' to refer to 'typography that concerns Roman script'.

81 Cf. https://www.google.com/get/noto/ (accessed September 15th, 2021).

82 This, ironically, is the opposite of the cultural typographic mimicry that was presented above in which Latin type is made to look like non-Latin type.

The situation regarding research on non-Latin typography resembles that of graphetic research on scripts other than Roman (consider, for example, the dominance of Roman-centred research in ⟶ Section 3.2). However, several recent projects have adopted a comparative perspective, describing and sometimes juxtaposing the typography of different scripts. Among them are the *Bi-Scriptual* project by Wittner, Thoma, and Hartmann (2019), which investigates many different scripts and their typography, Baur and Felsing's (2020) analysis of the coexistence of Chinese and Latin typography, Mariko Takagi's comparisons of Latin with Chinese (Takagi 2014) and Japanese (Takagi 2016), and Rjeily's (2011) attempt at 'bridging' Arabic and Latin typography.

3.4 Perspectives from emergent literacy

The preceding sections have focused on the general description of the material features of writing, their functions, as well as the question of how these are manifested in handwritten and typographic texts. Throughout, the physiological and cognitive processing of graphetic properties was mentioned as a relevant aspect of graphetic research. It now comes to the forefront as we turn to the question of how children acquire literacy. Commonly, research on literacy acquisition is concerned primarily with how children learn about the linguistic functions of writing, i.e., about how graphic units relate to linguistic units. It thus centres around graphematics. This prioritisation is tightly related to the perception that writing is *just* learned through instruction. While it is true that writing is not acquired 'naturally' like speech (⟶ Section 2.2, but cf. Anbar 1986, 2004), it would be inaccurate to claim that no aspects of writing are picked up by children without – or prior to – formal literacy instruction. Indeed, children notice many features of writing – especially graphetic features – apparently only by being surrounded by writing in the literate cultures in which they are raised. This had already been observed by Lurija (1977: 65), who wrote that "[t]he history of writing in the child begins long before a teacher first puts a pencil in the child's hand and shows him how to form letters". Investigating the acquisition of these features or, simply put, "what children know about writing [. . .] before being taught" (cf. the subtitle of Tolchinsky 2003) as a part of so-called *emergent literacy* research proves highly relevant. It reveals whether descriptively postulated graphetic features are physiologically and cognitively salient or 'real'.

Given that these features are not bound to specific languages, the question of which features are acquired by children – and when – is valuable in the search for graphetic universals of writing, which is, in turn, a central component of a theory of writing. Yet, as implied above, the investigation of these graphetic features appears to be a much smaller priority than research on how, in a next step, children grasp the linguistic functions of writing. Very roughly, thus, for the purposes of systematisation, we divide literacy acquisition into two major stages: (1) acquisition of graphetic features and (2) acquisition of graphematic features and functions. The transition between them is ushered in by the developing understanding in the child that writing is related to the language it speaks, i.e., the emergence of metalinguistic awareness. The focus of 'classic' research on literacy acquisition is precisely on various facets of this awareness. The most prominent is *phonological awareness* (cf. Blachman 2000; Anthony and Francis 2005; Gillon 2018), which most often is interpreted more specifically – and terminologically imprecisely – as awareness of phonological segments (i.e., phonemes) but technically also encompasses highly relevant syllabic awareness (cf. Høien et al. 1995 for the components of phonological awareness).[83] What is often relegated to the background is the equally paramount *morphological awareness* (cf. Carlisle 2010; Manolitsis et al. 2019; Tong et al. 2009; Wu et al. 2009) that is crucial not only in morphographic writing systems such as Chinese, as is often mentioned in the literature, but also in primarily phonographic writing systems (cf. exemplarily Schmidt 2018; Berg 2019 for morphography in German). As this section is not concerned with these important linguistic aspects of literacy acquisition, we will not go into detail about them.[84]

Before they learn to write, children usually already use a different graphic representational system in the form of drawing (cf. Taverna, Tremolada, and Sabattini 2020). Therefore, the main features of writing that are picked up by children in the context of their emergent literacy are those that distinguish writing from drawing. A first crucial feature is shared by both: artificiality. Both drawings and written utterances are artefacts in that they do not occur 'naturally' in our environment. For example, writing is not an 'inherent' part of entities existing in nature as are, for example, the stripes of a zebra (cf. Treiman and Kessler 2014: 105), and therefore it does not occur on natural surfaces such as a zebra's fur or on the leaves of a tree. What indicates that children acknowledge the artificiality of writing is that as early as at the age of two, they start using agentive verbs such as *make* or even *write* to refer to the process of writing (cf. Robins et al. 2012).

A first central difference between drawing and writing is their respective degree of iconicity. When drawing, children strive to create graphic representa-

83 A controversial question worth mentioning here is whether phonological awareness – and other types of metalinguistic awareness, for that matter – are interpreted as prerequisites or as by-products of literacy acquisition. Most often, the former is the case (cf. Birk and Häffner 2005).

84 The chapters in Verhoeven and Perfetti (2017) provide a comparative overview of how literacy is acquired across a range of different writing systems.

tions that visually resemble things they know from their environment – whether it be a house, their family, or a pet. Against this background, it is unsurprising that children transfer the expectation that graphic systems are pictorial (cf. Lavine 1977: 90) from drawing to writing and believe the shapes of writing resemble – and directly refer to – extralinguistic objects, i.e., those found in the(ir) 'real world'. However, today, most scripts and, in turn, writing systems of the world are not pictographic even though diachronically, they had been characterised by certain degrees of pictography (such as Chinese hanzi[85]). Most basic shapes in the world's scripts are thus abstract in that they do not (intentionally) resemble any objects. This formal arbitrariness makes shapes difficult for children to acquire (cf. Treiman and Kessler 2014: 171). Notably, children do implicitly differentiate between drawing and writing with respect to this feature, which becomes evident in the fact that when they are asked to write (vs. to draw), the scribbles they produce are abstract (i.e., non-pictographic) and thus differ markedly from their drawings (cf. Gombert and Fayol 1992). Furthermore, Brenneman et al. (1996) found that different motor plans are involved in drawing vs. writing:

> Children engaged in drawing made wide continuous circular movements, rotated their paper more often, filled in the outlined boundaries of represented objects and used referential appropriate colors. By contrast, when writing[,] they lift their pencil and interrupt their movements more frequently. (Taverna, Tremolada, and Sabattini 2020: 220)

Furthermore, in a study by Otake, Treiman, and Yin (2017), children used tools such as lined sheets and dark implements (e.g., black pencils) when asked to write, which differed from those they chose when they were instructed to draw.

An important difference between drawing and writing is their spatial organisation. Spatiality, as has been established above, is the governing feature of writing. Three features that are paramount in this respect are two-dimensionality, rectilinearity, and directionality.[86] While the first is shared by drawing and writing, the latter two are exclusive to writing. Drawing surfaces can be painted in a creative and random manner; by contrast, in writing, there are spatial conventions as to how material is organised on the surface. Specifically, writing does not exploit the two dimensions afforded by the surface freely but in a rectilinear fashion, i.e., in the form of lines. The reasons for this are arguably of cognitive nature: organising writing in lines makes it easier to produce and to read than if it were scattered randomly across the page. As a fundamental feature, rectilinearity

85 Cf. Xiao and Treiman (2012) for an investigation of the remaining iconicity in the contemporary Chinese writing system.

86 For an overview of children's knowledge of the spatial arrangement of writing, cf. Treiman, Mulqueeny, and Kessler (2015).

is acquired by children early on. Ganopole (1987: 426–427), for example, found that 87 % of 3-year-olds did not classify as writing strings of graphic material that was not arranged along a horizontal line. This is echoed in Lavine's (1977: 92) study in which children more often judged shapes that were arranged linearly as writing than nonlinear arrangements.

The second writing-exclusive spatial feature mentioned above is directionality. In the contemporary writing systems of the world, lines are oriented in a single direction. This is true regardless of the fact that multiple directions occur: in writing systems with horizontal lines, the direction can be left-to-right (i.e., dextrograde, such as in writing systems using Roman script) or right-to-left (i.e., sinistrograde, such as in the Arabic and Hebrew writing systems). If lines are vertical, they are always produced from top to bottom[87] and either from right to left (as in Chinese or Japanese) or left to right (as in Mongolian). Interestingly, the primacy of perception that has been mentioned above appears to manifest itself in the fact that children master the directionality of their writing system first in perception and only later in production. Tolchinsky Landsmann and Levin (1985: 329–330) found, for example, that most 3-year-olds participating in their study did not write in a consistent direction. A fascinating observation in which it appears that ontogeny recapitulates phylogeny is that some children switch the direction of their lines when they reach the ends of lines, i.e., the physical boundary of the writing surface. Thereby, they create an arrangement referred to as *boustrophedon*, which was prevalent in several writing systems in the past (cf. Coulmas 1996a: 49). Aside from having to acquire the correct direction of their writing system, which is a mesographetic aspect, children are also confronted with having to understand the rules of macrographetic spatial arrangement, i.e., higher levels of organisation. These, as has been elaborated above, escape mere linearity as they make use of two dimensions. Unsurprisingly, thus, understanding page arrangement proves more challenging for children than grasping the linearity and directionality of strings and is gradually acquired later.

The final noteworthy batch of features distinguishing writing from drawing includes its segmentality, finiteness, multiplicity, and alternation (cf. Meletis 2020a: 273–276). The segmental nature of writing is not shared by drawing, where the "composition is grasped as a whole, forms are hardly split up into single units" (Taverna, Tremolada, and Sabattini 2020: 220). The finiteness of writing – or better, of the units of writing – is also not found in drawing. While in writing, there is usually a closed set of units that can be used, and new units enter the

87 Top-to-bottom directionality appears to be universally preferred (cf. Treiman and Kessler 2014: 111) due to cognitive and physiological restraints.

system only in exceptional cases (e.g., when new Chinese characters are introduced, cf. Zhao and Baldauf 2008), in drawing, no such limitations exist. In other words, writing is a closed system, drawing an open system. The segmental and finite units of writing, now, due to the fact that they are used to represent language, usually occur in sequence, meaning that cases in which a single written unit stands alone, such as the indefinite article <a> in English, occur rather infrequently. This feature, which can be referred to as multiplicity (cf. Lavine 1977: 93), is picked up early by children, who are more likely to accept as writing strings of units rather than single units (cf. Ganopole 1987: 428; Treiman and Kessler 2014: 111–112). Notably, multiplicity as a defining feature of writing appears to be more important for younger children, as Lavine (1977: 92) found that around the ages of 4 and 5, "the unit itself takes on greater importance". An explanation for this is that at those ages, children across many writing systems have possibly understood that there can be well-formed written words that consist of only a single unit of writing. Related to multiplicity is the question of *how* and *which* units are combined with each other to form strings of writing. This leads to the feature of alternation, i.e., the fact that the same units of writing are usually not repeated in immediate sequence, but that writing is instead characterised by alternating units, i.e., "adjacent symbols within a string don't normally have the same shape" (Treiman and Kessler 2014: 112). Accordingly, in the preliterate stages of emergent literacy, children more likely consider strings with alternating units as writing than strings in which units are repeated (cf. Ganopole 1987: 428–429; Lavine 1977: 92; cf. also ⟶ Section 4.5 for graphotactics).

With the features described thus far, we focused on the differences between drawing and writing relevant in the context of emergent literacy and thereby highlighted the core graphetic properties that constitute writing as a distinct graphic representational system. What is also worth investigating, however, is which features more specific to different scripts are noticed by children. In other words, the question of whether children can identify 'their' script – i.e., the script employed in the writing system they are exposed to in their environment – and distinguish it from other scripts. According to Treiman and Kessler (2014: 168), this skill develops in children between the ages of 3 and 4. With more experience and exposure to their own system, it becomes more advanced. This was shown in the study of Lavine (1977) in which three different classes of scripts were presented to children. The first consisted of Roman script, the script used in the children's 'own' writing system, the second included units from scripts that share some graphetic features with Roman script (e.g., Hebrew script), and the third class was comprised of more visually dissimilar units such as Chinese characters or shapes from Maya script. Even the youngest children in the study (age 3) identified this latter third class as belonging to a system different from their own.

Due to certain overlapping visual features, however, the differentiation between the first and second classes proved more difficult, and only 5-year-olds significantly preferred units from their own script. This underlines that visually, scripts can be more similar or distinct from one another based on a spectrum of graphetic features that can be adhered to.

4 Graphematics

This chapter starts with a definition of graphematics and an illustration of its scope (Section 4.1). The focus is then shifted to graphematic units, beginning with the basic unit *grapheme* (Section 4.2). Next, Section 4.3 addresses larger units inherent in writing on the one hand and the question of how non-segmental linguistic units such as phonological syllables and words are represented graphematically on the other. Especially in the context of sentences and texts, punctuation marks become relevant; their functions will be discussed in Section 4.4 with a focus on a reader-based perspective. After that, Section 4.5 deals with *graphotactics*, i.e., the rules underlying the combination of graphematic units. The concept of *allography* is introduced in Section 4.6, where different types of written variation and structural allography will be presented. Finally, Section 4.7 opens up a psycholinguistic perspective to studying writing systems by examining reading processes and asking whether the graphematic units and concepts presented in this chapter play a role in processing, i.e., are psychologically real.

4.1 Definition

Graphematics (also referred to as *graphemics*[88]) is the core subfield of grapholinguistics. Its main goal is to investigate how the visual units of writing assume linguistic functions (distinguishing the meaning of words, for example) and how they relate to linguistic units such as phonemes and morphemes. In one of the few textbooks devoted to graphematics, it is defined as "the study of the writing system from the smallest units to the text" (Fuhrhop and Peters 2013: 180, our translation) with the main aim of identifying and systematically describing these units. However, as part of a comprehensive theory of writing systems, graphematics must achieve more than just a description of units. As a field of linguistics dealing with the eponymous (optional)[89] subsystem of language systems, graphematics shares important parallels with other linguistic subfields including phonology and morphology. Unsurprisingly, thus, several concepts relevant in those fields can be transferred to graphematics. To give an example: in his encyclopaedia of writing systems, Coulmas (1996a: 176) defines graphematics not only

88 Note that while these two terms are most often treated as synonyms, they are occasionally used with different meanings. For example, Fuhrhop and Peters (2013: 203) use 'graphemic' in a narrower sense in which it relates directly (and exclusively) to the unit grapheme and 'graphematic' in a broader sense to refer to graphematics both as a subsystem of language systems and writing systems in general.

89 As writing is an optional modality, not every language has a writing system, making graphematics an optional part of a language system (⟶ Section 2.1).

https://doi.org/10.1515/9783110757835-004

as the study of "writing systems based on a description of their elements" but also of "the graphotactic rules specifying the systematically permissible combinations" of said elements. The notion of graphotactic rules echoes phonotactics and morphotactics, combinatory rules for units in phonology and morphology, respectively. Furthermore, by analogy with allophony and allomorphy, Daniels (1991: 528) names allography as a concept that a graphematics must take account of; it represents a systematic approach to the structural variation exhibited by the units of writing systems.

The fact that several core concepts of graphematics have parallels in other subsystems of language makes it necessary to revisit a central question that was already asked in the context of the dependence and autonomy hypotheses (⟶ Section 2.3): is graphematics dependent on these other subsystems? The answer is no, at least not directly. *Grapheme*, *graphotactics*, *allography* – all of these concepts are analogues, not derivatives. As a subsystem of language systems equipped with writing systems, graphematics is in fact largely independent of the other subsystems of language. However, as a field of study, graphematics has borrowed concepts and methods from other linguistic subfields, which justifies the claim that it is to a large degree informed by them. The fact that these concepts *can* so neatly be transferred to graphematics actually underlines that it is as much a subsystem of language as phonology, morphology, and syntax. However, this does not mean that *every* concept that can be found in these subsystems has an analogue in graphematics. And vice versa, not everything in graphematics is expected to be found in those other systems or can be explained through a recourse to them – an example being capitalisation in alphabets with a case distinction.

At the outset of this chapter, it must be stressed once again that writing is a system in its own right, and graphematics studies those linguistic functions that are inherent and specific to writing. Only in a subsequent step, then, are the relation and the interaction between graphematics and the other subsystems of language studied, for instance how graphemes relate to phonemes, syllables, or morphemes (cf. Berg and Evertz 2018). Notably, graphematics deals not only with the segmental level, i.e., graphemes and their relations with units such as phonemes and morphemes, but also with the suprasegmental level, i.e., larger graphematic units (such as written words), their functions, and their relations and correspondences with other units of language such as syllables or words (cf. Eisenberg 1989).

In a definition of graphematics, it is paramount to distinguish it carefully from both graphetics and orthography, the two other central parts of writing systems as well as the eponymous grapholinguistic subfields that study them. As was shown in the previous chapter, graphetics deals with the material – predominantly visual – aspects of writing. It was argued that at the graphetic level, visual resources such as basic shapes are devoid of linguistic information and linguistic functions, which are instead provided by graphematics. However, graphetics *is* also concerned with functions given that the visual appearance of writing can contribute significantly to the meaning; this is evidenced by the fact that the same text printed in two vastly different typefaces can convey an altogether different meaning (⟶ Section 3.3.2.7). Crucially, however, these functions are semiotic but not linguistic in a narrow sense since they do not affect the linguistic structure of an utterance. In other words: they do not concern that level of writing that is associated with the denotative level of meaning. Thus, in a nutshell, graphematics is the domain of graphemes and larger graphematic units that *do* differentiate meaning at the denotative level and thus fulfil linguistic functions. Ultimately, graphetics and graphematics are complementary and best studied in combination, as only this allows arriving at a full picture of the functions of writing.

The differentiation between graphematics and orthography, on the other hand, is not quite as straightforward. Firstly, as will be elaborated in ⟶ Chapter 5, orthography, in its common reading as an externally codified regulation of writing, is only an optional part of writing systems. By contrast, graphematics is the obligatory core part of all writing systems without which they could not function. Secondly, but in close relation to that first point, graphematics is descriptive: it is the sum of all empirical regularities observed in the written utterances of a writing system's users and studies both the entirety of possible resources that the writing system offers and how users exploit them. Orthography, by contrast, is prescriptive and concerned with norms, i.e., with writing *correctly*. Graphematics does not have at its disposal this notion of 'correctness'. It can only evaluate whether a written utterance is possible and systematic within a given writing system, i.e., whether it conforms to its systematics. Crucially, within a given writing system, there is often more than one possibility of writing something (e.g., a string of sounds). Whether one of these possibilities is regarded as 'correct' is then determined by the orthography (if there is one).

Neef's concept of a *graphematic solution space* (Neef 2005, 2015) highlights this allocation of tasks. According to him, this space includes all possible variants of writing a given linguistic unit, e.g., a phonological string[90] such as /ˈɹaɪt/, which, in English, serves as the signifier of a variety of different lexical meanings

---

90 Neef's concept can, in our view, also be extended to non-alphabetic writing systems such as the morphographic system of Chinese. Here, the variants included in the graphematic solution space represent different possibilities of writing the same morpheme. However, as fine-grained phonological information is not present in Chinese graphemes and the correspondence between graphemes and morphemes is rather direct, the graphematic solution spaces for Chinese mor-

that are written in separate ways: <right>, <rite>, <write>, and <wright>, to name some of them (cf. Neef 2015: 716). One might observe that all of these variants are orthographically correct. This is true, but each of them is only correct for a given meaning (or given meanings) associated with the signifier /ˈɹaɪt/: <right> is either the opposite of *wrong* or *left*, whereas <write> is of course a verb central to the topic of this book. These spellings are not interchangeable, so <I will *right him a letter today.> is orthographically incorrect, as highlighted by the asterisk. Thus, for a given word that has both a pronunciation and a specific meaning, orthography selects one written variant as the 'correct' one (or sometimes more than one, such as English <doughnut> and <donut> or <disc> and <disk>), which is then codified as the correct spelling in rulebooks, dictionaries, etc.

Since all possible variants are included in the graphematic solution space, in the case of /ˈɹaɪt/, it also features variants such as *<ryte>. Such variants can be reconstructed against the background of the English writing system's systematics but do not actually represent the correct spelling of any English word. They are, thus, systematic, i.e., graphematic, but not normatively correct, i.e., orthographic.

As will be shown in the next chapter, orthography is phenomenologically primary. In other words, when people are dealing with writing (except when they are (grapho)linguists), they are dealing mainly with orthography and not with graphematics. Thus, reconstructing the graphematic regularities behind the normatively correct orthography, which is the writing system's surface representation, can pose a challenge. This is where an analysis of the use of the system becomes central, and with it, the distinction between language users' explicit and implicit knowledge. As Fuhrhop and Peters explain:

> Graphematics explores the writing system. It is not always about explicit knowledge, but about implicit knowledge that is revealed in the use of writing. Other grammatical subsystems such as phonology, morphology, and syntax also explore implicit knowledge of language users. (Fuhrhop and Peters 2013: 186, our translation)

The best example to further illustrate this are orthographic mistakes. According to orthography, they are mistakes precisely because they do not conform to the orthographic norm. Take *<definately>, a common English misspelling of <definitely>. If they are not mere typos, mistakes such as this one reveal something about the 'inner systematics' in the minds of writers, i.e., their implicit knowledge – in the sense of graphematic competence – about the writing system and

phemes are much smaller than those of words in alphabetic (or other segmental phonographic ⟶ Section 6.2.3) writing systems.

how, for example, graphemes relate to phonemes. Thus, the analysis of mistakes or, less prescriptively phrased, users' deviance from prevalent orthographic norms, is an important part of graphematic research.

Like many other aspects in grapholinguistics, graphematics has been studied primarily under a phonocentric lens. This becomes obvious in definitions such as Neef's: "The component of the writing system that captures the relation between letters and phonological units of the language system is what I call graphematics" (Neef 2015: 713). For a long time, the majority of scholars – to some degree even those who proclaimed that writing is autonomous with respect to speech – focused on this relation between speech and writing. However, given that writing is the representation of language (and not just phonology), other questions must also be investigated by graphematics (among them morphological and syntactic ones), not to mention the central issue of which features might be inherent to writing, i.e., independent of other linguistic subsystems not only in alphabets but possibly universally.

The value – and necessity – of comparing the graphematics of different writing systems was underlined by several scholars. Weingarten (2011), for instance, proposed a comparative graphematics in which comparable phenomena are identified and analysed across writing systems. To this day, however, these comparisons remain sparse,[91] and only few analyses have attempted to treat diverse writing systems within a single theoretical framework, i.e., with the same concepts, terms, and methods. This, however, is a prerequisite for arriving at graphematic concepts that are of general nature and thus escape language-specificity. In the following, we will present the basic concepts of such a comparative graphematic framework.

4.2 Grapheme

The grapheme is the basic unit of graphematics and thus arguably the basic unit of structural grapholinguistics in general. Yet, it is nowhere as established as other linguistic concepts, most prominently the phoneme or the morpheme. Ever since being coined by (most likely) Jan Baudouin de Courtenay at the beginning of the 20th century, the concept of grapheme has failed to gain traction. If it *was* addressed, this happened mostly in the context of a disagreement over how it

---

91 Some comparisons have been published in German: Meisenburg (1996) is a comparative analysis of Romance writing systems, Lindqvist (2001) an investigation of Scandinavian writing systems, and Fuhrhop (2018) a treatment of selected phenomena in alphabetic writing systems including French and Dutch, with the basis of the comparison being German.

should be defined in the first place (see below). It is for this dissent about a fitting definition that, since roughly the 1980s, the concept has started to attract considerable debate.

While a minority of scholars argue that the grapheme as a linguistic unit is unfeasible (cf. Daniels 1991, 2017),[92] others work with or at least acknowledge it. Yet, as mentioned, there is no consensus over a definition. What is also problematic is that many scholars resort to using the term without providing a clear – or sometimes any – definition. This admittedly evokes the impression that there cannot be a coherent conception of the grapheme, and this, in turn, is used by critics as an argument that it should be dropped from the study of writing entirely (cf. Share and Daniels 2016). By contrast, in our opinion, a unit that can be defined uniformly for the most diverse writing systems is a crucial requirement for their systematic analysis and comparison. Thus, the following sections are devoted to attempts of defining the grapheme and aim to condense from them the criteria that are relevant to a cross-linguistically applicable grapheme definition. At first, we will show that two main grapheme conceptions can be distinguished, which are closely associated with the two opposing views on the relationship between speech and writing (⟶ Section 2.3) and reflect the two core goals of graphematics.

4.2.1 Referential vs. analogical conception

Manfred Kohrt (1986) distinguishes two main ways of how the grapheme has been defined in the literature (cf. also Lockwood 2001): the first is the so-called *referential conception*. It reflects one of two core goals of graphematics: to study the relations between writing and other subsystems of language, most notably phonology. This goal is associated with the dependence hypothesis claiming that writing is dependent on speech. Accordingly, in the referential conception, graphemes are defined as 'depictions' of phonemes, as units of writing that merely *refer* to units of speech – hence the designation 'referential'. Take as an example the English word <sing>. Following this conception, it would consist of the three graphemes <s>, which depicts the phoneme /s/, <i>, which represents the phoneme /i/, and, crucially, the two-letter grapheme <ng>, which stands for the phoneme /ŋ/.

92 The most notable among them is Peter T. Daniels. His main argument for rejecting the grapheme is that unlike linguistic levels such as phonology and morphology, writing is "not an unconscious, built-in feature of a mind" (Daniels 2017: 88). Concerning this very question, Rogers (2005: 11) counters: "[. . .] the fact that the data of language and writing are different in nature does not preclude our using a similar theoretical framework".

Standing in stark contrast with the referential conception, the *analogical conception* has brought forth another central grapheme definition. Unsurprisingly, it is associated with the autonomy hypothesis, which holds that writing should be studied independently of speech and that interrelations between the two modalities should be investigated only in a subsequent step. Thus, it reflects the other, chronologically primary goal of graphematics: to study the structures of and in writing that are independent of other subsystems of language. 'Analogical' means that in this conception, the grapheme is defined by analogy with the phoneme, whose definition (at the time the analogical conception was introduced) hinged on minimal pairs. An example of a minimal pair in writing is <sing> vs. <sink>. These two words have different meanings due to the contrast of only one of their respective units, <g> and <k>, which are, thus, semantically distinctive. For this reason, following the analogical conception, these two units are considered graphemes. From this also follows that <ng>, which would be a single grapheme according to the referential conception, is interpreted as a combination of two graphemes, <n> and <g>, in the analogical one. It is important to stress that the analogical conception does not deny that <ng> is in a relationship with the phoneme /ŋ/, but it treats this relationship as one of correspondence rather than one of dependence. And, as mentioned above, these so-called grapheme-phoneme correspondences are of interest to the analogical conception only in a second step, i.e., after the graphemes of a writing system have been identified autonomously.

Instead of completely discarding any of these conceptions, it has been argued that both are in part accurate and must be combined in a grapheme definition (cf. Lockwood 2001). At the same time, it is obvious that they both have several drawbacks (cf. Kohrt 1986) that cannot be left unmentioned. The central problem of both conceptions is their restriction to alphabets, i.e., one type of segmental phonographic writing systems (⟶ Chapter 6.2.3.2). In the referential conception, this alphabetocentrism is based on the fact that what is studied is exclusively the written representation of phonemes. But it is also inherent in the analogical conception, whose definition of the grapheme is fundamentally dependent on the definition of the phoneme given the fact that it transfers the method of identifying phonemes through minimal pairs from structural phonology to writing.[93] Note that a restriction to alphabets (or in general to phonographic writing systems) is not a necessary requirement of these conceptions. In fact, we will illustrate below that the core principles of both conceptions can be extended and combined so

93 Ironically, it has been argued (e.g., by Schmidt 2018) that such alphabet-based conceptions are inadequate even for the description of alphabets. One argument is that since they are focused exclusively on a dependence on/an analogy with the phoneme, they are unable to capture other important aspects of alphabetic writing systems.

that they also account for non-alphabetic writing systems such as Chinese. First, however, the specific problems of the two conceptions shall be addressed, starting with the two main points of criticism against the referential conception.

Firstly, critics of the referential conception have pointed out that the interpretation of graphemes as mere depictions of phonemes implies that writing exhibits no systematics in and of itself. This, however, would render the assumption of a unit 'grapheme' as a basic unit of writing futile in the first place. And indeed, following the referential conception, grapheme inventories are merely lists of how a given language's phonemes can be represented in writing.

The treatment of variants in writing as well as the associated concept of allography (⟶ Section 4.6) also pose grave problems for the referential grapheme definition. In the referential conception, allographs are defined as different ways of writing a given phoneme. Thus, for example, <f, ff, ph, gh> would be conceived of as allographs of the phoneme /f/ in English as they represent it in words such as <fox>, <stiff>, <photo>, and <enough>, and <s, ss, sc, se, c> would be allographs of /s/ (cf. <sit>, <pass>, <scene>, <chase>, <city>). This association of allographs with phonemes rather than with graphemes has been fervently criticised (cf. Günther 1988: 76). Furthermore, as the referential conception of allography is reduced to variants of the mentioned kind, other types of variation that are found in the written modality and are unrelated to phonology (such as graphetic variation) are completely neglected. This is the most direct and palpable result of treating writing not as a system in its own right but as derivative of speech.

The analogical view has also been criticised for two important reasons, both of which have to do with the 'borrowing' of methods from phonology. In this context, Kohrt raises the question of whether it is reasonable to transfer a method that was originally established for speech – assembling minimal pairs – to the drastically different modality that is writing (cf. Kohrt 1986: 88–89; cf. ⟶ Section 2.2 for the differences between speech and writing). Indeed, writing is already segmented (with exceptions[94]), whereas speech is a continuous stream of sounds.[95] The second unresolved issue regarding the analogical conception is the interpretation of 'minimality': what is the truly minimal unit that is semanti-

94 Certain scripts are not pre-segmented, such as Arabic, where (most) basic shapes are connected with one another even in print. Also, even usually segmented scripts such as the Roman script can be connected when produced in cursive handwriting. Thus, segmentality is a prototypical but not a universal feature of writing – at least from a perceptual perspective and when finished products are analysed.

95 However, note that both in phonology and in graphematics, minimal pairs are not intended to merely identify segmental units but instead specifically those units that are semantically distinctive. This is seen as the decisive criterion of both phonemes and graphemes.

cally distinctive? For example, why is not the position of the horizontal stroke in minimal pairs such as <back> vs. <pack> (once appearing as an ascender in |b|, once as a descender in |p|) distinctive and considered a grapheme but instead the entire letters (cf. Lindqvist 2001: 10; cf. also Primus 2004, 2006 for a functional segmentation of letters)? This question is not addressed by the analogical conception. We will return to it below, but first an alternative non-segmental conception of the grapheme will be presented.

4.2.2 Suprasegmental conception

The conceptions illustrated above concern exclusively the segmental level: in case of the analogical conception the segmental level of writing itself and for the referential conception the question of how writing refers to the segmental level of speech (i.e., the level of phonemes). By contrast, more recently, German linguist Beatrice Primus (starting with Primus 2010) and her colleagues have worked on a suprasegmental model of graphematics in which the grapheme represents only one unit in a hierarchy of units – and, notably, a rather marginal one (cf. Berg, Primus, and Wagner 2016 for a recent version of the model).

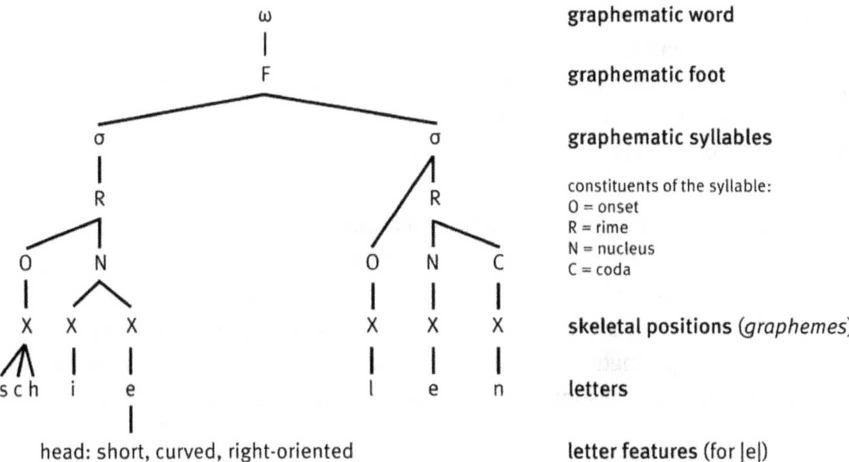

Figure 13: Suprasegmental graphematic hierarchy exemplified by the German word *schielen* 'to squint', adapted from Berg, Primus, and Wagner (2016: 351), cf. also Meletis (2019: 31).

When looking at Figure 13, we see that the smallest *unit* in this suprasegmental graphematic hierarchy is the letter. This reflects a departure for the German grapholinguistic tradition from its focus on the grapheme towards letter-based models (cf. also Neef 2005). Below the letter, another level is located, the level of *letter features*. These are parts of letters that are not considered 'units' but subsegmental building blocks. This level is based on Primus' (2004, 2006) ground-breaking assumption of form-function correlations in letters. She suggested that features of the Modern Roman script's letters (such as the [+length] of heads as in |d|, in which the head is the long stroke |l|) correlate with phonological features. Located above the letter is the level of so-called *skeletal positions*. In first iterations of the model, these were conceived of as graphemes. As the example in Figure 13 shows, they capture how certain combinations of letters such as the tri-letter <sch> are interpreted as functional units.

The reason that graphemes play a marginal role in this model (at least for German, for which it was devised) is that there is only a limited number of letter combinations that behave idiosyncratically, i.e., whose functions cannot be explained as being merely the sum of the functions of their constituent letters (cf. Schmidt 2018: 138). Indeed, in most cases, graphemes (or now skeletal positions) are associated with only one letter, implying that the level of letters is sufficient and rendering the grapheme level largely redundant – or at least subordinate (cf. Neef 2005). As for the terminological change, renaming this level 'skeletal positions' is a reaction to the fact that due to top-down factors it does not always represent graphemes: the nucleus of some strong graphematic syllables (which are the first syllables of bisyllabic graphematic trochees[96]) such as <e>, the nucleus of <le> in the German verb <lesen> /ˈleːzn̩/ 'to read', is associated with two skeletal positions. As Schmidt (2018: 129) points out, it is unreasonable to assume that one letter in a word manifests two graphemes at once. Through renaming this level 'skeletal positions', now, graphemes have effectively ceased to play any role at all.

We will not go into detail about the remaining units of the model, as the graphematic syllable and the graphematic word are addressed in dedicated subsections below. It is nevertheless paramount to note that the suprasegmental nature of the model allows for the systematic explanation of several phenomena that cannot (as easily) be explained in segmental conceptions. This is, for instance, the case for the doubling of consonant graphemes as in the word <filler>. It is modelled

96 The *graphematic foot* is a unit in the graphematic hierarchy and an analogue of the phonological foot. The canonical graphematic foot in English and German is the graphematic trochee, consisting of a strong syllable and a light syllable (cf. Evertz and Primus 2013; Evertz 2018). A noteworthy autonomous feature of English graphematics is the 'silent' <e> in words such as <like> or <rude> that serves to make them graphematic words. They are examples of graphematic trochees with a strong first syllable and a weak, reduced second syllable.

by analogy with the structure of words such as <filter>: the first <l> in both words is associated with a skeletal position in the nucleus of the first syllable (in both cases <fil>), while the second <l> in <filler> and the <t> in <filter> are associated with a skeletal position in the onset of the second syllable.

It is important to underline that the suprasegmental graphematic hierarchy presented here is inspired by the hierarchy of units in suprasegmental phonology (or prosody).[97] In the spirit of the analogical conception, this means that the graphematic units are not interpreted as being dependent on or even neatly corresponding with the phonological units of the suprasegmental phonological hierarchy but rather that they are modelled after them. Thus, the suprasegmental graphematic hierarchy is the result of a proposed modality-independent 'phonology' (⟶ Section 2.1) in which the core assumption is that distinctive meaningless structural units are combined to form larger meaning-bearing units. Notably, for both speech and writing, the so-called *strict layer hypothesis* applies (cf. Selkirk 1984 for the original formulation in phonology and Evertz 2016 for its application to graphematics). It states that a unit at any level – such as the graphematic syllable – must consist of a combination of units of the immediate lower level, in this case graphematic rimes (and optionally onsets),[98] which in turn must consist of skeletal positions, and so on.

At this point, it can be argued that a suprasegmental letter-based graphematic approach as sketched here is capable of modelling and explaining a great number of phenomena that occur in alphabetic writing systems. For these systems, thus, the model is of great value. However, in the vein of a comparative graphematics, it must be noted that the model is not easily generalisable since the question of how it could account for other, non-alphabetic systems such as Japanese or Chinese remains unclear (cf. Meletis 2017) – admittedly, however, no one has studied this question (yet). In the end, a broader conception of not only the grapheme but also of larger graphematic units is a necessity for the comparison of diverse writing systems.

97 To highlight this analogy with prosody, in his treatment of suprasegmental graphematic questions, Martin Evertz (2018) speaks of 'visual prosody'.

98 By analogy with the phonological syllable, graphematic syllables consist of onsets and rimes (cf. Figure 13). Onsets are consonant graphemes such as the <c> in <cat>. They are optional insofar as <at>, with a zero onset, is also a well-formed graphematic syllable. Rimes, on the other hand, are the core of graphematic syllables and must imperatively contain a nucleus. In most cases, the syllable nucleus is a vowel grapheme, cf. the <a> in <cat>. Optionally, rimes also contain a coda, i.e., a (consonant) grapheme that follows the nucleus, cf. the <t> in <cat>.

4.2.3 Criteria for a cross-linguistic grapheme definition

As has become evident in previous sections, all well-known conceptions of the grapheme to date are alphabetocentric. This is partially understandable given that they stem from works published in the context of German grapholinguistics and are centred on German and/or English. And yet, it is problematic that their applicability to other types of writing systems has not been tested and that they have not been extended accordingly. Such a language-specificity is uncommon for definitions of basic linguistic units. Phonemes and morphemes, for example, are defined in ways that apply to all languages, and it is likely that the same can be achieved for the grapheme.[99] The central question here is certainly which criteria are reasonable for a cross-linguistic grapheme definition that can accommodate all types of writing systems. In this section, we will discuss three such possible criteria (for more details, cf. Meletis 2019: 35–38). These, notably, were already inherent in the above-mentioned alphabetocentric conceptions but it was rarely – if ever – asked what they mean for writing systems other than alphabets.

The first criterion of a broad grapheme definition was already constitutive of the analogical conception: semantic distinctiveness. Graphemes are the smallest functional units of writing, and their function is not only to combine to build larger units of writing such as words, sentences, and texts, but also to distinguish between them. Not every segmental visual unit of writing, i.e., every basic shape (⟶ Section 3.2.1), automatically assumes such a function, and it is through the above-mentioned minimal pairs that their graphematic status can be tested. As elaborated above, the analogical conception faces limitations in that it assumes the grapheme to be parallel to the phoneme, i.e., the smallest distinctive – and, crucially, meaningless – unit of language. This definition is not applicable to morphographic writing systems such as Chinese, where the grapheme is parallel not to phonemes but to morphemes. Consequently, the grapheme in Chinese bears meaning and cannot always be broken down into smaller phonological or semantic parts (but see below for subsegmental graphematic components in Chinese).

This highlights a crucial distinction between phonographic and morphographic writing systems (⟶ Section 6.2.1): phonographic systems exhibit double articulation, morphographic systems do not (or to a lesser degree). Double articulation (also referred to as duality of patterning) is a core design feature of lan-

99 There is, of course, the possibility that given the diversity of writing systems, different types of graphemes need to be distinguished on the basis of their functions, e.g., phonographic graphemes that relate to phonemes and morphographic graphemes that relate to morphemes. But, as will be shown, the criteria described in this section render the assumption of multiple differing grapheme conceptions unnecessary.

guage (cf. Hockett 1960) and designates the fact that meaning-bearing units (such as morphemes) can be broken down into smaller, meaningless but semantically distinctive units, namely phonemes. To give an analogous graphematic example: written words such as <tree> can be broken down into the graphemes <t>, <r>, and two instances of <e>. This does not work for Chinese. It is, for example, impossible to segment the grapheme <木> *mù* 'tree' into smaller meaningless graphematic units (but cf. below for complex Chinese graphemes consisting of multiple components). In Chinese, thus, single graphemes can already be complete graphematic words and can thus themselves bear meaning. Note that this does not clash with semantic distinctiveness: trivially, two distinct graphemes (and their related morphemes) such as <木> *mù* 'tree' and <猫> *māo* 'cat' are, when contrasted, automatically also semantically distinctive precisely on the grounds that they have different meanings.

The second criterion for a universal grapheme concept is that graphemes are required to have linguistic value by corresponding with units of other linguistic subsystems, namely phonemes, syllables, or morphemes. This criterion responds to a problem of the analogical conception: if finding minimal pairs suffices to identify graphemes, then in German, <c> and <q> would be graphemes, cf. the minimal pairs <denken> 'to think' vs. <decken> 'to cover' (cf. Rezec 2013: 231) and <Qual> 'torment' vs. <Dual> 'dual'.[100] For |c|, many more minimal pairs can be found, whereas for |q|, in native words of German (i.e., excluding loanwords), there are none. In any case, even a single minimal pair should suffice to grant grapheme status, but minimal pairs fail to capture an important aspect that is considered in newer works (e.g., Berg 2019): |c| and |q| exhibit a conspicuous distribution in the German writing system as they do not occur throughout the system and thus do not behave like other graphemes. Most striking, of course, is that in native German words, |c| never occurs without |h| or |k|, and |q| never occurs without |u|.

Interestingly, the combinations <ch> and <qu> are considered graphemes of German even in the analogical conception.[101] The implicit reason for this is that

---

100 Note that it is unclear whether this example counts as a minimal pair as <Dual> is a Latin loanword, and on top of that, a linguistic technical term, the designation of a number in some of the grammars of the world's languages (such as Slovenian). <Qual>, on the other hand, is a native and common German word. A different example that is sometimes cited as a minimal pair for |q| is <Quelle> vs. <Duelle> (cf. Günther 1988: 83), but note that this is, strictly seen, also not a minimal pair as these words have different categorial structures (⟶ Section 4.6): <Quelle> 'source' is a singular and <Duelle> 'duels' a plural noun, which means they are not completely comparable paradigmatic alternatives.

101 <ck> is not regarded a grapheme but a special type of syllabically conditioned reduplication in the vein of the consonant doubling in <filler> (see above) – only that in this case, <k> is seldom reduplicated and most often accompanied by |c| instead.

these sequences, sometimes referred to as *digraphs*, correspond with linguistic units, whereas |c| and |q| alone do not: <ch> corresponds with the phoneme /x/ and <qu> with the phoneme sequence /kv/. As <qu> corresponds with /kv/ in German (or with /kw/ in English as in <query> /ˈkwɛ.ɹi/), one could assume that |q| corresponds with /k/. However, it is relevant to note, on the one hand, that it is not straightforwardly clear that it does so, as that would mean that <u> in <qu> stands for /v/, which it never does in any other context (cf. also Evertz 2018: 40). On the other hand, |q| alone never corresponds with /k/. Therefore, it is assumed that <qu> corresponds with /kv/ holistically and the assumption that |q| alone corresponds with no linguistic unit in German and English still stands. It is thus not a grapheme in these writing systems.

At this point, it is vital to stress that the perspective or 'direction' underlying this graphematic analysis is *writing* ⟶ *language*. The question is how units of writing relate to units of other subsystems of language and not vice versa. In other words, that the linguistic value criterion demands graphemes to correspond with linguistic units does not mean that graphemes are dependent on them. It also does not insinuate that *every* linguistic unit – for example every phoneme in a language's phoneme inventory – must have a corresponding grapheme or graphematic representation. And, as highlighted in Meletis (2019: 36), in order "to identify a unit as a grapheme, it is not necessary for it to refer to only one linguistic unit, and its linguistic reference does not need to be stable. It is only imperative that it has a linguistic value in all contexts in which it is used". Ultimately, what is of interest in assembling the grapheme inventory of a writing system is which of its script's visual units, i.e., its basic shapes, are graphemes, and which are not (such as |c| and |q| in German). This leaves open the crucial question of minimality.

In combination with the first two, the criterion of minimality can be applied straightforwardly to the definition of the grapheme: only the smallest units of writing for which both criteria of semantic distinctiveness and linguistic value apply are graphemes. Let us explain this with an example from above, the word <sing>: following the conception presented here, it consists of four graphemes, since for <s>, <i>, <n> and <g>, minimal pairs can be found in English, and all of them have an individual linguistic value by corresponding with phoneme(s). Notably, even though minimal pairs can also be found for the combination <ng>, which corresponds with a phoneme as well (in English /ŋ/), it is not a grapheme since both of its constituents – <n> and <g> – are already graphemes on their own. And here, it is not important that the sum of their functions does – in this example – not equal the function of the combination, as /n/ plus /g/ does not equal /ŋ/. Notably, even though sequences such as <ng> are not graphemes, they are relevant and have a graphematic function. In a nutshell, the criterion of minimality ensures economic grapheme inventories.

Inversely, there do exist graphemes that consist of more than one basic shape. Consider, again, German <ch>: as established above, |c| is not a grapheme since (in native words) it does not have a linguistic value of its own. It often is followed by <h>, which is an independent grapheme (as there are minimal pairs such as <hart> 'hard' vs. <zart> 'gentle') and has linguistic value, in the prototypical case by corresponding with the phoneme /h/. To explain how <ch> can be a grapheme when <h> is already one,[102] the conception proposed here needs to be refined: graphemes are conceived as either single basic shapes (such as <h>) for which the criteria of semantic distinctiveness and linguistic value apply, *or* as combinations of basic shapes (such as <ch>) for which both criteria apply although for at least one of their constituents (here |c|), one or both criteria fail to apply. Such combinations are referred to as *complex graphemes*.

Given the three criteria, it has become clear why the subsegmental head |l| in <back> vs. <pack> (see above) is not a grapheme although it is both minimal and semantically distinctive: it does not correspond with a linguistic unit.

Up until this point, we have relied on examples from alphabets to illustrate the criteria of a broad grapheme definition when, in fact, the universality of prospective criteria was the driving force behind uncovering them in the first place. Indeed, they do apply also to non-alphabetic phonographic writing systems such as abjads, abugidas, and syllabaries, as well as morphographic writing systems. This will be illustrated with four examples taken from Arabic, Devanāgarī, Japanese, and Korean. Note that at this point, only selected features of these writing systems will be addressed to show the universal applicability of our approach (for more detailed information on these types of systems ⟶ Chapter 6).

1) The identification of graphemes in other segmental phonographic writing systems – i.e., in which graphemes prototypically correspond with phonemes – is rather straightforward. In Arabic, for example, only consonant and long vowel phonemes are commonly represented graphematically. These graphemes are minimal, semantically distinctive, and correspond with phonemes. While long vowels are written, writing short vowels is optional. In contexts in which they are written, according to the definition above, they also count as graphemes as they fulfil all the criteria. It is noteworthy, however, that they are manifested graphetically by smaller shapes that visually orbit the larger consonant graphemes. In other words, while consonant graphemes occupy their own segmental spaces, short vowel graphemes are enclitic and cannot stand alone. Instead, they appear

102 An analogous question from phonology is whether the affricate /t͡ʃ/ should be considered a phoneme of English given that both /t/ and /ʃ/ are already phonemes, which is an issue also pertinent to diphthongs.

above or below consonant graphemes and share with them a single segmental space. Accordingly, consonant graphemes can be considered free graphemes while graphemes for short vowels are bound graphemes (cf. also Rogers 2005: 11–12). For example, Arabic <رَ> /ra/ is a combination of the free consonant grapheme <ر> /r/ and the optional and bound short vowel grapheme < َ > /a/.

2) The situation is quite similar in systems such as Thai, Tamil, or Devanāgarī (so-called abugidas ⟶ Section 6.2.3.4). The significant difference is that here, the graphematic representation of all vowels (save for the inherent vowel) is commonly obligatory. These systems raise a number of specific questions for the above-mentioned grapheme conception, one of which we want to mention (cf. Meletis 2019 for others): ligatures.[103] In Devanāgarī, for example, there exist written consonant clusters in which basic shapes are contracted and together form a new shape: <घ> /g^{ɦ}/ and <र> /ɾ/, for instance, are contracted to <घ्र> /g^{ɦ}ɾ/. Unlike in Chinese, where segmental graphemes that are minimised in size and used as subsegmental components cease to be individual graphemes (see below), this Devanāgarī ligature retains the original functions of its constituent graphemes. Thus, it corresponds with a phoneme sequence consisting of /g^{ɦ}/ and /ɾ/. This makes ligatures, similarly to combinations like <ng> in German, sequences of two graphemes instead of complex graphemes (like <ch> in German). However, the difference between ligatures and sequences is that the graphemes making up ligatures are subsegmental (and thereby lose their graphetic independence) while in sequences such as <ng> they retain their segmental status.

3) Since it is a fundamentally mixed writing system, Japanese is a special though uncontroversial case: the phonographic units from the kana syllabaries are graphemes given that they are semantically distinctive, correspond with linguistic units (in this case syllables – or moras ⟶ Section 6.2.4), and are minimal, i.e., cannot be broken down into smaller units. The morphographic part of the system, the kanji, function almost entirely the same way the hanzi do, the Chinese graphemes from which they historically derive. As for Chinese characters, in this broad grapheme conception, they can straightforwardly be conceptualised as graphemes, with the peculiarity that they are not overtly dually patterned (see above). Consequently, semantic distinctiveness is defined more broadly so that not only meaning-distinguishing phonemes but also meaning-bearing morphemes are interpreted as semantically distinctive. Given that many Chinese graphemes have a complex internal structure and in light of the fact that in other systems – such

103 Here, we speak of systematic and obligatory ligatures rather than (optional) typographic ligatures such as <fi> in Roman script.

as Arabic – subsegmental shapes (i.e., shapes that do not occupy an entire segmental space) can function as graphemes, we must turn to the important question of whether subsegmental components of Chinese graphemes are themselves graphemes.

Many Chinese graphemes have a complex subsegmental structure that warrants more attention. Take the two units <請> *qǐng*[104] *‘please, to ask’ and* <情> *qíng* ‘emotion’ (examples taken from Meletis 2019: 38). When contrasted with each other, it becomes obvious that they share a subsegmental element: a minimised form of the grapheme <青> *qīng* ‘green/blue’. In its isolated form, this character is an independent grapheme and occupies an entire segmental space (⟶ Section 3.2.2). However, it can also be used as a building block for other units; in this function, it serves as a so-called *phonological component* or *phonetic.* Notice how the pronunciation of all three graphemes differs only in tone, meaning their segmental phonological representation is the same. It is this pronunciation that is contributed by the minimised form of <青>, which appears on the right side of the respective graphemes. The meaning of this original grapheme is completely discarded as the meanings of the resulting complex graphemes have nothing to do with ‘green/blue’.

While phonological components typically occur on the right side (cf. Myers 2019: Chapter 2), so-called *semantic components* or *radicals* appear on the left side. They contribute to the meaning of a grapheme. In <請> *qǐng* ‘please, to ask’, the semantic component is a minimised form of the grapheme <言> *yán* ‘speech’. As evident from this example, the semantic contribution of such a component can be rather vague: the original meaning of ‘speech’ is only partially included in the meanings of the adverb ‘please’ or the verb ‘to ask’. A varying degree of the meaning of ‘speech’ will be found in most graphemes in which it is used as a minimised semantic component. The important question, now, is whether these subsegmental components are graphemes.

Both phonological and semantic components can form minimal pairs, so they meet the criterion of semantic distinctiveness. They are also minimal but, crucially, do not correspond with linguistic units. If used as subsegmental components, they can, as explained above, signal an approximate pronunciation, or give clues about the meaning of the resulting complex grapheme, but they effectively lose their original function of corresponding with particular morphemes,

104 The Mandarin variety of Chinese, from which the examples are taken, exhibits lexical tone, i.e., the pitch contour of syllables is lexically distinctive. Aside from the neutral tone, four tones exist, which are indicated with diacritics above the Pinyin Romanisation of syllables: the first tone (1) is a high-level tone (marked by a macron as in ā), the second (2) a rising tone (marked by an acute accent as in á), the third (3) a dipping tone (marked by a háček as in ǎ), and the fourth (4) a falling tone (marked by a grave accent as in à).

a function that they had in their full forms, cf. <青> *qīng* 'green/blue' and <言> *yán* 'speech'. Also, graphetically, what is striking is that they lose their independence and become spatially dependent on one another. As minimised forms, they cannot occur independently and need to be combined with other components. Only in combination are new graphemes formed.

Thus, we argue that complex Chinese characters are complex graphemes although, unlike in German <ch> (see above), where only one component cannot occur alone (in this case |c|), in Chinese complex graphemes, both segments cannot appear alone. Also, unlike in <ch>, Chinese components are subsegmental rather than segmental. Importantly, the fact that these subsegmental components are not considered graphemes does not mean that they have no graphematic function. Like there are graphematic units larger than the grapheme (see below), there are also graphematic 'units' or elements smaller than the grapheme.

4) An interesting case that remains to be discussed is Korean, which has a very transparent writing system as graphemes correspond straightforwardly with phonemes: <ㄱ>, for example, corresponds with /k/. While these units can uncontroversially be defined as graphemes since they fulfil all criteria presented above, it is their spatial arrangement that warrants further attention. Korean graphemes are not segmental but subsegmental as they are combined with other graphemes to form combinations of graphemes, combinations which then occupy a segmental space and correspond with phonological syllables (⟶ Section 6.2.3.2). An example is the graphetically segmental syllable block <각> which is made up of three graphemes and corresponds with the syllable /kak/. Korean graphemes, thus, are subsegmental and syllabically arranged (cf. Gnanadesikan 2017: 29). Note that this is a structural assessment; during reading and writing, syllable blocks might be processed holistically, which means it may be reasonable to interpret them as the basic units from a processing perspective.

Up until now, we have only mentioned default graphemes, i.e., those (sub)segmental units that represent the most important linguistic information by corresponding with core units of language such as phonemes and morphemes. What about other units, however, such as digits or special characters or, considering modern digital communication, emojis (for punctuation marks ⟶ Section 4.4)? Their graphematic status depends on the context and must be evaluated individually. Take digits such as <5> or special characters such as <§>. Arguably, they often fulfil all above-mentioned grapheme criteria, even if in different ways than default graphemes. For example, whereas <b> in alphabetic writing systems corresponds with a phoneme, <5> corresponds with a morpheme (or word), 'five'. It is, thus, used morpho- or logographically, which also highlights that most if not all writing systems to some degree incorporate features characteristic of other types of writing systems. In any case, even when digits and special characters are conceived of as graphemes, they are marginal graphemes in an alphabetic writing system given that they fulfil special functions. Furthermore, they can always be substituted by default graphemes, i.e., by spelling out <five> instead of using <5> or <paragraph> instead of <§>. Vice versa, this substitutability is not given. As for emojis such as ☺, while they can also be used graphematically in the same way as digits, specifically with a morphographic function to substitute morphemes/words (cf. Dürscheid and Meletis 2019), they are, nowadays, most often used semasiographically (⟶ Section 2.1), i.e., as visual resources that have a communicative function but not a linguistic meaning in a narrow sense.

4.3 Larger graphematic units

In the following, graphematic units larger than the grapheme will be discussed as the suprasegmental graphematic hierarchy that was introduced above will be revisited. Note that in this section, too, both major tasks of graphematics will be addressed: identifying independent graphematic units, i.e., units based in writing itself, but also investigating the interaction between graphematics and other subsystems of language. In other words, we will describe genuinely graphematic units as well as show how they relate to other linguistic units (such as phonological syllables). This way, both analytical directions *writing* ⟶ *language* (or decoding) and *language* ⟶ *writing* (or encoding), i.e., the question of how linguistic units are represented in writing, will be considered (cf. Fuhrhop and Peters 2013: 180; Neef 2005).

4.3.1 Syllables

First attempts at defining a graphematic syllable in alphabets date back to works of the late 1980s (such as Eisenberg 1989; Naumann 1989; Butt and Eisenberg 1990). They centred on the observation that plosive phonemes occurring at phonological syllable boundaries as in *dog* /dɒg/ or *but* /bʌt/ are 'depicted' by letters that have ascenders as in |d| or descenders as in |g|. By contrast, the cores or nuclei of syllables – in most cases vowels – correspond with letters that lack such ascenders or descenders, examples being |o| or |u|. Years later, the study of a syllabic structure in writing regained currency when Primus formulated a criterion for syllables that is modality-indifferent, i.e., holds for all modalities (spoken, signed, and written): syllables in all three modalities are characterised by the alternation of salient and non-salient units (cf. Primus 2003). While this conception *per se* might be indifferent to modality, the question of what is considered salient in each modality is not. In speech, more sonorous units are salient (e.g., vowels are more salient than nasals, which are more salient than fricatives), while in the signed modality as the primary modality of sign languages, movements are more salient than locations, and in writing, salience depends on the visual features of a given script. For the Roman script that Primus based her definition on, following her approach, it is the above-mentioned length of shapes (or their heads) that is salient.

This observation was taken up and operationalised by Nanna Fuhrhop and Franziska Buchmann, who proposed a graphematic syllable in German (cf. Fuhrhop and Buchmann 2009). In the vein of previous attempts at segmenting the basic shapes of Roman script – most importantly Brekle (1995) – they posit that lowercase basic shapes consist of a head (for Brekle, this was the so-called hasta ⟶ Section 3.2.3), which in most cases is a long vertical stroke and thus extends into the high space of the line, and a coda, an element that is attached to the head. Take as an example |d|: the vertical stroke |l| is the head, the half-circle |c| the coda. Notably, Fuhrhop and Buchmann's analysis is based purely on features inherent to writing. Unlike in the above-mentioned older conceptions, it is, at this point, of no relevance that those basic shapes exhibiting long heads correspond with, for example, plosive phonemes (but cf. Primus 2004 for a different view). Thus, this proposal of a graphematic syllable is clearly part of the autonomous graphematic paradigm. The following criteria are central for its definition:

a. Every letter has a head.
b. Every grapheme has a coda.
c. The head is the vertical segment which spans the central space by the shortest distance and may exceed it.
d. The coda is located in only one space (either central, upper, or lower space).

(adapted from Fuhrhop, Buchmann, and Berg 2011: 279)

Accordingly, every letter must have a head but not necessarily a coda. Instead, it is every grapheme that must have a coda, which marks a categorical difference between letters and graphemes and provides a heuristic to distinguish between them.[105] It is important to note that heads being 'long', i.e., exhibiting a feature called length, is not interpreted absolutely. Length, accordingly, is not conceived of as a binary but rather as a scalar feature that gives rise to a length continuum (cf. Fuhrhop and Buchmann 2009: 138). Also, length is not determined purely vis-

105 Following this conception, |c| is not a grapheme since it only consists of a head but lacks a coda. By contrast, basic shapes such as |l| and |o| are being analysed as consisting of both a head and a coda although visually, like |c|, they also consist of only one element. With that, they are regarded as graphemes. It is these aspects of the conception that were partially criticised.

ually, i.e., graphetically, as additional criteria are taken into account. These criteria have at times been criticised as opaque and as assumed in a top-down manner driven by the desired outcome of the analysis (cf. Rezec 2010). With length being a scalar feature, now, a so-called *length hierarchy* can be assumed in which the letters (or more generally, basic shapes) are ordered according to the length of their heads (cf. Figure 14).

This hierarchy is important for the concept of the graphematic syllable as it is the basis of the *length sequencing principle*,[106] a rule used to evaluate a given syllable's well-formedness: "The graphematic syllable core is occupied by the most compact grapheme. The length of the segments increases monotonously toward both syllable edges" (Fuhrhop, Buchmann, and Berg 2011: 283). An example of a well-formed graphematic syllable in English is <flat>. According to the length hierarchy, |f| is longest (as it has a long head), |l| is not as long (as it has a short straight head and a non-bent coda), and |a|, being the syllable nucleus, is shortest (since it exhibits a short bent head). Following this nucleus, the length of heads increases again, and |t|, with its long head, serves as a prototypical graphematic syllable boundary. Notably, the length sequencing principle reflects the above-mentioned alternation that is central to Primus' (2003) syllable definition, namely that salient visual units alternate with less salient visual units.

Long head	Slant head	Short straight head				Short bent head
		Connected at the top	Not connected at the top			
		Bent coda	Non-bent coda		Bent coda	
b, p, d, g, k h, t, ß, j, f	v, w, x, z, s	m, n	r, l	i	u	a, e, o

← **Increasing Length**

Figure 14: Length hierarchy, from Fuhrhop, Buchmann, and Berg (2011: 282).

This marking of syllable boundaries is assumed to be functionally relevant for reading processes as it helps the recognition of syllabic structures by making them stand out visually (cf. Fuhrhop and Peters 2013: 219–220; Eisenberg 2020: 323–324). Crucially, this is important insofar as syllables are believed to be salient units for processing not only in speech but also in writing (cf. Daniels 1992, 2018: 136–139

106 This principle is obviously inspired by the sonority hierarchy in phonology.

and ⟶ Section 6.4). This is likely also the motivation behind historical processes that have led to an optimisation of the graphematic syllable structure. In this context, Fuhrhop and Schmidt trace several diachronic changes in German: the gradual replacement of non-long |c| with long |k|, for example, because the latter is a more optimal marker for syllable boundaries. Likewise, they describe the ousting of long |y| from the position of syllable nucleus and its 'relegation' to the syllable edge position (at least in native German words; it remains in nucleus position in loanwords such as <Rhythmus> 'rhythm') (cf. Fuhrhop and Schmidt 2014). In a functional view of writing, these changes can be interpreted as results of human processing pressure on the structure of writing.

Notably, the length sequencing principle is not an absolute rule, which means it can be violated (cf. Fuhrhop and Buchmann 2016: 361–368). Basic shapes that violate it in English are, for instance, |s|, but also the aforementioned |y|. The former violates the well-formedness of graphematic syllables in words such as <speak> or <stake> in which |s|, as a shape with a slant head, precedes |p| and |t|, respectively, shapes with long heads that should appear only in the outermost positions of the syllable. Thus, in these syllables, length is not at its maximum at the syllable boundary, and |s| violates otherwise perfectly well-formed graphematic syllables such as <peak>. If, as in this example, it violates the length sequencing principle either before or after a well-formed graphematic syllable (both of which is the case in <speaks>), it is referred to as an *extra-syllabic grapheme*. |y| also behaves peculiarly in English, where it marks – as in German – loanwords such as <rhythm> but can also function as a syllable nucleus as in <shy> or to mark word boundaries as in <lady> (where it alternates with |ie|, cf. <ladies>).

An interesting question concerns the graphematic syllable's independence of phonological syllables. At first glance, there are many parallels between the two. And indeed, in the majority of cases, they converge. There are, however, also notable differences (cf. Fuhrhop and Peters 2013: 228). One of them concerns the marking of vowels. In graphematic syllables, syllable nuclei are always vowels, whereas phonologically, sonorants can also serve as syllable nuclei: thus, <gen>, the second syllable of German <legen> 'to put' has the vowel grapheme <e> as a syllable nucleus while one of the standard phonological representations of the word is /le.gn̩/, in which the syllable nucleus of the second syllable is the nasal /n/. Also, phonological syllables in German usually have onsets as a consonant precedes the vocalic syllable nucleus. In cases in which a syllable seemingly starts with a vowel, a glottal stop appears syllable-initially. By contrast, graphematic syllables can have a zero onset, which is, however, also due to the fact the glottal stop is not represented graphematically. Vowel-initial graphematic syllables such as the first syllables in <alle> 'all' or <Ende> 'end' are thus common. The bottom line is that the visual salience of graphematic syllable structures afforded by the feature [+length] is of importance regardless of whether it mostly reflects phonological syllable structures or is an autonomous feature of writing.

As is the case with many phenomena described in this chapter, given that most of the graphematic literature has focused on alphabets – and specifically German –, the remarks thus far have been alphabetocentric. And in this case, due to the script-specific nature of graphetic features, they were even restricted to the Roman script. Interestingly, though, the feature [+length] can also be found in other alphabetically used scripts such as Greek, Armenian, and Georgian (cf. Meletis 2020a: 123–126). However, for them, no fine-grained graphetic/graphematic analyses have been carried out yet. Furthermore, as mentioned above, in the typologically alphabetic Korean writing system, the graphemes are graphetically subsegmental and arranged syllabically, i.e., in syllable blocks that occupy segmental spaces, resulting in a situation where a graphematic syllable is visually salient despite being – unlike the types of graphematic syllable discussed above – graphetically segmental.

To shift the focus from alphabets to other types of writing systems, an important comment must be made about syllables in non-segmental (i.e., syllabographic and/or morphographic) writing systems. Here, the above-mentioned concept of graphematic syllable ceases to have any relevance. As was shown above, the graphematic syllable is meant to make visible *autonomous* structures of writing that are larger than graphemes and smaller than words, the latter of which are (Eurocentrically) defined as visual units between two blank spaces (see next section). When considering the units of the Japanese kana inventories or the Chinese hanzi, both of which were defined as segmental graphemes above, it becomes obvious that the phonological syllable plays a central role for them: the graphemes of the Japanese kana scripts correspond with phonological syllables and Chinese graphemes correspond with morphemes, which almost all have monosyllabic phonological representations, meaning Chinese graphemes indirectly also relate to phonological syllables. Consequently, we are dealing with situations in which segmental written units, i.e., graphemes, correspond with non-segmental linguistic units. Japanese kana graphemes such as <の> *no* and Chinese graphemes such as <猫> *māo* 'cat' are, thus, directly or indirectly, syllabographic graphemes. Here, crucially, *syllabographic* indicates their linguistic correspondence. However, they are not graphematic syllables in the sense characterised in this section since they do not make visible larger structures in writing. Unlike in Korean (see above), the graphemes in Japanese and Chinese cannot be broken down into units that correspond with phonemes but are rather interpreted holistically. This leads to the conclusion that in syllabographic or morpho(syllabo)graphic writing systems such as Japanese and Chinese, there are no suprasegmental graphematic syllables. These can only exist in more fine-grained, i.e., segmental writing systems (cf. Meletis 2020a: 126–130).

This observation also raises the question of the phonological syllable's relevance for writing. In this context, Daniels (1992) famously suggested that the syllable plays a special role as the linguistic unit most salient for writing. He observed that both "[a]ll new writing systems [. . .] invented by nonliterates who know that writing exists" (Daniels 2017: 84) and the independently created writing systems Sumerian, Mayan, and Chinese are or were syllabographic – in the case of these latter three systems even morphosyllabographic. This indicates a syllabic origin of writing that has led to the stronger claim of a general primacy of the syllable in writing (⟶ Section 6.4). Moreover, segmental phonographic writing systems such as alphabets, after having reached the typological stage of segmentality, appear to undergo certain developments resulting in suprasegmental written structures that correspond with syllables becoming more salient. This leads to the above-characterised graphematic syllable, which also underlines the importance of the syllable for writing. Additionally, there is experimental psycholinguistic evidence from processing backing up the assumption of a primacy of the syllable (cf. Daniels 2017: 76; Meletis 2020a: 305–308).

4.3.2 Words

The next larger unit beyond the syllable is the graphematic word. As in the previous section, we will first look at the proposal of an autonomous graphematic word and then move on to the questions of how such a unit could be conceptualised in non-alphabetic systems and finally how the 'word', a somewhat elusive linguistic unit, can be represented in writing.

The concept of a graphematic word presented here was proposed by Fuhrhop as follows: "The graphematic word stands between two spaces and does not contain any spaces internally" (Fuhrhop 2008: 193, our translation). As established in ⟶ Section 3.2.2, there exist several different spaces at various levels of writing. Some of them are occupied by visual material while others are empty, i.e., blank. In alphabets, the blank space relevant for the graphematic word is the one that is perceptibly larger than the blank space positioned between basic shapes. For instance, in <writing system>, the space between <w> and <r> in <wr> is smaller than the space between <g> and <s> in <g s>. Like the criterion of length that is central to the graphematic syllable in some scripts such as Roman, this blank space is defined visually, i.e., graphetically. It is not universal as it does not occur in all writing systems of the world. Unsurprisingly, thus, as the graphematic word (like all larger graphematic units treated here) was first proposed for German, it is not readily applicable to other writing systems, not even to all other alphabetic writing systems that exhibit the relevant type of blank space Fuhrhop's definition is based on. Considering compounds in English, for example, it is questionable whether graphematic words can have spaces internally. Is <apple pie> one graphematic word or two?

Fuhrhop (2008: 194) does add three more criteria to her definition of the graphematic word in German that help to distinguish prototypical graphematic words from marginal ones: prototypical graphematic words (1) consist of one or more graphematic syllables (as defined in the section above), are (2) unbroken sequences of default graphemes, and (3) contain a maximum of one uppercase grapheme word-initially. An example of a well-formed graphematic word of English is <cat>. At this point it is also noteworthy that there exist graphematic words consisting of only one grapheme. This sole grapheme simultaneously serves as the syllable nucleus of a graphematic syllable, cf. the English indefinite article <a> in <a house>, or the Spanish conjunction <y> 'and'. Interestingly, instances of such one-grapheme words overwhelmingly represent function words rather than content words.

The second criterion mentioned by Fuhrhop refers to cases in which sequences of graphemes can be 'broken up' by punctuation, specifically the word marks apostrophe <'>, hyphen <->, and abbreviation period <.> (cf. Buchmann 2015). Accordingly, <don't>, <mother-in-law>, and <approx.> are all well-formed but marked graphematic words. Of these, only the period after abbreviations does not stand between two graphemes but at the end of graphematic words, which means it is followed by a blank space.[107] This, then, raises the question of whether sentence marks that cliticise onto the preceding default grapheme such as the colon <:> count as parts of graphematic words. Fuhrhop (2008: 217) negates this, claiming that, for instance, <writing.>, <writing:>, and <writing,> are merely positional variants as the question of which sentence mark occurs in these cases is dependent on the position of the word in a sentence. Furthermore, the respective mark is not part of the word itself. Consequently, since combinations of graphematic words and sentence marks such as <writing.> are predictable, assuming them as distinct units would violate the general theoretical principle of economy (cf. Evertz 2016: 391).

Finally, the third criterion addresses capitalisation and filters out marginal cases including acronyms like <EU> or <NATO>. Like the entire definition itself (as illustrated by the example of English <apple pie>), this criterion cannot even

107 The abbreviation period has the same form as the full stop, the syntactic punctuation mark used at the end of graphematic sentences, which has a different function. Making a formal distinction between these two punctuation marks poses a challenge and is also a problem for the definition of the graphematic sentence (cf. Schmidt 2016).

be extended to all other alphabets that use Roman script: in Dutch, for example, in words starting with the digraph <ij>, both constituents are capitalised, as in <IJzer> 'iron'.

Concerning the correspondence of graphematic units with other linguistic units, it was established above that graphemes relate to diverse linguistic units depending on the type of writing system in question while graphematic syllables in alphabetic and several other segmental phonographic writing systems correspond largely with phonological syllables. What about the graphematic word as characterised above? Fuhrhop and Peters (2013: 251) observe that it does not relate to the phonological word, which is frequently 'shorter' in length. For instance, while German <Fußballweltmeisterschaftsqualifikationsspiel> 'soccer world cup qualifying match' is one (admittedly untypically long) graphematic word (made possible by excessive compounding), the corresponding unit of speech consists of at least three phonological words: /ˈfuːsˌbal/, /ˈvɛltˌmaɪ̯stɐʃaft/, and /kvalifikaˈt͡si̯oːnsʃpiːl/. By contrast, the graphematic word does relate more directly to units at the morphological and syntactic levels (cf. Evertz 2016: 394). Indeed, morphosyntactically, <Fußballweltmeisterschaftsqualifikationsspiel> is one word. This correspondence with the morphological level underlines not only that writing is often independent of speech but also serves as a fitting transition to the question of how the graphematic word could be conceived of in non-alphabetic writing systems.

The largest issue in this respect is raised by writing systems that lack blank spaces between what we identify as 'words'. Three major examples are Chinese, Japanese, and Thai. Chinese is still often referred to as a 'logographic' writing system (from Greek *lógos* 'word'), which insinuates that its graphemes (which actually correspond with morphemes, making Chinese morphographic ⟶ Section 6.3) always represent full-fledged independent words. Actually, however, the majority of words in Chinese is bi- or polysyllabic (cf. Yen et al. 2012: 1009). Given that Chinese morphemes are monosyllabic, now, most Chinese written words actually consist of several morphographic graphemes. Since blank spaces, however, remain the same between all graphemes (whether they belong to the same word or separate words), it is not Chinese 'words' that are made visible by blank spaces but morphemes. From a purely structural point of view, thus, there is no 'graphematic word' in Chinese.

As a mixed writing system, Japanese also lacks blank spaces between words. What users can exploit instead as information signalling word boundaries is the alternation between the system's constituent scripts: the morphographic kanji on the one hand and the syllabographic scripts hiragana and katakana on the other. Since these scripts are used for different purposes, they indicate word boundaries: specifically, hiragana graphemes are used to write, among other things, inflectional suffixes, which operate mostly at the end of words, while kanji represent lexical stems (cf. Smith 1996). Thus, the sequence 'hiragana grapheme followed by kanji grapheme' often marks the beginning of a new word between them.

Thai is the most problematic case. It is a segmental phonographic writing system that lacks blank spaces between words and fails to offer any other type of cues about where word boundaries might be located. It is thus up to the reader to identify words in the reading process.

The lack of spaces in the above-mentioned systems affects users' perception of words: specifically, if 'words' as defined for alphabetic writing systems are not indicated by blank spaces, users have fuzzier intuitions about what 'words' are. This raises the question (already introduced in ⟶ Section 2.5.1) of whether some linguistic concepts such as the 'word' are brought into users' consciousness only through writing. Or, as Davidson (2019) claims, might they even be constituted by writing? Claims like these lead to the assumption of graphic relativity (cf. Bugarski 1993), implying that users perceive language through the concepts or 'tools' afforded by their specific writing system. In that sense, in systems in which 'words' remain unmarked in writing, they might play a secondary role for users in general. And in languages that lack a written modality altogether, words might not play an important role at all. As Davidson remarks, the

> word is not a concept that applies to speech. [. . .] because contemporary preliterate and illiterate language users do not show any awareness of [words] it is unlikely they were parts of the mental grammars of pre-literate peoples. (Davidson 2019: 140)

One can argue similarly for the sentence, a unit that likewise has no clear-cut spoken equivalent. However, at least in writing, through the rather universal nature of punctuation marks such as the full stop (see below), a 'graphematic sentence' (cf. Schmidt 2016 for German) appears to be a more prominent unit in the world's writing systems than the graphematic word (cf. Meletis 2020a: 137–142).

4.4 Punctuation

In the previous sections, we dealt with default graphemes, which were defined as those units of writing systems that are semantically distinctive and correspond with linguistic units such as phonemes, syllables, and morphemes, and we also addressed larger graphematic units made up of combinations of such default graphemes. Punctuation constitutes another important part of many of the world's writing systems. In this section, the focus will explicitly be on a small set of punctuation marks that originally developed in alphabetic writing but have since also been adopted by other writing systems such as Chinese, Japanese, and Korean (cf. Taylor and Taylor 2014: 374–377). Notably, whether the punctuation marks discussed here also count as graphemes is an interesting question. In some conceptions, they are treated as graphemes, while in others, they are not; often, they remain altogether unmentioned. When applying the aforementioned grapheme criteria (⟶ Section 4.2.3) to punctuation, what can be observed is that punctuation marks can indeed be distinctive, although not at the lexical but rather at the syntactic level. This becomes obvious when considering a type of 'minimal pair' that is prominent on the internet and has, in various versions, even become a meme proclaiming that "Punctuation saves lives":

Let's eat, grandma!
Let's eat grandma!

Examples such as these are abundant and also concern other punctuation marks, cf. *Hello!* vs. *Hello?*, where the difference is arguably not (primarily) syntactic but located at the semantic and/or pragmatic levels. When moving on to the second criterion of identifying graphemes, the linguistic value criterion, an analysis of punctuation runs into certain difficulties. While punctuation marks certainly convey linguistic information of some sort, they themselves do not correspond with linguistic units of any kind. Consequently, we argue that punctuation marks are not graphemes the same way default graphemes are. If they are to be modelled as graphemes, the definition of grapheme has to be extended (which makes it more imprecise) or another class of graphemes has to be defined that behaves differently both structurally and functionally.

When turning to the function of punctuation, it is first worth mentioning that for a long time, punctuation was analysed from a prosodic perspective. A well-known assumption was, for instance, that commas indicate pauses in speaking. At one point, though, the focus was shifted at least partially to syntax (cf., for example, Behrens 1989). Ultimately, as Frank Kirchhoff (2016: 414) shows, the impression that punctuation was prosodic is actually tied to the fact that punctuation is associated with syntactic structures. It is these structures, then, which are tightly connected to prosody and provide a link between punctuation and prosody. Notably, while this observation is a good start for a structural analysis, from a functional point of view, it is short-sighted since the fact that punctuation marks occur in many diverse syntactic constructions insinuates a polyfunctionality of punctuation (see below).

It was this multitude of different structures associated with a single mark that led to a fundamental shift in the treatment of punctuation underlying the work of Bredel (2008, 2011).[108] Prior to her analysis, most approaches to punctuation – not only in German grapholinguistics – were, as mentioned, structure-oriented and attempted to explain punctuation by tying it to certain linguistic phenomena. Examples of such an analysis include that “the full stop <.>” is used “to mark the end of a sentence; the colon <:> to introduce a new idea, a quotation or an enumeration [. . .]”, etc. (Coulmas 1996a: 421). Bredel refers to this construction-based approach as the *offline perspective*. She proposes an alternative: a functional processing-based view, the so-called *online perspective*. It focuses on how punctuation marks instruct readers in the course of the reading process. Thus, rather than associating punctuation marks with certain constructions, they are assigned specific instructions that they supply to readers whenever they are encountered in texts. For example: “The full stop instructs the reader to conclude syntactic parsing, i.e., not to parse the material preceding and following the full stop together as one unit” (Bredel 2011: 5, our translation).

This approach solves two closely related problems that had previously plagued the investigation of punctuation. Firstly, it frees the analysis of elusive constructions such as ‘sentences’, the many forms of which greatly complicate the search for a coherent definition of the functions of punctuation. This, in turn, also makes obsolete the assumption that punctuation marks are polyfunctional. The comma’s occurrence in the context of different linguistic constructions, for instance, ceases to be a problem when the basis of an analysis is the instruction it provides readers, which remains the same in all constructions that exhibit a comma (see below). Furthermore, it is noteworthy that the online perspective appears reasonable also from a diachronic perspective given that punctuation developed primarily to aid perception, more specifically silent reading processes.

By comparison with larger sets of marks classified as punctuation in other approaches (cf. Carter and McCarthy 2006; Nunberg, Briscoe, and Huddleston 2002), the inventory that Bredel analyses is a narrow set: < . ; , : - – . . . ’ ? ! ( ) „“>. It results from four features that distinguish punctuation from default graphemes as well as from digits, special characters such as <&>, and the blank space. According to these features, punctuation is, firstly, (1) identifiable without context. This means that unlike the blank space, which is visualised only by material surrounding it, punctuation can be perceived and classified by users even in the absence of other graphic material. Secondly, punctuation is (2) not recodable (i.e., verbalisable), unlike graphemes which correspond with phonemes or morphemes, digits,

108 To this day, Bredel’s analysis, which was published in German, has received little attention in English-language research. An overview in English is given in Kirchhoff and Primus’ (2016) chapter in *The Routledge handbook of the English writing system*.

and special characters: <&>, for example, is verbalised as ‘and’. Furthermore, punctuation marks are (3) not freely combinable (but cf. for the graphotactics of punctuation below). This distinguishes them from default graphemes, which are combined to form larger graphematic units, and digits, which can also combine with each other to form larger numbers. Finally, punctuation marks are (4) not paired, separating them from the default graphemes of most alphabetic systems, which are available in both uppercase and lowercase versions.

A striking feature of Bredel's analysis is her proposal of form-function correlations based on a graphetic analysis grounded in the three-space schema of the line (⟶ Section 3.2.2). Three graphetic features are relevant: (a) [±empty] distinguishes marks that touch the base line from those that do not, rendering <: ; . , ! ? „“ ( )> [–empty] and <- – . . . ’> [+empty]. The second feature, (b) [±vertical], characterises marks that extend into the high space of the line, i.e., <! ? „“ ( ) . . . ’>, which are [+vertical], while the rest, i.e., <: ; . , - –>, is [–vertical]. The third feature, (c) [±reduplicated], concerns the question whether marks (or parts of marks) occur more than once: Accordingly, <: – „“ ( ) . . .> are reduplicated while <; . , ’ - ! ?> are not.[109] Given these features, every punctuation mark can be assigned a triple of feature values: the full stop <.>, for example, is [–empty, –vertical, –reduplicated]. As we will see below, these feature values give rise to graphetic feature classes, and the marks in these classes exhibit similar functions.

In addition to these features, Bredel distinguishes two types of punctuation marks based on their graphotactics (see next section), i.e., the way in which they combine with each other and occupy different spaces of the writing surface. In short, *fillers* are those punctuation marks that occupy their own segmental space, while *clitics*[110] attach to other units inside a single segmental space. Fillers are [+empty] and thus include the marks <. . . – - ’>. Their context is symmetric, i.e., they are surrounded by units of the same class. The hyphen <->, for example, is surrounded by two graphemes as in <ground-breaking>. By contrast, the clitics <( ) „“ . , ; : ? !> are [–empty]. This distinction is relevant because fillers and clitics assume different functions. To illustrate this, Bredel notes that “already through its pure materiality, writing makes linguistic units visible” (Bredel 2011: 24, our translation).

109 Bredel works with the historical forms of two punctuation marks to arrive at certain feature values: quotation marks <„“> are [–empty] because they were formerly written as < ⟩⟨ >, and the ellipsis mark <. . .> formerly appeared in the form of three strokes in the high space < /// >, rendering it [+empty] and [+vertical] (cf. Bredel 2009: 120). Furthermore, the dash <–> is [+reduplicated] because it is interpreted as a reduplicated hyphen <--> (cf. Bredel 2008: 29).

110 This marks a terminological analogy to clitics in morphology, defined as morphemes that have properties of words but depend phonologically on other words or phrases (cf. the contracted form of the verb form *am* in *I’m*).

Indeed, for the recognition of some linguistic units in their written form, it suffices to glance at a page without even reading it. In other words, we recognise them by merely scanning the page. This is precisely where clitics come into play: they help readers in the scanning process by marking graphetically coded units. The hyphen, for example, marks a deviance from the default graphetic structure of words and thus reveals visual information crucial for the reading process. Fillers, on the other hand, do more than that: they are not just visual cues by virtue of marking linguistically coded units. Instead, they aid readers by telling them how, for example, to parse sentences, i.e., build syntactic structures out of what is currently being read. Thus, following Bredel, they do not serve scanning but processing. As mentioned above, the full stop, for instance, instructs readers to conclude syntactic parsing and begin textual parsing, in other words, to associate the sentence that was just read with the following sentence that first must also be parsed syntactically.

This leaves open the question of the functions associated with the graphetic features [±reduplicated] and [±vertical]. The former reveals at which linguistic level punctuation marks operate: marks that are [+reduplicated] have as their scope the text level, while [–reduplicated] marks work at the word and sentence levels. Finally, punctuation marks can have a mainly cognitive function, by structuring the parsing process, or a communicative function, by signalling a change of communicative roles in the reading process. This is where [±vertical] comes into play: marks with the feature value [–vertical] are concerned with parsing, whereas marks that are [+vertical] are pragmatically relevant as they signal a change of reader/writer roles.

As for communicative functions, according to Bredel, marks characterised by the feature triple [–empty, +vertical, –reduplicated], i.e., <?> and <!>, assume epistemic functions by assigning different states of knowledge to the reader and the writer.[111] By contrast, marks that are [–empty, +vertical, +reduplicated], i.e., <( )> and <„“>, aid in understanding interactional meaning. The parentheses, for example, signal a change of roles from ‘covert writer/reader’ to ‘overt writer/reader’. Specifically, outside of parentheses, writers are ‘covert writers’, i.e., stay in the background and do not write in their own voices, whereas inside parentheses, they become ‘overt writers’. As overt writers, they reveal themselves as authors of the text and open up side discourses, frequently by commenting on what is written outside of the parentheses. When readers encounter parentheses, this is accompanied by a symmetrical change in their role from covert to overt readers.

111 The question mark <?>, for example, “instructs the reader to assume the role of the knowing party and, in this role, to look for the element of knowledge that the writer lacks – independently of the construction that it marks” (Bredel 2011: 24, our translation).

The quotation marks indicate a change of role, too, albeit a different one: as in the case of citing direct quotes, quotation marks signal that what is enclosed in them was said by someone else (cf. Bredel 2011: Chapter 6). To sum up, Figure 15 provides an overview of how the graphetic and graphotactic features of punctuation marks correlate with their respective instructive functions in the reading process.

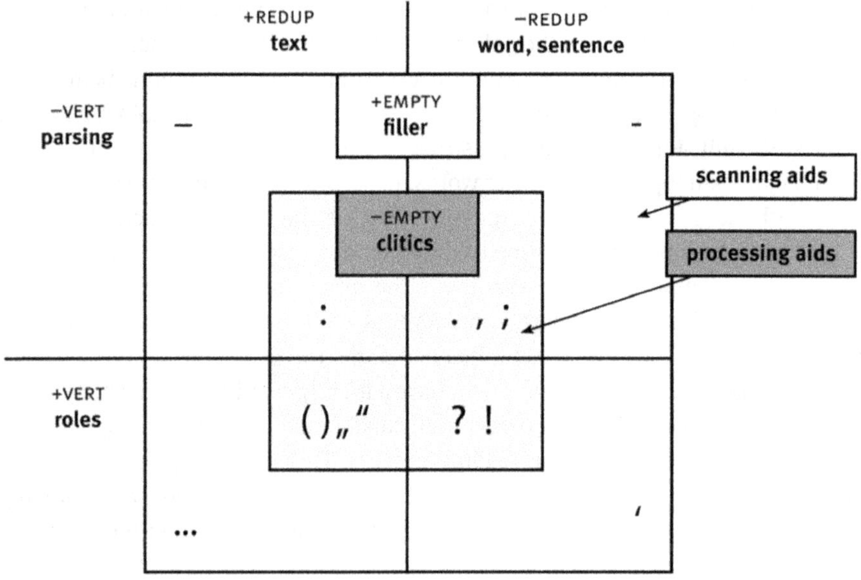

Figure 15: Form-function correlations of punctuation marks, adapted from Bredel (2011: 30).

The comma is arguably the most important punctuation mark and warrants further attention. In Bredel's processing-based approach, along with the full stop, the colon, and the semicolon, the comma is treated as a syntactic punctuation mark as it is involved in syntactic parsing. The general instruction that it gives readers is to block syntactic subordination. In other words: not to interpret the structures that precede and follow the comma as parts of the same syntactic constituent. This instruction is modelled by Primus (2007: 106–107) in the form of optimality theoretic constraints to capture the comma's basic cross-linguistic function:

A. Syntactic sisterhood: If two syntactic units are not sisters at the syntactic level, there is no comma between them.
B. Non-subordination: If two syntactic units are not connected to each other by the subordination options of the language, there is no comma between them.

The first constraint, SYNTACTIC SISTERHOOD, "prohibits a comma between two syntactic units if there is no node that immediately dominates them", i.e., if they are not part of the same sentence (Kirchhoff and Primus 2016: 98). Thus, in <Peter went. To Berlin.>, for example, no sentence node dominates the two (graphematic) sentences the way it does in <Peter went, to Berlin.> in which <to Berlin> is a prepositional phrase attached to the phrase *Peter went* (cf. Kirchhoff and Primus 2016: 98 for details). The second constraint, NON-SUBORDINATION, concerns syntactic 'sister' constituents that are not associated by subordination, i.e., are not syntactically dependent on each other but equivalent.

An example of subordination is <Today I will cook dinner.>, in which *cook* syntactically subordinates *dinner*. The comma, thus, is not licensed between them and <*Today I will cook, dinner.> is incorrect, at least if the exact same meaning of the sentence is intended. Filtering out subordination leaves two syntactic relations that license the comma: (1) coordination, as in <This is a story of dogs, cats and mice.>[112] and (2) dislocation, as in <This is, I believe, the title of the book.>, in which <I believe>, a so-called comment clause, is dislocated. As for coordination, there exist two main types: syndetic coordination, in which elements are coordinated with a conjunction (such as *and*), and asyndetic coordination, in which they are not. The comma is required in asyndetic coordination in many writing systems, including English, German, Dutch, Russian, and Spanish (cf. Primus 2007).

An additional constraint can explain typological variation in the comma's function across diverse writing systems: "If two subordinated syntactic sisters are separated by a clause boundary, there is a comma between them" (Kirchhoff and Primus 2016: 105). This constraint is active in German and Russian, for example, but not in English. Thus, in German, it must be <Hunde, die bellen, beißen nicht.>, whereas in English, it is <Dogs that bark don't bite.>.[113]

---

112 Notably, this could also be <This is a story of dogs, cats, and mice.>; the final comma before the conjunction <and> is a serial comma (often referred to as Oxford Comma). Officially, it is optional in most written varieties of English, with some favouring its inclusion and others largely omitting it. In the end, it is a matter of style that is addressed in many style guides such as *The Chicago Manual of Style* or *The Oxford Style Manual*.

113 Note that the pronoun *that* introduces restrictive phrases, i.e., phrases essential to the meaning of a sentence. By contrast, *which* commonly introduces non-restrictive phrases. Unlike restrictive phrases, they must be separated from the main sentence by preceding and following commas: <The kitten that I adopted, which had been a stray on the streets of Greece, always purred so loudly.>. However, matters are complicated by the fact that *which* can also serve in the same function as *that*, introducing restrictive phrases.

4.5 Graphotactics

Graphematic units – as building blocks – are not the only relevant part of graphematics, which has as its centre also "restrictions on ways in which" these graphematic units "may combine with each other" (McCawley 1994: 115). By analogy with terms such as *phonotactics* and *morphotactics*, these restrictions are termed *graphotactics*. They include rules of how written units of various kinds may be combined to form well-formed units at a higher level as well as rules that constrain the positions that smaller units may occupy inside these larger units. Importantly, graphotactic rules are not explicit and codified rules, which are characteristic of orthography (⟶ Section 5.3). They are rather a core part of the very systematics of a writing system – its graphematics. As such, they also underlie the above-mentioned graphematic solution space by restricting which combinations of units are even possible. Notably, like everything graphematic, they are part of the implicit knowledge of users.

For example, users of English likely know that <v> is almost never the final letter of words (with the exception of marked words such as <lav> or <rev>) and that an <e> is almost always added after it, cf. <have>, <give> (cf. McCawley 1994: 117; Berg 2016a: 2). This knowledge that *<hav> and *<giv> would be unsystematic spellings of English is implicit graphotactic knowledge. What these examples also illustrate is that from a purely phonographic perspective, these words (*have* /hæv/ and *give* /gɪv/) do not require a word-final <e> in their graphematic representation. It is not motivated by the graphemes' correspondence with phonemes but graphotactically, underlining that notwithstanding the great number of parallels between phonotactics and graphotactics, the latter is not necessarily dependent on the former. This is also the gist of the argument that graphematics is its own subsystem of language – it obviously exhibits distinct and idiosyncratic systematics.

It is noteworthy that graphotactics is a core aspect of graphematics and yet research on it is scarce and limited to specific graphotactic phenomena (such as the graphotactics of monosyllabic nouns in German, cf. Balestra 2017). Nevertheless, in the following, we will attempt to sketch a non-exhaustive overview of a number of phenomena in different writing systems to exemplify various forms of graphotactic restrictions. We will mention examples that concern the well-formedness of (1) graphemes, (2) larger graphematic units, and (3) punctuation.

In the presentation of grapheme criteria, we discussed the internal structure of complex Chinese graphemes that consist of both a phonological and a semantic component. These types of components prototypically appear in respective positions: semantic components are located in the left part of characters while phonological components occur in the right part (cf. Taft, Zhu, and Peng 1999: 498). Such is the case in <妈> *mā* 'mother', where the semantic component on the left signals the meaning 'female' and the phonological component on the right evokes the pronunciation /ma/. These preferred positions are an example of subsegmental graphotactic constraints. For any given character, they "determine whether the character is legal or not" (Ho, Ng, and Ng 2003: 853). In other words, if the two types of components occur on 'their' side of a grapheme, they contribute to form either an existing grapheme or a well-formed pseudographeme. By contrast, if they appear in 'illegal' positions, the result is a nongrapheme.[114] Users' knowledge of these graphotactic constraints is tested in so-called character decision tasks, the results of which suggest that even first graders utilise this knowledge to reject nongraphemes and judge pseudographemes as acceptable (cf. Shu and Anderson 1999).

When it comes to grapheme combinations, a number of heterogeneous graphotactic phenomena can be found in the world's writing systems. One of them concerns the permissible length of words. The English writing system provides a well-known example here in the form of the so-called *three-letter rule* formulated by Kenneth H. Albrow (1972): content words (as opposed to function words) in English must consist of at least three letters. As McCawley (1994: 117) notes, except for a few cases of doubt (e.g., the treatment of *do* and *go* as function words), this rule holds up remarkably well. It can explain, for instance, the differences between <sow> vs. <so>, <buy> vs. <by>, and <inn> vs. <in>. A second phenomenon concerns permissible grapheme sequences. McCawley (1994: 117–118) illustrates it by means of the alternation between <y> and <i> in English. Many instances of this alternation can be explained by assuming that an underlying <y> is replaced by <i> before any suffix, as in <glory> vs. <glorious> and <carry> vs. <carried>. However, there is a noteworthy exception: <y> remains when <-ing> is added, as in <carrying>, <spying>. This exception could be based on a graphotactic constraint to avoid <ii>. This constraint, however, cannot be absolute, since in inflected forms of words ending in <i>, <ii> does occur, cf. <skiing>. But there are also absolute constraints in the world's writing systems, such as that <jj>, <vv>, or <ww> are not allowed in German within single morphemes[115] (cf. Berg and Evertz 2018: 193).

114 The distinction between pseudo- and non-units corresponds with what is systematic (i.e., located inside the graphematic solution space) but is not actually in use (= pseudographemes) vs. what is unsystematic, i.e., not part of the system in the first place (= nongraphemes).

115 Note that at the lexical level, due to compounding, these doublets can occur, for example in <Kollektivversagen> 'collective failure', where a morpheme boundary is located between the two instances of <v>.

Our final example concerns punctuation and its use in many alphabetic writing systems (see the previous section). Here, graphotactic constraints concern the positions in which punctuation marks occur as well as their combination with written units of other classes – such as default graphemes – and with each other (cf. Bredel 2011: 19–22). As described above, fillers occupy their own segmental space whereas clitics attach to other units in their respective segmental spaces. Furthermore, the fillers <. . . – - '> are characterised by the fact that their surroundings are symmetric. Also, fillers such as the dash <–> can (at least in German) occupy both the initial and the final segmental space in a line. Clitics, by contrast, have asymmetric surroundings and can only occupy the final but not the first segmental space of a line. An example is the comma that attaches to, for instance, a default grapheme (or a digit), as in <example,> and is followed by a blank space. Additionally, clitics can be subdivided in two groups based on whether they exhibit the feature [±vertical]: [+vertical] clitics, i.e., clitics that extend into the high space, may combine with each other, as in <really?!">, where the sequence <y?!"> occupies a single segmental space. By contrast, clitics which are [–vertical], <. , ; :>, are not combined with each other. Bredel (2011: 22) assumes this is because only one clitisation position is available for these marks, and when it is already occupied by one, it is blocked for all the others (cf. also Nunberg 1990).

4.6 Written variation and allography

4.6.1 Definitions of variation and allography

Although choices between different alternatives are involved in practically every aspect and at every level of writing – graphetics, graphematics, and orthography – variation in writing has not been studied extensively. A term that is closely associated with written variation is *allography*. Like *grapheme* or *graphotactics*, it is a term that has been coined in analogy with terms prominent in other linguistic subfields, most notably *allophony* and *allomorphy*. In fact, as we will see below, there exist different types of allography that are similar to either allophony or allomorphy. It is, however, also important to note upfront that not every type of variation in writing has a parallel in other linguistic subsystems, and not every instance of variation automatically counts as allography.

Before turning to different types of written variation and allography, it is necessary to first give a general definition of variation with respect to writing. For this, Kristian Berg's approach proves useful, as he describes how linguistic expressions can differ on various levels of linguistic structure (cf. Berg 2016b). In languages that have a writing system, linguistic expressions such as the word *tiger* can be analysed at four structural levels: (1) graphematic structure (GS): <tiger>, (2) phonological structure (PS): /ˈtaɪgə/, (3) semantic structure (SS): ‘tiger’, and (4) categorial structure (CS), which bundles the morphosyntactic features of the word’s (or expression’s) constituent structure such as {NOUN, SINGULAR, . . .}.

Table 6: Different types of variation between the four structural levels of linguistic expression, adapted from Berg (2016b: 15).

Type	GS	PS	SS	CS	Example
a	+	+	+	+	<dog>/<write>
b	+	+	+	–	<cat>/<mouse>
c	+	+	–	+	<laugh>/<laugh+ing>
d	+	+	–	–	<start>/<begin>
e	+	–	+	+	<right>/<write>
f	+	–	+	–	<sight>/<site>
g	+	–	–	+	<phobia>/<-phobia>
h	+	–	–	–	<advisor>/<adviser>

Table 6 lists types of variation that are characterised by the structural levels on which two given expressions vary (with variation being indicated by a plus sign). In *Type a*, words differ on all structural levels: <dog> is a noun, <write> is a verb. They have different meanings and are both pronounced and written differently. Further down the table, expressions differ only with respect to some but not all structural levels. Take, for instance, *Type e*, exemplified by the pair <right> and <write>. Expressions of this type are pronounced the same but have differing graphematic, semantic, and categorial structures. In *Type f*, expressions are even more similar, as they additionally exhibit the same categorial structure: <sight> and <site>, for instance, are both nouns.

Analogous examples can also be found in other writing systems: Chinese <世> *shì* ‘generation’ and <事> *shì* ‘work’ are pronounced the same but have different meanings and a different graphematic structure, which also applies for <พาย> /phaay/ ‘paddle’ and <ภาย> /phaay/ ‘part (of space or time)’ in Thai (cf. Brown 1988: 44). Next, expressions of *Type g* have the same phonological structure but differ with respect to their graphematic and categorial structures: while <phobia> is its own word, <-phobia> is a suffix used to designate specific phobias such as <agoraphobia>, meaning these two expressions do not have the same categorial structure. Also, given that <-phobia> never occurs alone in writing, they manifest differently at the graphematic level.

Finally, *Type h* is relevant for our investigation of variation in writing. Here, expressions differ exclusively with respect to their graphematic structure – an example being <advisor> vs. <adviser>.[116] Only this type is considered written variation. By contrast, *Types b–g*[117] are not considered types of written variation because they also (or at times only) include variation with respect to other structural levels (cf. Berg 2016b: 17).[118] Take <right> and <write>: they are homophones but not homographs and, crucially, they have different meanings. Accordingly, their graphematic structures differ only secondarily. In other words, the fact that they are written differently is determined by other reasons, in the case of <right> vs. <write> their different meanings.

As we will show, three types must be considered for a comprehensive picture of written variation. They were already differentiated by Daniel Bunčić (2016), who, with his colleagues, investigated sociolinguistically conditioned written variation within one language or between two (or more) very similar languages. The goal was to make possible better sociolinguistic descriptions of situations in which different written variants co-occur in a given context. An example of such a situation is the complex alternation between the Cyrillic and Roman scripts in the use of the Serbian writing system (⟶ Section 5.5.3.1). In the resulting typology, three types of variation are distinguished according to the three structural levels of writing systems: following the terminology in our book, we call them graphetic, graphematic, and orthographic variation.

In the following sections, we will take a closer look at these types of variation and their corresponding types of allography (cf. also Meletis 2020b). At first, however, the important conceptual distinction between variation and allography must be clarified: written variation as in <advisor> vs. <adviser> might be constituted by differing segments (such as <o> vs. <e> in this example) but, given that the benchmark is the word level, variation actually concerns a larger graphematic level rather than that of individual graphemes.[119] Furthermore, written

116 However, the fact that they are not distinctive at the denotative level does not mean that their difference cannot carry social meaning, as Sebba (2007: 7, emphasis in original) notes: "In English today, *vulcanising a tyre* is not exactly the same as *vulcanizing a tire* [. . .] and in Galician, *dia* is distinct in its connotations, though not in its reference, from *día*".

117 Note that in *Type a*, expressions differ on all structural levels, making them altogether different words. Thus, they are not variants in any respect, which is why one cannot speak of variation (cf. Berg 2016b: 17).

118 Berg (2016b) refers to both types as graphematic variation but considers *Type h* to be graphematic variation in the narrow sense and *Types b–g* graphematic variation in the broad sense.

119 This means that the alternation between <e> and <o> in this example is not an inherent feature of the writing system that occurs throughout the system (which would be the case for graphematic allography) but is instead specific to a given set of words.

variation can be embedded in complex sociolinguistic situations and can involve multiple (varieties of) writing systems such as the American English and British English varieties in the case of <color> vs. <colour>. Accordingly, we use *variation* here in a broad sense to denote alternations that concern higher levels than the individual grapheme and are potentially intersystemic (i.e., involve multiple writing systems or at least different varieties of one system). Additionally, variation may also be determined by orthographic regulations that may exist in a writing system: <acetose> and <acetous>, for example, are both orthographically licensed in English.

By contrast, *allography* is defined more narrowly. It exclusively captures alternations of units at the segmental level – either between basic shapes or graphemes. These alternations occur only within a given writing system, i.e., they are intrasystemic. Finally, unlike variation, allography is always constituted by the system and cannot be determined externally, i.e., by sociolinguistic factors, among them orthographic regulation.

4.6.2 Graphetic variation and allography

Graphetic variation is constituted by different instantiations of units written in the same script, e.g., Roman script. It can be chirographic or typographic. Think of ten people writing the word <milk> by hand. They all use Roman script, but the fact that they all have individual handwriting results in graphetic variation. And given that every manifestation is unique this is the case even when their handwriting is visually very similar.[120] Similarly, when a word such as <milk> is once printed (or digitally presented) in Times New Roman and another time in Arial (<milk>), this also represents graphetic variation. Crucially, graphetic variation is entirely visual and concerns the assignment of graphs to their corresponding basic shapes. The concrete graphs that are produced either in handwriting or typography, no matter how much they vary at the visual level (within boundaries, that is, see below), materialise the same abstract basic shapes that belong to the same script.

At this point it is noteworthy that from a perceptual, i.e., reader-based perspective, the different types of written variation as well as their corresponding types of allography can be distinguished based on the knowledge required to classify variants as belonging to the same unit. From this perspective, graphetic

120 Note that this is technically also the case when one person writes the word repeatedly: all instantiations are unique, no matter how much they are visually similar.

variation does not pose a challenge to readers who are literate in a given script as they know the script's basic shapes and thus recognise variants of them, meaning graphetic variation usually does not disturb the reading process. In fact, it actually serves as a valuable resource of writing as it contributes a layer of meaning in addition to the purely denotative meaning conveyed by graphematic units. The graphetic features of a written utterance always transport information of various kinds, e.g., social information about the producer of a given text. Therefore, they can be used by individuals and groups to position and (self-)identify themselves socially through the visual appearance of their writing (⟶ Section 3.3.2.6). Thus, graphetic variation is highly relevant to the social and symbolic functions of writing.

As evident from the <milk>-example above, graphetic variation may occur at the suprasegmental level, i.e., concern sequences of graphs. There are several important types of this kind of suprasegmental variation, among them *italics*, underlining, or colour (cf. Gallmann 1986: 49 and Günther 1988: 65 for more types). Italics, bold print, and, as a matter of fact, the above-mentioned choice of typeface are what Günther classifies as *integrative* variation as they alter the appearance of the graphs themselves, i.e., are 'integrated' into them.[121] By contrast, underlining is *additive* given that it merely adds an element to the graphs but does not directly affect their appearance. Finally, colour is what Rezec (2009: 60) refers to as *non-form changing*: graphs are neither altered by it nor is anything added. Notably, these types can overlap, as colour is arguably also – if not in the same way as italics or bold print – integrative, whereas l e t t e r s p a c i n g is non-form changing and, in a way, additive, as additional space is added between graphs.

The type of allography associated with graphetic variation is accordingly termed graphetic allography. It hinges on visual similarity, which makes it similar to allophony, where non-distinctive phones – such as [r] and [ɹ], among others, for the English phoneme /r/ – must be phonetically similar in order to be considered allophones of the same phoneme. Two subtypes of graphetic allography are distinguished: syntagmatic and paradigmatic graphetic allography. Syntagmatic graphetic allography captures allographs that co-occur in sequence in the context of the same graphetic inventory, be it a given person's handwriting (at a specific moment in time)[122] or a specific font such as *10 pt italic Times New Roman*. For

---

121 It is important to note that in the context of graphetic variation, basic shapes (usually) do not change but only the graphs that materialise them. However, in some typefaces, when changing a portion of text from roman to italics, some basic shapes might be switched out. An example of this is Times New Roman, in which roman |a| changes to |*a*| in italics (see below).

122 Note that a person's handwriting usually changes over the course of their lifespan, so even one person's handwriting from two different points in time may differ markedly.

example, when a person writes the word <kitten> by hand, two graphs instantiating the basic shape |t| are produced, and the same applies when the word is printed, as in <*kitten*>. In both cases, thus, two instances of |t| occur. These two instances, as unique physical events, are concrete graphs and are syntagmatic variants of the same basic shape. They can be considered free allographs as they can be replaced by each other: the two instances of |t| in <*kitten*>, for example, might be switched. Note, however, that there may be effects of coarticulation, especially in handwriting: the graphomotoric movements of the hands and writing tools involved in production may affect the forms of the preceding and following graphs and thus also the shape of the two instances of |t|, making them dependent on their specific position and, thus, visually variable and non-exchangeable.

By comparison, the second subtype, paradigmatic graphetic allography, concerns the relation between graphs across inventories, i.e., different people's handwritings or different typefaces and fonts. For example, the |t| in the handwritten version of <kitten> and the |*t*| in the typographic version are paradigmatic graphetic allographs of the basic shape |t|. Since they are part of different inventories, they cannot occur together in a minimal context such as the word <*kitten*> because it is uncommon to change the inventory in the middle of a minimal context such as a single word, e.g., [?]<*kitten*>. Instead, as they instantiate the same basic shape, they occur in the same slot in a given written/printed word. In sum, all possible graphs that can materialise a given basic shape in a given position in an utterance are considered paradigmatic graphetic allographs.

4.6.3 Graphematic variation and allography

Graphematic variation, as the second type of written variation, differs from graphetic variation in that it does not necessarily involve visual similarity. Instead, variants are identified by having the same linguistic function.

In a sociolinguistic context, Bunčić (2016) mentions as instances of graphematic variation situations in which two different scripts are simultaneously used for writing one – or two very similar – languages. An example that concerns two languages (or two varieties of one language, which is often debated) is Hindi, which is written in Devanāgarī, and Urdu, which is written in Arabic script. Notably, the spoken modalities of Hindi and Urdu are so similar that they are mutually intelligible, and it is the written modality that is meant to clearly mark them as two different languages (cf. Gumperz 1957). The use of different scripts is in this case conditioned mainly by religious reasons as both scripts signal different faiths (Devanāgarī is associated with Hinduism and Arabic script with Islam). In this situation, the same (or very similar) linguistic units are represented by different, visually dissimilar shapes – Devanāgarī shapes in one case and Arabic shapes in the other. In the absence of visual similarity, readers need to be biliterate to be able to read both. This means that the knowledge involved is graphematic, not graphetic. Because Hindi and Urdu are so similar as spoken languages, linguistically, this example of graphematic variation could arguably be considered intrasystemic. From a political point of view, however, it is intersystemic as the different scripts are actively utilised to give the impression of two distinct languages.

Another example is a type of intrasystemic suprasegmental graphematic variation in alphabets that have a case distinction: all caps. At times considered to be graphetic variation, it is in fact graphematic, since in all caps, the lowercase basic shapes in a word are switched out for the uppercase basic shapes, which are sometimes visually dissimilar, cf. <Danger!> vs. <DANGER!> (cf. Dürscheid 2016b). Here, too, the knowledge that |r| and |R| are variants of one grapheme is graphematic rather than graphetic (cf. below for capitalisation).

The corresponding type of allography is called graphematic allography. It deals with different basic shapes that are assigned to the same grapheme; these may be but need not be visually similar.[123] In this respect, graphematic allography is conceptually similar to the morphological concept of allomorphy, where allomorphs can be phonologically similar (such as the English plural allomorphs [s], [z], [ɨz] in *cats, dogs,* and *houses*, respectively) but do not have to be (such as *go* and *went* as allomorphs of the lexeme GO). As with graphetic allography, two types of graphematic allography are distinguished: paradigmatic and syntagmatic graphematic allography.

Paradigmatic graphematic allography pertains to those basic shapes that occupy the same slot and thus do not occur together in any context. Examples from Roman script are |a| and |ɑ| as well as |g| and |ɡ|. The units in these pairs are visually too dissimilar to count as graphs of one basic shape. They are rather distinct basic shapes that are – in the writing systems of English and German, for example – assigned to two graphemes, respectively: <a> and <g>.[124] Again, the knowledge necessary to identify them as variants of one unit is graphematic: it comes from knowing that they have the same linguistic function and not from recognising a (non-significant) visual similarity that may exist in these examples

123 In fact, even if they are visually similar, the difference between them must be bigger than the difference between graphetic allographs, which are usually visually very similar. In other words, the visual difference must be big enough for them to count as two distinct basic shapes.
124 Notably, in other writing systems, the different basic shapes might be used as the visual signifiers of distinct graphemes.

but is absent from many other instances of graphematic allography.[125] Ultimately, the choice between them is free, but in a given context it is nonetheless fixed: once |g| has been chosen, switching to |ɡ| in the immediate context, e.g., a portion of text such as a word or a sentence, is very uncommon (but not impossible or orthographically prohibited), cf. $^{?}$<bigger>.

Paradigmatic graphematic allography can also be found in the Chinese writing system (⟶ Section 6.3) in the form of so-called *yìtǐzì* (異體字), translated as 'variant characters'. As Chinese is a morphographic system, these variant characters are basic shapes that relate to the same morpheme and do not individually have any other function besides that. Examples include |峰| and |峯| for *fēng* 'mountain top', |群| and |羣| for *qún* 'group, flock', and |册| and |冊| *cè* for 'booklet' as well as |裏| and |裡| for *lǐ* 'inside' (cf. Galambos 2015). The units in these pairs are functionally equivalent, but as with |g| and |ɡ|, it would be strange to use them together in the same minimal context in a text (e.g., the same sentence or even the same paragraph). By contrast, in a (slightly) larger context such as the front page of a newspaper, it would not be strange when the two allographs occur in different minimal contexts, e.g., when one of them occurs in the headline and the other in the running text. The same applies also to headlines which might be printed in sans-serif typefaces (and thus feature |ɡ|) while the running text is printed in serif typefaces using the variant |g|.

Syntagmatic graphematic allography concerns basic shapes that occur together in a given context but are complementarily distributed, i.e., never occupy the same slots. This type of allography is reminiscent of complementarily distributed allophony as exhibited by the allophones [ç] as in *ich* /ɪç/ 'I' and [x] as in *Nacht* /naxt/ 'night' for the German phoneme /x/, which never occur in the same positional contexts. The most prominent example in writing is positional allography in writing systems using Arabic script. Here, most graphemes have four different positional allographs: an allograph that occurs in isolation and three connected allographs that occur either at the beginning, the middle, or the end of a word or string of basic shapes. For example, the grapheme <ب> has |ب| as its isolated form, |بـ| as its initial form (at the beginning of words), |ـبـ| as its medial form (between two other basic shapes) and |ـب| as its final form (at the end of words). Another well-known example of syntagmatic graphematic allography comes from Greek, where the grapheme <σ/ς> has two positional variants: |σ| occurs word-initially and word-medially, while |ς| occurs only word-finally.

125 Arguably, |ɑ| is not more similar to |a| than to |o|. If we believe to see a visual similarity here, this is likely influenced top-down by the graphematic knowledge that – in the writing systems we are familiar with – they 'mean' the same.

This leads us to a complex case of allography: capitalisation, i.e., the distinction between uppercase and lowercase units in alphabets that exhibit both sets of units. It concerns writing systems using the Roman, Cyrillic, Greek, and Armenian scripts and raises the question of whether corresponding uppercase and lowercase units are individual graphemes or allographs of one grapheme. Sampson (2015: 16) claims that in English, they are individual graphemes, arguing that the case distinction is significant (but cf. for a different view Daniels and Share 2018: 109, where they are treated as allographs). He mentions as an example reverential and thus pragmatically motivated capitalisation of <He> as opposed to the default, lowercase use of the pronoun, <he>. However, uppercase and lowercase units usually do not occupy the same positions in contexts such as words and sentences. Therefore, it is proposed that they are not separate graphemes but syntagmatic graphematic allographs that are dependent on their positions within sentences. This is most evident when considering sentence-initial capitalisation, which exists in all alphabets that feature a case distinction. By marking the beginning of a graphematic sentence, it serves a purely graphematic function (cf. Schmidt 2016). The situation is more complex when it comes to sentence-internal capitalisation (cf. Fuhrhop and Peters 2013: 207–208). For example, in German, the capitalisation of address pronouns as in polite <Sie> is determined pragmatically (similar to the English capitalisation of <He>), and proper names, brand names, and toponyms are likewise capitalised. And what is often explained morphologically as the capitalisation of a specific part of speech, the noun, can actually be better explained on syntactic grounds: heads of noun phrases are capitalised (cf. Maas 1992). In a nutshell, uppercase variants are licensed in some contexts while lowercase variants appear in others. Their alternation is explainable, but due to the necessity of referring to other linguistic levels in doing so, this type of graphematic allography is considered externally determined (cf. Meletis 2020b: 257).

An important difference between paradigmatic and syntagmatic graphematic allography is that the former can be deemed free (in the sense that one is free to choose an inventory that uses either |g| or |ɡ|, for example) and thus predominantly stylistic in nature, whereas the latter is a core feature of the system: for instance, to write in conformity with the graphematics of the system, one is required to use all of the allographs of Arabic graphemes in their required positions. This renders syntagmatic graphematic allography obligatory and system-inherent.

4.6.4 Orthographic variation

Orthographic variation can concern variants across writing systems (intersystemic variants) or variants within one writing system (intrasystemic variants). It affects the spelling of entire words and thus the suprasegmental level, even when in given examples it seemingly only affects the segmental level (as in the choice of an 'orthographically correct' grapheme in a word). Orthographic variation is common in the different writing systems of pluricentric languages. In most varieties of German, for example, there is a grapheme <ß>, whereas in Switzerland and Liechtenstein, the linguistic unit represented by that grapheme is written <ss>. Consequently, the German word for 'big' is written <groß> in Germany and Austria and <gross> in Switzerland and Liechtenstein. Something similar is observable in the varieties of English: in American English, one writes <color>, <realize>, and <center>, whereas in British English, one writes <colour>, <realise> (or optionally also <realize>), and <centre>.

Another example of orthographic variation comes in the form of pluricentric Chinese characters that are in use in a number of Asian countries such as China, Taiwan, Japan, and South Korea. In the 1950s and 1960s, in the course of an orthography reform, the government of the People's Republic of China simplified many characters by reducing their number of strokes. The goal was to make them easier to learn and to thereby promote literacy (⟶ Section 5.5.3.4). The resulting simplified characters were also adopted in Singapore and by the Chinese community in Malaysia but not in Hong Kong and Taiwan, for example, where the original, unchanged characters – referred to as traditional characters – remain in use to this day. This also applies to the writing systems of Japanese and Korean, where traditional Chinese characters are in use as kanji and hanja, respectively. Examples of the difference between traditional vs. simplified are the respective characters for the word/morpheme 'language': the traditional variant is |語|, the simplified one |语| (cf. also ⟶ Section 6.4). Note that intersystemic variation with respect to Chinese characters results not only from simplification. An example that illustrates general orthographic variation is the character corresponding with respective related morphemes that have different meanings from 'door' to 'family'. The morpheme is written |户| in mainland China and Hong Kong, |戸| in Japan, and |戶| in Taiwan and South Korea. Neither traditional vs. simplified variants nor these latter kinds of regional variants are interchangeable, i.e., only one of them is orthographically correct in a given writing system.

As mentioned above, orthographic variation can also be intrasystemic and, although it always affects entire words (or even phrases, when it concerns variation of punctuation ⟶ Section 5.2), manifests itself not only at the suprasegmental but also at the segmental levels. In German, for example, both variants <Typographie> and <Typografie> are orthographically correct. This apparently gives rise to the segmental variation between <ph> vs. <f> which, however, concerns only (a limited number of) loanwords (cf. Dürscheid 2016b). At the suprasegmental level, there exist orthographic variants of words that differ holistically, i.e., with respect to more than one segment. An English example is <doughnut> and <donut>, a German example *<Majonäse> vs. <Mayonnaise>. Both English spellings are orthographically licensed, i.e., regarded as correct, and for a certain period, the same applied to the German pair of variants. However, as the asterisk highlights, the variant *<Majonäse> was dropped in 2016 by the *Council for German Orthography* responsible for regulating correct spellings and is thus no longer regarded as correct.

4.7 Perspectives on reading processes

So far, in this chapter we have dealt with graphematic concepts that are useful in a structural and functional description of writing systems. Such an approach is static and oriented towards the description of the product, which means that it does not reveal anything about the role that the proposed concepts play in the actual use of writing. For this reason, we now open up a psycholinguistic perspective. The core questions at the interface between psycholinguistics and structural grapholinguistics deal with processes of reading and writing – how these are acquired in a first or second language (for the acquisition of basic graphetic features ⟶ Section 3.4), how they proceed in healthy individuals, and what types of impairments potentially affect them. We will exemplarily take a closer look at the stage of word recognition as a core part of reading processes[126] and present relevant models before turning to the specific question of whether the structural units graph, basic shape, and grapheme as well as concepts such as allography and graphotactics have psychological correlates – and how these are manifested.

4.7.1 Models of word recognition

The psycholinguistic literature on the various stages involved in reading processes is vast, and myriad models have been proposed with the aim of explaining what exactly happens at these stages. Notably, reading is not a uniform process but a complex bundle of processes that includes, among others, eye movements, word identification, syntactic parsing (i.e., the mental building of sentences out of what has been/is being read), and discourse processing, which is necessary "to

---

126 Aside from reasons of space, we focus on reading rather than writing processes firstly because more research has been carried out on reading and secondly because in the literature, as mentioned before, it is often assumed that perception is primary to production (cf. Primus 2006: 10), partially since members of literate communities more often read than write.

connect the meanings of individual sentences into more global representations that support text comprehension" (Rayner and Reichle 2010: 791). In the following, the focus will be on models of word recognition, a process that can itself be broken down into smaller subparts. We choose to highlight this level because even though structural grapholinguistics usually focuses on the segmental level (but cf. Schmidt 2018 for a different, word-based view), what is perceived and recognised during reading is not individual graphemes but larger chunks of texts, in which words – regardless of how elusively they might be defined across writing systems (⟶ Section 4.3.2) – assume a central role.

One of the models that suits the structural graphematic framework described in this chapter remarkably well was developed in the early 1980s: the *Interactive Activation Model* (short IA model), a computational model by James McClelland and David Rumelhart (cf. McClelland and Rumelhart 1981). Prior to the proposal of this model, general consensus was that word recognition works bottom-up as well as serially: readers recognise parts of letters, which in the next step leads to the recognition of entire letters, and this in turn adds up to the identification of words. While this assumption seems perfectly plausible, it has a flaw in that it cannot explain the *word superiority effect* (first described by James Cattell in 1886): readers can more easily recognise letters that are part of existing words (as in <work>) than when they are presented as part of nonwords (as in <wkor>). If readers perceived every letter of a (non)word in sequence, it would be expected that they require the same amount of time to recognise the four letters of both <work> and <wkor>, which are precisely the same set, or that they can recall the four letters of both of these sequences equally well after having perceived and recognised them. This, however, is not the case, and the IA model presented an explanation of this effect.

It consists of the three levels of letter features, letters, and words. The innovation, now, was the assumption that it is not only lower levels that activate or inhibit higher levels in a bottom-up fashion but that the same also occurs in the opposite direction. Thus, if readers have recognised three letters of a four-letter word such as <wo_k> but are missing the fourth letter (e.g., because it is written illegibly or not clearly visible for some reason), this missing letter may be 'filled in' due to the help of top-down information. Specifically, the context of the entire word activates possible letters for the missing spot that would result in well-formed words and inhibits others that would lead to nonwords. At the same time, additional information may come from the lower level of letter features, where specific features activate the letters which they are a part of and at the same time inihibit others. Thus, all three levels provide information necessary for recognition and interact with each other in both directions, i.e., with respective lower and higher levels.

The three levels of the model fit the structural assumption of elementary forms (= letter features), graphs (= letters), and graphematic words (= words). This reveals one of the model's shortcomings: it does not feature visual and functional levels of abstraction at the segmental level (i.e., basic shapes and graphemes). Instead, concrete elementary forms (which are, on top of that, all straight, i.e., feature no curves)[127] are combined to build concrete graphs, and these, in sequence, form words. As will be shown in the following section, however, concrete visual information plays a role only in very early stages of processing, after which it is processed in a more abstract form. Other weaknesses of the model are its neglect to factor in the roles played by both meaning, i.e., semantics, and phonology in word recognition, and that it fails to account for the influence of the context provided by levels higher than the word such as sequences of words (especially collocations) or entire sentences (cf. Eysenck and Keane 2020: 438–439). Furthermore, the model is limited to the recognition of four-letter words; whether it can explain the processing of longer words is uncertain. Lastly, the model overemphasises the importance of exact letter positions. However, it was shown that readers can – without much added effort – recognise words even when (some of) their letters are jumbled, i.e., presented out of order.[128]

Two more types of word recognition models shall be presented here. Like the IA model, both are computational models, i.e., use programs to simulate word recognition. Notably, they both focus on reading aloud and not on silent reading, although the latter is arguably the default. What is of particular interest is the differences between the two models, especially concerning one of the expectations

127 The model utilises 14 'features' – concrete visual segments of basic shapes – proposed by Rumelhart and Siple (1974). All of them are straight lines that are differentiated by the direction in which they are slanted and the spatial position they assume within a basic shape. Thus, what is conceived of as 'feature' here is actually a mixture of elementary forms (i.e., basic visual segments such as lines) and distinctive features thereof (e.g., Watt's proposed feature of [PROG] that characterises elementary forms that are slanted in the direction of writing, cf. Watt 1980); ⟶ Section 3.2.3 for the important distinction of these two concepts.

128 This was shown particularly clearly by an email that started circulating around 2003 and referred to (fake) research at Cambridge University (cf. Velan and Frost 2007: 913). Its first part reads "Aoccdrnig to a rscheearch at Cmabrigde Uinervtisy, it deosn't mttaer in waht oredr the ltteers in a wrod are [. . .]". Because of this email, the fact that readers can still read texts despite letters being jumbled is often referred to as *Cambridge University effect* (cf. http://www.mrc-cbu.cam.ac.uk/people/matt.davis/cmabridge/ for more information; last accessed September 16th, 2021). This effect has attracted considerable attention from the reading research community and has led to the proposal of word recognition models that allow for a certain flexibility concerning the position of letters; examples are the *SERIOL model* (cf. Whitney 2001), the *SOLAR model* (cf. Davis 2010), the *open bigram model* (cf. Grainger and Van Heuven 2004), and the *overlap model* (cf. Gomez, Ratcliff, and Perea 2008).

that most models of reading claim to meet: explaining how reading proceeds in individuals with certain impairments such as the different types of dyslexia.

The first of the models, the *dual-route cascaded model* (cf. Coltheart et al. 2001), assumes two routes for recognising words that are both employed in parallel by healthy readers: a (1) non-lexical route in which grapheme-phoneme correspondence rules are used to arrive at a word's phonological representation, and a (2) lexical route, which is itself divided into two sub-routes, (2a) one that incorporates semantic information and (2b) one that does without it. The other part of the model's designation, 'cascaded', refers to the fact that unlike serial models, it assumes that processing at a following level can begin before processing has been completed at the previous level. The non-lexical route, now, is meant for reading words that are regularly pronounced, as the systematic use of a set of grapheme-phoneme correspondences can account for them but not for irregular pronunciations. Surface dyslexics, it appears, use this route as they have difficulty reading irregular words (cf. Eysenck and Keane 2020: 444). The second, lexical route is based on the fact that trained readers can easily and quickly recognise thousands of familiar words. Put differently, accessing them proceeds more directly than through the mediation of grapheme-phoneme correspondence rules: visual perception of a word activates its entry in the orthographic lexicon, after which its meaning is received in the semantic system (this step may be bypassed depending on the sub-route taken), before finally, its pronunciation is obtained in the phonological output lexicon. The exclusive use of the lexical route can explain what happens in individuals affected by phonological dyslexia: they can recognise familiar words (whether pronounced regularly or irregularly) but, due to the lack of grapheme-phoneme correspondence rules, face problems in processing words unfamiliar to them, both existing words and pseudowords regardless of whether they are regular or irregular.

The second influential type of model is the *triangle* model, also known as *parallel distributed model* (cf. Plaut et al. 1996). It differs from the dual-route cascaded model in a number of crucial ways. Firstly, it lacks lexicons for orthographic or phonological words as well as grapheme-phoneme correspondence rules. Instead, it is conceived of as a connectionist distributed model. It assumes that during reading, three types of information – phonological, orthographic, semantic – contribute simultaneously to word recognition – hence the term 'triangle' in the model's designation. This is supported by evidence showing that while reading, brain regions responsible for phonological, orthographic, and semantic processing are all active (cf. Hoffman et al. 2015). Secondly, while the dual-route cascaded model aims to explain how already acquired reading skills function, it cannot explain their acquisition; this is different in the triangle model, which "learns to produce the correct output (i.e., spoken word or nonword) from the input (i.e., written word or nonword) using back-propagation [. . .] by comparing actual responses against correct ones" (Eysenck and Keane 2020: 447). In the triangle model, too, there are two pathways for the recognition of words: a direct pathway from orthography to phonology and an indirect pathway in which a detour is made through semantics. The former pathway is used when high-frequency regular or consistent words are encountered, whereas the indirect pathway is responsible for reading low-frequency irregular and inconsistent words. This brings us to the concept of consistency, which is not the same as regularity. A word has a high consistency when its pronunciation is in line with those of its orthographic neighbours; crucially, it is irrelevant whether this pronunciation is regular according to grapheme-phoneme correspondences. The pseudoword *taze*, for example, is consistent given that similarly spelled words are all pronounced consistently (*haze, laze, maze*); the same is not the case for *tave*, whose neighbours are characterised by different patterns of pronunciation (*have* vs. *gave*, *rave*, *save*; examples taken from Harley 2017).

How can reading affected by different types of dyslexia be explained with the triangle model? For surface dyslexia, it is assumed that the brain's semantic system is damaged, while for phonological dyslexia, an impairment of phonological processing is assumed. As this implies, the reliance of the three different components (phonological, orthographic, semantic) that work in parallel results in rather straightforward explanations for different types of dyslexia (for a more thorough discussion of how the dual-route cascaded and triangle models account for them, cf. Eysenck and Keane 2020: 449–451).

At this point, two remarks must be made about the presented models. First, it is important to note that they only represent starting points, and for both of them, there exist many modified variants and further developments. They were first assumed on the basis of English, which underlines a certain 'alphabetism' in reading science (cf. Share 2014). This is important to note as English orthography, due to the complexity of its grapheme-phoneme correspondences, is different from most other alphabets, i.e., typologically related writing systems, making it an 'outlier' rather than a good representative of the alphabetic type (cf. Share 2008). Reading in more transparent systems such as Finnish or Greek, for example, relies partially on different processes than in English, and certain assumptions (such as multiple routes of reading) might not be as justified when judged from a more universal perspective. Yet, since most types of writing systems are in some way phonographic (whether alphabetic or not ⟶ Section 6.2), an attempt to transfer these models' tenets to processes involved in reading in these systems appears reasonable. This is notably different for writing systems that are morphographic or have a significant morphographic component (Chinese, Japanese). Different studies have tested the mentioned models' assumptions against the background of these writing systems: Yu and Reichle (2017) compare cognitive processes in reading English vs. Chinese, Wang and Yang (2014) test the models' usefulness in classifying different types of dyslexia in Chinese children, and Sato (2015) asks how the models can contribute to explaining dyslexia in Japanese. Generally, a push for more comparison of diverse systems and the ensuing universality of models is palpable despite being a rather recent phenomenon (take, for example, Frost 2012 for the discussion of a universal model of reading and Verhoeven and Perfetti's 2017 edited volume on literacy acquisition in seventeen different writing systems; cf. also ⟶ Section 6.4).

In a nutshell, it has become clear that not only concerning structural but also for psycholinguistic questions in grapholinguistics, concepts and models must be found that transcend language-specificity. Crucially, this is not meant to undermine the reality that in vastly diverse systems, different concepts and processes may be relevant, but rather accounts for the fact that despite this, all these systems must still have a shared core. This core is arguably more easily found in their use (subsuming their processing) than in their structure, which is why structural assumptions should echo or even be grounded in what we observe in their use. The following section reflects this by asking whether the structural concepts that have been described throughout this chapter have psychological correlates.

4.7.2 Psychological correlates of grapholinguistic units and concepts

The smallest structural level of interest for the study of recognition and reading processes is that of 'letter' features, i.e., subsegmental visual elements that are the building blocks of basic shapes (cf. the IA model above). Notably, this is a level that is not only challenging to investigate in experiments and thus underrepresented in reading research (cf. Finkbeiner and Coltheart 2009: 1) but also one whose very existence is controversial. It is not universally agreed that segments making up shapes – in graphetic terms, we referred to them as elementary forms – even play a role cognitively, with the alternative possibility being that shapes are processed holistically. The first question that comes up in the investigation of perceptually relevant elementary forms, now, is what they could possibly be; this echoes that even in purely descriptive terms, scholars have not agreed on any segmentation of shapes (⟶ Section 3.2.3). In their study, Pelli et al. initially assumed that elementary forms (in their terms 'features') are irrelevant because processing them instead of whole shapes would be inefficient:

> Efficient letter identification demands use of receptive fields that each match a whole letter. If, instead, the visual system uses receptive fields that each pick up a feature that carries

> only a small fraction of the energy of the letter, making individual yea/nay decisions about each feature, then the observer's threshold for the whole letter will be limited by the energy of each feature, a small fraction of the energy of the whole letter. Demonstrating that human observers are highly efficient at identifying letters would rule out independent feature detection as an explanation of their performance, unless letters themselves are features. (Pelli et al. 2006: 4647)

They discarded this initial assessment based on their own results, which suggest that in all of the scripts they tested (Roman script used for English as well as the Arabic, Chinese, Devanāgarī, and Hebrew scripts, and several invented ones), 7±2 'features' were necessary to identify a shape. The reciprocal relation between efficiency of shape recognition and shape complexity points strongly to the perceptual relevance of the subsegmental level: "simple forms are seen efficiently, complex forms inefficiently, as though they could only be seen by means of independent detection of multiple simple features" (Pelli et al. 2006: 4665). Crucially, knowing that 'features' play a role does not reveal to us *which* features are relevant. In that respect, Fiset et al. (2009) and Rosa, Perea, and Enneson (2016) found that junctions between elementary forms (e.g., edges where two lines meet) are important, as deletions at these junctions disrupted the recognition process more than deletions within elementary forms. For example, a part missing from within the stroke making up the shape |I| is a less grave distortion than when the intersection between the two strokes in |X| is deleted.[129] A noteworthy drawback of Pelli et al.'s above-mentioned study (and, in fact, many recognition studies) is that its results may be specific to the given typeface in which the shapes were presented. As implied in the discussion of the descriptive concept of graphetic solution spaces in ⟶ Section 3.2.1, the concrete appearance of graphs does seem to play a role. And if graphs assigned to a given basic shape differ visually, their concrete 'features' also differ automatically. This leads to the vital question of how relevant concrete visual information is in recognition processes. In other words: do we even recognise graphs or is what we recognise already located at the abstract level of basic shapes?

Modern imaging techniques have made it possible to study where and when stimuli evoke a reaction in the human brain. With the help of electroencephalography (EEG), event-related potentials (ERPs) can be studied – the brain's electrophysiological responses to sensory, cognitive, or motor stimuli. They help us better understand the stages at which written signs are recognised and processed.

---

129 This, then, also highlights the perceptual relevance of topology, which had been addressed in descriptive terms in ⟶ Section 3.2.1. Cf. also Changizi et al. (2006) for the role of topology in the makeup of basic shapes in the world's scripts.

As Rey et al. (2009) have found, in the first 100–200 ms after a letter is presented, lower cognitive processes take place: more specifically, subjects perceive that 'something' is located in their visual field and can already identify that it is a specimen of a known category ('letter'). Between 120 and 180 ms after the presentation of a stimulus, higher cognitive activity starts, which is interpreted as a result of readers detecting the visual features necessary for the recognition of a specific letter. When what is studied is the perception of a writing system using Roman script, then at this stage, the activated 'letter' representation is still case-specific (see below). Next, at around 220 ms, an abstract 'letter' representation devoid of concrete visual information is activated, and at 300 ms, subjects can react to the presented 'letter', which means that they have successfully – and consciously – recognised it. Subsequently, they are able to follow instructions that require prior recognition (cf. Thiessen et al. 2015: 177–178; Keage et al. 2014: 83–84).

While everything just described applies to the recognition of letters of alphabets using Roman script, Carreiras et al. (2013) studied Arabic and found that recognition processes involved in reading it follow many of the same principles. Notably, in Arabic, it is not 'letters' (or, more generally, basic shapes, which is why we put 'letters' in quotation marks here) of different cases (lowercase vs. uppercase) which are at some point subsumed by a more abstract representation but rather visually distinct positional allographs. The fact that case variants and positional variants are processed similarly supports the fact that structurally, they are treated as allographs rather than as individual graphemes, and more specifically, that they are both classified as instances of syntagmatic graphematic allography (⟶ Section 4.6.3).

Returning to the concrete visual input, a relevant descriptive concept we had discussed is graphetic allography (⟶ Section 4.6.2). It is based on the fact that the specific material substantiation of writing – whether in handwriting or print – is highly variable. Transferred to psycholinguistics, now, the question is whether the concrete visual appearance of graphs plays a role in the (approximately) first 220 ms of recognition in which no abstraction has taken place yet. Keage et al.'s (2014) study offers interesting findings that suggest the specific appearance of a typeface is indeed relevant. They tested four different typefaces, of which they categorised two as 'fluent' (i.e., easier to read) and the other two as 'disfluent' (i.e., harder to read). The fluent typefaces were Arial and Times New Roman, the disfluent ones Lucida Blackletter ('Lucida Blackletter') and Edwardian Script ('Edwardian Script'). The authors found that the specific typographic makeup of writing affects the first stages of recognition; particularly, for the disfluent typefaces, the abstraction process from graph to basic shape is more difficult for readers. Furthermore, writing presented in disfluent typefaces "captures more attention than material written in fluent typeface" (Keage et al. 2014: 87). Interestingly, the findings also suggest that the concrete visual appearance influences not only the first stage of recognition but also later stages, "which could suggest a feedback loop between abstract letter representations and lower-level visual processing areas" (Keage et al. 2014: 88). In any case, this evidence clearly points to visual appearance being relevant, supporting the assumption of the structural concept of graphetic allography – and the graph level, for that matter.

All these findings suggest that the structural units of graph, basic shape, and grapheme are indeed psychologically real: first, concrete visual information is processed, meaning what is perceived is essentially a graph (or a sequence of graphs). Next, based on the features of this graph, a specific abstract category (a bundle of visual features) is activated – a basic shape. At this point, however, an important question is whether what is recognised is indeed 'only' a basic shape – which is still devoid of linguistic information – or already a basic shape as a specific manifestation of a grapheme that has a specific linguistic function. Most models of reading (cf. the preceding section) assume some sort of interaction of bottom-up and top-down processes, meaning it is likely that the recognition of graphemes (i.e., relations between visual units and linguistic units such as phonemes) facilitates, at a lower level, visual processing including the recognition of basic shapes. In any case, after the recognition of a basic shape has successfully led to the activation of an abstract linguistic representation independent of visual information (= a grapheme), its actual visual identity fades into the background, which is why experimental evidence suggests that after being presented Roman basic shapes, subjects could recall correctly the grapheme associated with the basic shape they had seen but not the basic shape's case (i.e., whether it had been lowercase or uppercase; cf. Friedman 1980).

This immaterial representation that is thus activated has been given various names, among them *abstract letter identity* (ALIs, cf. Coltheart 1981: 247) and *abstract letter unit* (ALUs, cf. Finkbeiner and Coltheart 2009: 4).[130] It is, of course, already a psychological correlate of the grapheme, which leaves open the question of what psychological role – if any – the intermediate step, the basic shape, assumes. In this step, visual aspects such as case (in Roman script and others) and positional variant (in Arabic, or for subsegmental components in Chinese graphemes) are still relevant. Like the feature level, the level of basic shapes is underrepresented in reading research. Psychologically, basic shapes appear to be quite elusive, and only few proposals exist on how to conceptualise them, one

130 While it was initially proposed for Roman script, this concept was also found to be relevant for other scripts such as Chinese, where it was termed *abstract radical identity* (ARI), cf. Li et al. (2021).

of them being the so-called *case-specific letter unit* (cf. Finkbeiner and Coltheart 2009: 5; Petit et al. 2006) that is positioned between specific visual information and abstract linguistic representation. The assumption of such a unit is supported by the fact that specific visual information often differs vastly for uppercase and lowercase graphs (at least in Roman script,[131] cf. |d| vs. |D| as an example), and the processing of such distinct information likely first leads to the activation of abstract units that hinge on this specific visual information before entirely immaterial linguistic units are activated.

Note that the term *case-specific letter unit* is typologically too narrow: firstly, it cannot account for variants for which case is irrelevant as they stem from writing systems with other distinctions, e.g., the above-mentioned Arabic, where it would be position-specific units instead. Secondly, it cannot even account for cases within Roman script such as |g| and |g|, which also do not differ in case yet are distinct basic shapes. A terminological alternative could be *abstract shape units*, highlighting that what we are dealing with here are abstractions of visual information for which, however, configurations of shape do still play a role. Given this as well as the aim of shaping a more universal terminology rid of alphabetocentrism, *abstract letter units* could analogously be renamed to the more general *abstract grapheme units*.

This leads to another crucial open question: what exactly, in psychological terms, are these latter abstract letter units that have been proposed in the literature? More specifically, how do they correspond to the grapheme, and which grapheme exactly, given the many disparate definitions that have been proposed for it (⟶ Section 4.2)? In a nutshell, abstract letter units correspond with a more autonomous grapheme definition in line with the analogical conception. They are, thus, written linguistic units of processing largely independent of phonological information. Ironically, when the term 'grapheme' is used in psychological research, it mostly refers to the referential structural definition of the grapheme in which it is conceived of as a shape (or a sequence of shapes) that represent(s) a phoneme. As psychologist Leslie Henderson (1985: 137–138) notes in his survey of the use of 'grapheme' in psychology, this referential meaning of the term was not always predominant in psychological research. One of its proponents, however, was Coltheart, a primary architect of some of the most influential models of reading (see above). Unsurprisingly, thus, this reading of the term has gradually become largely accepted in psychology. In the most recent edition of a popular

131 This claim is script-specific. In Cyrillic script, for example, the situation is different, where lowercase basic shapes in most cases are simply relatively smaller versions of their uppercase counterparts, cf. |Ш| vs. |ш|.

textbook on cognitive psychology (Eysenck and Keane 2020: 444, emphasis in original), for example, the grapheme is defined as "[a] small unit of written language corresponding to a phoneme (e.g., the *ph* in *photo*)". It is unfortunate that the structural and psycholinguistic definitions do not match, but this does not take away from the fact that the structural grapheme has a psychological correlate in the abstract letter unit (or, as proposed above, abstract grapheme unit).

In sum, during processing, graphs are superseded by basic shapes, which are then superseded by graphemes.[132] Both graphetic and graphematic allography assume crucial roles here. However, it must be stressed once more that recognition does not occur at the segmental level, i.e., segment by segment, but suprasegmentally, meaning that even before all graphemes in a written word have been successfully recognised, the representation of the entire word may have already superseded them (cf. the IA model presented in the previous section). For sequences of graphemes, now, the concept of graphotactics introduced in ⟶ Section 4.5 is essential as it captures rules and regularities of how graphemes may combine in a given writing system. Indeed, graphotactics has become an important topic in psycholinguistic research on spelling in both children (cf., for example, Pacton et al. 2013) and adults (cf. Treiman, Decker, and Kessler 2019), showing that readers are implicitly aware of graphotactic constraints and employ them during reading to judge, for example, whether or not presented strings of graphemes are systematic, i.e., in line with the workings of their writing system.

Needless to say, both structural and psychological concepts have their raison d'être independently of each other. However, given grapholinguistics' interdisciplinarity and the overall aim of constructing a comprehensive theory of writing that accounts for the structure as well as the use of writing – especially since they interact with each other in complex ways –, attempting to align their assumptions with each other, as was done here, appears to be a valuable endeavour.

---

132 This match between descriptive units and units relevant in reading processes also supports the purported primacy of perception over production.

5 Orthography

This chapter is devoted to the systematic aspects of orthography as the standardisation and regulation of writing systems. First, we provide a definition of orthography and present its different types (Section 5.1). The following sections will then address general features of orthographies (Section 5.2), characterise different types of orthographic rules (Section 5.3), and present diverse features that are subject to orthographic regulation in typologically distinct writing systems (Section 5.4). Then, in Section 5.5, the focus will be shifted onto one of the central perspectives in the study of writing and especially orthography: sociolinguistics. To introduce it, the three aspects of system, practice, and ideology will be differentiated (Section 5.5.1) and important general cornerstones of the sociolinguistics of writing will be presented (Section 5.5.2). The next sections will then return to the topic of orthography to shed light on some of its most important sociolinguistic aspects, beginning with how it can represent social action (Section 5.5.3). Four issues are exemplarily discussed: the choice of an orthographic standard (Section 5.5.3.1), the development of an orthography for a hitherto unwritten language (Section 5.5.3.2), the potential social meaning of deviations from the orthographic norm – including their functions as well as attitudes and sanctions associated with them (Section 5.5.3.3), and orthographic reforms and the metadiscourses surrounding them (Section 5.5.3.4).

5.1 Definition and types of orthography

At the beginning of this chapter, it is imperative to define the term *orthography* and properly explain its different readings and uses. The term's etymology helps in underlining what it denotes: its first part derives from Greek *orthós* 'correct'. Accordingly, orthography is about the existence of rules that both urge users of a writing system to write correctly and tell them how to do so. This makes orthography prescriptive and distinguishes it from the descriptive, usage-oriented graphematics treated in the preceding chapter. In turn, the following cannot be emphasised enough: *orthography* is not to be interpreted as an equivalent or synonym of either *writing system* or *graphematics*. Yet, especially (but not exclusively) in the Anglo-American realm, these terms are often used interchangeably, with *orthography* serving as a descriptive term.[133] In our opinion, orthography is only one part of a given writing system. Even more so: as Neef established in his multimodular theory of writing systems (cf. Neef 2015), orthography is only an optional part. Consequently, not every writing system is equipped with an orthographic subsystem or module – as Neef calls it. Such an

133 An example of such a descriptive use of the notion *orthography* also in German grapholinguistics is the title of Nanna Fuhrhop's textbook *Orthographie* (Fuhrhop 2015), which is actually concerned with the graphematics of the German writing system.

https://doi.org/10.1515/9783110757835-005

orthographic module prescribes which of the variants included in the graphematic solution space of a linguistic unit (such as a word) is/are orthographically licensed as the correct one(s). Take, for example, *<phox>, *<foks>, and <fox>[134] as possible spellings for the English word *fox*. All of them are theoretical possibilities of how to represent the word graphematically. However, as the asterisk – commonly used in grapholinguistics to mark incorrect spellings – shows, only <fox> is deemed 'correct' by the module of orthography.[135]

Thus, an orthography is prescriptive, it is an external regulation of a writing system. In rulebooks and dictionaries, orthographic rules codify those spellings that are regarded as correct. It is important to reiterate that not every writing system is equipped with such a module. Instead, there exist different types of writing systems, distinguished by how they are standardised.

First, there are (1) unstandardised writing systems. These are systems without an official orthography. This type is ontologically primary given that new writing systems are often (but not always, see the next type) developed without being standardised right from the start. In many cases, writing systems belonging to this type are, as mentioned, relatively young, having been created only recently, often in the course of a literalisation program intended to bring literacy to a hitherto oral culture (⟶ Section 5.5.3.2). Frequently, however, such systems are, eventually – rather earlier than later – also provided with an orthography, at which point they become (2) writing systems with an artificial orthography. What the relatively vague attribute 'artificial' refers to is best understood when contrasted with the third and final type, which nowadays subsumes the majority of writing systems: (3) writing systems with a naturally developed orthography.

---

134 Usually, in grapholinguistics, no distinction is made between the notation of graphematic units on the one hand and orthographic ones on the other: both are presented in angle brackets < >. Notably, in publications focused on questions of orthography, units that are possible graphematically but not licensed orthographically are often marked with an asterisk – as is done here. In the context of discussions of graphematics in which orthography is not of primary concern, orthographically unlicensed forms are often not specifically marked.

135 In Neef's (2005) original formulation of the graphematic solution space, it only includes possible spellings for phonological strings. However, this alone does not suffice to arrive at the correct spelling of a word. In German, for example, for a word like *Walfang* 'whaling' (the phonological representation of which is /ˈvaːlˌfaŋ/) the graphematic solution space may include, among others, the entirely phonographic spelling <walfang>. Thus, there must additionally exist a second filtering level at which it is decided, for example, whether the word is capitalised as in <Walfang> and, since it represents a compound, whether its constituents are written without separation or separated by a hyphen, as in <Wal-Fang> (both of which are possible in the graphematics as well as licensed by the orthography of German). The internal structure of the graphematic solution space, thus, might be more complex, as it consists of various levels (cf. also ⟶ Section 5.3).

The decisive difference between (2) and (3), i.e., artificial and naturally developed orthographies, is, simply put, whether they are based on the previous use of the system, making time a crucial factor. Writing systems such as German or English, for instance, had existed and been in use without a standardisation, i.e., as writing systems of the first type presented above, for an extended period of time. This gave members of these literate communities the chance and opportunity to implicitly negotiate which spellings they prefer for the words of their language. However, while during this formative time, it was not officially deemed correct or incorrect to choose a given variant for a word, after the very first period of usage, some variants were still employed more commonly than others. Eventually, it was precisely those variants that became conventionalised. Crucially, for this very reason, it is short-sighted to assume that unstandardised systems automatically represent 'non-orthography'. Instead, the analysis of such systems must be more fine-grained and allow for the assumption of a different kind of standardisation – 'orthography' in a broader sense of the word. In this context, Mihm (2016) speaks of premodern orthographies.[136] These were negotiated by members of a given literate community and were, thus, implicit public orthographies. Here, 'implicit' refers to the fact that in most cases, conventions were not explicitly communicated but simply 'silently' agreed on by users.

It is important to note that even without an official and codified orthography, user-based conventions were influenced by many factors, which is underlined by Elmentaler (2018: 144, our translation), who states that "[t]he graphematic variation in premodern manuscripts and prints is by no means arbitrary and random but is rather controlled by numerous factors both external and internal to the language system". Some of the external factors are of regional, social, or confessional nature, to name only a few types. In any case, what must be noted is that in the investigation of such premodern orthographies, it poses a "challenge to detect those underlying rules, which made the written communication successful at that time" (Mihm 2016: 271). What is meant by 'detecting' rules is that they must be reconstructed theoretically because they were not explicitly communicated – they were not written down or, using the technical term, codified, which is a constitutive feature of modern orthographies (⟶ Section 5.2).

From a diachronic perspective, when premodern orthographies were codified as 'official' orthographies, it was often the conventionalised spellings that had been preferred by users up until that point that were elevated to an official status.

---

136 Many of such premodern orthographies of Europe – including English, German, Spanish, Italian, French, Swedish, and others – are dealt with in the different chapters of the edited volume *Orthographies in early modern Europe* (cf. Baddeley and Voeste 2012).

The remaining spellings that were not codified can nowadays only be ‘detected’ in diachronic grapholinguistic analyses. In other words, in such scenarios, the codified orthography grew out of prior usage, out of conventions which users had gradually agreed on. In a nutshell, the biggest difference between an implicit public orthography and an explicit orthography is that the latter 1) is deemed official as it is implemented and enforced by authorities of linguistic policy and 2) is codified (i.e., its rules do not need to be reconstructed since they are written down, e.g., in a rulebook).

By contrast, in writing systems that have been created only recently (for a range of examples, cf. the case studies in Cahill and Rice 2014), it is not possible to base codified rules on prior usage since such usage simply does not exist. This is why orthographic rules in such systems are necessarily somewhat ‘artificial’. There may exist compelling linguistic (or other) reasons to codify given spellings in such young writing systems, spellings that may indeed even be grounded in the systematics of the system, but in the end, they are still not based in the actual use of the system. It is for this reason that, in the context of discussing such newly created writing systems, Karan (2014), in the title of her article, provocatively asks: “Standardization? What’s the hurry?”.

Consider a scenario in which, at least for a limited period of time, users of a writing system were granted the freedom to write graphematically, that is without a “normative expectation” (Karan 2014: 109). In such a situation, they would be allowed to make use of the full set of resources and systematics offered by the system they have acquired instead of being expected to adhere to an orthographic standard right away. In this case, their usage and the variation it exhibits might reveal preferred spellings, which can, in a next step, be regulated orthographically. To revisit an earlier example: before either <phox>, <foks>, or <fox> is codified as correct, users can (mostly unconsciously) decide which variant they prefer, and collective preferences may reveal important features of the writing system’s graphematics and how it is processed. Given these benefits, as Karan (2014: 109) puts it, “[. . .] it may be best to allow a standard to evolve naturally instead of prescribing right from the start how a given language should be written”.

It is paramount to emphasise that the three types presented above are not mutually exclusive. They rather represent different diachronic stages in a writing system’s development: at first, most writing systems – unless they are created in controlled settings of literacy development and thus devised and codified as orthographies right from the start – are commonly unstandardised, i.e., of type (1). When time has passed and the implicit conventions negotiated by users are considered at the point at which an orthography is officially codified, a writing system turns into type (3). If, however, no such time is allowed to pass, or – what must be mentioned as an additional possibility – time has passed but established conventions are purposefully disregarded in the design of an orthography, a writing system becomes one of type (2). Notably, natural orthographies can at any given point in time still be superseded by 'artificial' ones when they are subjected to reforms (⟶ Section 5.5.3.4). In this case, the resulting modified rules may no longer be oriented towards actual usage but instead driven (mainly or exclusively) by other considerations.

Given the fact that orthography is merely an optional part of a writing system, it is justified to ask why the term is so dominant in grapholinguistics, or phrased more specifically: why is it that *orthography* is sometimes used *pars pro toto* as a designation for *writing system*? The reason for this might lie in the dominant and salient nature of orthography. As Schmidt (2018) argues, when a writing system is equipped with an orthography, this orthography inevitably becomes phenomenologically primary as it is more present in our perception and awareness. The reason for this is rather straightforward: once an orthography has been implemented, users have to adhere to it – not in the sense of a law, but in the sense of a perceived social obligation (see the next section). This is instilled in them as early as in literacy instruction, in the course of which pupils do not merely learn to write, but to write correctly, i.e., in accordance with the norm. Thus, right from the start, deviances from the norm are regarded as mistakes, seen as undesirable, and are socially sanctioned in various ways. The consequence is that arguably the vast majority of members of literate communities strive to produce orthographically correct written utterances as best as their respective degree of knowledge of orthographic rules allows them to. Deviance, thus, becomes the exception, whether it is unconscious (in the form of mistakes) or conscious (e.g., in advertising). Both of these types have additional social meaning that is unintended in the former and mostly intended in the latter (⟶ Section 5.5.3.3). This, in turn, leads to the situation that users of orthographically regulated writing systems are, on a daily basis, confronted predominantly with correct writing. In other words, orthographically correct writing becomes (almost) the sole face of writing, its surface representation.

As has already been noted, this also poses a challenge for grapholinguistic research, as users' adherence to the norm effectively conceals the graphematics behind orthography. Indeed, it is impossible to know whether a person arrived at the correct orthographic output through their knowledge of the underlying system[137] (i.e., on the basis of internal norms that incidentally produce correct

---

137 Notably, adhering to the regularities of the underlying system does not necessarily lead to orthographically correct spellings, as these may deviate from graphematic regularities (see below).

spellings) or whether the correct spelling is merely the result of obeying the orthographic rules (i.e., adhering to external norms, cf. ⟶ Section 5.3). This, ultimately, renders deviances from orthography a relevant phenomenon for an analysis of both the graphematics and the orthography of a writing system as well as their interaction.

A central issue that remains to be addressed is raised by the fact that we cannot take orthography as granted. What, then, is the purpose of orthographies as standardisations of writing systems? In her German textbook on orthography, Ina Karg claims that the motivation behind an orthography is "that someone writes down something that can be read by others, and that in doing so, he or she adheres to the given specifications which, to this day, most language communities have agreed on in forms which are binding to varying degrees" (Karg 2015: 5, our translation). In other words, one important goal of an orthography is allowing writers to communicate in a way that ensures they are understood by others who adhere to the same norms. This is necessary in cases in which understandability is not already afforded by the graphematic module alone. A benefit closely associated with this is that orthography usually serves readers as the uniformity of correct spellings should allow for efficient and routine reading.

While this, in principle, is also echoed by Maas, who has worked extensively on issues of orthography, he criticises the bindingness of orthographies (see the next section), i.e., their perception and treatment as law-like rules by authorities of linguistic policy and users alike. The purpose of an orthography, he argues, should not be to sanction what is incorrect but instead to act as a guideline, to support members of literate communities in writing sensibly. This calls for a shift of perspective from the maxim "write by the rules" to "write how you want to be read" (Maas 2015: 3, our translation). It must be noted that this argument stems from a bottom-up perspective that focuses on how people perceive orthography. However, the motivation behind the development of orthographies and their status as rigid sets of rules rather than loose guidelines is crucially influenced by top-down factors (⟶ Section 5.5.3.4).

5.2 Features of orthographies

As standardisations of writing systems, orthographies in general exhibit a bundle of characteristic features, the most important of which which have been described by Nerius (2007, 2020). The features he focuses on are based on an investigation of German orthography; therefore, they may be generalised and applied to other orthographies only with caution. Nonetheless, as we will see, given their broad nature, the majority of them do also apply – to varying degrees – to orthographies of other, including non-alphabetical, writing systems. Orthographies are commonly:

1. externally codified, i.e., authorities of linguistic policy (such as councils, language academies, publishers of dictionaries) decide on and codify orthographic rules and correct spellings.
2. socially binding, i.e., users commonly adhere to orthographic norms and simultaneously perceive them to be binding while ascribing to them the feature of being binding. This bindingness also leads to social sanctions of deviance from the norm.
3. characterised by limited variability, i.e., in most cases there will be one unambiguously correct way of spelling something.
4. static, or, in other words, only changeable in the course of orthography reforms.

The first described feature of orthographies is that they are (1) external and codified standardisations. While 'codified', as already mentioned above, means that orthographic norms are systematically laid down in written form as rules, 'external' refers to two aspects: firstly, orthographic rules are commonly prescribed by outside regulators rather than being internal norms (or better: conventions) that users mainly arrive at through their own implicit graphematic analysis of the writing system (see also the next section). Secondly, 'external' also refers to these very outside regulators: behind most orthographies, there stand authorities who have the power to either decide on the norms or codify them – or both. For the pluricentric German, for example, both of these tasks are carried out by the *Council for German Orthography* (German *Rat für deutsche Rechtschreibung*) in which 41 members from seven countries and regions decide on orthographic regulations and, in the next step, codify them by means of a rulebook, the so-called *Amtliche Regelung* 'official regulation'. While the *Amtliche Regelung* codifies general rules of the orthography as well as distinct spellings in an additional word list (the last version of which includes roughly 12,000 entries), dictionaries – such as the *Duden* or the *Wahrig* – which are not associated with the *Council for German Orthography* codify single words according to the rules laid out in the official regulation. Accordingly, German orthography is codified twice – in an official rulebook including a word list as well as in separate dictionaries. Notably, only the rulebook has a binding and official status; the dictionaries, by contrast, are merely dependent on it, meaning the spellings listed in them are derived from the rules codified in the general rulebook.

The orthography of the English writing system, by comparison, is not regulated by any single external authority, and no official rulebook is published. Instead, the only thing that is available for English that resembles such rulebooks is theoretical reconstructions of the orthography that were developed by scholars – in most cases linguists.[138] Yet, the writing system of English does have an orthography, as there do exist dictionaries in which users can look up spellings that are conventionally considered to be *correct* spellings. These spellings have become conventionalised naturally (see the preceding section) as the English writing system, including its orthography, is a self-regulating system (cf. Berg and Aronoff 2017). However, given that the general consensus is that dictionaries state correct spellings, the publishers of dictionaries still exercise a certain authority over linguistic policy. The fact that there are dictionaries but no official rulebook, now, renders English orthography singly codified (and even this single codification is not 'official'). In this context, it must also be underlined that it is more accurate to speak of *orthographies* of English since there exist a number of different orthographic regulations dependent on the variety of English in question, cf. differences such as those between <-or> and <-our> in <color/colour>, where the first variant is considered correct in American English and the second in British English. The same applies, for instance, to <ß> and <ss> in Standard varieties of German: the former occurs in all varieties but those used in Switzerland and Liechtenstein, where only the latter is used (cf. also ⟶ Section 4.6.4).

Examples of other external regulators include the *Académie Française* for French (as well as the *Superior Council of the French language* appointed in the late 1980s with working on a reform of French orthography), the *Committee of Ministers of the Dutch Language Union* for Dutch, the *Sciences Academy of Lisbon* and the *Brazilian Academy of Letters* in the case of the pluricentric Portuguese orthography, or the *Royal Society of Thailand* in the case of Thai orthography. The latter, for example, not only codifies orthographic rules but also publishes the *Royal Institute Dictionary*, meaning that Thai orthography, similar to German, is doubly codified – however, unlike in German, here, the ruling authority also publishes its own official dictionary.[139] Furthermore, types of codifications can

138 The fact that presentations of English orthography are reconstructions of a system rather than lists of externally codified rules actually blurs the line between graphematics and orthography, which, together with the fact that English orthography is self-organised, might be the reason why in the Anglo-American tradition, *orthography* is often perceived as a descriptive notion (cf. also Meletis 2021a).

139 In this sense, thus, unlike Thai orthography, German orthography is – officially – only singly codified precisely because the dictionaries are not official dictionaries published by the *Council for German Orthography* but instead merely based on the Council's official rulebook. However, as mentioned, the Council does publish a word list with approx. 12,000 entries, which is available at https://www.rechtschreibrat.com/DOX/rfdr_Woerterverzeichnis_2016_veroeffentlicht_2017.pdf (September 17th, 2021) and includes, among others, some (not all, see below) spellings that cannot be reconstructed from the Council's official rulebook.

take many different forms and do not exist only in the form of rulebooks laying out entire orthographies. Other examples from non-alphabetic writing systems include two documents of 1956 and 1964 in which Chinese character simplifications were issued (cf. Hu 2015) and also several guidelines listing kanji for general use in Japanese (from 1946, 1981, and 2010). In a nutshell, in a comparative analysis of orthographies one must consider various types of regulators as well as various types of regulations and, in turn, differing codifications that also depend on the nature of a given writing system's features that are in need of orthographic standardisation (⟶ Section 5.4). Capitalisation, for instance, is of course only an issue in writing systems in which there even is a case distinction.

The second central feature of orthographies is their (2) bindingness. It needs further clarification since – as noted in the introduction to this chapter – orthographies are not binding by law. Thus, there are no legal ramifications if a person makes an orthographic mistake or decides consciously to deviate from orthographic rules. Instead, orthographies are characterised by a form of social bindingness that results from the collective attitudes that members of literate communities have towards an orthography. Commonly, writers perceive an orthography to be binding and simultaneously actively confer to it this status. The special situation that in the case of orthographic norms (unlike for other linguistic norms such as syntactic norms) rules are externally codified leads to a certain awareness of the written norm on behalf of users. In turn, they largely adhere to this norm and thereby contribute to its stability. Furthermore, as the external norms of orthography are being internalised by users, thus eventually becoming internal norms (see below), orthography is, to a large degree, equated with linguistic correctness. Interestingly, users are not only aware of and accept that orthography is binding – they apparently want it to be. They expect an orthography to be capable of telling them which spellings are correct and prefer clear and unambiguous rules rather than, for example, the existence of variants from which they can and actually *must* choose themselves (cf. Sebba 2009: 44).

Another factor that contributes to the bindingness of orthography is that orthographic rules are by default absolute as they distinguish between what is correct and what is incorrect. There are also, however, special norms that are looser in nature and conceive of correctness more as a gradual matter in the sense of degrees of acceptability, thus differentiating between what is more or less correct (cf. the integration of foreign material in Chinese below). Finally, what must also be mentioned is that while the social bindingness of orthography is not associated with legal ramifications, it can still result in the imposition of various social sanctions for users when they unconsciously or consciously deviate from the orthographic norm (⟶ Section 5.5.3.3).

This remark serves as a fitting transition to the third feature: (3) limited variability. Orthographies are characterised by the fact that they leave little leeway for variation. In other words, orthographic rules are typically unambiguous, meaning that in most cases there is one and only one way to correctly spell a given word. In fact, the sometimes-criticised purpose of an orthography is actually to curb variability by selecting a correct spelling from among the variants that are included in the graphematic solution space.[140] This leads to a situation in which variability is considered an undesirable feature of orthographies. In the 2006 amendment of the 1996 reform of German orthography, for example, a number of orthographic rules (such as the placement of commas) were loosened, which resulted in an increase of possible alternative variants that are now all deemed correct. Given that users prefer unambiguous rules and actually expect an orthography to tell them exactly how to write, increased variability and the freedom to choose may lead to frustration and confusion on their part. Thus, as regards the example of German, Nerius (2020: 369) observes that the *Council for German Orthography* has actually reversed its course again and is now likely moving towards a renewed reduction of variability. Of course, if viewed from a different perspective, orthographic regulation nowadays effectively curbs linguistic freedom and creativity, as is observed by Maas (2015). This leaves users who wish to adhere to the norm only with little opportunity to express their creativity. However, users can precisely achieve this very effectively by deviating from the norm (⟶ Section 5.5.3.3).

The level that most writing systems' orthographies are focused on is the word level: both orthographic rules and dictionaries tell users how to correctly spell words. For this reason, as has been argued by some scholars (cf. Stetter 1994; Schmidt 2018), the correct 'spelling' of specific sounds of a language that make up words – when seen from a referential perspective (⟶ Section 4.2.1) – is actually a top-down phenomenon constituted by the spelling of entire words. To illustrate this with an example: without knowing whether we intend to write <rose> as in the flower or the homophonous but semantically unrelated <rows> as in lines of seats in a theatre, we cannot know how to correctly spell the sound sequence /ɹəʊz/. Thus, the sometimes 'vast' variability of possible ways to 'write sounds' in given writing systems such as English and German may result from the variability of writing words, i.e., the graphematic representation of units that have distinct meanings.

140 Notably, sometimes even variants that are *not* included in the graphematic solution space are codified as correct. They are, thus, unsystematic.

A similar situation pertains to units larger than the word: through the orthographic regulation of punctuation in many writing systems, the correctness of written sentences also appears to be regulated by orthographies. While this is basically true, it must be noted that aside from basic rules such as capitalisation at the beginning of sentences in alphabets and the use of sentence-final full stops in many (including non-alphabetical) writing systems, there is a lot of room for punctuation-based variation at the syntactic level. One example is the choice of punctuation marks to highlight parenthetical phrases such as <not the tiger> in <The lion (not the tiger) is the king of the wilderness.>, which could also be enclosed by two commas or two dashes instead of the opening and closing parentheses. Note that at even higher levels, variability increases remarkably: take the textual level, at which there are no explicit orthographic rules of where or how to start a new paragraph, for example.

A remaining issue that is worth mentioning with respect to variability within the norm is the question of what parts of the system it primarily concerns, i.e., which aspects of graphematic representation are primarily regulated. In this context, what can be observed for German orthography arguably applies to most if not all orthographies: licenced variability occurs mostly in the spelling of loanwords or, more generally, foreign material. It is caused by the integration (or lack thereof) of foreign material into the systematics of the native writing system. Accordingly, foreign and 'native' spellings often coexist, as is the case for <Orthographie> and <Orthografie> 'orthography' in German. This is arguably an issue for every writing system and its respective orthographic regulation (if it has one) as it touches on questions such as how foreign graphemes are dealt with. Are they included into the native system as new graphemes or are they substituted by existing native graphemes? Another question concerns units from writing systems that use different scripts and the question of whether they are transliterated. To provide an example from a non-alphabetic writing system, let us describe how the name *Eisenhower* is written in Chinese (cf. also Coulmas 2016: 49–51).

As the writing system of Chinese is morphographic, its graphemes correspond with morphemes. These morphemes, of course, have a signifier, which in most cases is a monosyllabic phonological representation. This 'pronunciation' is not directly indicated by graphemes and users can arrive at it only by knowing how a given morpheme is pronounced. Simply put, what is written is meaning, not sound (⟶ Section 6.3). This poses a challenge for the integration of foreign material, especially proper names (which are commonly not included as entries in dictionaries) given that there are no graphemes that correspond with phonemes, which could be used to write names phonographically and as faithfully as possible. Importantly, no new characters are introduced for writing foreign material, "probably for typographic reasons and/or due to the lack of familiarity with newly created characters" (Hsieh 2015: n. p.), meaning writers must use existing characters. The first challenge users face in this process of integration, now, is to modify a given foreign name so that it conforms to the phonotactics of Chinese phonology (characterised by a limited number of well-formed syllables). Possible ways of doing that for the English name *Eisenhower*, for instance, are *ai-sen-hao-wei-er* or *ai-sen-hao*, depending on whether material of the original word is deleted or new material is inserted (cf. Li 2007: 54). Another example is *wei-mu-bo-dun* or *wen-bu-dun* for *Wimbledon*.

Once a user has decided on Chinese syllables with pronunciations approximating the original, the next and central question is which graphemes should be used to write these syllables. Due to the small number of possible syllables, Chinese is characterised by numerous homophonous morphemes. In writing, these are unambiguously distinguished since graphemes refer to meaning rather than pronunciation. The result of all this is that for most Chinese syllables, there exist a great number of possible graphemes with different meanings. Users have to choose from them when writing foreign material phonographically, for example when writing *ai* in *ai-sen-hao-wei-er*. Notably, for many – especially well-known – foreign names and words, there exist standardised spellings. They can be consulted in lists and handbooks such as *Names of the World's People* published by the *China Translation Cooperation* and are used in more formal and official contexts, e.g., by print media. In more informal contexts, by comparison, users are free to write the names in a way they choose. In that latter scenario, there still exist certain loose 'rules' that users of Chinese may adhere to when deciding on a grapheme for a syllable. For instance, no graphemes that have negative meanings (such as 'death', for example) or meanings with negative connotations should be chosen. Also, graphemes that are visually too complex, i.e., consist of too many strokes, should be avoided. These 'rules', arguably, require rather subjective evaluations, as writers have to decide themselves what counts as a negative meaning and what is visually complex. Some guidelines also recommend using graphemes with low frequency in order to indicate the 'foreignness' of the words in which they are used, a strategy that is, however, discouraged by some institutions such as the *Xinhua News Agency*, which underlines that these are not codified orthographic rules. In other words: while these loose norms may reduce the variants of how to write a given proper name or other foreign material that exist inside the given graphematic solution space, they do not pinpoint to one and only one correct spelling.

The fourth feature of orthographies and the last listed by Nerius is their (4) staticity, which results from their restricted changeability. As established above, an orthography is usually an external codification and not a 'natural' system. Thus, while graphematics can change through being subject to constant use or, put differently, can be interpreted as the dynamic product of this continuous use, orthographic rules are static and, officially, remain the same unless they are officially changed. This curbs any organic changes of graphematics since, when put to use, these changes would represent deviances from the norm that most users attempt to adhere to so faithfully (see above). Consequently, a language's normatively regulated written modality and its dynamic spoken modality potentially drift apart, i.e., become increasingly dissimilar. And this, in turn, raises the question of whether a given orthography should be changed.

Indeed, orthography can potentially be changed – but only by official decree in the process of orthography reforms. These reforms introduce official changes through alterations of the orthographic norm. As (re-)codifications of the existing orthography, they are decided on by an authority of linguistic policy – often the one that had introduced the original orthography in the first place. In the case of German orthography, reforms are helmed, as already mentioned, by the *Council for German Orthography*. In the case of English, by contrast, no such supranational authority of linguistic policy exists (see above). Interestingly, in cases in which there are actual external authorities such as the *Council for German Orthography*, reforms can create certain tensions because users interpret orthography as a common good and, consequently, have (often strong) opinions about how it should or should not be changed. This, in turn, can lead to heated debates (⟶ Section 5.5.3.4), which underlines that orthography is a deeply social matter and, in turn, a central subject of the sociolinguistic study of writing (cf. the final section of this chapter). Given users' strong reactions to reforms, one might argue that they regard orthographies as stable (which is a positive spin on 'static'): through remaining the same, orthographies can provide users with a sense of continuity and (linguistic) security. It is in part the perceived disruption of this stability and the question of who is allowed to prompt it that leads to emotional debates surrounding orthography reforms.

5.3 Types of orthographic rules

To better understand how orthographies function and which kinds of rules are involved, it is necessary to take a closer look at the interaction between three components: the system, its use, and the norm. Although this distinction is of fairly general linguistic nature, our focus will remain specifically on writing. System, here, designates the underlying systematics of a given writing system, i.e., its resources and regularities. Provided that a writing system is actually in use, it is in a state of constant flux. In other words, because it is being employed by writers, it is dynamic in nature and subject to change. For example, new elements can be added to the system when new words enter a language and must then be provided with a written form (see above) or, inversely, older words and spellings may fall out of use. Together, the system and the use that constitutes it form the graphematics of a writing system. However, as established above, not only in writing systems with a codified orthography do conventions, i.e., norms, exist. In the following, we will nevertheless focus on those systems that exhibit official externally codified orthographies – systems in which we are not dealing merely with implicit conventions but with explicit rules. Figure 16 schematically shows how the three phenomena of system, use, and norm partially overlap but also display distinct areas. It is taken from Mesch and Noack (2016), who also discuss norms in writing.

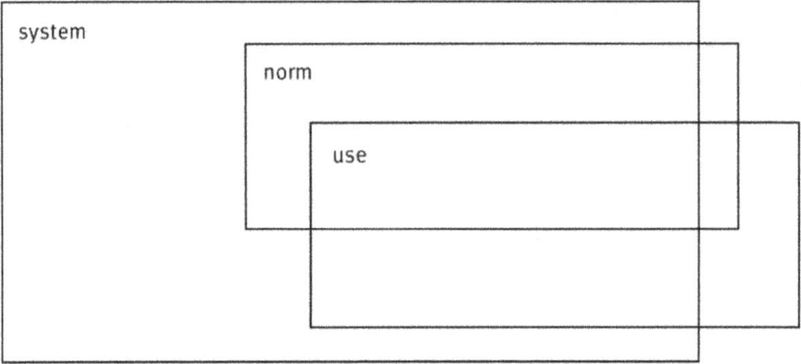

Figure 16: Rough visualisation of the relationship between system, use, and norm, taken from Mesch and Noack (2016: 4).

In the case of writing systems that have an orthography, 'norm' refers primarily to a set of orthographic rules. Importantly, the nature of these orthographic rules is different from the nature of rules or regularities in other linguistic subsystems such as phonology, morphology, syntax, and – crucially – graphematics. These latter regularities are descriptive. Accordingly, what users require in order to be able to evaluate a syntactic unit such as a sentence as 'correct', or more appropriately, as grammatical and/or well-formed, is knowledge about regularities that they have acquired through their prior experience with syntax.[141] In the case of graphematics, this knowledge provides users with internal norms that guide their

141 Note that the question of the genesis of this knowledge is highly theory-dependent (cf. the generative paradigm, for instance). However, at least for writing, 'internal' norms can, in fact, not be guided by an innate language faculty since writing, unlike language in general and speaking (or signing) as its main modality, is never acquired naturally – it has to be learnt. The internal

communicative written behaviour. By contrast, orthography is prescriptive. It is construed of external norms which, in the form of rules (or conventions),[142] tell users what to do in order to write correctly.

Now, in an optimal scenario, orthography overlaps (almost) completely with graphematics. Within this overlap, internal norms and external norms would be identical. We thus call these external norms *pre-existing rules* (or *given rules*), referring to the fact that these rules are already present in the graphematics of the writing system. Notably, in this case, users would likely produce a spelling that is deemed correct even in the absence of a pre-existing orthographic rule since their corresponding internal norm leads to the same result as the external norm. By contrast, rules that do not overlap with the graphematic regularities of the system, i.e., which are located in that part of the norm that does not overlap either with the system or its use (cf. Figure 16), are referred to as *set rules*. They are exclusively of external nature and exist only in their codified form. Indeed, they "only function because of being explicitly recorded" (Ewald 2007: 42, our translation) – they are *set* by authorities of linguistic policy.

This shows: internal norms can be externalised, which occurs when authorities consider the actual use of writing in their design of rules. What this also means is that technically, pre-existing rules (also) become set rules as soon as they are codified. This is most obvious when, due to diachronic changes (such as changes in the pronunciation of words), the original systematic basis and internal norm for the rule ceases to exist. After that, it is not a pre-existing rule anymore and remains only as a set rule. Inversely, external norms can also be internalised. An example is the correct placement of commas: at first, during literacy acquisition and early literacy, it is often governed by external norms. Later, with experience, users often execute it through what they feel are 'intuitions', with these intuitions being precisely external norms that have been internalised. Arguably, external norms not only have the potential to be internalised but are actually expected to be (cf. Kohrt 1990: 118).

Neef (2015) distinguishes between two types of orthography which roughly correspond with the distinction between internal and external norms: systematic and conventional orthography. The basis for this distinction is the graphematic solution space. In Neef's original version, this space includes all those spellings that in a writing system represent a given phonological string, which usually

norms of graphematics, thus, are necessarily of a different nature than the internal norms relevant in other linguistic subsystems such as syntax.

142 In the case that no codified orthography exists in a writing system, conventions known and followed by users also constitute norms. However, in this case, these are implicit norms, whereas codified orthographic rules are explicit norms.

serves as the signifier of one (or more than one) word(s). As we have established, without an orthography, users would not necessarily adhere to any notion of correctness and, thus, all of the variants included in the graphematic solution space would or could be used. However, this is not entirely accurate, as not all of the variants are exactly equivalent, and one crucial factor distinguishing them is, as already mentioned above, usage, and the implicit conventions users in a literate community have agreed on and established among themselves. Neef, in this context, considers the literate community to be a norm-giving authority, and its users' conventions are part of what he calls *systematic orthography*. In the terms introduced above, these conventions are pre-existing rules which, however, are semi-external due to being conventions of the literate community. At the same time, they are implicit as users have not *explicitly* agreed on them, i.e., communicated them to each other. Since they exist without rule explications, i.e., are uncodified, they can only be reconstructed, as Neef notes:

> In any case, it is probable that this authority [= the entire literate community, DM/CD] makes its decisions not in an absolutely random way but that it follows some precepts or guidelines in selecting the specific spelling of a word from its graphematic solution space. It is the task of the linguist to detect these precepts and to reconstruct them as a system. Taken together, these guidelines form an optional component of the writing system theory which I call 'systematic orthography'. (Neef 2015: 716)

With this systematic orthography, we have not yet arrived at the reading of orthography that is predominantly used in this chapter, i.e., orthography as an externally codified regulation of the writing system. This, now, is what Neef calls *conventional orthography*. It is relevant primarily in those cases in which the user-based systematic orthography does not suffice to unambiguously pick one variant from the graphematic solution space, i.e., in cases in which a pre-existing rule results in more than one possible correct spelling:

> This reduction does not necessarily leave one fixed spelling of the word but usually a larger set. Conventional orthography in the end decides which of these options the correct one is. This means that conventional orthography cannot be fully reconstructed as a theoretical system, but only partially. (Neef 2015: 720)

Thus, the choices made by external authorities and regulators – such as the *Council for German Orthography* – are part of conventional orthography. This, in theory, automatically renders all writing systems which have an externally codified orthography conventional orthographies. As Neef remarks, not all rules of conventional orthography can be systematically reconstructed as not all of them overlap completely with the rules of systematic orthography. Crucially, this means that some part of conventional orthography must be considered unsystematic. This unsystematic part includes those set rules that codify as orthographically correct either a variant from inside the graphematic solution space that is not part of systematic orthography, i.e., not the obvious choice according to implicit given rules that users have agreed on, or a variant that is not even found inside the graphematic solution space. An example of the former scenario is the German spelling *<Majonäse> which was codified as a nativised variant of the foreign-looking spelling <Mayonnaise> for the loanword 'mayonnaise' even though users had not actually used it prior to its codification. It also did not come into use after having been codified as correct (probably in part since it was introduced only as a variant and not as the sole correct spelling), so – as the asterisk highlights – it was later rescinded and is therefore considered incorrect again.

The last necessary distinction of different types of rules concerns their scope. Firstly, there are rules that do not operate on single words but are stated in more general terms, with respect to a larger context. They have a global scope and commonly apply to a large number of words. Often, they take the form "in context x, use grapheme y", an example of which is the (phonographic) spelling of <ß> in most German-speaking countries (apart from Switzerland and Liechtenstein): when /s/ occurs after a long vowel or a diphthong and is not followed by a consonant in the stem of the word, <ß> must usually be written. Rules of this kind are termed *general rules* and clearly constitute the most important orthographic rules. However, the fact that in most cases, they fail to apply to all words that include the context stated in them gives rise to the second type, so-called *particular rules* (also referred to as *singular rules*; cf. Ewald 2007: 44–48). In essence, particular rules tell users how to spell exceptions from general rules.

Notably, the distinction between general and particular rules is related to the potential double codification of orthography: general rules are stated in rulebooks while particular rules usually take the form of entries in dictionaries or word lists. Another example from German can highlight this: the official regulations state that "in a few words, the diphthong [aɪ], as an exception, is spelled <ai>" (Amtliche Regelung: 24, § 18, our translation) instead of <ei>, which is its usual spelling. While the rule goes on to list a few of these exceptions, including <Hai> 'shark' and <Mai> 'May', these are by no means exhaustive. Accordingly, the general rule fails to inform users of all the words in which <ai> is written instead of <ei>. This is precisely where word lists and dictionaries and their entries as particular rules come into play.

In the case of the self-organising English orthography, one could argue that particular rules are primary given that what is codified in dictionaries is not a result of decisions made by external authorities and associated rulebooks. Inversely, general rules are of secondary nature as they are reconstructed by linguists on the basis of abstracting a great number of particular rules.

5.4 Orthographic regulation in different writing systems

With the exception of a small number of examples from other writing systems such as Chinese, most remarks up until this point have centred on alphabetic writing. This reflects the fact that with respect to orthography in the sense of a standardisation of writing systems, research has been predominantly alphabeto-centric. In fact, due to the above-mentioned perceived synonymity of *orthography* and *writing system*, often, when works announce that they investigate a given orthography, what they are actually focused on is a description of the writing system. Consequently, actual discussion of prescriptive orthographic regulation is relegated to research on linguistic policy, which is carried out primarily from a sociolinguistic perspective, a crucial perspective that we will adopt below in the final part of this chapter. This, however, leaves open many questions regarding the structural nature of orthographies, and in particular the question of which aspects are even in need of and subject to standardisation in typologically diverse writing systems. This question is vital for a comparison and an understanding of the big picture of how orthographic regulation works.

That this is by no means trivial becomes obvious when looking at Coulmas' (1996a: 379) list of fields frequently regulated in orthographies: grapheme-phoneme correspondence, word division, hyphenation, capitalisation, and the spelling of loanwords. Strikingly, the *only* phenomenon of these that is relevant to many diverse orthographies is the spelling of loanwords and foreign material in general (see above). Meanwhile, all other aspects are specific to given writing systems: capitalisation to those with a case distinction (which not even all alphabets have, cf. the monocase Georgian alphabet), and grapheme-phoneme correspondences are restricted to segmental phonographic writing systems (aside from alphabets, these include abjads and abugidas → Section 6.2.3). Notably, however, even with respect to different alphabets, the orthographic regulation of such correspondences is of vastly varying importance. For example, in alphabets such as Italian and Finnish, these correspondences are rather transparent and straightforward, which is why these systems are often referred to as shallow. In them, fewer orthographic rules are necessary than in, for example, a system such as French, in which these correspondences are opaquer and which is thus considered a deep system.[143]

As for word division, there exist writing systems without it, most prominently Chinese and Japanese. In these systems, thus, word division is no issue

143 For the original definition of deep vs. shallow orthographies in the context of the formulation of the so-called *orthographic depth hypothesis*, cf. Katz and Frost (1992) and → Section 6.4.

relevant in orthographic regulation. Hyphenation, too, occurs in some but not all writing systems: in most writing systems using Arabic script, for example, there is no hyphenation, and there is none in the writing systems of Chinese, Thai, and Korean; it is, by contrast, relevant in Hebrew and Devanāgarī, to name two non-alphabetic systems. What these observations call for is a more fine-grained comparative orthography that considers diverse writing systems. As of yet, such an endeavour apparently does not exist, which is why Coulmas observes (in a publication released twenty years after the one from which his above-cited list was taken):

> [. . .] most research about standardisation and prescriptive grammars has paid little attention to the writing system as a potential variable, that is, to the question of whether different writing systems impact the process of standardisation differently. (Coulmas 2016: 40)

While at this point, we cannot address this question in detail, its relevance for future research needs to be emphasised. In this vein, we will mention a few examples of what can potentially be regulated by orthographies in different systems.

When looking at diverse writing systems, as has been exemplarily done above, it quickly becomes apparent that the subject(s) of prescriptive rules can vary considerably depending on the systems' distinct structures. An illuminating example comes from Chinese in which the stroke order involved in the production of characters is prescribed. This fixed stroke order has been "distilled from Chinese handwriting going back thousands of years" and "contributes to the correct, fast and aesthetic production" of characters (Zhang 2014: 424). Notably, it also reflects an interesting weighting of the relation between graphetics and graphematics: as the basic shapes of the Chinese script number in the thousands, are frequently visually complex and, importantly, can become visually very similar to each other so much so that "a small difference in the stroke pattern can make it look like another character with a different meaning" (Kenner 2004: 76), orthographic regulation is also imposed upon the graphetics of the writing system. This, conversely, is not as relevant in writing systems with smaller inventories of basic shapes and graphemes, such as alphabets, where orthographic regulations largely disregard graphetics and are focused exclusively on graphematics.

The obvious starting point for an investigation of the aspects regulated in different writing systems appears to be their respective graphematic solution spaces, and in particular their sizes. The central assumption is the larger the graphematic solution spaces for relevant units (in most systems, these are words), the more orthographic regulation will be needed. An example that is noteworthy in this respect is the writing system of Japanese, which represents a unique mixture of scripts that assume different graphematic functions: the two kana scripts are used syllabographically while the kanji have morphographic functions. In theory, now, every Japanese word could be written exclusively with syllabographic kana graphemes, and this is indeed sometimes done in instructional material for literacy acquisition.[144] Although the purposes that the different scripts serve in the system as a whole are rather clear, the possibilities that the system's entire combined resources offer are often exploited in playful and creative ways. Apparently, the notion of orthographic 'correctness' differs markedly from that in most alphabetic systems. In this context, Terry Joyce and Hisashi Masuda discuss whether the notion of graphematic solution space might be applicable to Japanese or not. As they note:

> Certainly, there are 'standard' orthographic conventions associated with each component script, which, taken together, largely establish the foundations of contemporary written Japanese. However, it is also essential to realize that these are far from absolute rules that can never be deviated from, and, thus, [. . .] graphematic variation – the co-existence of multiple graphematic representations – is a prevailing characteristic of the [Japanese writing system]. (Joyce and Masuda 2019: 248)

To arrive at similarities and differences between orthographic regulations more systematically, six aspects listed by Coulmas (2016: 41) appear useful: the question of (1) sequence concerns the order of elements of a writing system. The (2) type of codification examines, for instance, how entries are arranged in dictionaries. This is often closely associated with their sequence, e.g., that in English dictionaries, entries start with A, proceed with B, etc. With (3) key principles of orthography, Coulmas most likely refers to the most important graphematic regularities of writing systems. In our approach, this would mainly be their graphematic solution spaces and the graphotactics underlying them. Next, he lists the issue of (4) purism, i.e., whether there are tendencies to assimilate foreign material to suit the systematics of the native system or to rather leave it in its original form (cf. the above-mentioned German example *<Majonäse> vs. <Mayonnaise>). Another aspect is the relation between the writing system and (5) linguistic change. Finally, Coulmas mentions the sociolinguistically relevant phenomenon of (6) diglossia, i.e., the question of whether the written and spoken modalities in a language are used for distinct purposes.

As he applies these aspects to different writing systems, Coulmas reveals that some of them are more prone to differences between orthographies than others (and he offers an insightful summary table, cf. Coulmas 2016: 52). The two that

144 As it is the alternation between kana and kanji that offers cues as to where word boundaries are located, text presented solely in kana lacks these boundaries, making oral recitation – in the course of which word boundaries are 'discovered' with one's voice – a crucial part of elementary reading instruction in Japan (cf. Sakamoto and Makita 1973).

show considerable variation are purism and the key principles of orthography, leading back to the graphematic solution space and the system-specific challenges of the graphematic representation of words across different writing systems. In any case, what the considerations in this section show is that a comparative investigation of orthography, which is still in its infancy, is a worthy endeavour and a necessity in the investigation of the "question whether the structural differences between them [= writing systems, CD/DM] have any implications for prescriptive rules" (Coulmas 2016: 41).

5.5 Perspectives from sociolinguistics

5.5.1 Systems, practices, and ideologies

One of the main goals of sociolinguistics is to "strive towards an empirically-based description (rather than prescription) of everyday language use" (Lillis and McKinney 2013: 419). Accordingly, with respect to writing, sociolinguistics describes how society affects writing or, more loosely, in which ways the two interact.

To understand how sociolinguistic perspectives relate to the structural perspective adopted in this book, it is useful to refer to the following three aspects (cf. Busch 2021): as has become evident, the main focus of this book is the structural description of writing systems as precisely that – systems. It includes questions such as: How are they built? What units are they comprised of? Which concepts play a role in their analysis? And how can the diversity of the world's writing systems be dealt with in a unified framework? As important as these linguistic questions are, as already outlined above with respect to orthographies, no system that is in use is static. Thus, a complete study of the spoken language – and the same applies to writing – must consider not only the system but, given that it is heavily influenced by its users, also its use. Furthermore, it must be investigated how usage affects linguistic structures (and vice versa, how linguistic structures affect their use). To apply this specifically to writing, from a sociolinguistic perspective, the most important aspects writing systems are affected by are (1) how they are used (for sociocommunicative purposes) and (2) what beliefs people hold about both them as systems and about how they are used.

The first of these aspects deals with practices of use. When using language – regardless in which modality – users engage in many different practices. The nature of these practices depends on, among other factors, the context, possible other interlocutors and addressees, and the degree of formality. Speaking at a conference in front of an audience is a different communicative practice than writing a letter to a friend (⟶ Section 2.4). When the focus is specifically on the use of writing, communicative practices are referred to as literacy practices (cf. Street 1993). They come in many forms and include everything users do with, by, and through writing. Aside from the mentioned writing of letters, examples include keeping diaries, jotting down shopping lists, filling out forms, carving initials into the bark of trees, composing text messages or emails, taking notes while listening to a lecture, spray painting graffiti, and working on scientific papers. While these practices focus on text production, practices that focus on text reception include immersing oneself in books, skimming newspaper articles, and reading bedtime stories to children. Crucially, literacy practices such as the ones just listed are not universal but vary depending on factors including region, period, or culture (⟶ Section 2.5). In sum, all communicative practices and the circumstances in which writers and readers (like speakers and listeners) engage in them are highly relevant from a sociolinguistic perspective.

But the sociolinguistic study does not stop at that point. Not only do we use writing, we also have certain attitudes towards it. And these attitudes concern both writing itself (for instance the difficulty of comma rules) and – arguably primarily – different literacy practices. Indeed, we often reflect on and discuss these practices, an example being the increasing popularity of emoji use. Many people have a strong – either positive or negative – opinion on this topic, making it the subject of debates in the media and public forums (such as online message boards or comment sections on social media). This 'thinking and talking about the system and its use' reveals people's ideologies with respect to writing.[145] Indeed, "considerable metadiscursive activity with regard to 'writing' – what it is and what it should be – is clearly evident in both public discourse and in the field of sociolinguistics" (Lillis and McKinney 2013: 420), meaning both users and scholars have certain ideologies when it comes to writing.

Take another much-discussed example in this respect: the deviation from orthographic norms in what is often considered 'informal' writing, e.g., in WhatsApp or on social media. While some people do not mind the omission of punctuation or the neglect of capitalisation, to name two widespread practices, others do, which underlines that attitudes most often involve evaluations of some

145 Thinking and talking about the use of language or writing means engaging in metapragmatic discourses. Pragmatics – as a linguistic subdiscipline – deals essentially with language use and how it contributes to linguistic meaning. When we talk about certain communicative (i.e., pragmatic) practices and thus make them the focus of our conversation, we are situated at a metapragmatic level. At yet another metalevel, we have metadiscursive discourses, which refer to, simply put, thinking and talking about how people think and talk about communicative practices.

sort. In sum, language ideologies and, by analogy, writing (system) ideologies subsume all attitudes towards and beliefs about languages and writing systems. They interact with both the structure of systems and practices of using them and thus become a central sociolinguistic matter.

5.5.2 The sociolinguistics of writing

Now that we have discussed usage-based aspects in general terms, let us turn to several issues faced by the sociolinguistics of writing, a subdiscipline that has emerged only recently. In 2013, sociolinguists Theresa Lillis and Carolyn McKinney assessed that "writing has largely been ignored as a significant empirical object of study in sociolinguistics" (Lillis and McKinney 2013: 415). Instead, the focus was on speech, a situation highly reminiscent of the general linguistic stance towards writing (⟶ Section 1.2). Consequently, the sociolinguistics of writing is still practically in its infancy. In the introduction to the writing-themed special issue of the *Journal of Sociolinguistics* edited by them, Lillis and McKinney outline some of the challenges that this paradigm of studying writing must overcome. Specifically, they name three perspectives instrumental in achieving a full-fledged sociolinguistics of writing. The first is an (1) ethnographic perspective. As already mentioned briefly in ⟶ Section 2.5.2, various paradigms such as the New Literacy Studies attempt to describe "the ways in which writing figures in everyday lives" (Lillis and McKinney 2013: 422), i.e., to capture the above-mentioned literacy practices in all of their variety and thus give a realistic picture of the use of writing. Two different methods are predominant: studying literacy practices in different communities such as those of villagers in Iran (cf. Street 1984) – to give an example – or studying literacy practices in specific domains such as prisons (cf. Wilson 2000). Sometimes, studies focus on both a specific community and domain, e.g., Häcki Buhofer's (1985) description of literacy practices in a Swiss industrial plant.

Next, following Lillis and McKinney, the (2) educational perspective is of relevance. Literacy is often seen through the lens of education simply because it is considered the desired outcome of formal schooling. A central question here concerns the observation that some individuals are more successful than others in mastering the literacy practices taught in school. The assumption that has frequently been made in this respect is that success, here, depends on the (dis)similarity of the literacy practices of formal schooling and those practiced in the home and/or local communities. Specifically, people whose 'home literacy practices' have been similar to those relevant in school are advantaged. Against this background, the educational perspective comes to the forefront "in considering ways in which sociolinguistic understandings can be used to redress inequalities in educational experience and outcomes" (Lillis and McKinney 2013: 422).

It must be stated here that the sociolinguistics of writing, and especially this educational perspective, is plagued by a normative view that must actively be challenged – a view that distinguishes sharply between 'standard' and 'error' (cf. Lillis and McKinney 2013: 425). One consequence of this view is that in sociolinguistics, writing has long been reduced mainly to the role it plays in the standardisation of languages (where it does admittedly play a vital role, cf. ⟶ Section 5.5.3.1). Another important reflection of this normativity is that writing, unlike speech, is often judged as correct or incorrect. Indeed, this normative expectation that we have of writing is the very foundation of the notion of orthography that is the topic of this chapter. However, judging writing as correct or incorrect from a systematic orthographic perspective (i.e., the system) differs sharply from judging writing from the perspectives of practice and ideology, to return to the three aspects mentioned above. Omitting punctuation or neglecting capitalisation in WhatsApp messages may in all cases be orthographically incorrect, but at the same time, from the perspective of literacy practices, it cannot be evaluated as either 'standard' or 'error' but rather as more or less appropriate/fitting for a given context. In one of the following sections, we will discuss such 'deviances' from the 'norm' that are used to evoke special social meanings. In this context, it is crucial to interpret the term 'deviance' as well as the stance of correct vs. incorrect that it evokes from the perspective of the system. As mentioned, if seen from the perspectives of practice and ideology, on the other hand, such choices are not deviances but have important sociolinguistic functions.

The example of WhatsApp messages already introduced the (3) digital perspective (cf. Lillis and McKinney 2013: 423–424). It is quickly gaining currency as new media are becoming more and more popular and important. Considering the effects of digitalisation is vital for a sociolinguistics of writing insofar as the shift from analogue to digital written communication affects the system as well as practices and ideologies of use. Also, it challenges sociolinguistics to change its predominantly monomodal view, which was already insufficient for many analogue products of writing such as print advertisements that combine text with other modes. In general, writing, much like speech, is frequently not only verbal but embedded in complex (combinations of) signs that include non-verbal material such as emojis, photos, etc. (cf. also Heyd 2021). Even more so, it is not only this additional material that is non-verbal but certain aspects of writing itself: as shown in ⟶ Section 3.3, certain features such as typeface (or style of handwriting), size, or colour are inherent to writing but do not provide linguistic information in a narrow sense.

5.5.3 Orthography as social action

Starting with this section, we will return specifically to the concept of orthography and reconsider it from a sociolinguistic perspective. As established, unlike the graphematics of a writing system, which is unconsciously shaped by all members of a literate community but accessible only through theoretical reconstructions by grapholinguists, orthography is palpable by existing in the form of rules and involves everyone as everyone is expected to learn, master, and adhere to these rules. This connects the structural and social sides of the orthographic medal. Most things that users do by means of writing are done through the filter of orthography in a sphere in which normativity has become the benchmark. Crucially, here, it is not orthography in the sense of the systematic norm constraining the resources of a writing system that is of primary relevance but orthographic ideologies, i.e., what users *believe* to be orthography, what they believe is correct. In other words, writing is "looked at through the lens of dominant ideologies about what completed writing should be/look like" (Lillis and McKinney 2013: 429). This notably also applies to situations in which writers willingly break the rules, such as in dialect writing, online communication, or in advertising. In cases in which users actively engage with or negotiate orthography, it is, in essence, social action in the form of written communication (see this section's title).[146]

Accordingly, in the following subsections, we will mention exemplarily a range of different phenomena that reveal the social nature of orthography: the choice of an orthographic standard among several varieties of a language (⟶ Section 5.5.3.1), the development of an orthography for a hitherto unwritten language (⟶ Section 5.5.3.2), the social meaning of deviations from the systematic orthographic norm that renders 'deviation' a form of social action (⟶ Section 5.5.3.3), and the question of how orthographic regulations can be changed through orthography reforms, including a discussion of types of discourses surrounding these reforms (⟶ Section 5.5.3.4).

5.5.3.1 Choice of orthographies and scripts

What all questions discussed in the following have in common is that they are highly affected by language-external factors of various nature: politics, religion, or economy, to name only a few. The first of these questions concerns the genesis of orthographies, i.e., the question of how they are designed and implemented in the first place. This often entails choosing the variety of a given language that is to

146 Cf. also the title of the edited volume *Orthography as social action – Scripts, spelling, identity and power* (Jaffe et al. 2012).

serve as the standard variety since frequently, languages exhibit a number of different (regional, social, . . .) spoken varieties. Notably, prior to the creation of an official orthography, these multiple varieties may also be used in writing but, crucially, all writing technically occurs in an unstandardised manner as no codified orthography exists (yet). At one point, a need for a written standard and its codification may arise, for example because a common orthography "may enhance the status and prestige of [a] language and may help create a sense of unified identity" (Jones and Mooney 2017: 1). In this context, the central question that emerges is which variety should be chosen as a standard. It can become a "contentious and divisive issue" (Jones and Mooney 2017: 7) as the choice authorities of linguistic policy ultimately make may be interpreted as "deliberate favoritism" (Karan 2014: 116) through privileging one variety (and its users) over the others.

This impression of favouritism is arguably most pronounced in the (1) *unilectal approach* in which a single variety is chosen to serve as the basis for a standard. Potential reasons underlying the decision to choose it can be its large number of speakers or that it is spoken in a region of particular political relevance. While the danger of coming off as favouritism represents a risky drawback, the choice of a single variety as basis of a language's orthography simultaneously fulfils a unifying function that is not only symbolic politically but may also be linguistically functional. The latter is the case in Chinese: despite the fact that its different spoken varieties are sometimes considered separate languages due to their mutual unintelligibility, 'Chinese' is commonly regarded as one language thanks to its unified writing system, which allows all writers of Chinese to communicate with one another.[147]

By contrast, in the (2) *dialectal approach*, multiple orthographies are devised based on different varieties. While this may please speakers of these different varieties, it bears the risk of conveying social fragmentation and simultaneously diminishes the linguistic usefulness of each standard as it only applies to its respective variety instead of to the whole language.

There are also a number of compromises, the first of which is the (3) *multilectal approach* that seeks to reconcile features from various varieties in one standard. This potentially supports building a common identity for the speakers of different varieties but, in fact, only replicates the divisive problem of choosing between varieties at a lower level as "the question of how best to accommodate

---

147 Speakers of the different mutually unintelligible varieties can still communicate through the written modality due to the fact that the Chinese writing system is morphographic. The morphemes represented by graphemes are, however, pronounced distinctly in the varieties.

different varieties within a single orthography leads directly to issues of power and authority" (Sebba 2007: 112). Thus, this approach circles back to the favouritism of the unilectal approach. Crucially, it also poses a challenge from a linguistic point of view, for example when a feature that is prominent and salient in one variety and therefore included in the orthography is redundant in another variety, in which case the result is a suboptimal match between the graphematics and the orthography.

The (4) *common-core approach* is another compromise, although one that has seldom been implemented successfully in the past. Its goal is, as the name suggests, to reconstruct the common historical core of a language's different varieties. This core then serves as the basis of the orthography. While this approach could help ease tensions given that no single dialect is favoured over another, it has a quite significant linguistic drawback: no users of any variety are familiar with the standard as it is 'artificial' to all of them and thus may not fulfil the functions expected from a standard, including the facilitation of literacy instruction; instead, the common-core approach introduces a complex situation of diglossia in which spoken varieties and the written standard are distinct.

The preceding remarks concerned the choice of one variety among a number of varieties in the design of an orthography. By contrast, a special situation arises when there is no definite choice but multiple written varieties are already in use simultaneously, a phenomenon that has been termed *biscriptality*. It is highly relevant sociolinguistically since users are, in different situations, still often faced with having to choose from a language's coexisting available varieties. This choice is in most cases not arbitrary but guided by certain factors. Specifically, biscriptality is defined as "the simultaneous use of two (or more) writing systems (including different orthographies) for (varieties of) the same language" (Bunčić 2016: 54). At the structural grapholinguistic level (⟶ Section 4.6), three types of variation can be distinguished: (a) between different variants of one script, which Bunčić calls *glyphic variants*, e.g., the typefaces Times New Roman and Arial in Roman script, (b) between different scripts such as Devanāgarī and Arabic script, and (c) between different orthographies, e.g., the orthographically regulated use of <ß> vs. <ss> in German varieties. The second and more important level in Bunčić's typology, however, is the sociolinguistic level at which it is not relevant *what* is alternating but *how* and *why*. With respect to these questions, he distinguishes (1) privative, (2) equipollent, and (3) diasituative variation.

A (1) privative opposition is constituted by variants one of which exhibits a feature that the other lacks. Which of the two is used can then depend on a variety of factors including register, social class, and writing material. Here, Bunčić speaks of *diglyphia* (for glyphic variants), *digraphia* (for scripts), and *diorthographia* (for different orthographies). By contrast, in an (2) equipollent opposition, two variants are distinguished by the fact that they each are characterised by a different feature, an example being the alternation between Devanāgarī and Arabic script in the writing systems of Hindi and Urdu, respectively, where Devanāgarī is associated with the feature [Hindu] and Arabic with [Muslim]. Reasons for choosing either variant can include, obviously, confessional or religious reasons but, in other cases, also geographic or ethnic ones. Depending on which structural level is affected, Bunčić terms the corresponding phenomena *glyphic pluricentricity*, *scriptal pluricentricity* (as in the case of Hindi vs. Arabic script), and *orthographic pluricentricity*, the latter of which is, for example, exhibited by the use of traditional Chinese characters in some regions and simplified ones in others. Finally, in (3) diasituative oppositions, there is no clear-cut criterion that can predict the choice of a given variant. Bunčić offers as an example the Serbian writing system in which, in addition to confession, a number of other factors can influence the choice of either Roman or Cyrillic script: "the number of participants in a communicative setting; the relationships among participants concerning age, education, sex, etc.; time and duration of the communicative act; the topic; the degree of publicity; and many more" (Bunčić 2016: 61). This type of diasituative variation is called *biglyphia*, *bigraphism*, or *biorthographism* depending on the structural grapholinguistic level in question.

In a nutshell, by combining the grapholinguistic and sociolinguistic dimensions, Bunčić constructs a fine-grained typology for the description of sociolinguistically motivated variation, and the comprehensive volume *Biscriptality: A sociolinguistic typology* (Bunčić, Lippert, and Rabus 2016) provides detailed and illustrative examples of each type.

5.5.3.2 Literacy development

A context in which orthography's double status as social action and core concern of linguistic policy reveals itself very clearly is so-called *orthography development* (Lüpke 2011), which is sometimes also – more neutrally – referred to as *literacy development*. It refers to the process in which a writing system is developed for languages that hitherto were only spoken. This is especially relevant for endangered languages (cf. Jones and Mooney 2017) and indigenous languages (cf. Cocq and Sullivan 2018). Considering the term 'orthography development', it can be argued that in many cases, it is indeed an orthography that is created right from the start rather than a 'mere' unstandardised writing system. The main goal of literacy development is to bring literacy to people, which a written standard (including the possibility of immediately making available instructional material such as textbooks and dictionaries) is believed to support. This is the reason that, as Karan has criticised (→ Section 5.1), there often is no period of unstandardised graphematic usage of writing prior to the implementation of a binding orthographic standard.

In general, literacy development represents a fruitful context for the investigation of the sociolinguistics of writing. From the recent past until this day, it has occurred in controlled environments and many instances of it are well documented in the literature. The environments are controlled given that literacy development is often conducted and/or overseen by so-called *script mediators* (alternative terms are *orthography mediators* or simply *orthographers*, cf. Sebba 2009; Jones and Mooney 2017) who are most often linguists or experts from other fields invested in language. They enter into communities from the outside with the goal of developing a writing system either with or without community involvement. With respect to this latter question, it is often emphasised just how vital input from the local community is and that devising a writing system without it can have detrimental effects (cf. Karan 2014: 132).[148] Community involvement is expected to heighten the acceptance of the new writing system which is a (if not *the*) key factor in the success of literacy development. Jones and Mooney list important factors that can increase the acceptance on behalf of communities:

> (i) the usefulness of a literacy programme must be recognized and approved by traditional community members (e.g., elders, politicians, religious leaders); (ii) local contexts for literacy must be identified and approved by community members; (iii) there must be continued widespread use of the [. . .] language; (iv) there must be support for the maintenance of local literacy by (local) educational systems. (Jones and Mooney 2017: 6)

A special situation arises when unstandardised writing systems already exist and are in use in (parts of) these language communities. These systems are referred to as *legacy orthographies* (cf. Jones and Mooney 2017: 30) and must imperatively be considered in the design of the new and standardised writing system to ensure that people who use them do not feel disregarded or overlooked and that they accept the newly created writing system.

In the process of designing a writing system/an orthography, involved community members often express a slate of socioculturally motivated wishes for how it should be structured and what factors need to be considered. In this context, Peter Unseth (2005) lists three prominent wishes: (1) identification with a group, (2) distanciation from a group, and (3) participation on a larger scale. All these

148 For examples of community involvement, cf. Bow (2013), who describes how native speakers of four Bantu languages of Western Zambia worked on writing systems for their respective languages (Fwe, Mashi, Makoma, and Kwangwa), or Page (2013), who, together with community involvement from two Southeast Asian language communities, worked on first orthography proposals for their languages.

needs highlight the fundamentally social nature of orthography. More specifically, the first two frequently involve asymmetrical and complex hierarchical relations between a dominant and a dominated group that often simultaneously represent distinct language communities. Here, the dominated community either wants their writing system/orthography to be similar to that of the dominant group to signal belonging to said group or, on the contrary, wishes to indicate distance from the dominant group by choosing a dissimilar writing system. Distance is sometimes desired when communities wish to "create ideological independence from former colonial powers" (Jones and Mooney 2017: 25), ostentatiously underlining the frequently involved power asymmetries. The third and final objective addressed by Unseth describes a community's wish to be able to use their newly gained literacy to participate in global communication. This is often the major driving force behind literacy development in the first place as the possibility of communicating through writing "clearly influences a group's preparedness to interact with other groups outside their circle, regionally or internationally" (Unseth 2005: 27).

Another crucial factor that must be mentioned in this context and that is related to the wish of participating on a larger scale is not primarily social but also has to do with hegemony and power: technology. To make communication possible, technology (computers, printers, smartphones, etc.) must not only be available but the devised writing system/orthography must also be suitable for it (cf. Cahill 2014: 9). This may lead to the decision of adopting scripts that are already encoded in Unicode,[149] in most cases Roman script, which (due to the tight association of Roman script with alphabets) also often entails the choice of the alphabetic type.

5.5.3.3 Deviance as social action

This section addresses the question of how non-orthography, i.e., writing that is located outside of the norm, can convey significant social meaning precisely on the grounds of breaking orthographic rules. Note that, as mentioned above (⟶ Section 5.5.2), the sociolinguistics of writing wants to challenge the notion that writing is always 'standard' and everything that deviates from the stand-

149 Unicode is "the universal character encoding, maintained by the Unicode Consortium. This encoding standard provides the basis for processing, storage and interchange of text data in any language in all modern software and information technology protocols". It "covers all the characters for all the writing systems of the world, modern and ancient. It also includes technical symbols, punctuations, and many other characters used in writing text" (http://www.unicode.org/faq/basic_q.html, accessed September 20th, 2021). A list of all scripts and information on whether they have already been encoded in Unicode or not can be found at http://www.worldswritingsystems.org/ (accessed September 20th, 2021).

ard is considered an 'error'. Thus, it is important to note that here, we interpret 'deviance' not as deviance with respect to the use of writing but with respect to the system, i.e., the codified orthographic norm of a writing system. The focus is on how deviance is used in literacy practices and what ideologies are associated with it.

First, a number of necessary distinctions between different ways of deviating from orthographic rules must be made. Following Corder (1967), we differentiate between errors and mistakes. Regarding orthography, errors are deviations from the norm resulting from the fact that a person lacks the knowledge required to spell (part of) a written utterance – e.g., a word – correctly. Errors are, thus, non-corrigible in that people will not become aware of them even when, for instance, they proofread what they have written. Mistakes, on the other hand, are deviations that occur even though a person knows how to spell a word correctly. A typical example is the typo as the result of mistakenly typing the wrong key on a keyboard. While both errors and mistakes, especially the way how they are perceived, are socially relevant, social meaning comes to the forefront when mistakes are not unintentional and unconscious, as is the case for typos, but intentional and conscious. An example of intentional deviance is when writers actively choose to write an English email entirely in lowercase, ignoring capitalisation in the contexts in which it would be required – and do this not because they do not know how to capitalise correctly but because they wish and prefer to do so (for several possible reasons).

Another distinction is paramount: that between licensed and unlicensed variation. We are dealing with the former when there is an orthographically licensed choice, as in German <Orthographie> vs. <Orthografie>, both of which are officially codified as correct (see above). This means that a writer must choose between them. And while neither choice deviates from the norm, both have the potential to bear social meaning, for example when one variant is seen as more old-fashioned or traditional (<Orthographie>, with <ph> conforming to the old, 'original' spelling of Greek loanwords with /f/) while the other, in this case newer variant (<Orthografie>, which was licensed as orthographically correct at a later point in time) is being perceived as more modern. There are numerous factors like this such as regional or even ideological connotations that licensed variants may evoke. Unlicensed variation, by contrast, occurs when users choose a variant that is not orthographically licensed and thus actively deviate from the norm. Notably, this may still happen in a systematic fashion. In fact, as Sebba (2007: 32) notes, the deviation must "be close enough to the norm to be recognisable to other members of the language community". In other words: one cannot simply substitute an <u> for an <x>, for example, or write *<whule> instead of <whale>. In terms of the structural grapholinguistic framework presented in this book, the deviation should be located inside the graphematic solution space (⟶ Section 4.1).

From the perspective of potential social meaning, that part of the graphematic solution space that includes the variants not codified as orthographically correct can be conceived of as the "zone of social meaning" (Sebba 2007: 34). As mentioned above, since they are located inside the graphematic solution space, Sebba (2007: 46) observes that variants used for conscious and intentional 'mistakes' are "not necessarily unsystematic". In a nutshell, the deviation must be designed in a way that "allows the original meaning to be conveyed, along with additional social meaning which derives from defying the conventions" (Sebba 2007: 30). This means that the question of how much potential a writing system offers for socially meaningful deviations from orthography ultimately depends on the size of its graphematic solution space. If it, for example, overlaps almost completely with the codified orthography, which is the case in transparent writing systems such as Finnish, the choices users may have to deviate are more limited than in a system in which the graphematic solution space provides more variants for a given utterance.

An example of a deviation that carries additional social meaning is *<skool> for English <school>, for which Sebba (2007: 30–31) remarks that it "has the merit of being recognisable as a representation of the word 'school', but at the same time defiantly refusing to conform to the standard spelling form for this word". In general, for alphabetic writing systems, numerous strategies of consciously deviating from the norm exist (cf. Sebba 2007: 34–41). They include the use of

(1) grapheme-phoneme correspondences that are conventional (i.e., systematic) but 'wrong' for the particular word, cf. *<woz> for <was>,
(2) spellings that represent non-standard pronunciations, for example colloquial, local, or regional pronunciations, such as *<runnin'> for <running> or *<tings> for <things>,
(3) single graphemes of the alphabet or non-alphabetic graphemes, especially numbers, as substitutions for grapheme sequences, with very prominent examples being *<u> for <you> and <8> in spellings such as *<l8> for <late>,
(4) archaic or pseudo-archaic spellings such as the use of <w> in Swedish that has an archaic connotation since it was, in the early 20th century, officially replaced by <v> (cf. Carney 1994: 450),
(5) language-external symbolism, which, crucially, unlike the other types, involves users' knowledge of writing systems *other* than their own. An example is the use of <x> and <z> in German fanzines to indicate a subcultural identity (cf. Androutsopoulos 2000), where the social meaning of these graphemes works only if users perceive the relation with the English writing system (cf., for example, *<Zeux> for colloquial German <Zeugs> 'stuff').

> The same also goes for spellings such as *<ashtändig> (for *<aschtändig> 'decent', itself a colloquial spelling) that are used in Swiss German youth language varieties. Here, the substitution of German <sch> with English <sh>, both of which represent /ʃ/, establishes an association with African-American English varieties characteristic of US-American hip hop (cf. Dürscheid and Spitzmüller 2006: 26).

An interesting question with respect to types of deviance from the norm is where, i.e., in which contexts they are practiced. As established above, the notion of correctness introduced by orthography is interpreted absolutely: a given word is spelled either correctly or incorrectly with respect to the orthographic norm, and officially, there is nothing in between. However, when considering the contexts in which deviation occurs, the additional and looser notion of acceptability must be considered, specifically as regards the question of how acceptable deviance is in different communicative situations and associated registers. Indeed, in some contexts, writing appears to be generally less strictly regulated than in others. In schools and publishing houses, for example, orthographically correct writing is demanded. By contrast, in certain types of digital communication such as text messaging through SMS or services such as WhatsApp or Chinese WeChat, orthographic norms may not be adhered to as rigidly (cf. Figure 17).

Crucially, however, the degree of orthographic regulation has nothing to do with the form of communication *per se* but is dependent on the specific situation. This subsumes factors such as the intended purpose of a text, its potential addressee(s), the formality of the situation, etc. These factors are also relevant in determining what consequences potentially arise from orthographic deviation. And the key word 'consequence' leads to another important facet of deviation from the norm: sanctions. As was mentioned in ⟶ Section 5.2, being perceived as binding is a central feature of orthographies. However, their bindingness is not of legal but of social and administrative nature.

Thus, if a person makes an orthographic error or mistake, the consequences are in most cases also of social nature. Even if no additional social meaning was intended by the person making the mistake, unconscious deviation still carries important social meaning and is central for ideologies surrounding orthography. As Simon Horobin observes in his book *Does spelling matter?*, "[r]ather than being seen simply as mistakes, incorrect spellings are often viewed as a reflection of a person's intelligence, social class, and even morality" (Horobin 2013: 250). Note that the literature on this provocative claim is, however, inconclusive, with some studies suggesting that deviation from orthography is not associated with an assumed level of a person's intelligence (cf. Kreiner et al. 2002) and others claiming that it is (cf. Figueredo and Varnhagen 2005). In any case, it is impor-

Figure 17: WhatsApp chat showing some deviations from orthography, e.g., lack of punctuation, lack of capitalisation (*<royal bank plaza>), and use of emoticons such as < :) >.

tant to emphasise that not all deviation is treated the same. A prerequisite for this is that readers are capable of distinguishing between, for example, errors and mistakes (cf. Boland and Queen 2016). They treat them differently given that mistakes are corrigible, meaning the writers who made them could have spotted and corrected them, e.g., by attentively rereading their text a second time before sending it. Recipients of such texts can interpret the failure to correct them as an unwillingness to allocate sufficient time to composing the text which, in turn, can be seen as a lack of respect for the addressee. Furthermore, users can also distinguish unconscious deviation from conscious deviation (cf. Scott et al. 2014) and have sophisticated implicit knowledge about different registers and non-standard spellings.

The sanctions mentioned above can vary from context to context: in school, for example, deviation can result in bad marks, and if mistakes or errors are part of CVs or cover letters included in job applications, HR managers might factor the (lack of) orthographic competence into their decisions. This means that orthography is not only social action but power, and it is instrumentalised to create social hierarchies. Those who know how to spell correctly can succeed in a literate community in which there is a codified orthography while those who do not are likely put at a disadvantage in various respects. This is true also for examples of modern literacy practices in which the ascription of characteristics such as 'unintelligent' to orthographic deviation can have social consequences of varying severity. Take online dating, for instance, where lack of orthographic knowledge can act as a gatekeeper as erroneous profile texts or private messages may hinder the potential initiation of a personal relationship.

From a diachronic perspective it is also noteworthy that in the past, up until the High Middle Ages, literacy was reserved to certain circles – generally the elite – and the very knowledge of how to read and write alone marked a crucial social distinction of power (cf. Maas 2010: 122). A demotisation of literacy followed only at a later stage, together with a shift from the distinction between 'those who know how to write vs. those who do not' to 'those who know the orthographic rules vs. those who do not', which has prevailed as the predominant distinction in modern literate communities. It is accompanied also by the crucial knowledge of writing (and spelling) in ways that are appropriate in different situations.

With respect to sanctions, the acceptance of sanctioning orthographic deviation also varies: a striking example that illustrates this is the practice of *orthographic shaming*, i.e., correcting or commenting on others' errors or mistakes in public contexts, especially on the internet, which in many cases is carried out in a degrading manner (cf. Meletis 2020a: 378–380). People who engage in this behaviour are frequently referred to as *grammar nazis* or *spelling nazis*. This practice is often met with negative reactions, either by the person who was the target of the correction or by third parties who choose to intervene. It is often regarded as a technique employed to distract from the actual discussion with the goal of discrediting the opponents' arguments by insinuating that, because they are not orthographically competent, their argument must be faulty, too.

5.5.3.4 Orthography reforms and their metadiscourses

A central feature of orthographies discussed in → Section 5.2 is that they are rather static, which results from their very restricted changeability. Given that orthographies are codified sets of rules, changes of orthography must be made per modifications of the current rules and must themselves be codified. This usually happens by decree in the process of reforms. To clarify the terminology, however, it is important to note that even though all changes (no matter how small they are) must be official changes, they do not automatically constitute 'reforms'. Instead, the term *orthography reform* (or *spelling reform*) should be reserved for larger changes that affect general rules (→ Section 5.3) and, in most cases, numerous graphematic aspects such as the spelling of words, word division, and punctuation (cf. Nerius 2007: 40). By contrast, the recent official introduction of an uppercase <ẞ> in German orthography by the *Council for German Orthography*, for example, is not regarded as a reform but as a smaller, isolated modification of the orthography.

The general goal of orthography reforms is, as Coulmas (2014: 107) notes, "to secure the functionality of the system by simplifying its rules and thus to facilitate the task of children becoming literate". However, ironically, even though their main motivation is simplification, orthography reforms are anything but simple matters. In the course of reforming an orthography, linguistic, social, political, economic, and numerous other factors converge (and simultaneously clash), which means reforms cannot simply be decided on and then implemented by an authority. That orthography "is the most conspicuous linguistic subsystem which non-linguists tend to take as representing the language itself, its history and symbolic value as a marker of identity" (Coulmas 2014: 122) results in the fact that it is largely perceived as a common good. In other words, many of its users interpret orthography *pars pro toto* as language, which means changing orthography equals changing (their) language. Consequently, the acceptance of an orthography reform by the community is essential. The underlying motivation of reforms is usually the above-mentioned improvement of the system for the sake of simplifying the rules, yet opponents of orthography reforms argue against them, citing various drawbacks (see below).

The complexity and delicacy of the situation are only increased by the fact that numerous stakeholders from different areas have a vested interest in orthography and engage in both specific and general discourses about it (cf. Eira 1998). Scientific discourses are one example; they are led mostly by linguists and educationalists and centre on the goal of making an orthography more systematic, especially for the purpose of literacy instruction. Politicians have their own motivations, which may be of symbolic nature – e.g., grounded in the wish to signal affiliation to a given regime. An economic drawback, on the other hand, is the need to modify and reprint official documents, teaching material, etc. following the implementation of a reform, which can be a costly affair (cf. Karan 2014: 110). Moreover, the media, especially print media, are incredibly invested in matters of orthography given that any changes of codification affect them directly.[150] Additionally, they serve as a forum for other stakeholders to discuss the contents of

150 Notably, they often have their own rules, so-called *in-house orthographies* that may deviate from the codified orthography (cf. exemplarily Schimmel-Fijalkowytsch 2018: Chapter 7 for in-house rules of a number of Swiss media).

an orthography reform, which is how the public is both informed and invited to participate. And indeed, the public is opinionated when it comes to orthography. Change, it seems, is perceived as an intrusion into the personal space since orthography 'belongs' to everyone in a literate community. Also, change is often perceived as diminishing the effort that was involved in learning the old rules and at the same time bodes new efforts as the reformed orthography is of course also expected to be mastered by everyone, necessitating the learning of new rules. This, ultimately, ignites resistance and the members of the public feel "both entitled and qualified to voice their opinions about writing their language" (Coulmas 2014: 125).

Unsurprisingly, then, there are opponents to virtually every orthography reform, as is illustrated by four recent and prominent reforms of European orthographies: French (1990), Dutch (1995), German (1996, with modifications later on), and Spanish (2010). The German orthographic reform of 1996 is a remarkable example, as in 1995, when public discussions surrounding it began, "a storm of protest erupted" (Coulmas 2014: 117) almost immediately. This even led to proceedings in the Federal Constitutional Court as users legally challenged the reform, arguing that it violates their constitutional rights. In the end, the court decided in favour of the reform, after which it could be implemented (cf. Johnson 2002). However, the controversies never completely died down, and in 2006, a compromise was agreed on in the form of amendments that rescinded some of the changes made in the original 1996 reform. The modifications at that time centred on grapheme-phoneme correspondences, capitalisation, the spelling (specifically the division) of compound words, hyphenation, and punctuation (especially the placement of the comma before conjunctions that precede main clauses).

As Coulmas (2014: 116) rightly argues, due to their "political embeddedness it is difficult to make generalizations about spelling reforms, their success and failure, and the extent of public support and opposition". Figure 18 visualises a series of steps of decision making inherent in most orthography reforms. The development starts with competing views on the established orthography, with the majority of 'lay users' accepting it and resisting change while other groups bemoan deficiencies that could be eliminated to improve the system. Notably, this identification of deficiencies is also by no means a straightforward process in which all experts agree, so that even among proponents of the idea of an orthography reform there can be major disagreement as to what should be reformed (and how). At this point, different stakeholders voice their opinions and the entire web of discourses surrounding the reform becomes highly complex, resulting in the fact that the reformed orthography will inevitably represent but a compromise. If a reform is eventually implemented, the public's acceptance determines what happens next. In case there is a lack of acceptance, the old, superseded norm may remain in use as some users consciously decide to adhere to the now officially incorrect old rules, signalling their disapproval of the reformed orthography. If this rejection persists, as the example of the 1996 reform of German orthography clearly shows, decisions can be reversed or amended. Generally, orthography reforms are never final as their result might become subject to yet another reform further down the line.

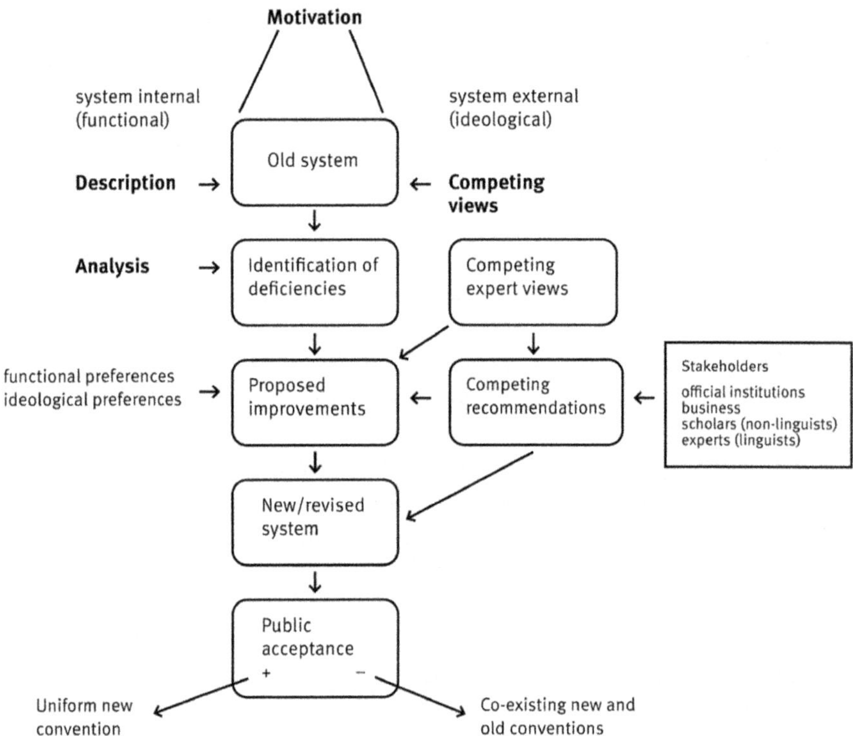

Figure 18: Decision making in the process of reforming an orthography, adapted from Coulmas (2014: 124).

A special type of reform not yet mentioned is arguably even more invasive as it switches out entire scripts. The change of Arabic script to Roman script for the writing system of Turkish in 1928 (intended to strengthen ties to Europe) is one of the best-known examples of script reforms. Another striking example is the script changes for the writing system of Azeri, from Arabic to Roman to Cyrillic and back to Roman, all of which occurred in a relatively short span of time (cf. Hatcher 2008). As was established in → Section 3.1, the visual appearance of a writing system has symbolic meaning and power. And replacing a script with a different one changes a writing system's visuality to a maximum degree. Also, such a switch significantly heightens the effort required by users to 'stay' literate. Different scripts are not only visually dissimilar but, in most cases, involve different graphematic relations with linguistic units (whether these are phonemes, syllables, or morphemes), partially because they consist of a different number of basic shapes. This means that in the context of script changes, users have to first learn a different script and its basic shapes' graphematic values. In a way, this equals learning an entirely new writing system.

Notably, in some cases, a switch of scripts even entails a change of a writing system's type. For instance, if the writing system of Chinese were Romanised, (which was in fact proposed, cf. Coulmas 2014: 111–112), this would not merely constitute a switch from Chinese script to Roman script but also one from the morphographic type to the phonographic alphabetic type. This would result in wide-reaching consequences for the entire system, one of which is that the speakers of mutually unintelligible spoken varieties would no longer be able to understand each other when communicating in the written modality. It is because of such profound side effects that even more than orthography reforms, script reforms "constitute a disruption of intellectual life and a break with the past, making literature in the old script inaccessible to the non-specialist" (Coulmas 2014: 116). This is rather drastic, for example in that new generations who become literate through the new script are completely cut off from literature written in the old script – i.e., cut off from older literature written in their native language.

6 Writing system typology

This chapter starts with a discussion of the purposes a typology of writing systems should serve as well as the challenges it faces (Section 6.1). The following two sections are devoted to the major types of writing systems, which can be subsumed under the headings of phonography and morphography. Thus, Section 6.2 deals with subtypes of phonography; first, three types of segmental writing systems, namely alphabets, abjads, and abugidas, and then the non-segmental type of syllabary. Morphography is at the core of Section 6.3. Following this treatment of diverse types, in Section 6.4, we consider universal tendencies in the world's writing systems. Finally, in contrast to the predominantly synchronic nature of the preceding sections, a diachronic perspective is adopted in Section 6.5 to highlight the history of writing systems, particularly commonalities in their development, and to investigate how these are connected to the types of writing systems we assume today.

Typologies in general deal with classifications and categorisations, so the aim of different kinds of linguistic typologies is to group together languages that share certain properties. The choice of a specific criterion underlying the classification results in the assumption of different types that subsume together languages behaving similarly or even identically with respect to this criterion. In the case of a prominent morphological typology, for example, the criterion is case inflection, while one of many possible syntactic typologies focuses on canonical word order. Crucially, linguistic typology is, in the first instance,[151] not interested in genetic affiliations between languages, meaning unrelated languages such as Japanese and Turkish can very well be part of the same type – in the case of a morphological typology because they are both agglutinating.

The same essentially applies to typologies of writing systems as they are intended to find commonalities and differences between systems and thus categorise them into types. Yet, writing system typology – as it has usually been practiced – differs from language typology in one important respect: while languages are independent semiotic systems and language types are assumed on the basis of features inherent to them (such as the above-mentioned inflection or word order), writing systems are not (only) systems with independent features but are also always tied to specific languages. In terms of the different views on writing presented in ⟶ Section 2.3, traditional writing system typology apparently (and implicitly) follows the dependence hypothesis in elevating the structural level of language that is primarily 'represented' by the basic units of writing systems to the status of an uncontested main criterion. The broadest relevant distinction that is drawn by means of this criterion is between writing systems whose basic

151 Genetic affiliation can, of course, be useful to *explain* why certain languages belong to one type, although even this is secondary in linguistic typology (see below).

https://doi.org/10.1515/9783110757835-006

units relate to sound (phonography ⟶ Section 6.2) and those whose units refer to linguistic meaning (morphography ⟶ Section 6.3).[152]

Notably, such a focus inevitably puts autonomous properties of writing systems out of focus. These include features of their scripts, i.e., their visual appearance, but also the question of how words and other linguistic units are demarcated by graphetic means, e.g., by word spacing or the alternation of scripts. This underlines that the common practices of writing system typology should be assessed critically as to what they can and cannot achieve. Therefore, the purpose(s) of typologies as well as some of the challenges they face will be discussed before the main types of writing systems proposed thus far in the literature will be presented. The focus will be on an overview that highlights core features of types on the one hand and central (open) issues of writing system typology on the other. All of this will be done from a synchronic perspective, which must be explicitly stated in advance given that a diachronic treatment of writing system typology would look markedly different (cf. also Tranter 2013). Some general questions concerning the history of writing systems will, however, be broached in the final section of the chapter (⟶ Section 6.5). At the end of this introduction, it is important to note that this chapter provides no comprehensive overview of existing writing system typologies but rather a treatment of the most relevant questions and ongoing debates. These will at times be discussed in-depth to demonstrate how detailed and intricate issues negotiated in this field can be.

6.1 Purposes and challenges of typologies

The main purpose of the field of writing system typology in general is "to establish criteria for assigning any writing to one of a number of meaningful types" (Coulmas 1996b: 1380). The first challenge, here, is to choose a suitable criterion to serve as the basis. Making this decision requires walking a fine line between criteria that are too broad on the one hand (which could lead to too few types that may still differ from each other in significant respects), and criteria that are too narrow on the other hand, resulting in an abundance of types which may still share relevant features that warrant grouping them together. Aside from the scope of criteria, their very nature is also relevant – as Coulmas (1996b: 1381) remarks, it is vital that they be "informative and analytically valuable". This means that

152 An even broader distinction is made between glottography and semasiography (⟶ Section 2.1). Given that we adhere to the narrow definition of writing here, this distinction is not conceived of as part of writing system typology but rather part of a typology of graphic (communication) systems; thus, only glottography is treated in this chapter.

criteria pertaining to geography, such as 'Central American writing', and based on genetic affiliation, such as 'Chinese-derived writing', should be excluded. The reason for this is that regional vicinity or proximity as well as genetic affiliation may be the causes for the similarity of systems, rendering typologies on this basis uninformative. 'Central American writing', for example, is not actually a criterion but already the type based on it, and one that does not reveal anything about how the included systems work. The criterion that writing system typology has relied on instead is of structural nature and centres on the question of how writing systems relate to the languages they are tied to.

There exist relatively few ways in which writing systems relate to their underlying languages. Identifying them reveals important aspects about the fundamental relation between writing and language. The criterion based on this relation has been and still is at the core of writing system typology and can be referred to as *dominant level of representational mapping*[153] (cf. Joyce and Meletis 2021). Specifically, this criterion identifies the linguistic level that the graphemes of a writing system primarily relate to (or, in terms of the dependence hypothesis, 'represent'). The basic options are the segmental phonological level (= phonemes), the syllabic phonological level (= syllables and potentially moras, see below), or the morphological level (= morphemes). These types of relations lend the remainder of this chapter its structure as individual sections will be devoted to the resulting types of writing systems. At first, however, four important criticisms of a sole focus on this criterion shall be mentioned: (1) it is unable to capture certain features that are inherent to writing as a graphic and spatial semiotic system of its own; (2) it is too broad and therefore incapable of drawing relevant fine-grained distinctions; (3) it is commonly not combined with other criteria; and (4) it conflates different types of phonography and morphography with each other. In the following, we will address these issues in more detail.

(1) Basing a typology (or multiple typologies, see below) solely on the relation between graphemes and linguistic units inevitably leads to categorisations that are exclusively linguistically structural. Writing, however, is also a graphic modality. What, thus, about the visual variety found in the world's scripts? Visual similarity or distinctiveness is completely disregarded in traditional writing system typology. What visual criteria could potentially reveal about the (linguistic) nature of writing systems may not be straightforwardly clear, but that does not make them altogether trivial (cf. Meletis 2020a: Chapter 1.3). Notably, graphetic aspects are often not tied to graphematics, meaning a difference in visual

153 Trigger (1998: 44) calls it a writing system's *predominant organising principle*.

appearance does not necessarily entail different functionality. Writing systems using distinct scripts (such as Roman, Cyrillic, and Georgian script), for example, can relate to respective languages in the same way (in this case, they are alphabets, i.e., phonographically segmental).

Aside from the scripts employed by writing systems, there are other features that are unaccounted for in writing system typologies based on the dominant level of representational mapping. Coulmas (1996b: 1380) mentions "higher-level organizational principles of writing, e.g., chapters, sections, paragraphs, and sentences by means of which text is segmentable, or properties of text such as direction (left, right), axis (horizontal, perpendicular) or lining (top to bottom, bottom to top)" as well as punctuation, while Gnanadesikan (2017: 14–15) lists "a set of signs, the spatial arrangement of the signs, [. . .] and language-specific orthographic rules by which the signs are interpreted" (cf. also Joyce and Meletis 2021 for several other criteria). Some of the features they mention, such as aspects concerning the spatiality of writing, refer to material aspects and would, thus – following the structural trichotomy introduced in this book – lead to graphetic typologies, whereas the 'orthographic rules' that Gnanadesikan names are the basis of orthographic typologies (a first rough proposal of which can be found in ⟶ Section 5.1). In comparison, most typologies of writing systems proposed thus far, given their focus on the relation between units of writing and other units of language, are graphematic typologies.

Table 7: Typological grid with higher organisational structures.

level	*linguistic units*	writing systems / TYPES	**Korean (FEATURAL) ALPHABET**	**German ALPHABET**	**Thai ABUGIDA**	**Arabic ABJAD**	**Japanese (kana) SYLLABARY**	**Chinese MORPHO-GRAPHIC**
phono-logical	*feature*		[x]	[x]				
	phoneme	*consonant*	[X]	X	X	X		
		vowel	[X]	X	X, x	(x), X:		
	syllable		X	[X]	[X]	[X]	X	X
morpho-logical	*morpheme*		[X]	[X]	[X]	[X]	[X]	
	word		X	X	[X]	X	[X]	[X]
syntactic	*phrase, sentence*		X	X	X	X	X	X
textual	*larger units*		X	X	X	X	X	X

Table 7 shows such a graphematic typology that was proposed in Meletis (2020a: 148). While it is also based on the criterion of dominant level of representational mapping, it additionally considers higher organisational levels. Rather than a traditional typology that assumes different broad types, it represents a typological grid into which individual writing systems can be entered. The columns in Table 7 show representatives of the major types described in traditional writing system typology merely for presentational purposes. The rows, on the other hand, are assigned different linguistic levels that can be represented in writing systems. As for the notation: if a level is represented graphematically, the respective table cell in a writing system's row includes either an uppercase X for graphemes or larger graphematic units or a lowercase x for graphematic information that is secondary in some respects, such as the short vowel graphemes in Arabic. Square brackets [ ] indicate that a unit is not made visible by empty space(s) around it, i.e., does not fulfil the empty space criterion (⟶ Section 3.2.2), while normal brackets ( ) mean that the representation of this level/unit is optional. Finally, the empty cells indicate that a given linguistic level is not at all represented in the writing system, while cells with a grey background highlight the levels with which the graphemes in the given writing system correspond.

While this presentation is not innovative, it systematically summarises and visualises certain core issues of writing system typology. Note that what it reveals depends crucially on the writing systems that are included in it. In the rendition here, it shows, for example, that graphemes are almost uniformly the smallest units that fulfil the empty space criterion, i.e., are visually salient by being the smallest segmental units. The only outlier is Korean, where graphemes are subsegmental and the smallest segmental 'unit' corresponds with the phonological syllable. This exception, now, echoes an ongoing discussion about the typological status of Korean (⟶ Section 6.2.3.2). Moreover, the grid highlights differences in the representation of vowels that motivate the assumption of different kinds of segmentaries (see below). What it also visualises is that the writing system of Chinese is morphosyllabic – although it is not specifically indicated that the syllable level is not directly represented but only melded with the morpheme level. To name a final example, the word level can be used to distinguish the systems that are unspaced – in this case Thai, Japanese, and Chinese – from those that are spaced. Most of the mentioned issues will be revisited in the course of this chapter.

(2) The second problem concerns the scope and depth of existing typologies as it has been criticised occasionally that they cannot account for fine-grained distinctions between writing systems assigned to the same type. Weingarten (2011: 12) formulates this critique as follows: "The types proposed to date [. . .] may highlight certain basic characteristics of a writing system but they cannot, for example, elucidate the fundamental differences between the French and the Italian writing system, which both belong to the alphabetic type". Therefore, he

arrives at the rather drastic conclusion that writing system typology is still in its beginnings. It is, of course, obvious that writing systems subsumed by the same type must differ in some respects, but the complex question is at which point their differences become so significant that they warrant a new (sub-)type. With respect to this question, the typological grid introduced above could be modified and improved to show more specific information – for example what percentage of vowel graphemes is transparently indicated by graphematic units in two different alphabets – so that it uncovers differences also between writing systems that are commonly assigned to the same type.

(3) Furthermore, one of the core constraints or – evaluatively put – shortcomings of writing system typologies is that they are based on only one main criterion.[154] Different criteria may additionally be incorporated to distinguish between subtypes, but that is not the same as using them as base criteria, in which case the typology as a whole may appear fundamentally different. One can, for example, ask which alphabets, morphographic systems, etc., exhibit spaces between 'words' and which do not, but if done this way, this merely adds information about types that had already been assumed. By contrast, if we were to take word spacing as a main criterion, then writing systems such as Chinese, Japanese, and Thai would be grouped together as unspaced and contrasted with spaced systems, which represent the majority. Note that this would be a typology wholly different from traditional ones, as the graphemes of Chinese, Japanese, and Thai relate to units at different linguistic levels.

This thought experiment highlights an important general point: there exist many possible base criteria for typologies of writing systems that could lead to illuminating groupings. However, before applying a specific criterion (such as spaced vs. unspaced), it is paramount to reflect on what the purpose of the resulting typology is. Whether a writing system has spaces between words (or other units) or lacks them, for example, may not be of primarily structural significance but could be highly relevant for the processing of these systems given that spacing is important for several processes involved in reading (e.g., eye movements and word identification). Such possible criteria for 'alternative' typologies

154 What Anderson (1992: 322) claims for morphological typology could also be applied to writing system typology: "We can conclude that the parameters of a typology ought to be ones from which something follows: that is, they ought to identify groups of properties that co-vary with one another, so that knowing how one thing works entails knowing about others as well, as a direct consequence of whatever it is that motivates the typological labels". The 'shortcoming', now, is that typological labels in grapholinguistics are only motivated by a single 'parameter' and do not necessarily identify co-varying properties.

of writing systems can broadly be assigned to three categories: those concerning the relation between writing systems and (a) their respective languages, (b) the way the systems are physiologically and cognitively processed by users, and (c) their embedding in a specific cultural context as well as the sociopragmatic needs of their users. Accordingly, the criteria are either primarily (a) structural (such as dominant level of representational mapping), (b) psycholinguistic, or (c) sociolinguistic (cf. Meletis 2018, 2020a). These labels, of course, are merely idealisations, as criteria can often be assigned to more than one of these categories. The above-mentioned spacing, for example, is both a structural and a psycholinguistic criterion. In reality, thus, these three general categories commonly interact, which means every typology that is based on only one criterion will in some ways be reductive. However, no one has claimed that there must or can only be one typology. In fact, if multiple typologies based on different criteria were combined with each other, this could reveal much more about how writing systems can be similar or different than a single typology is capable of.

(4) An important aspect worth elaborating is that although writing systems are classified as either morphographic or phonographic, which refers to their dominant and basic level of representational mapping (cf. the introduction to this chapter), this is commonly not the only level at which they correspond with linguistic units or structures. Thus, we propose that the dominant level of representational mapping be terminologically highlighted by referring to writing systems whose units correspond with phonemes or syllables (or moras, see below) as *primarily* phonographic and to those whose units correspond with morphemes as *primarily* morphographic. To give an example, according to this distinction, the English writing system is primarily phonographic, the Chinese writing system primarily morphographic. 'Primary' implies the existence of a secondary level that is either embedded in the primary level or superimposes it. In the case of Chinese, morphographic graphemes include phonographic subcomponents that – with a varying degree of reliability – give hints about the pronunciation of the morphemes that the graphemes relate to in their entirety (⟶ Section 4.2.3 and below). Overemphasising the relevance of this secondary phonographic level occasionally even led scholars to classify Chinese as phonographic (see below).

Vice versa, secondary morphography 'superimposes' phonography in systems such as English or German.[155] Firstly, phonographic graphemes are combined to

155 For non-phonographic graphemes in phonographic writing systems – such as digits and special characters ⟶ Section 4.2.3.

form larger units (such as graphematic words ⟶ Section 4.3.2) that relate to morphemes and words. But secondary morphography also occurs at the segmental level: when the graphematic solution space includes multiple possibilities for the graphematic representation of a phoneme, the choice of one of them can be motivated morphographically (cf. Eisenberg 1983). An example often mentioned is the spelling of German <Kälte> 'the cold', where the choice of <ä> for /ɛ/ rather than <e> (which would be the default) is determined by the noun's morphological relation to the adjective <kalt> 'cold'. In other words, <a> and <ä> graphematically (or orthographically)[156] highlight a morphological connection. Phonographic transparency, or at least unmarked phonographic representation, is 'sacrificed' in such cases at the expense of a graphematic indication of morphological association. Note that in describing this situation, the verb 'superimpose' must be used cautiously as recent conceptions (cf., for example, Schmidt 2018) treat the morphological level – and thus the spelling of morphemes and words – as dominant also in primarily phonographic writing systems (specifically German). According to such models, the choice of phonographic graphemes and thus grapheme-phoneme correspondences at the segmental level are merely epiphenomenal.

In a nutshell, it is vital not to conflate what we refer to as *primary* level of representational mapping, which reflects the linguistic units that the graphemes of a writing system relate to, and any possible *secondary* levels, which are concerned with any additional linguistic levels that are represented in a writing system, often at the sub- or suprasegmental levels (cf. also Osterkamp and Schreiber 2021). As will become evident below, such a conflation is inherent in several proposals of writing system typologies. Note that since they are the unmarked types, we will refer to primary phonography and primary morphography as phonography and morphography, respectively. By contrast, the secondary types will always be terminologically marked.

Despite its weaknesses, given that it has been at the core of writing system typology thus far, the focus of the following sections will also be on the relation between the basic units of writing systems and linguistic units. However, mentions of other possible criteria will be interspersed throughout.

---

156 This is a good example to show how deliberate orthographic regulation can favour different possibilities afforded by the graphematics of a writing system. In fact, in German, the 'morphological principle' illustrated by the example <kalt> and <Kälte> was a factor in some of the decisions made in the German orthographic reform.

6.2 Phonography

6.2.1 The phonography/morphography dichotomy: open questions

Most writing systems of the world are phonographic systems (with *phono-* deriving from Greek *phōnḗ*, 'sound', 'voice') as their graphemes relate to units of sound – either segmental (phonemes) or non-segmental units (syllables or moras). Moreover, writing systems which are morphographic also often incorporate secondary phonography (see below). As established above, phonography is one of only two basic options for the functioning of writing systems, the other one being morphography. This fundamental distinction is made in almost all proposed typologies of writing systems (cf., for some examples of modern typologies, Hill 1967; Coulmas 1996b; Daniels 1990, 2001, 2017; Sampson 2015; for a synoptic discussion, cf. Joyce and Borgwaldt 2011).[157]

Notably, phonography and morphography are often not regarded as categories of equal weight due to the prevalent view of phonocentrism. It describes a situation in which phonography is seen as superior and writing's relationship to sound is foregrounded at the expense of other linguistic structures that are likewise represented in it. This view is stated boldly in John DeFrancis' (1989) influential book *Visible speech*, whose name basically already says it all. Essentially, he claims that all writing is phonographic (for some counterarguments, cf. Sampson 1994). As a sinologist, he specialised in Chinese, the only language that nowadays has an exclusively morphographic writing system, which makes his claim especially impactful. The argument that even Chinese writing is phonographic hinges to a large degree on the secondary phonological components that are found in a significant proportion of Chinese graphemes and integrate phonographic elements into morphography (⟶ Section 4.2.3). Furthermore, one could argue that due to double articulation, i.e., the fact that all meaning-bearing morphemes are necessarily made up of meaning-distinguishing phonemes (even if this is not reflected overtly in writing), all writing is ultimately related to phonological structures and thus phonographic. In this view, however, the important and inevitable 'detour' that is made through morphography is disregarded. In psycholinguistic terms, in morphographic systems such as Chinese, readers can only arrive at the phonological representation of a morpheme through recognising the morpheme first.[158] Phonological components, thus, are secondarily phonographic as

157 An excellent overview of most proposed typologies of writing up until the early 2000s is given in Voß (2003).

158 Of course, some graphemes or phonological components that are almost exclusively used for their phonographic value may already be completely desemanticised in processing.

they – in the vast majority of cases – receive their phonological value through being morphographic. Furthermore, DeFrancis' argument loses much of its force when considering Japanese kanji, which are derived from Chinese graphemes (cf. Sampson 1994: 128–129) but one of whose readings is a native Japanese reading with a Japanese pronunciation. Since Japanese and Chinese are genetically unrelated, the phonological components in the graphemes borrowed from Chinese lose their ability to reliably signal the associated morphemes' pronunciations. Thus, in their native reading, Japanese kanji are completely devoid of phonography (cf. Daniels 2017: 82) and the claim that all writing is phonographic is debunked (cf. also ⟶ Section 6.3).

Given the example of Chinese, it is obvious that a challenge faced by an absolute distinction between phonography and morphography is that most writing systems are, to some degree, mixed systems in that they combine elements of both in different ways (cf. Günther 1988: 43; Rogers 2005: 272).[159] The phonological components in Chinese graphemes underline this. Importantly, now, the fact that phonography and morphography most often co-occur in some way has resulted in several typologies in which they are not treated as two distinct categories but as interacting dimensions.[160]

In the two-dimensional typology proposed by computational linguist Richard Sproat, which is shown in Table 8 (cf. Sproat 2000; it was later also modified by Rogers 2005), phonography is assigned to the x-axis and is – yet again – understood as a basis in that all writing systems are assigned to one type of phonography. Morphography (or, in Sproat's terminology 'logography', cf. ⟶ Section 6.3 for a discussion of the terminology), on the other hand, is added to phonography or superimposes it on the y-axis. Note that as described above, this conception conflates primary phonography and morphography with secondary phonographic and morphographic elements. However, the differences between the writing systems included in a two-axial typology such as this are not merely of quantitative nature, i.e., by differentiating the 'amount of logography'. There

---

159 An exception is, ironically, the writing system of Japanese. While it is fundamentally mixed in the sense of containing important phonographic components in the form of the kana scripts, the label 'mixed' applies only when the system as a whole is assessed. The system's individual components are themselves largely unmixed (at least synchronically): the kanji are morphographic, the kana are phonographic (see below).

160 An important question that will not be addressed here but that is treated extensively by Osterkamp and Schreiber (2021) deals with the fact that not just entire writing systems are "taxonomically messy" (Rogers 2005: 272) but sometimes also individual graphemes: in primarily morphographic writing systems that also employ phonographic elements such as Chinese or Japanese, for example, it may not always be straightforwardly clear whether a grapheme is a morphogram or a phonogram.

are also crucial differences in the quality of both phonography and morphography across various writing systems (cf. Osterkamp and Schreiber 2021: 53). Essentially, there exists no straightforward way of comparing the morphography in primarily phonographic systems such as English with the morphography in primarily morphographic systems such as Chinese. This is concealed by the practice of using an underdifferentiated terminology, i.e., referring to various types of graphematic representation of morphological information as 'morphography' (or 'logography') regardless of how much they differ.

Table 8: A two-dimensional typology of writing systems, taken from Sproat (2000: 138).

			Type of Phonography			
	Consonantal	**Polyconsonantal**	**Alphabetic**		**Core Syllabic**	**Syllabic**
Amount of Logography ↓	W. Semitic		English, Greek, Korean, Devanāgarī	Pahawh Hmong	Linear B	Modern Yi
	Perso-Aramaic					
						Chinese
		Egyptian			Sumerian, Mayan, Japanese	

6.2.2 Tone

Before turning to segmentaries, a remark must be made about a phonological phenomenon that is crucial for many languages and their writing systems but that is largely neglected in writing system typology: tone. There exist many tonal languages in the world; however, just because a language is tonal does not mean that its writing system (if it has one) will also represent relevant tonal distinctions. The Chinese varieties, for example, have different tones that are lexically distinctive, but this is not reflected in the morphographic writing system, so much so that even the phonological components used in many Chinese graphemes disregard tone. For example, the component |青| (Mandarin) *qīng*, which originally carries high tone, is also used to indicate pronunciations with low or rising tones. Of course, tone *can* be graphematically represented, and there are various ways in which this is achieved. The most systematic description of the graphematic representation of tone that has been proposed is, however, restricted to alphabets, and even more specifically to those that are written with the Roman script: David Roberts developed a typology of how tone is represented on the basis of six intricately interacting parameters that will only be characterised briefly here (for details, cf. Roberts 2011).

(1) *Domain* is, essentially, a different term for the criterion of dominant level of representational mapping as elaborated above and, thus, concerns the linguistic level represented by the graphematics of a writing system. (2) *Target* is a subparameter of *domain* and specifies what exactly is 'targeted' by the graphematic representation of tones: if the domain is phonography, tonal graphematic representation is straightforward as it may target the tones themselves (such as high, mid, and low tone) and different tones are written with corresponding diacritics, for example. If the domain is morphography, on the one hand, the target may be grammatical information, e.g., when a language uses tones to indicate verb inflection. On the other hand, the lexicon may also be targeted, e.g., when tone is marked in cases in which two written words would otherwise be homographs. Notably, there are also 'dual strategies' (cf. Roberts 2011: 85–86) in which both tone and grammar are targeted. (3) *Symbol*, as the name suggests, concerns the graphetic resources used to write tone, including superscript numbers, punctuation, and diacritics such as accents. A second mainly graphetic parameter is (4) *position*, which captures where the tone symbols are positioned relative to either segmental graphemes or larger graphematic strings. (5) *Density* refers to 'tone diacritic density', which is "precisely quantifiable by calculating the number of tone diacritics in a natural text [. . .] as a percentage of the number of tone bearing units" (Roberts 2011: 90). In other words, how many of the tonal distinctions are actually reflected in the writing system? Finally, the arguably most complex parameter, (6) *depth*, deals with the levels of linguistic representation that are targeted by written tones: in surface (i.e., phonetic) notation, it is post-lexical phonological output, in shallow or transparent graphematic representation, it is lexical phonological output, and in deep graphematic representation, it is lexical phonological input (cf. Roberts 2011: 93–101 for details). Notably, while these parameters have been proposed for alphabets using Roman script, they can likely be extended to account also for the representation of tone in both alphabets using other scripts and other types of writing systems in general.

6.2.3 Segmentaries

6.2.3.1 A more fine-grained typology of segmental phonography

The question of whether a system's graphemes relate to phonemes or syllables leads to an important distinction of phonographic subtypes: *segmentaries* and *syllabaries*. A segmentary – a term proposed by Amalia E. Gnanadesikan – is a writing system "all or most of whose signs are used in such a way as to encode individual phonological segments" (Gnanadesikan 2017: 21). Within the type of segmentaries, yet another important categorisation must be made, as systems in which all classes of phonemes in a language's phoneme inventory are represented (i.e., both consonants and vowels) must be differentiated from those in which only consonants (and no or some but not all vowels) are written. Crucially, with respect to vowels, it is not just relevant whether they are represented but also how many of them are represented – and how.

Subtypes of segmentaries have been proposed by numerous scholars. The arguably most influential typology was developed gradually by Daniels (2017); the structure of this section is based on it. Daniels assumes three basic segmental subtypes: *alphabets*, in which both consonants and vowels are graphematically represented, *abjads*, in which consonants (and no or some vowels) are written, and *abugidas*, systems in which consonant graphemes additionally indicate an inherent (and thus unmarked) default vowel, and other vowels are represented through a systematic graphetic modification of consonant graphemes. As for the terminology, the labels for the two latter categories were coined by analogy with the well-established term *alphabet* and are thus formed from the first – in both cases four – graphemes of systems belonging to the designated type: *a, b, j, d* from the (original order of the) Arabic writing system, and *a, bu, gi, da* from the Ethiopian writing system[161] (cf. Daniels 1990: 730).

For the sake of completeness, what must be mentioned regarding phonography is that aside from types based on relations with segmental or larger phonological units, an additional type has been proposed; it is based on the relation between features of graphemes (specifically visual features of their basic shapes) and phonological features of corresponding phonemes, making the relation subsegmental at both ends. Such a type was first assumed by Sampson ([1985] 2015), who termed it *featural*. Subsequently, several other scholars (among them Daniels) incorporated it into their typologies. Importantly, the sole writing system in use today in which such a featural relation can be (uncontroversially)[162]

161 With respect to *abugida*, it has been criticised that Daniels chose a rather marginal writing system to coin the term. Most abudigas are found in Asia, with Devanāgarī being one of the most important contemporary representatives of the type (⟶ Section 6.2.3.4). In a footnote, Daniels (2017: 90, emphasis in original) responds to this by writing: "Recently, the letter-order of both consonants and vowels in ancient India has been recognized [. . .], and if I were devising a term for the writing-system type today, I might choose *arepiconu*".

162 A 'featural' relation between visual features of basic shapes and phonological features of corresponding graphemes was also claimed for the Roman script (as used for the alphabets of many languages) by Primus (2004, 2006). Notably, this proposal has neither been widely adopted as it has not (yet) been received outside of German grapholinguistics, nor has it been convincingly debunked (cf. the lone criticism in Rezec 2010, 2011).

observed is Korean. As will be argued below, however, this is best conceptualised as an additional property of the Korean writing system, which can otherwise be classified as an alphabet (⟶ Section 6.2.3.2).

While Daniels' above-mentioned typology has been widely adopted,[163] there exist proposals for refinements. In her own 'typology of phonemic scripts' (where she uses 'script' in the meaning of *writing system* here), Gnanadesikan (2017: 19) posits that typologies "such as Daniels [sic] (2001) abjad-abugida-alphabet-featural script, are on the one hand incomplete, and on the other hand too fragmented, in that they do not acknowledge the similarities between the various scripts that encode segments". Thus, a typology such as Daniels' supposedly runs into both problems mentioned at the outset of this chapter: it is in some respects too narrow and at the same time too broad. To improve the situation, Gnanadesikan proposes a typology based on four categories which are presented in Table 9.

Table 9: Typological criteria and terminology, taken from Gnanadesikan (2017: 28).

Category	Values	Term
Characters (basically) represent segments	Yes	Segmentary/Phonemic script/Segmental script
	No	Other
Other structures represented (other than those in 'higher-order structures' below)	Features	Featural
	Moras	Moraic
	None	(omit)
Higher-order structures represented	Peak/margin	*Āksharik*
	Syllables	Syllabically arranged/spaced
	None	Linear
Inclusion of vowels	All	Fully vowelled
	Most	Mostly vowelled
	Some	Partially vowelled
	None	Consonantal

In this typology, in addition to the well-established criterion of segmental vs. non-segmental phonological correspondence, three more criteria serve to distinguish between different types of segmentaries. The criterion that functions as the basis of the widely accepted alphabet-abjad-abugida trichotomy is 'inclusion of vowels': alphabets are fully vowelled, abjads are either consonantal or – and this is crucial – partially vowelled, and abugidas are either mostly or fully vowelled. This

163 One reason for this wide adoption is likely that Daniels has written important chapters on writing systems in handbooks aimed at a general linguistic audience (e.g., Daniels 2017).

already highlights that 'abjad' and 'abugida' as defined by Daniels are underdifferentiated types with respect to how the systems assigned to them deal with vowels.

The remaining two criteria allow for a more fine-grained description of special properties segmentaries may exhibit. As introduced above, Korean has been identified as featural in the past. Following Gnanadesikan, 'featural' is not to be regarded as its own type but as an additional subsegmental structure that is represented in the writing system (see below also for moraic structures). Yet another special property of Korean can be captured by the criterion 'higher-order structures': Korean graphemes relate to phonemes, but they are arranged in syllable blocks that occupy a single segmental space on the writing surface. In Gnanadesikan's approach, this does not make Korean a syllabary, as the syllabic arrangement is also merely an additional feature. In sum, this means that the Korean writing system can be classified as a fully vowelled syllabically arranged featural segmentary. As for the terminology, while such a precise descriptive label is "not as simple" as terms like *alphabet* and may even be perceived as cumbersome, fully specified designations of this kind "recognise a wider range of segmental scripts" (Gnanadesikan 2017: 28). It is thus only for the sake of terminological simplicity (and the space available for section titles) that the following sections are based on Daniels' terminology. It is crucial to note that Gnanadesikan's contentions are kept in mind throughout, meaning we understand *alphabet*, *abjad*, and *abugida* as broad types which need to be and will be further differentiated with the help of the additional criteria presented here.

6.2.3.2 Alphabets

Structurally, an alphabet is a segmentary in which both types of phonemes – consonant as well as vowel phonemes – are represented by graphemes of equal status, which means there is a "lack of distinction in the treatment" (Daniels 2017: 77) of graphemes for consonant phonemes and vowel phonemes. This renders alphabets fully vowelled segmentaries. Crucially, for this classification it is not required that in a language written with an alphabet, every consonant or vowel phoneme is graphematically represented. What it rather means is that in general, graphemes with an equal material and functional status correspond with both consonants and vowels. What 'equal status' refers to will become obvious in the discussion of abjads and abugidas below, where vowel graphemes are secondary for one or more of several reasons: because they are optional, because they are written with basic shapes that are smaller than the ones used to write consonant graphemes, because they do not occupy their own segmental spaces, etc. At a more abstract level, the main difference between types of segmentaries, i.e., their inclusion or treatment of vowels, amounts to the question of (under)representation. In other words: how graphematically underrepresented (or, in seldom cases, overrepresented) are phonemes in alphabets, abjads, and abugidas?

'Alphabet' is likely the best-known and most-used term in the context of writing system typology, the study of writing in general, and likely also the public's knowledge of and discourses about writing. One reason for this is that it is frequently being used in a generalised sense (intended to be) synonymous to *writing system*.[164] An example of such a use is found in the book *The story of nine Asian alphabets* (cf. APCEIU 2015), which is targeted at young, non-expert readers: most of the writing systems discussed in it (including Chinese, Thai, Arabic) are, obviously, not correctly classified as alphabets. Another reason for the terminological overreliance on 'alphabet' lies in a special type of the above-characterised phonocentrism: when mixed with Eurocentrism, it results in the special and predominant type of alphabetocentrism, describing a situation in which the alphabet is held to be the most ingenious human invention and, thus, as superior to all other types of writing systems (cf. Logan 1986). Crucially, this alleged superiority of the alphabetic type also fostered assumptions of teleologies concerning the history of writing according to which all writing systems necessarily undergo several developmental stages, the last and most advanced of which is the alphabet (cf. Gelb 1963 and ⟶ Section 6.5). While these views have been dispelled, grapholinguistic research continues to disproportionately focus on alphabets. The obvious reason for this is that English, not only an academic but a general lingua franca, uses an alphabet (albeit, ironically, not a prototypical one) as its writing system. As an effect, not only structural descriptions of writing systems but also much psycholinguistic research is, to a certain degree, distorted. In this vein, Share (2014) speaks of an 'alphabetism' in reading science that results in alphabets – again, more specifically, the English alphabet – being the basis of most models of reading, which renders them incapable of accurately accounting for processes occurring in other types of writing systems.

Although most alphabets in use today employ Roman script, it is important to mention other scripts that are used for alphabets, including, on the one hand, Cyrillic, which was also adopted for many writing systems, and Georgian, Armenian, and Korean on the other, which are more specific to given alphabets. This highlights the relevance of differentiating between the concepts of script and type (of writing system): within a given type such as the alphabet, different scripts can

---

164 Another, slightly less generalised use is observed by Buckley (2018: 27), who notes that the term is used for what was defined as *segmentary* above, i.e., a writing system whose units relate to phonemes, regardless of whether all, some, or no vowels are written in it (cf. also Gnanadesikan 2017: 21).

be found since scripts are not tied to types (and in myriad cases also not to specific writing systems). Consequently, two writing systems using the same script do not necessarily belong to the same type. Take the writing systems of Uyghur, a Turkic language spoken by the Uyghurs (mostly in China), and Persian, a Western Iranian language. Both are written in Arabic script (with some modifications), which is predominantly employed for writing systems that are classified as abjads (see below). Persian is indeed an abjad; by contrast, in Uyghur, all vowels are written, making it an alphabet typologically (cf. Hahn 1991; Kaye 1996).[165]

Notably, this also means that while all writing systems using Roman script are indeed alphabets, one should still refrain from calling it the 'Roman alphabet' as it could be used by writing systems of all types. Of course, Roman script as we know it today is based on the Roman alphabet in the sense of the alphabetic writing system that was historically used by Romans, so from a diachronic perspective, in a very specific sense, there is also a 'Roman alphabet' (cf. Daniels 2018: 29–30). Nowadays, however, the many alphabets that use Roman script merely employ its basic shapes – or 'letters' – whose graphematic values not only differ from those they once had in the Roman alphabet but also vary across writing systems. Thus, an <e> may have similar values but is not exactly the same in English, German, Italian, Swedish, etc., as all these alphabets are distinct systems associating the basic shapes of Roman script with different phonemes. In a nutshell, even if two alphabets use the same script, they are still distinct writing systems because they put into writing distinct languages (cf. Weingarten 2011), which means two writing systems 'looking' the same should not trick us into believing they are the same writing system or even belong to the same type, as the examples of Uyghur and Persian show.

Since the functioning of alphabets is in general rather straightforward, only one example shall be mentioned briefly. Table 10 shows the 33 graphemes of the Georgian alphabet with their pronunciations. Both vowels and consonants are represented by graphemes of equal graphetic and graphematic status. The basic shapes stem from *Mkhedruli*, the standard script in which modern Georgian is written. Two other scripts – *Asomtavruli* and *Nuskhuri* – exist but are used only by the Georgian Orthodox Church.

165 Notably, Persian and other abjads using Arabic script can optionally also be fully vowelled. However, as short vowels are then written with vowel 'diacritics' which are secondary to consonant or long vowel graphemes (see next section), one could discuss the typological classification of such fully vowelled abjads as alphabets. Bright (2000: 70), for example, considers them alphasyllabic rather than alphabetic for precisely this reason (cf. also Gnanadesikan 2017: 32; see below for the term 'alphasyllabary').

Table 10: Georgian alphabet in Mkhedruli script.

ა	ბ	გ	დ	ე	ვ	ზ	თ	ი	კ	ლ	მ
[ɑ]	[b]	[g]	[d]	[ɛ]	[v]	[z]	[tʰ]	[ɪ]	[k']	[l]	[m]
ნ	ო	პ	ჟ	რ	ს	ტ	უ	ფ	ქ	ღ	ყ
[n]	[ɔ]	[p']	[ʒ]	[r]	[s]	[t']	[ʊ]	[pʰ]	[kʰ]	[ɣ]	[q']
შ	ჩ	ც	ძ	წ	ჭ	ხ	ჯ	ჰ			
[ʃ]	[tʃʰ]	[tsʰ]	[dz]	[ts']	[tʃ']	[x]	[dʒ]	[h]			

A feature that is typical of alphabets but absent in Georgian (and Korean, see below) is capitalisation,[166] i.e., there are no pairs of lowercase and uppercase graphemes. The Georgian alphabet is noteworthy for being an alphabet that almost lives up to the expectations of the 'ideal' alphabet because it is "almost perfectly phonemic" (Holisky 1996: 365) and thus almost maximally phonographically transparent. This means that each grapheme corresponds with a single phoneme and each phoneme is represented only by a single grapheme. Furthermore, features that are often perceived as 'deficits' and are pervasive in other alphabets – among them silent letters (e.g., in French) – are kept to a minimum in Georgian.

As a much less prototypical instance of an alphabet that "has been plagued by typological confusion" (Gnanadesikan 2017: 19), Korean Han'gŭl shall also be mentioned here. In principle, classifying the Korean writing system as alphabetic is not controversial: it has graphemes that correspond with consonant phonemes and ones that relate to vowels. However, two above-mentioned aspects set them apart markedly from graphemes of other alphabets: firstly, they are graphetically subsegmental as they are syllabically arranged (cf. Gnanadesikan's view above), i.e., positioned inside syllable blocks that occupy segmental spaces.

Figure 19 shows the individual consonant graphemes <ㅅ> *s*, <ㄹ> *r*, <ㅁ> *m*, and the vowel grapheme <ㅏ> *a* as well as how they are arranged in the two syllable blocks <사> *sa* and <람> *ram* to write the word <사람> *saram* 'person'. The reason behind this arrangement is for Han'gŭl to be "in accord with the appearance of the prestigious Chinese script" (Daniels 2017: 83); more specifically, "[t]he organisational principle of the frame in Chinese is so strong that all other East Asian writing systems that have been influenced by Chinese [. . .] make strict use of an idealised square" (Tranter 2013: 5). There are different views as to whether this has a bearing on the structural classification of the Korean writing system: while most scholars argue that Korean is a 'syllabic' alphabet (cf. Rogers 2005;

166 In the past, there were attempts to introduce capital letters, but none of them were successful.

Daniels 2018), i.e., an alphabet with the syllabic arrangement treated as an additional feature, some – including Pae (2011) – argue that Korean is an alphabetic syllabary, with the syllable being the dominant unit structurally (and psycholinguistically).[167]

In this latter view, the perspective is turned around and the fact that the syllable block can be segmented into smaller graphematic units is considered a surplus. From a strictly structural point of view – and if graphemes are allowed to be subsegmental (⟶ Section 4.2.3) – we adhere to the former view and agree that Korean is an alphabet. However, this debate is still justified as it raises questions such as: is the graphetic feature of segmentality (i.e., the occupation of a segmental space) salient enough to warrant syllables in Korean being treated as basic units? And should the psychological reality of how graphemes and larger graphematic units are actually processed be considered in a structural definition?[168] If so, how? (cf. ⟶ Section 4.7 for similar questions).

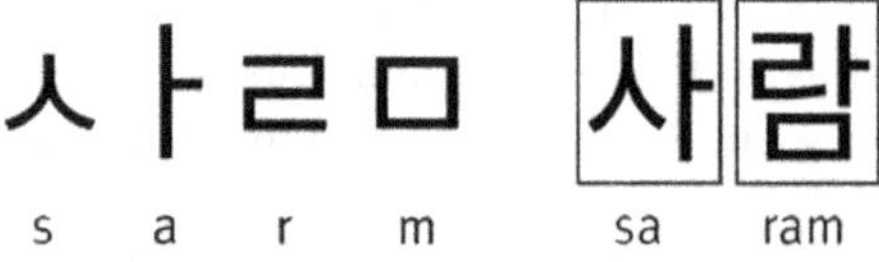

Figure 19: Individual subsegmental graphemes arranged in two syllable blocks.

The second peculiarity of Korean graphemes is that their visual shapes partially relate to phonological features (particularly place/mode of articulation). Notably, this relation is not arbitrary (i.e., symbolic) but iconic: the visual shapes pictographically resemble the places of articulation they relate to (cf. Kim 2011 and Figure 20). While a striking feature, it arguably does not warrant its own subtype of phonography. As one reason, Rogers (2005: 277) mentions that the overall inventory of Han'gŭl shapes "is sufficiently unsystematic as to the relationship between features and shapes" and concludes that "the presence of features does not mean that they form the basic structure of the system" (Rogers 2005: 278). Of

167 Arguably, at least in literacy acquisition, the syllable is foregrounded as the Korean writing system is taught to children as a syllabary (cf. Taylor and Taylor 2014).

168 Rogers (2005: 277) negates this, although not in the context of classifying Korean as a syllabary but as a featural system (see below): "Some people have argued against the featural analysis on the grounds that Koreans learn the system by memorizing entire syllable glyphs. Although I reject the featural analysis, this argument is unpersuasive since linguistic systems and human conscious awareness of them are often quite different" (cf. also Sproat 2000 for a similar argument).

course, the other convincing reason to discard a featural type in a general typology of writing systems is that such a relation does not occur in other major writing systems.

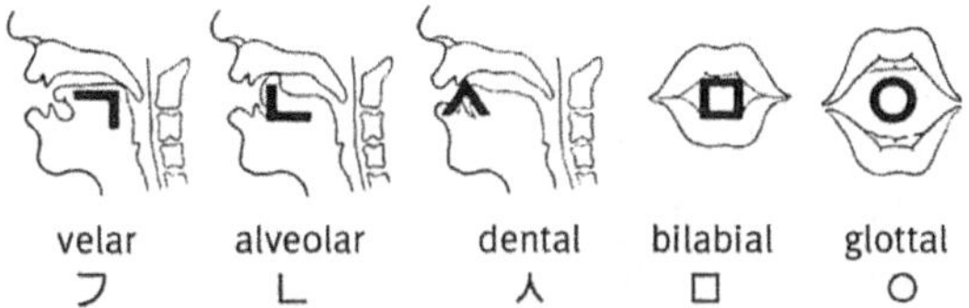

Figure 20: Iconic representation of places/modes of articulation in Han'gŭl.

6.2.3.3 Abjads

An abjad, according to the classification proposed by Gnanadesikan (2017), can either be a consonantal or a partially vowelled segmentary. This widens Daniels' (2018: 37) narrow definition of an abjad as a writing system "that notates only the consonants of its language", which accounts for the diachronic origins of abjads but does not capture the synchronic reality. In the major abjads in use today – the sinistrograde writing systems of Arabic and Hebrew – some vowels are always graphematically represented (and optionally all of them, see below). For early Semitic writing such as the Phoenician writing system, Daniels' definition is accurate, as it represented no vowels. It was during their development that both Hebrew and Arabic came to use certain consonant graphemes to write long vowels. In both systems, graphemes with this function are referred to as *matres lectionis* (Latin 'mothers of reading'). In Arabic, they are *alif* <ا>, which usually – word-initially – carries a *hamza* (<أ>) and then corresponds with /ʔ/, for /a:/,[169] *wāw* <و>, commonly corresponding with /w/, for /u:/, and *yā'* <ي>, whose consonantal correspondence is /j/, for /i:/ (cf. Table 11 for Arabic consonants, where the matres lectionis are marked with asterisks). In Hebrew, the ones most commonly used are <י> for /i:/ and /e:/ and <ו> for /u:/ and /o:/; their default consonantal correspondences are /j/ and /w/, respectively (cf. Rogers 2005: 127, 135). Synchronically, thus, both writing systems are always partially vowelled. What is interesting to note about the long vowel graphemes is that they originally correspond with consonants that are categorised as semivowels or glides.

As mentioned above, Arabic script can also be fully vowelled, as can be Hebrew. This is because in both systems, secondary vowel graphemes were

169 If, word-initially, alif does not carry a hamza, it has no phonological value; if it carries a *madda*, which visually resembles a tilde, in this position (i.e., <آ>), it is pronounced as initial /a:/.

developed. In this respect, Rogers (2005: 133) observes “interesting structural and sociolinguistic parallels between the Arabic and Hebrew writing of vowels” as in both systems, the graphematic representation of short vowels was motivated by the wish to more (faith)fully indicate the pronunciation of religious scripture so that it would not be lost.[170] The secondary graphetic status of the short vowel graphemes, now, is due to the fact that both Hebrew and Islamic scholars did not want to drastically alter sacred text by inserting vowel graphemes of the same size as consonant graphemes. This resulted in respective sets of vowel diacritics. In Hebrew, most of them are points – the practice of using them is accordingly referred to as *vowel pointing*, and texts in which they are employed are *pointed texts* (cf. Rogers 2005: 127). The three diacritics used to represent short vowels in Arabic are shown in Figure 21. Notably, in both Hebrew and Arabic, texts are commonly not fully vowelled, notable exceptions being texts for beginning readers (children or L2 learners).

Table 11: Arabic consonants; the ones marked with asterisks are also used as long vowels.

ا	ب	ت	ث	ج	ح	خ	د	ذ	ر	ز	س
*	[b]	[t]	[θ]	[ʤ]	[ħ]	[x]	[d]	[ð]	[r]	[z]	[s]
ش	ص	ض	ط	ظ	ع	غ	ف	ق	ك	ل	م
[ʃ]	[sˤ]	[dˤ]	[tˤ]	[ðˤ/zˤ]	[ʕ]	[ɣ]	[f]	[q]	[k]	[l]	[m]
ن	ه	و	ي								
[n]	[h]	[w]*	[j]*								

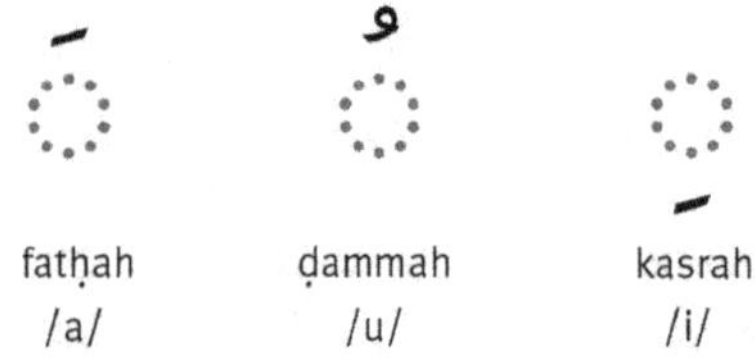

Figure 21: Short vowel graphemes (‘diacritics’) in Arabic.

170 Cf. Daniels (2018: 50–55) for more details on the graphematic representation of vowels in abjads.

6.2.3.4 Abugidas

Commonly, in abugidas, most vowels – most frequently all vowels but one – are graphematically represented, which makes them mostly vowelled segmentaries according to Gnanadesikan's (2017) typology (but see below for other cases). Specifically, the respective 'unmarked' vowel in an abugida – by default a phonetic rendition of the vowel /a/ – is not graphematically represented, at least not when it follows a consonant. Thus, an "abugida is a writing system in which each basic character represents a consonant *and the 'unmarked' vowel that follows it*" (Daniels 2018: 67, emphasis in original) or an individual vowel, although such independent vowels occur only word-initially.

The central unit of abugidas is the so-called *akshara* (from Sanskrit *akṣara* 'syllable, letter'). It corresponds neither straightforwardly with phonological syllables nor with graphemes. Instead, aksharas represent phonological units or sequences which consist of a short or a long vowel that may be preceded but not followed by a consonant or consonant cluster. Thus, possible structures that aksharas correspond with are V, CV, CCV, etc. (cf. Patel 2010: 3). Figure 22 illustrates how the boundaries of phonological syllables and those of aksharas diverge. Notably, given that in most abugidas, consonant graphemes by default also exhibit an inherent vowel value, aksharas can be vowelless although their corresponding phonological syllables have overt vowels as syllable nuclei. Thus, conceiving of aksharas as graphematic syllables in a broad sense implies only that there is a significant suprasegmental graphematic structure; it does *not* mean that this structure corresponds with phonological syllables, i.e., that abugidas are syllabaries. This is also stressed by Daniels (cf. McCawley 1994: 121–122 for the same view):

> The Sanskrit word *kārtsnya* 'totality' is spelled कार्त्स्न्य = क *ka* + आ *ā* + र *r* + त *t* + ष *s* + न *n* + य *ya*. The word provides a spectacular example of why Indic writing systems should not be considered syllabaries: the writing-units do not denote syllables! An entire sequence of up to five consonants followed by a vowel (or a *virama*) is a single writing-unit; the name for such units is *akshara*. [. . .] र्त्स्न्य *rtsnya* is an *akshara*. Clearly, *rtsnya* is not a syllable; the syllables of the word *kārtsnya* are *kārts-* and *-nya*. No matter whether a syllable boundary falls in a sequence of consonants, all the consonants combine in a single *akshara*.
>
> (Daniels 2018: 69–70)

The script in Daniels' example is Devanāgarī, which is the most prototypical representative of abugidas and is used in India and Nepal for the writing systems of Hindi, Marathi, Nepali, as well as, in modern publications, Sanskrit (cf. Gnanadesikan 2017: 18). There exist myriad other abugidic writing systems across South Asia that function very similarly; they all descend from Brāhmī script (cf. Patel, Pandey, and Rajgor 2007; Patel 2010). Table 12 shows the vowel graphemes and Table 13 the consonant graphemes of Devanāgarī.

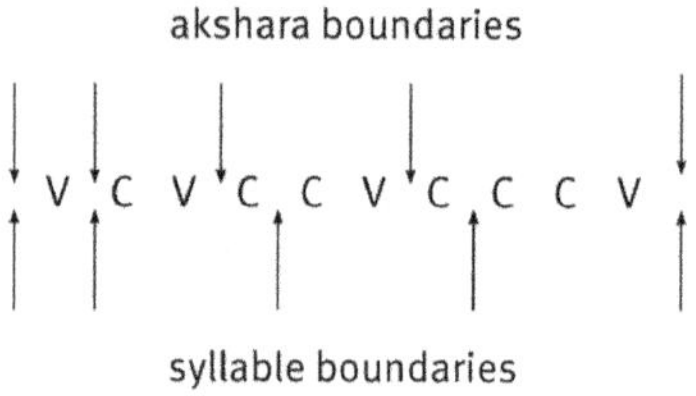

akshara boundaries

V C V C C V C C C V

syllable boundaries

Figure 22: Diverging akshara and (phonological) syllable boundaries, taken from Gnanadesikan (2017: 26).

Table 12: Devanāgarī vowels (independent, as diacritics, and exemplified with consonants <र> *r* and <व> *v*).

	a	*ā*	*i*	*ī*	*u*	*ū*	*r*	*r̄*	*l*	*l̄*	*e*	*ai*	*o*	*au*	–
V	अ	आ	इ	ई	उ	ऊ	ऋ	ॠ	ऌ	ॡ	ए	ऐ	ओ	औ	
C_V	–	◌ा	◌ि	◌ी	◌ु	◌ू	◌ृ	◌ॄ	◌ॢ	◌ॣ	◌े	◌ै	◌ो	◌ौ	◌्
r-	र	रा	रि	री	रु	रू	रृ	रॄ	रॢ	रॣ	रे	रै	रो	रौ	र्
v-	व	वा	वि	वी	वु	वू	वृ	वॄ	वॢ	वॣ	वे	वै	वो	वौ	व्

Table 13: Devanāgarī consonants.

k	*kh*	*g*	*gh*	*ṅ*	*c*	*ch*	*j*	*jh*	*ñ*	*ṭ*	*ṭh*	*ḍ*	*ḍh*	*ṇ*	*t*	*th*
क	ख	ग	घ	ङ	च	छ	ज	झ	ञ	ट	ठ	ड	ढ	ण	त	थ
d	*dh*	*n*	*p*	*ph*	*b*	*bh*	*m*	*y*	*r*	*l*	*v*	*ś*	*ṣ*	*s*	*h*	
द	ध	न	प	फ	ब	भ	म	य	र	ल	व	श	ष	स	ह	

The first common feature of (most) abugidas exemplified by Devanāgarī, which is written from left to right, is the existence of individual vowel graphemes that occur only word-initially. These graphemes have the same graphetic status as consonant graphemes as they are of the same size and occupy their own segmental spaces. It is exclusively in this word-initial position that the vowel /a/ is represented by a grapheme, <अ>. All remaining short and long vowels have corresponding diacritical versions called *matras* (cf. Daniels 2018: 67) that are used together with and are dependent on the consonant graphemes, which serve as 'carriers'.[171] Like the short vowel diacritics in Arabic and Hebrew mentioned above, these post-consonantal vowel graphemes are – at least graphetically – secondary: they cannot occur alone, they are visually less salient (because their

171 Gnanadesikan (2017: 25) refers to this situation of two existing sets of vowel graphemes as 'semi-dependent vowels' and mentions as an example "Devanāgarī, in which initial vowels have their own symbols but vowels that follow consonants are written as diacritics on those consonants".

shapes are in most cases smaller than the shapes of the consonant graphemes they attach to), and they do not occupy their own segmental spaces on the writing surface, which means they can be conceptualised as something like graphetic clitics. For some pairs of short and long vowels, the diacritics for the long vowels are iconic graphetic reduplications of the short vowel diacritics, cf. <ृ> for short and <ॄ> for long vocalic /r/.

Another graphetic feature that has a bearing on the graphematic level as well as reading processes is the position of the diacritical vowel graphemes: they can occur above (such as <े> *e*), below (such as <ु> *u*), to the right (such as <ी> *ī*), or to the left (such as <ि> *i*) of the consonant grapheme. If they occur on the left, i.e., before the consonant grapheme, there is a mismatch between the sequence of graphemes and corresponding phonemes, as written <vC> is pronounced as /Cv/; such vowels have been referred to as *misaligned vowels* (cf. Winskel 2009 for Thai). In Table 12, the consonant graphemes <र> and <व> are shown together with the different secondary vowel graphemes.

The reason that abugidas have at times been classified as syllabaries is that every consonant grapheme, whether in isolation or in combination with a vowel grapheme, corresponds with a phonological CV sequence. As Daniels (2018: 69) notes, this makes writing open syllables – whether they include the graphematically unrepresented vowel /a/ or any other vowel – rather straightforward. However, there is also a need to write closed syllables in Devanāgarī, which is where things get considerably more complicated. If a closed syllable appears at the end of a word, a 'vowel killer', the so-called *virāma*, may be used. It appears as the diacritic <्> below the consonant (cf. the last row of Table 12). As Gnanadesikan (2017: 18, emphasis in original) notes, "in practice in the modern languages, the *virāma* diacritic is almost invariably omitted, the presence or absence of the /a/ vowel being predictable from the prosodic structure of the language". By contrast, if there are consonant clusters within a word, sometimes complex aksharas (also referred to as *ligatures*) are formed by conjoining the graphemes' basic shapes: examples of such complex aksharas conjoining two, three, or four shapes are <त्व> *tva*, <ङ्क्ष> *ṅkṣ*, and <र्ष्ट्र> *rṣṭr*, respectively (cf. Daniels 2018: 68 for examples of four modifications that occur when shapes are conjoined).[172]

As for the type of abjad above, it is important to also address Gnanadesikan's reservations concerning the abugida, especially how, if defined so broadly, it subsumes systems that among themselves exhibit significant differences of typological relevance. That the classification of such a category (or categories)

---

172 At *Omniglot*, one can find a table of all conjunct consonants: https://omniglot.com/writing/devanagari_conjuncts.php (accessed September 21st, 2021).

is challenging is reflected by a variety of terms that have been used to refer to it, including *semi-alphabet, semi-syllabary, semi-syllabic script, syllabic alphabet, alphasyllabary, neosyllabary, segmentally coded syllabically linear phonographic script, akṣara system*, and *āksharik script* (cf. Gnanadesikan 2017: 18–19 for the sources of these terms). What this terminological breadth reveals is a strong tendency to classify systems such as Devanāgarī as something in between alphabets and syllabaries, capturing how they exhibit features of both. This is most evident in Bright's (2000: 65)[173] term *alphasyllabary*, which he notes is common among South Asian specialists (cf. also Salomon 2000). While one might think that the term is a competitor of *abugida*, the two actually denote different phenomena as they have different priorities: abugidas are defined functionally, i.e., graphematically (by the fact that one of the vowels is not represented because it is inherent in consonant graphemes), while alphasyllabaries are defined formally, i.e., graphetically (as vowel graphemes are graphetically secondary, see above).[174] This means the two concepts "disagree as to whether to give priority to *what* segments are being represented or to *how* the representation of those segments is arranged" (Gnanadesikan 2017: 22, emphasis in original). Bright elaborates:

> Daniels prefers a typology based on the 'functional' criterion of correspondence between sound and symbol, in particular the importance of the 'inherent' vowel and its replacement by other vowel symbols. But my own preference, which he calls 'formal', is for a typology which gives more attention to the graphic arrangement of symbols. For this purpose, I accept the terms 'alphabet' and 'abjad' as Daniels defines them; but in defining the alphasyllabary, I focus on the predominantly 'diacritic' status of the vowel symbols.
> (Bright 2000: 66)

This is not the end of the story, however. The two terms not only foreground different criteria but are in fact independent of each other in that "the use of an inherent vowel and the use of vowel diacritics do not always co-occur" (Gnanadesikan 2017: 23). Examples mentioned by Gnanadesikan include, on the one hand, the Thaana script used for the writing system of Dhivehi, which uses vowel diacritics but has no inherent vowel(s), and 'Phags-pa on the other, which has inherent vowels, but vowel graphemes are not secondary. Gnanadesikan's (2017: 28) modification of a typology of segmentaries prioritises the functional criterion,

---

173 Bright (2000) is a reprint of his 1999 article in *Written Language & Literacy*, which was not available to us.

174 In a similar vein, Rimzhim, Katz, and Fowler (2014) have argued that writing systems derived from Brāhmī are structurally (i.e., descriptively) āksharik, i.e., based on the graphematic unit of akshara, but functionally alphabetic. Cf. Share and Daniels (2016) for a rebuttal.

i.e., the two possible choices with respect to inherent vowels, and distinguishes between mostly vowelled āksharik segmentaries and fully vowelled āksharik segmentaries. While the former can either be abugidas or alphasyllabaries, the latter, following Bright's criterion of the graphetic status of vowel graphemes, are either alphasyllabaries (when vowel graphemes are secondary) or alphabets (when they are primary).

In sum, it can be concluded that in its common use, as defined by Daniels, *abugida* "picks out a certain combination of behaviours (inherent vowels and vowel diacritics) that do not in fact always combine" (Gnanadesikan 2017: 23). Its meaning in this book is broader, as it acknowledges the fine-grained and important distinctions established by Gnanadesikan by accepting as abugidas systems that have both an inherent vowel and vowel diacritics but also systems that exhibit only one of those features.

A special challenge for the distinction of syllabaries (or moraic writing systems, see below) and abugidas that intermeshes graphetic features with graphematic functions is the classification of the Cree writing system (cf. McCarthy 1995). In Cree, as generally in abugidas, a given grapheme corresponds with a consonant phoneme plus a vowel phoneme. The unique property, now, is that differences in the vowels that accompany consonants are not represented through graphetic additions to the consonant graphemes. Rather, different vowels are consistently marked by a rotation of the basic shape, so that what graphematically indicates different vowels is the shapes' orientation: <ᑕ>, for example, corresponds with *ta* and <ᑌ> with *te* (cf. Table 14).

Table 14: Cree graphemes.

	–	p	t	k	ch	m	n	s	y
a	ᐊ	ᐸ	ᑕ	ᑲ	ᒐ	ᒪ	ᓇ	ᓴ	ᔭ
e	ᐁ	ᐯ	ᑌ	ᑫ	ᒉ	ᒣ	ᓀ	ᓭ	ᔦ
i	ᐃ	ᐱ	ᑎ	ᑭ	ᒋ	ᒥ	ᓂ	ᓯ	ᔨ
o	ᐅ	ᐳ	ᑐ	ᑯ	ᒍ	ᒧ	ᓄ	ᓱ	ᔪ

The fact that this feature systematically corresponds with different vowel phonemes distinguishes the writing system of Cree markedly from other syllabaries or moraic systems such as the Japanese kana, in which the graphemes correspond with CV sequences holistically and there is no graphetic similarity between graphemes' shapes that correspond with either the same consonant onsets or vowel nuclei (see below). Yet, if Cree were classified as an abugida, the definition of abugida would have to be extended to account for its unique properties. Depending on the way one interprets it, either all or no vowels are represented.

Graphetically, vowels are not anything that is visibly *added* to the basic shapes that correspond with consonants. We still argue that all vowels *are* represented; inspired by Günther's (1988: 65) approach, the way orientation indicates a correspondence with vowels can be conceived of as an integrative linear suprasegment which, in this case, has a graphematic value (⟶ Section 4.6.2). Following the view that all vowels are represented can, of course, also lead to classifications of the system as an alphabet, although what would have to be explained in that case is the lack of independent graphemes for vowels. According to Gnanadesikan's (2017: 29) typology, Cree can be defined as a fully vowelled āksharik segmentary. Lockwood (2001: 310) leans towards classifying Cree as an abugida and notes that the differences in marking vowels from more prototypical representatives of the type should be captured by assuming two subtypes: *diacritic abugida* (such as Devanāgarī or Thai) and *orientational abugida* (such as Cree). Note, however, that given Cree's unique status, such a distinction may not be warranted, as Gnanadesikan concludes:

> It is an open question [. . .] whether the spatial arrangement of the vowels – in the sense that they overlap in space with the consonants rather than being diacritics on consonants – is an important typological distinction to make. In terms of which vowels are represented and how they form larger linguistic units with the consonants, it may not in fact be an important difference. (Gnanadesikan 2017: 29)

6.2.4 Syllabaries

The phonographic types treated in the previous sections are based on relations between graphemes and segmental phonological units. By contrast, syllabaries are, as their name suggests, based on relations between graphemes and syllables, i.e., larger phonological units that are themselves comprised of segments. As shown above, the basic units of abugidas in many cases also correspond with CV syllables. However, aside from the fact that aksharas do not always correspond with syllables, another crucial difference between abugidas and syllabaries is that syllabographic graphemes relate to syllables holistically. In other words, one cannot identify, isolate, or recover in them parts that systematically and consistently relate to the components of the represented syllables (e.g., mainly the onset or the nucleus, in cases of CVC syllables also the coda). Thus, in a syllabary, the basic shapes of graphemes that correspond with the syllables /ha/ and /ma/ or those used to write /ma/ and /me/ are not visually similar even though these pairs of syllables share a syllable nucleus or onset, respectively. Take as specific examples the graphemes that relate to these syllables in the Cherokee syllabary (see below): <Ꭽ> /ha/ vs. <Ꮉ> /ma/, and <Ꮉ> vs. <Ꮍ>

/me/. It is impossible to state which parts of these graphemes' basic shapes relate to the vowel /a/ or the consonant /m/. In abugidas, by comparison, the shapes of graphemes relating to the same consonants are stable, as are the secondary vowel graphemes.

The system these examples stem from, the Cherokee syllabary, was invented in the 19th century by Sequoyah (ca. 1770–1843), a monolingual and illiterate speaker of Cherokee, an indigenous Iroquoian language of the Americas that is now endangered-to-moribund.[175] Upon realising that there existed graphic marks relating to the English language, he created a writing system for Cherokee that he presented to the public in 1821. A mere three years later, awareness of the system was already widespread among the speakers of Cherokee (cf. Scancarelli 1996: 587). That Sequoyah was inspired by other scripts in the design of his own is implied by the fact that many Cherokee basic shapes visually resemble Roman or Greek shapes, cf. <Ꮃ> which relates to /la/ or <Ꮀ> which relates to /hu/. As Table 15 shows, there are 85 graphemes in the Cherokee writing system that derive from a combination of six vowels (a, e, i, o, ə̃[176]) and twelve consonants/consonant clusters (g, h, l, m, n, qu, s, d, dl, ts, w, y).

It is noteworthy that the writing system of Cherokee is underdifferentiated with respect to certain phonological distinctions relevant in the language: for example, null onsets and onsets including a glottal stop are not distinguished from each other (e.g., <Ꭱ> corresponds with both /e/ and /ʔe/), and onsets with unaspirated stops are not differentiated from those with aspirated stops except in five cases: <Ꭶ> *ga* /ka/ vs. <Ꭷ> *ka* /k^{h}a/, <Ꮣ> *da* /ta/ vs. <Ꮤ> *ta* /t^{h}a/, <Ꮥ> *de* /te/ vs. <Ꮦ> *te* /t^{h}e/, <Ꮧ> *di* /ti/ vs. <Ꮨ> *ti* /t^{h}i/, and <Ꮬ> *dla* /t^{l}a/ <Ꮭ> *tla* /t^{lh}a/ (cf. Rogers 2005: 249; Scancarelli 1996: 590). Furthermore, vowel length is not indicated. Also, since every grapheme represents a consonant and an accompanying vowel (with the exception of <Ꮝ>, which corresponds with /s/), consonant clusters are written by simply 'ignoring' the vowel values of syllabographic graphemes (cf. Daniels 2018: 9). Similar phonological distinctions are also left unrepresented in other syllabaries, illustrating that graphematic underdifferentiation and underrepresentation are prevalent in this type of writing system. Of course, how well syllabaries suit the phonology of a language depends on the phonology's structure (and/or additional features of the writing system). Japanese CV (or CVC) syllables, for example, can be represented rather fully with kana graphemes (see below) as well as several additional diacritical modifications, meaning not

175 Cf. https://www.ethnologue.com/language/CHR (accessed September 21st, 2021).
176 In Table 15, the vowel [ə̃] is transcribed as <v>.

all syllabaries necessarily underrepresent important distinctions inherent in the phonologies they correspond with.

Table 15: Cherokee graphemes.

a	e	i	o	u	v [ə̃]
Ꭰ a	Ꭱ e	Ꭲ i	Ꭳ o	Ꭴ u	Ꭵ v
Ꭶ ga Ꭷ ka	Ꭸ ge	Ꭹ gi	Ꭺ go	Ꭻ gu	Ꭼ gv
Ꭽ ha	Ꭾ he	Ꭿ hi	Ꮀ ho	Ꮁ hu	Ꮂ hv
Ꮃ la	Ꮄ le	Ꮅ li	Ꮆ lo	Ꮇ lu	Ꮈ lv
Ꮉ ma	Ꮊ me	Ꮋ mi	Ꮌ mo	Ꮍ mu	
Ꮎ na Ꮏ hna Ꮐ nah	Ꮑ ne	Ꮒ ni	Ꮓ no	Ꮔ nu	Ꮕ nv
Ꮖ qua	Ꮗ que	Ꮘ qui	Ꮙ quo	Ꮚ quu	Ꮛ quv
Ꮝ s Ꮜ sa	Ꮞ se	Ꮟ si	Ꮠ so	Ꮡ su	Ꮢ sv
Ꮣ da Ꮤ ta	Ꮥ de Ꮦ te	Ꮧ di Ꮨ ti	Ꮩ do	Ꮪ du	Ꮫ dv
Ꮬ dla Ꮭ tla	Ꮮ tle	Ꮯ tli	Ꮰ tlo	Ꮱ tlu	Ꮲ tlv
Ꮳ tsa	Ꮴ tse	Ꮵ tsi	Ꮶ tso	Ꮷ tsu	Ꮸ tsv
Ꮹ wa	Ꮺ we	Ꮻ wi	Ꮼ wo	Ꮽ wu	Ꮾ wv
Ꮿ ya	Ᏸ ye	Ᏹ yi	Ᏺ yo	Ᏻ yu	Ᏼ yv

The best-known and most researched syllabaries are indeed the two *kana* inventories of Japanese, *hiragana* and *katakana* (cf. Table 16). As mentioned above, among writing systems in use today, Japanese is unique: it relies on type mixing by using several scripts that are graphematically linked to different types of linguistic units. While one big component of the writing system consists of morphographic graphemes, the *kanji* (cf. next section), which were borrowed from Chinese, the other component is syllabographic (or moraographic, see below).[177] In the very beginnings of writing down the Japanese language, only the morphographic part existed. This presented various challenges since Japanese, as an agglutinating language, is typologically far removed from the structure of isolating Chinese. Analogous situations have occurred many times in the adaptation of writing systems, with some of them representing core moments in the diachronic development of writing in general (⟶ Section 6.5). Handel (2019) aptly illustrates patterns in the strategies employed by languages adapting writing systems that are not suited for them, patterns that also extend to adaptations beyond those of sinography (i.e., writing with Chinese origin), one example being the adaptation of Sumerian writing for Akkadian. Concerning the adoption and ensuing adaptation of Chinese graphemes, not only Japanese but also Korean, both of which are polysyllabic and agglutinating languages,

177 The third component is *rōmaji*, an alphabetic component using the shapes of Roman script.

> will put more emphasis on disambiguating borrowed sinograms through sequential use of phonograms as phonetic determinatives, and will represent morphological affixes through desemanticized graphs that will tend to simplify in structure and come to form a fixed set of phonograms. (Handel 2019: 311)

Thus, it was the need to graphematically represent grammatical affixes that led to the development of the syllabographic kana inventories. A first stage emerged with the so-called *man'yōgana*, kanji used only for their phonological values. Hiragana developed from cursive man'yōgana, whereas katakana are the result of "reducing a sign [. . .] to one of its elemental components" (Masayuki 2011: 54). Some hiragana and katakana graphemes corresponding with the same syllables derive from the same man'yōgana (such as <か> and <カ> for /ka/, both developed from <加>), others from different ones (such as <け> and <ケ> for /ke/, developed from <計> and <介>, respectively).

Synchronically, the two kana scripts fulfil different functions in the writing system: hiragana, the default kana, are used for writing grammatical information and are attached to the morphographic kanji, which represent lexical roots. Also, in some texts, such as texts for beginning readers, kanji are not used at all as such texts are written completely in hiragana. Katakana, on the other hand, mostly serve to write foreign or borrowed words as well as foreign names and toponyms for which there are no kanji. Additionally, they are used for onomatopoetic expressions, to signify emphasis, or for technical and scientific terminology (cf. Smith 1996). A special use of kana is as so-called *furigana*, smaller kana – mostly hiragana, in rarer cases katakana – which are positioned above (when the writing direction is horizontal) or (in vertical writing) to the right of kanji to indicate their pronunciation. They are found predominantly in written materials intended for children or L2 learners.

Table 16: Hiragana and katakana inventories.

					Hiragana					
	–	**k**	**s**	**t**	**n**	**h**	**m**	**y**	**r**	**w**
a	あ	か	さ	た	な	は	ま	や	ら	わ
i	い	き	し	ち	に	ひ	み	–	り	–
			shi	chi						
u	う	く	す	つ	ぬ	ふ	む	ゆ	る	–
				tsu		fu				
e	え	け	せ	て	ね	へ	め	–	れ	–
o	お	こ	そ	と	の	ほ	も	よ	ろ	を
										o (wo)
–					ん					

Table 16 (continued)

	Katakana									
	–	k	s	t	n	h	m	y	r	w
a	ア	カ	サ	タ	ナ	ハ	マ	ヤ	ラ	ワ
i	イ	キ	シ shi	チ chi	ニ	ヒ	ミ	–	リ	–
u	ウ	ク	ス	ツ tsu	ヌ	フ fu	ム	ユ	ル	–
e	エ	ケ	セ	テ	ネ	ヘ	メ	–	レ	–
o	オ	コ	ソ	ト	ノ	ホ	モ	ヨ	ロ	ヲ o (wo)
–					ン					

Thus far, syllabaries were discussed as if it was self-evident that their graphemes relate to syllables, which is suggested by the designation 'syllabary'. In fact, however, their linguistic unit of correspondence is still a matter of debate, and most modern accounts classify systems such as the Japanese kana as moraic or 'moraographic' (for this term, cf. the footnote in Daniels 2018: 62; we adopt it here because it is parallel to the other typological terms). Cherokee is also often treated as based on moras, and following claims first laid out by William Poser (1992),[178] Rogers (2005: 276) holds that, in fact, most writing systems classified as syllabic are in fact moraic.[179] Moras (alternative plural: morae, symbolised in phonology with μ) consist of more than one phoneme but are smaller than syllables (symbolised in phonology with σ). They are the building blocks that syllables are composed of, and syllables can be monomoraic (or short) or bimoraic (long); in rare cases, they can also be trimoraic. The syllable nucleus can equal one mora in the case of short vowels or two moras in the case of long vowels or diphthongs. Since syllable onsets do not count as moras, the sequence CV (i.e., consonant and short vowel) is a monomoraic syllable while CVV (i.e., consonant with a long vowel) is bimoraic. In some languages – such as in Japanese – codas also count as moras, rendering CVC (with a short vowel and a coda) a bimoraic syllable.

178 Poser has never published his ideas, which he first presented in talks in the early 1990s. According to his CV, the first of them – titled "The structural typology of phonological writing" – was held at the University of British Columbia in 1991. He would go on to give talks with the same title ten more times until 1997 (cf. http://www.billposer.org/Papers/cv.pdf, accessed September 21st, 2021). Though unpublished, his claims have spread quite widely (cf., for example, Ratcliffe 2001).

179 Others even treat several writing systems that are commonly classified as segmentaries as (at least additionally) moraic: Daniels (2018: 62–63), for example, describes moraic structures in the Arabic abjad while Gnanadesikan (2012) conceives of the writing system of Thaana as a moraic alphabet.

The mora, thus, is a unit that indicates syllable weight, as the number of moras distinguishes light syllables from heavy syllables. A core point of arguing that 'syllabaries' are in fact based on moras, now, is that in actual syllabaries, bimoraic syllables such as CVC in Japanese should be written with a single grapheme. As Rogers (2005: 276, emphasis in original) puts it: "If Japanese *kana* and Cherokee were true syllabaries, there would be separate symbols for the closed syllables, and a syllable such as /kun/ would be represented by a single symbol". This is not the case in any of the systems thus far presented in this section. In Japanese hiragana and katakana, all graphemes correspond with moras, which means syllables ending in /n/ are written with two graphemes, the first for the onset and the syllable nucleus and the second – the vowelless <ん> in hiragana, <ン> in katakana – for the coda /n/. Some 'true syllabograms' for closed CVC syllables are, according to Rogers (2005: 277), found in Sumerian cuneiform (cf. also Buckley 2018: 34).

As evident above, the 'moraic view' gained acceptance among scholars of writing: Rogers extended it quite productively to re-classify syllabaries, and Daniels' (2018) comprehensive book covering a wide range of types of writing includes a dedicated chapter on systems based on moras. Others, such as Sampson (2015), neither explicitly endorse nor oppose the view. Considerable scrutiny comes from Buckley (2018), who essentially argues that in what are claimed to be moraographic writing systems, core syllables are written instead of moras (cf. also Sproat 2000: 136), i.e., CV syllables that merely coincide with moras. Accordingly, the central graphematic relation is between graphemes and such core syllables, and any correspondence with moras is only secondary or epiphenomenal. Important points raised by Buckley include the fact that in modern phonology, both simple onsets such as in CVC syllables and consonant clusters in complex onsets such as CCCVC are usually conceived of as being linked to the syllable (so-called *syllable linking*) and not to the mora (*mora linking*). In other words, CVC is phonologically modelled as $[C[V]_{\mu}[C]_{\mu}]_{\sigma}$ instead of as $[[CV]_{\mu}[C]_{\mu}]_{\sigma}$ (cf. Buckley 2018: 30).

According to this approach, syllable onsets are not part of moras, which means graphemes corresponding with CV (such as the Japanese kana graphemes) but also more complex sequences such as CCCVC are not, in fact, moraographic but syllabographic.[180] Another relevant point raised by Buckley (2018: 26–27) is that "a central prediction one would expect in a moraic system, that purely moraic differences of vowel and consonant length are crucial, is contra-

180 Note that in the suprasegmental graphematic model proposed for the writing systems of German and English (⟶ Section 4.2.2), the mora also plays no obvious role (but cf. Evertz 2018 for a more thorough picture).

dicted by the well-known fact that these distinctions are among the most ignored in writing". As one type of potential strong evidence that would point to the mora being the actual unit of representational mapping in writing systems, he mentions the distinction of moraic and non-moraic codas (cf. Buckley 2018: 47). The question of whether systems such as the Japanese kana or Cherokee are based on (core) syllables or moras will not be conclusively answered here. Yet, in a comprehensive account of modern writing system typology, it is vital to at least mention it since it is a relevant ongoing debate.

To now turn to a possibility that was briefly introduced in the context of the graphematic syllable (⟶ Section 4.3.1), it is necessary to reiterate that the phonological syllable may enjoy a primacy with respect to the emergence and further development of writing on the grounds that it is a perceptually salient unit. Given that this is a broad hypothesis that concerns all writing, it will be discussed further in the context of universals of writing (⟶ Section 6.4). Notably, aside from the undeniable acoustic salience of the syllable as the linguistic unit of correspondence, there are also disadvantages that are often addressed in association with syllabaries. One of them is that systems with small grapheme inventories such as most segmentaries are easier to acquire; this contributes to the belief that the alphabet is superior. Thus, the perceptual inferiority of the phonological segment to the syllable is compensated by the superiority of a smaller set of units that must be acquired and mastered. Note, however, that this view is challenged by recent research suggesting that syllabaries are, in fact, more easily learned despite consisting of larger inventories (cf. Asfaha, Kurvers, and Kroon 2009; Inkelas et al. 2013). Furthermore, in the instruction of alphabetic writing, the syllable often assumes a central role, and this affinity to syllabic methods existed also in the past as "from Roman times until the nineteenth century reading and spelling were taught syllabically rather than alphabetically" (Trigger 1998: 49).

Another way in which syllabaries and alphabets are compared with each other is their suitability for different types of phonologies and, in extension, languages. Specifically, syllabaries are often thought to be fitting only for phonologies with simple syllable structures in which CV is the default syllable type and in which, for example, no or only few consonant clusters are allowed in onsets and codas (see above). However, this is only an idealisation that does not capture reality, which is underlined by the existence of syllabaries for languages with rather complex syllable structures, one of which is Cherokee (cf. Voogt 2021). Yet, as noted above, writing such a language with a syllabary does entail 'sacrificing' the graphematic representation of some phonological distinctions, which would not be necessary (to the same degree) if such languages used segmentaries.

6.3 Morphography

Turning from the different types of phonography to morphography, it quickly becomes evident that the latter is one major type that is commonly not divided into subtypes. In morphographic writing systems, as the designation implies, the core graphematic principle is that basic shapes relate to morphemes, thereby constituting morphographic graphemes (sometimes referred to as *morphograms*). As mentioned above, due to the double articulation of language, morphemes – with the exception of null morphemes – always have a phonological representation, meaning they can be pronounced. Thus, morphographic graphemes are (in a loose sense) automatically also secondarily phonographic. An example is Chinese <米> (Mandarin) *mǐ*: as a morpheme, *mǐ* has the meaning 'rice', but it can also be used just for its pronunciation *mi* (with or without the specific tone), for example to write non-Chinese names. Vice versa, this is by default not the case; phonographic graphemes like the ones used in alphabets are 'meaningless' as they relate to phonological units which are themselves only parts of morphemes. This fundamental distinction is captured by French (1976: 118, cf. also Haas 1976: 152–153 in the same volume), who classifies morphographic writing systems as *pleremic* (from Greek *plḗrēs* 'full') since their graphemes are semantically informed and phonographic writing systems as *cenemic* (from Greek *kenós* 'empty') given that their units are devoid of meaning.

Terminology is contentious when it comes to morphography, as the term itself is not universally accepted. Indeed, one can still often find the term 'logography' in research addressing morphographic writing systems. Interestingly, as Joyce (2011: 59) observes, 'logography' also continues to be used by scholars who readily admit that 'morphography' is more accurate; examples include Daniels (1996), Gnanadesikan (2009),[181] and Sampson (2015). Joyce criticises this practice:

> As the central motivations driving terminological distinctions should be to provide more accurate descriptions and develop more realistic theoretical accounts of the phenomenon under consideration, clearly getting the terminology right is vital. (Joyce 2011: 59)

Indeed, maintaining 'logography' to refer to morphography just because it has traditionally been the predominant term is not a convincing enough argument.[182]

181 Cf. Gnanadesikan (2009: 7, emphasis in original): "Writing systems that concentrate on representing morphemes – as complete meaning-pronunciation complexes – are called *logographic* (the name, meaning 'word-writing,' is traditional, though it ignores the difference between morphemes and words)".

182 Cf. Meletis (2021a) on the need of re-evaluating some established (grapholinguistic) terms, illustrated by the descriptive use of 'orthography'.

Crucially, if taken literally, logography and morphography actually do not designate the same phenomenon. Terminologically, 'logography', from Greek *lógos* 'word', refers to word-writing. As will be argued in the following section, there are no modern writing systems in which the word level (i.e., the polymorphemic level) is the dominant level of representational mapping. One could still argue that 'logography' is accurate when what is written in a system are single free lexical morphemes since these already represent independent words on their own. The major challenge for the concept of 'logography' thus comes in the form of bound morphemes: in Chinese, one of the two major writing systems in which morphography is central to this day, graphemes relate to bound morphemes the same way they relate to free morphemes. Suffixes, for example, are represented by single graphemes the same way lexical morphemes are (cf. Osterkamp and Schreiber 2021: 49). However, it is paramount to note that the accuracy of classifying such a system as morphographic and thus rejecting the notion of 'logography' is biased synchronically. As Osterkamp and Schreiber (2021: 48) point out, in Old Chinese, graphemes did actually correspond with entire words, the crucial point being that these could not only be mono- but also polymorphemic. Thus, from a diachronic perspective, the existence of a concept of logography – in a narrow sense based on a literal reading of the term – may be justified.[183] Since this section is devoted to the synchronic classification of writing systems (even when it is used to classify writing systems no longer in use, see below), we will adhere to 'morphography'.

As mentioned, synchronically, the morphographic type of writing systems is only represented by Chinese and one component of the multi-script Japanese writing system, the kanji. What is interesting is that in Sproat's and Rogers' two-axis typologies (⟶ Section 6.1), Japanese is claimed to incorporate a larger amount of morphography than Chinese. The reason for this is that Chinese graphemes include phonological components indirectly providing readers with information about the pronunciation of respective graphemes that include them (⟶ Section 4.2.3). In Japanese, the situation is much more complex, as the kanji, most of which were originally adopted from the original Chinese hanzi, have more than one reading, i.e., effectively relate to more than one linguistic unit (or variants of one unit, see below). For example, the Chinese word (= free lexical morpheme) *shān* 'mountain' was borrowed into Japanese as *san*, which is written with the likewise borrowed grapheme <山>. As time passed, the native Japanese

183 As an alternative, Daniels (2018: 99) also mentions the terms 'heterogram' (and, analogously, 'heterography'), which originates from Iranian studies, and argues that "[s]ince it is noncommittal as to the level of grammatical analysis involved – it doesn't specify 'word' or 'morpheme,' just otherness – it might be convenient to adopt it for general use".

morpheme for 'mountain', *yama*, also came to be written with the same shape. At that point, <山> had (at least) two readings: the former, Sino-Japanese reading (or *on-reading*) and the latter, native Japanese reading (*kun-reading*).

The situation is made even more complex by the fact that both Chinese words and graphemes were borrowed into Japanese during three different periods, the result of which is often multiple on-readings. The question of how to conceptualise this coexistence of multiple readings for one shape cannot be answered simply. Joyce (2011: 62) speaks of an "interesting form of allomorphy", which is to be understood as one morpheme such as 'mountain' having different pronunciations (on- vs kun-readings) in different contexts. While this analysis appears plausible, how does it translate to a corresponding grapholinguistic analysis? It means that the same basic shape can relate to different allomorphs of a morpheme depending on the morphological context (which is indicated by the surrounding morphographic graphemes). What can be conceptualised as syntagmatic graphematic allography according to the framework presented in ⟶ Section 4.6.3 is complicated by the fact that the visual shape does not change along with the shifting linguistic referent (i.e., allomorph). This, however, is not much different from analogous situations in phonographic writing systems. In German, for example, the complex grapheme <ch> refers to different allophones depending on the phonological context (and also depending on the regional variety of German in question). Accordingly, varying linguistic values – especially if they are 'only' allophones or allomorphs – do not challenge the graphematic concepts introduced in this book.

There is another noteworthy difference between Chinese and Japanese that can be interpreted as rendering the latter 'more' morphographic: the native Japanese morphemes that the graphemes borrowed from Chinese were (re)associated with are often not monosyllabic. This means that in their kun-readings, graphemes potentially relate to morphemes that consist of multiple syllables. This undoes the morphosyllabicity of Chinese in Japanese as graphemes in most cases correspond exclusively with morphemes and not (also) indirectly with syllables.

This typological property of morphosyllabicity also serves as a fitting transition from synchrony to diachrony. In the past, morphography was also prevalent in other writing systems, making it relevant for diachronic research on writing but also the comparative study of writing in general. In fact, all of the first (independently invented, see below) writing systems – which, aside from Chinese, include those of Sumerian and Mayan – were to large degrees morphographic. When asking why it is exactly these languages in which writing first arose, the complex answer includes their typological features, most importantly the fact that they were essentially morphosyllabic. Thus, cognitively salient units (free lexical morphemes = words) collapsed with acoustically salient units (syllables) to constitute units that are perceptually suitable to serve as correspondence units for graphemes (see the following section). Another crucial feature that these first writing systems shared is their incorporation of pictography (cf. Figure 23 for examples), at least in their earliest stages. Thus, the basic shapes of many graphemes iconically resembled the meaning of the corresponding morphemes. This intimate connection between morphography and pictography is not difficult to explain: as units that bear meaning, morphemes provide something that can be 'written' or rather rudimentarily 'drawn'. This, of course, applies only to morphemes with concrete meanings such as *tree* or *bird* that can be depicted and not to those with abstract meanings such as *freedom* or *love*, which could be written only with the help of strategies such as semantic and phonological extension (⟶ Section 6.5).

Figure 23: Oracle Bone shape (early Chinese) iconically resembling water, Mayan glyph resembling the blossoming of a water lily, and Egyptian hieroglyph resembling waves (from left to right).[184]

The most important commonality of these systems, however, is that they are not only morphographic but also use similar strategies of including secondary phonography. An interesting though (thus far) little-received proposal for a comparative analysis comes from Tranter (2013). He terms his approach *layering* and characterises it as follows:

> [. . .] the analysis of writing systems under consideration must recognise the (potential) existence of more than one layer of composition and posits three fundamental units corresponding to different layers: logogram, component, and element. (Tranter 2013: 8)

As will be shown with an example, the element, at the lowest level of analysis, has a function in the writing system as a whole and relates directly to the function of the component it is a part of; however, it is itself not a component. The same relation is repeated at a higher level: the component has a function, meaning, or value that relates directly to the logogram (understood here as 'morphogram') it is a part of, but it is not a logogram itself. Finally, the logogram "is defined as the smallest complete unit of writing that corresponds to a unit of

184 The Mayan glyph (*JA'/HA'* 'water') is taken from Tokovinine (2017: 14).

meaning in the spoken language, typically a word in a very loose sense" (Tranter 2013: 9). To exemplify this, Tranter (2013: 9–10) analyses the Chinese grapheme <菇> (Mandarin) *gū* 'mushroom' (cf. Figure 24). At the component level, we find the phonological component |姑| that derives from the independent grapheme <姑> (Mandarin) *gū* 'paternal aunt' and the semantic component |艹| that indicates PLANT and thus hints at the meaning of the logogram; the latter does not exist as an independent character. That the process of combining semantic and phonological components is recursive becomes obvious in a further analysis of the component |姑|: it combines the semantic component |女| WOMAN with the phonological component |古| *gǔ*, both of which derive from independent morphographic graphemes, <女> *nǚ* 'woman', and <古> *gǔ* 'old'. Notably, these latter two components of the grapheme <姑> are not classified as components but as elements with respect to <菇> because they do not directly contribute to the value of the logogram as a whole: *mushroom* has nothing to do with WOMAN, and the pronunciation of the logogram derives (directly) from |姑|, not |古|.

Figure 24 also shows examples from Sumerian[185] and Mayan. Notably, they differ from the Chinese example in that here, components can also consist of further components.[186] In the Sumerian example, thus, |𒇉| is a component not only of |𒀀𒇉| but also of <𒀀𒇉𒌓𒄒𒉣> *buranun* 'Euphrates' because it relates directly to the entire logogram's meaning. Aside from the different proposed layers, another achievement valuable for a comparative grapholinguistics is the four component types that Tranter (2013: 14–19) describes: S (+semantic, –phonological), P (–semantic, +phonological), X (–semantic, –phonological), or Ψ (+semantic, +phonological); cf. Figure 24 for examples of S and P. Importantly, components are not required to be etymologically or otherwise diachronically motivated and do not even have to derive from independent morphographic graphemes (or 'logograms'), as "[a]ll that is required is that the value that we assign to them occurs synchronically as a component in more than one logogram" (Tranter 2013: 9).[187] Thus, as alluded to above, Tranter's proposal is synchronic

185 For other interesting comparative studies of Chinese, Sumerian, and Egyptian writing, cf. Gong (2006) and Gong, Yan, and Ge (2009).

186 For Chinese, Tranter (2013: 9–10) describes a 'two-component maximum principle'; logograms involving three components do exist, but unlike in the other mentioned writing systems, they are rare.

187 To give an example from Chinese, "the WOMAN component is attested in a large number of characters representing morphemes involving women or activities involving women. It is from its recurrence in these characters that we identify it synchronically as WOMAN rather than from its occurrence as an independent logogram writing 'woman'" (Tranter 2013: 9).

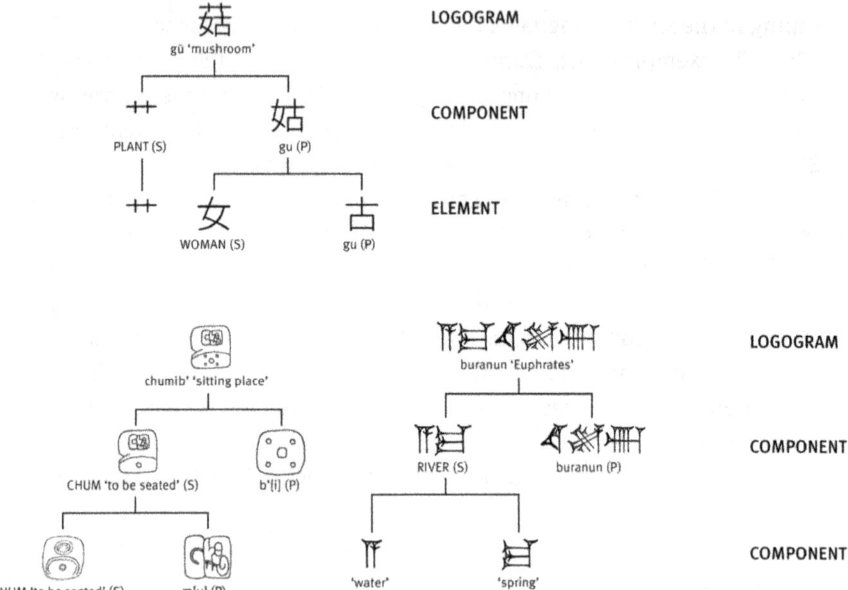

Figure 24: Layering in Chinese, Mayan, and Sumerian.

although he is interested in the structure and use of ancient writing systems that are – with the exception of Chinese – no longer in use.

At the end of this section, secondary morphography shall not be left unmentioned. As introduced above, it concerns the – in most cases suprasegmental – graphematic representation of morphological information in otherwise cenemic phonographic writing systems. Some scholars deem it so relevant they even devote a subtype to it. Among them is DeFrancis (1989), who divides the alphabetic type into what he calls 'pure' phonemic systems such as Greek, Latin, and Finnish, and morphophonemic systems, as examples of which he lists English, French, and Korean. Interestingly, the attribute 'pure' is inherently evaluative and reflects the underlying ideal expected from phonographic writing systems: one-to-one correspondences between units of writing and units of sound. Any morpho(no)graphic information that superimposes 'purely' phonographic correspondences can thus quickly be discarded as nuisance. This perception is also present in the orthographic depth hypothesis (cf. Katz and Frost 1992) according to which writing systems that adhere to the one-to-one ideal are classified as shallow, whereas others that include – among other things – morphographic components are deemed deep. This assessment is motivated psycholinguistically, as the hypothesis aims to explain differences in how children learn to read in different writing systems. However, what has often been pointed out in the literature is that beginning readers and advanced readers have different needs, with the latter actually benefitting from a certain degree of morphography as it allows them to access the meaning of written words more directly.

6.4 Universals of writing

The preceding presentation of different types has highlighted the diversity of writing systems. In this section, the perspective is reversed, and the focus is shifted to the universality or 'unity of writing systems' (cf. Daniels 2017). An investigation of what is universal about or in writing as opposed to what is unique to distinct (types of) writing systems is a worthwhile endeavour because it is expected to uncover important aspects about the general nature of writing. Indeed, the grapholinguistic approach adopted in this book is shaped by this view, and many of the ideas established in earlier chapters – for instance descriptive graphematic concepts such as the grapheme, allography, and graphotactics – are intended to be universally applicable. Defining such broad tools is possible only because regardless of how diverse they appear superficially, at their core, writing systems share certain structural and functional features: with respect to the mentioned concepts, for example, they all consist of abstract basic units of which there are variants of different types, and they are all governed by certain regularities and rules (regarding the combination or permissible length of units, to name two central aspects).

These traits are universal as they stem from the basic facts that (1) writing systems are semiotic systems that relate to language and, in order to be used successfully for communication, (2) must be processed physiologically and cognitively by humans. But why, given these two fundamental aspects, are there so many diverse writing systems? Firstly, because each writing system relates to a specific language, which means writing systems reflect the sheer diversity of the world's languages, and secondly, because writing is a cultural technique. Thus, writing systems are shaped by the cultures in which they were conceived and in which they are used. In a nutshell, universality in writing is conditioned by the paucity of ways in which writing can relate to language in general on the one hand and universal human cognitive processes on the other, whereas the diversity of specific writing systems is largely a reflection of the diversity of languages and cultures (cf. Meletis in press). In the following, several important universal tendencies in writing systems as well as the tension between universal and diverse traits will be discussed. Before this can be done, however, it is vital to examine why Sampson (2016a: 566), as an authority in the study of writing systems, believes that "issues of typology [and universals, DM/CD] are unusually contentious" with respect to writing – and whether such a view is justified.

In essence, Sampson's argument rests on the fact that "there are few independent examples" (Sampson 2016a: 565), meaning few writing systems that are unrelated. As will be shown below, historically, writing indeed emerged in different settings fewer than a handful of times, and all writing systems in use both in the past and today have developed from this extremely limited number of 'original' systems. For example,

> [a]ll fully-alphabetic scripts (that is, with letters for vowels as well as for consonants) descend with only minor changes from the adaptation of some version of the Semitic alphabet, probably by a single individual Greek-speaker on a particular occasion, to write Greek. (Sampson 2016a: 565)

Consequently, claims such as that of the naturalness[188] of using a single grapheme to represent the phoneme sequence /ks/ in most alphabets could be misguided since such phenomena may amount to nothing more than historical accidents:

> The Greek who first learned the alphabet must have struggled to interpret the alien sounds of a Semitic language in terms of the phonology of his own language, and perhaps came up with the interpretation /ks/ for a single Semitic sound. Ever since then, speakers of Greek and of most languages written with the Roman alphabet [= in our conception different alphabets using Roman script, DM/CD] have used a single letter for that pair of phonemes. (Sampson 2016a: 566)

While this is why Sampson regards writing system typology a contentious field, both the assumption of meaningful types of writing systems and the search for universals are arguably not this controversial, which is based on the simple fact that in such a line of argument, a vital aspect is disregarded: just like languages, writing systems change, and this process relies crucially on the interaction between the structure of writing systems and their use by members of literate cultures. With respect to the mentioned /ks/-example, this means that if representing this sound sequence with a single written unit had not in a way been 'natural', whatever this means in a given context, users of writing systems descending from Greek could have (unconsciously or consciously) changed it. They could have, for example, dropped the letter or altered it (cf. Daniels 2006). In fact, in alphabets using Cyrillic script such as the Russian writing system, no single grapheme exists for the sound combination, which is written as <кс> /ks/ instead (as in <текст> 'text'). Similarly, in some alphabets employing Roman script such as the Danish alphabet, <x> is used only in exceptions while <ks> is the default. In any case, changes do occur, and they (re)shape the synchronic structure of writing

188 For the concept of naturalness in writing and the proposal of a *Natural Grapholinguistics*, cf. Meletis (2018) and Meletis (2020a: Part III).

systems. Dismissing all such observations as historical accidents would mean disregarding users' (conscious and unconscious) influence and agency. Investigating the forces involved in the diachronic development of writing systems helps to understand why certain universal tendencies have prevailed, highlighting the intimate connection between the history of writing (⟶ Section 6.5) and the universals that emerge in its course.

Watt (1983) describes four forces of change: homogenisation, facilitation, heterogenisation, and inertia. Homogenisation makes units of writing systems more similar to each other, facilitation leads to them becoming easier to produce and/or to perceive. Heterogenisation, as the counterforce to homogenisation, intervenes when units threaten to become too similar, and, finally, inertia is essentially a passive force that reflects the human preference for maintaining the status quo. Accordingly, inertia could be responsible for many alphabets retaining the practice of using a single letter for /ks/, which is reinforced by the general features of writing, specifically its material permanence (⟶ Section 2.2). Notably, all of the mentioned forces are based in human capacities, be they physiological, cognitive, or sociopragmatic. This reflects what neuroscientist Stanislas Dehaene hypothesises with respect to the interaction between human nature and the structure of writing systems:

> In brief, our cortex did not specifically evolve for writing – there was neither the time nor sufficient evolutionary pressure for this to occur. On the contrary, writing evolved to fit the cortex. Our writing systems changed under the constraint that even a primate brain had to find them easy to acquire. (Dehaene 2009: 150)

By establishing that "developmental pathways [. . .] result from universal features of human cognitive processing", Handel (2019: 312) provides valuable evidence supporting this hypothesis. While some specifics surrounding his findings will be presented in the following section, it suffices to mention here the core claim that both "human cognition and linguistic typology have a determinative influence on how early logo-syllabic writing can develop and be adapted" (Handel 2019: 311). When the second part of this sentence, which focuses on the first writing systems ever created as well as the ways they were adapted (see below), is rephrased to 'how writing systems can develop', the result is an even broader hypothesis. And indeed, above, human cognition and linguistic typology were suggested as driving forces behind the universality and diversity of writing systems, respectively. This makes it worthwhile to take a closer look at how they assume these crucial roles.

Few 'true', that is, absolute universals of writing have been identified. One that has been observed in the literature is determined by both human cognition and the fact that writing is a modality of language. It concerns the criterion we have referred to as dominant level of representational mapping (⟶ Section 6.1), which has shaped traditional writing system typology as outlined in this chapter. Specifically, all levels that possibly serve as the dominant level of representational mapping – and, in turn, all possible types of writing systems – are based on units of language that form (relatively) closed classes (cf. Sampson 2015: 32). As we have seen, in segmentaries, written units relate to phonemes, in syllabaries to syllables or moras, and in morphographic writing systems to morphemes. Every language's phoneme inventory is closed, exceptions being the (rather seldom) borrowing and integration of foreign phonemes together with loanwords. Likewise, due to phonotactic constraints, every language allows only a limited number of syllables that are deemed well-formed. Finally, while the level of morphemes is, in theory, open, as new morphemes do enter languages, this happens much less frequently than new words being formed from existing morphemes (through processes such as derivation, composition, etc.).

By contrast, at least synchronically, there exist no writing systems whose basic units relate to polymorphemic units, i.e., words, let alone sentences, precisely because these inventories are open (cf. Unger and DeFrancis 1995). If a writing system's graphemes referred to sentences, there would need to be an infinite number of graphemes, which of course is not possible – mainly due to constraints of our cognitive system and the fact that, if such sentence-graphemes existed and were to be used for communication, they would have to be(come) conventionalised and accepted by all members of a literate community. Given the productivity of syntax, this is an impossible scenario.

A second potential universal of writing that was briefly mentioned above appears promising but is not unequivocally accepted (cf. Klinkenberg and Polis 2018: 59): what Daniels (1992, 2017, 2018) has termed the primacy of the syllable (cf. also Meletis 2020a: 305–308). Evidence for it comes from observations regarding the creation/invention of writing systems (what Daniels calls 'grammatogeny'):

- "All new writing systems [. . .] invented by nonliterates who know that writing exists are syllabaries. This suggests that syllables might be paramount in grammatogeny.
- All three languages involved in creations of writing systems from nothing [Sumerian, Chinese, ancient Mayan, DM/CD] share a typological similarity. They are essentially monosyllabic." (Daniels 2017: 84)

Writing systems for which the first point applies – among them Cherokee and Vai (see below) – are syllabaries (or moraographic systems) because, arguably, the phonological syllable is the most salient unit of speech accessible to speakers of a language even in the absence of sophisticated metalinguistic knowledge or 'phonological awareness'. Within the spoken modality, the syllable's salience is compared to that of the phoneme, which is frequently claimed to be less accessible to users (cf. Daniels 2017: 76), resulting in blanket statements such as "[a] more natural unit than the phoneme is the syllable" (Sampson 2016b: 49). However, it is important to note that while the syllable is the prominent unit of speech, it is not the most salient unit of language in general, a role that is arguably assumed by the word (or free lexical morpheme) mainly because it bears a concrete meaning and is thus most graspable for users (cf. Trigger 1998: 55). However, if the structure of a language is not suited for morphography,[189] for example because most of its words are polymorphemic or it involves a large degree of morphonography, the syllable level proves to be the next best candidate for becoming the dominant level of representation in a writing system.

The second point raised by Daniels refers to the original independent creations of writing. The question of why it was specifically these languages (and cultures) in which writing first emerged – in the form of morphographic writing systems, notably – is a lucky typological coincidence: Sumerian, Chinese, and ancient Mayan were not only, as Daniels states, monosyllabic, but, importantly, morphosyllabic. In other words, morphemes consist(ed) of a single syllable, creating 'super-salient' units that were accessible both acoustically because they are syllables and cognitively because they were meaning-bearing morphemes. Here, the two aspects mentioned by Handel converge: human physiology and cognition (what can we hear and process?) as well as linguistic typology (how are languages built?). This underlines that both aspects must be consulted together in any search of universals of writing.

Noteworthy research focusing on universals of writing was carried out by John S. Justeson. In line with Joseph Greenberg's influential work on language universals, Justeson (1976, 1978) attempted to uncover universals of writing by analysing a large sample of writing systems. Notably, his search was restricted to the representational function of writing, i.e., its relation to language and, at least in a first instance, to phonography (cf. Justeson 1976: 59). This must be noted because excluding purely or largely morphographic systems such as Japanese and Chinese constrains the scope of possible universals to be found. On the basis of his sample, Justeson identified a total of 38 universals of phonography. However, only two of them are considered absolute universals: (1) "[a]ll writing

189 Daniels (2018: 9) briefly mentions that Sequoyah, the inventor of the Cherokee writing system, initially attempted to create it as a logographic writing system. Here, 'logographic' is understood literally since (polymorphemic) words would have been written. As argued above, the word level of a language is open and thus not a suitable candidate as a basis for (the creation of) writing systems.

systems distinguishing any phonemes contain signs distinguishing some consonantal phonemes", and (2) "[n]o writing system represents either long or geminate consonants" (Justeson 1976: 61). It is the first of these – an implicational universal – that is much more interesting, as aside from the above-mentioned preference for syllables, it suggests another primacy, that of consonants over vowels.[190] And indeed, with abjads, there exist major writing systems in which consonants are graphematically represented but not (all) vowels, and in most abugidas, vowels are secondary, whereas there exist no writing systems in which vowels but not consonants are written or vowels are primary and consonants secondary. Gnanadesikan (2017: 29) captures this by writing that "[i]n the distinction between consonants and vowels, consonants are the consistent winners". While some of the other universals proposed by Justeson reveal interesting facets about the fundamental functioning of writing systems – examples being "[f]ew writing systems distinguish all their phonemes" and "most writing systems over-represent some of their phonemes" (Justeson 1976: 61) – others are less interesting from a purely grapholinguistic perspective because they merely echo general universals of language (such as "no nasal vowel is represented unless some oral vowels are represented", Justeson 1976: 69).

In a subsequent study, Justeson (1978) also included discussion of possible universals that concern the morphological and semantic levels. The former are relevant for morphographic writing systems. An example is that no writing system "represents all its morphemes by individual signs" (Justeson 1978: 94), which is similar to the situation in phonographic writing systems as cited above. The semantic universals, on the other hand, apply to semantic determinatives as found in Egyptian and Akkadian. In general, Justeson's description of these non-phonological universal tendencies remains vague, which is in part due to the small sample size available for such systems. This leads back to the problem mentioned by Sampson (2016a: 565) that "[t]he only logographic scripts used to any serious extent in the modern world are Chinese script and its adaptations to write the languages of countries neighbouring China".

Whether they are grounded in human physiology and cognition (such as the primacy of the syllable, especially when it converges with the morpheme) or merely echo universals found in language (such as the majority of the universals proposed by Justeson), all universals mentioned thus far concern the 'classic' cri-

---

190 To complement this structural observation with data from processing, psycholinguistic research has suggested that in some alphabetic writing systems (using Roman script), consonant graphemes prove more important for recognition processes than vowel graphemes (cf. Carreiras and Price 2008). Notably, a study by Pae, Bae, and Yi (2019) suggests that this consonant primacy is script-specific as it was not found in the reading of the Korean writing system.

terion of writing system typology, (dominant level of) representational mapping. In other words, they are structural universals that focus exclusively on writing as a modality of language. Two relevant perspectives are neglected in such an approach: the use of writing and writing as a spatial system that exhibits features independent of language.

As for use, the universals of reading acquisition described by Verhoeven and Perfetti (2022) can be mentioned as a promising example. They are based on descriptions by respective experts of how children learn to read in different writing systems (these individual contributions are collected in Verhoeven and Perfetti 2017). While this question favours perception over production, it would, of course, also be possible to study universals of writing by hand[191] or typing, to name only two production-oriented examples. Moreover, in their study, only one – if an important – aspect of perception is singled out, namely reading acquisition. By contrast, possible general universals of reading (i.e., ones relevant once literacy has been acquired) are suggested in Frost (2012) and discussed in many stimulating responses in the open peer commentary.[192] The writing systems Verhoeven and Perfetti consider as a basis of their generalisations are

> Asian (Chinese, Japanese, Korean, Kannada), West Semitic (Arabic, Hebrew), Romance (Italian, French, Spanish), Germanic (German, Dutch, English), Slavic (Czech, Slovak, Russian), Greek, Finnish, and Turkish. (Verhoeven and Perfetti 2022: 150)

While this sample may be broad as it covers many individual systems, it does not represent all types of writing systems equally. Unsurprisingly, alphabets are highly overrepresented while there are only two abjads, one abugida (Kannada), and two morphographic systems. The only syllabaries included are Japanese kana. Especially the lack of abugidas is acknowledged by the authors, who, however, frame it geographically by stating that their sample "underrepresents the languages read in South Asia and Sub-Saharan Africa" (Verhoeven and Perfetti 2022: 151).

Verhoeven and Perfetti's focus is on the mapping principles of writing, i.e., once again the relation between units of writing and units of language. In this vein, they formulate several so-called *operating principles* (OP) that allow children to grasp said mapping principles. These OP "apply to the three major aspects of learning to read: becoming linguistically aware, acquiring word identification

191 With respect to handwriting, Goodnow and Levin's (1973) so-called 'grammar of action' is worth mentioning. It describes processes in handwritten production that – save for differences due to varying writing directions – are possibly universal (cf. Thomassen and Tibosch 1991).
192 Cf. *Behavioral and Brain Sciences* 35 (2012): 279–329.

skill and learning to comprehend" (Verhoeven and Perfetti 2022: 154). They are assumed to be universal mainly because reading involves the engagement of a reading network in the brain regardless of the writing system that is being read. The authors sum up their proposed OP as follows:

> Thanks to the (re)structuring (OP1) and increasing awareness (OP2) of the phonological infrastructure of spoken language, and as a result of a learned specialization to recognize (OP3) and extend orthographic codes (OP4), visual word forms are stored in memory which increase in number, specificity (OP5) and redundancy (OP6) through reading exposure. A connection can then be made between these lexical building blocks and basic unification blocks with morphological (OP7) and syntactic relations (OP8), on the one hand, and general knowledge (OP9), on the other. (Verhoeven and Perfetti 2022: 161)

These listed OP are, of course, the results of a high degree of generalisation. However, the authors do underline that the specific influences of given writing systems on learning to read should not be neglected. Indeed, they close their paper by stating that the "story of learning to read [. . .] is one of universals and particulars" (Verhoeven and Perfetti 2022: 161): universals because writing, regardless of the specific system in question, by definition always relates to language (see above) and thus all children learning to read essentially face the same challenge of grasping this relation, and particulars because the unique features of individual writing systems do matter. With respect to the latter particulars, Verhoeven and Perfetti emphasise the representational function of writing by claiming that in literacy acquisition it is paramount not only that but "*how* different levels of language – morphemes, syllables, phonemes – are engaged; this in turn depends on the structure of the language and how its written form accommodates this structure" (Verhoeven and Perfetti 2022: 161, emphasis added). This underlines how traditional writing system typology is tied to language typology.

It also serves as a fitting transition to the question of what the reason is behind the sheer diversity found in the world's writing systems (see also the next section). The first level at which we – quite literally – 'see' diversity is the scripts used to give writing systems their graphic form. There exist, of course, many more scripts than types of writing systems, as a single type such as the alphabet may be exemplified by various scripts. By contrast, there are fewer scripts than specific writing systems, as every language that has a written modality has its own writing system, and different writing systems may employ the same script. As the material manifestation of writing, scripts are symbolically charged and thus come to signify cultures. Thus, one reason underlying visual diversity is, broadly put, culture, which is in line with the fact that writing is a cultural technique. Here, 'culture' is globally defined and subsumes, for example, the materials that are being used for writing in a given culture (because they are available in a specific region, affordable, . . .), which – especially in the past given the absence of digital technology – have also frequently shaped the visual makeup of scripts and thus contribute(d) to graphetic diversity: Burmese script, written on leaves, is very round, whereas cuneiform, carved on clay, is angular.

Diversity can, of course, also be found at the graphematic level. What was mentioned as a challenge of writing system typology is that types are always idealisations, and systems belonging to them differ, sometimes considerably so. That, for instance, both the French and Finnish writing systems are classified as alphabets does not mean they function exactly the same. In such cases, differences are found at the system-specific level because of the way a given (type of) writing system is suited – or not – to the features of the language it relates to. Thus, graphematic diversity is determined by the differences between the world's many languages on the one hand and the degree of how well writing systems fit the structure of their respective languages on the other. This latter 'linguistic fit' (cf. Meletis 2020a: Chapter 6) can capture how typologically similar languages whose writing systems we would expect to be alike actually rely on different graphematic strategies and solutions. Therefore, not every language 'gets the writing system it deserves' (cf. Frost 2012), at least not in structural terms. This is due to the myriad influences that only in (complex) combination determine the makeup of writing systems, including cultural, religious, commercial, and political factors (cf. Verhoeven and Perfetti 2022: 154).

What must also be mentioned here is that even if at the graphematic level, a writing system has a 'good' linguistic fit, superimposing orthographic regulations can still intervene and disturb the relation between graphematics and linguistic levels such as phonology and morphology. An illuminating example of this provided by Handel (2013) concerns the externally regulated simplification of Chinese characters: the previously transparent relation between semantic components occurring in different positions across traditional (i.e., unsimplified) graphemes was opacified when some of them were simplified in one position (i.e., on the left of a character) but not in another (i.e., at the bottom); Figure 25 shows the SPEECH radical (number 149) |言| as an example (cf. Handel 2013: 45). Thus, conscious, external orthographic standardisation is another reason why writing systems of similar languages can exhibit significant differences.

Finally, we briefly turn to universals that concern writing as its own semiotic system. They have, thus far, been most neglected in grapholinguistic research; indeed, most of what was described above deals with the representational function of writing. An example of a universal that highlights writing as its own

tr. <訁 > simplified to *s.* <讠 >
left position: *tr.* <語> ⟶ *s.* <语>
tr. <課> ⟶ *s.* <课>
bottom position: *tr./s.* <警>, <譬>

Figure 25: Simplification of traditional (tr.) |訁| to simplified (s.) |讠| on the left but not on the bottom of Chinese graphemes.

system is Justeson's (1976: 61) statement that "[f]ew writing systems distinguish all their phonemes". While superficially, this universal tendency also appears to concern the representational function, it actually reveals something different: that writing systems, for some reason, underrepresent phonological information (and the same applies to morphological information in morphographic systems). Thus, this uncovers fundamental information about how writing generally functions independently of the specific language it relates to or the way it relates to it.

Furthermore, many of the features that distinguish writing markedly from speech stem from its materiality, which brings graphetic questions to the fore of potential autonomously grapholinguistic universals. In their above-described study on universals of reading acquisition, for example, Verhoeven and Perfetti discuss graphic complexity and the way it is associated with other variables (such as type of writing system; cf. also Miton and Morin 2021). It is calculated with the help of *GraphCom* (Chang, Chen, and Perfetti 2017), a measure that "in addition to perimetric complexity, includes the number of simple features, number of connected points, and number of disconnected components" (Verhoeven and Perfetti 2022: 152). In the conception proposed in this book, 'simple features' are elementary forms, and the way GraphCom functions resembles Altmann's quantitative approach to measuring graph complexity (⟶ Section 3.2.3).

Several possible graphetic universals can also be postulated when considering the graphetic features acquired by children prior to formal literacy instruction (⟶ Section 3.4), many of which are spatial in nature. Examples are (1) directionality, as all writing systems exhibit top-to-bottom directionality, (2) rectilinearity, given that all writing systems are rectilinear, i.e., written in lines, and (3) segmentality and alternation, since in all writing systems, distinct segmental (or segmentable)[193] units are combined with each other to form larger units. What these examples share is that just like the finiteness of units of

193 From a perceptual perspective, graphemes might not come pre-segmented, such as in the Arabic writing system, where they are connected. However, they are segmentable as even connected writing is a sequence of segments – unlike speech, which is a sound continuum (cf. Dürscheid 2016a: 32–33). Arguably, in writing, visual continua formed by graphic connectedness are secondary to segmentality, whereas in speech, segmented sounds are secondary to the otherwise continuous stream of speech.

writing systems and the primacy of the syllable (see above), they are most likely determined by cognition.

The same applies to universal graphetic tendencies that have been presented in recent literature: they include the fact that the average number of elementary forms that basic shapes in the world's scripts are comprised of is three as well as the fact that half of the graphetic information stored in basic shapes is redundant (cf. Changizi and Shimojo 2005). Other noteworthy examples are that the structures of "visual signs have been culturally selected to match the kinds of conglomeration of contours found in natural scenes because that is what we [humans, DM/CD] have evolved to be good at visually processing" (Changizi et al. 2006: E117), which again emphasises the interaction of processing and structure. To name a final example, what has also been observed is that "the orientation of strokes inside written characters massively favors cardinal directions" (Morin 2018: 664), i.e., horizontality or verticality rather than diagonality, which incidentally also applies at a higher level to the above-mentioned types of directionality in writing systems.

The discovery of further universal tendencies like these – be they graphetic, graphematic, or even orthographic in nature – is clearly an important grapholinguistic desideratum. As has been advocated throughout this section, it is one in which considering the interaction between cognition and the structure(s) of writing is central – and one that cannot rely on a synchronic perspective alone.

6.5 Perspectives on the history of writing

The additional perspective opened up at the end of this chapter highlights the history of writing (systems). The focus is thus shifted from a predominantly synchronic treatment of writing, which characterised both the previous sections in this chapter and generally the preceding chapters, to relevant diachronic aspects that should not be neglected, not least because they can fundamentally inform synchronic research. At the outset of this section, it is important to note that it will provide a descriptive presentation of neither the history of writing in general nor specific writing systems. Such descriptions – many of which are excellent – already abound (cf., for example, Diringer 1948; Février 1948; Cohen 1958; Friedrich 1966; Jensen 1969). Furthermore, many prominent textbooks and overview works on writing such as Coulmas (2003), Rogers (2005), or Daniels (2018) adopt a predominantly descriptive and historical perspective as they aptly trace the history of different systems.

The main question dealt with in this section is instead how a diachronic lens can enrich grapholinguistics. The tentative and very broad answer is that it allows sketching relevant trends of development in writing that reveal important aspects about its nature. As underlined above, the study of features shared by writing systems can provide us with such valuable insight. Crucially, the universal tendencies previously mentioned in many cases did not exist from the outset but are precisely the result of common diachronic developments. Indeed, commonalities in the origin, transmission, and development of writing systems potentially represent cornerstones of a theory of writing that extends beyond description. For instance, the fact that early writing systems initially exhibited a remarkable degree of pictography that gradually decreased and was superseded by arbitrariness and abstractness (see below) is not a coincidence but an interesting observation that points to some of the underlying driving forces in the development of writing – in this case primarily the tendency to facilitate the production of units of writing, which is determined cognitively and physiologically. In the following, we will concentrate on such broad strokes, i.e., tendencies in the history of writing.

The fact that this treatment of diachronic aspects of writing is embedded in the chapter on writing system typology may appear arbitrary given that it could have been integrated into any other chapter. However, it is actually very fitting since research on the history of writing is frequently concerned with how systems developed from one (idealised) type such as morphography to another like the alphabet. Such trajectories from one type to another have even been the subject of controversial – and nowadays refuted – teleologies propagated by prominent scholars of the study of writing. Although such assumptions are inherent in many (especially early) typologies of writing systems,[194] the most important one was formulated by Ignace J. Gelb in his influential *A study of writing*: the so-called *principle of unidirectional development* (cf. Gelb 1963: 201). Its main claim holds that

> writing, whatever its forerunners may be, must pass through the stages of logography, syllabography, and alphabetography in this, and no other order. Therefore, no writing can start with a syllabic or alphabetic stage unless it is borrowed, directly or indirectly, from a system which has gone through all the previous stages. (Gelb 1963: 201)

This principle is problematic for two reasons: firstly, and most importantly, it is factually incorrect, as was pointed out by Daniels (1990, 2018: 133–135). To name just two examples that serve as counterevidence: syllabaries can develop from alphabets (the Caroline Islands syllabary developed from an alphabet), and seg-

194 Among them are the typologies of Taylor (1883), Virl (1949), Diringer (1962), and Gaur (1984), which Voß (2003: 37–48) classifies as 'evolutionistic typologies'.

mentaries can develop from morphography (the segmental hieroglyphic graphemes that corresponded with consonants and had developed from morphograms in Egyptian did not constitute a syllabary). In order for Gelb's principle to hold, he had to classify the writing systems of Hebrew and Arabic, among others, as syllabaries, which is inadequate. Furthermore, writing systems such as Chinese or Japanese have either remained morphographic or retained core morphographic components to this day (in the case of Chinese, after thousands of years of development), which fortunately is no longer interpreted as a sign of 'backwardness'. The fact that it once was already highlights the second major problem that plagues teleologies: the Eurocentrism inherent in proclaiming the alphabet as the final stage or pinnacle of (Western) civilisation – an ideal that every literate culture using a non-alphabetic writing system is judged against and that serves as grounds for an unjustified devalorisation of those literate cultures (cf. Dürscheid 2016a: 125–126). Even rather recent publications are not free from ethnocentric undertones of this kind:

> It [= the alphabet, DM/CD] is unlikely ever to surrender its hegemony. The Chinese will learn to use the alphabet, but alphabet users will not learn to use Chinese. In this sense one can think of the alphabet as a superior system, because it is transcendent and because in its attachment to human speech it is a force for unifying the world.[195] (Powell 2009: 254)

Opposing this view, several authors have pointed out that devaluing non-alphabetic writing (especially morphography) at the expense of the 'superior' alphabet (which is also practiced by, for example, Hannas 1997, 2003) is no longer tenable – and has never been, for that matter. Indeed, with respect to both economy and education, countries or administrative regions with (partially) morphographic writing systems including China, Taiwan, Hong Kong, and Japan have in many respects surpassed countries with alphabetic literacy (cf. Trigger 1998; Sampson 2016a; Voogt 2021). This ostentatiously emphasises how, in the study of the history of writing, teleologies with inherent value systems are greatly misplaced. In other words, the focus should be on the non-evaluative description and explanation of changes and developments rather than on instrumentalising them to contrast levels of cultural or intellectual advancement in diverse and not straightforwardly comparable literate cultures. As Mignolo (1989: 62) aptly formulates, "the history of writing is not an evolutionary process driving toward the alphabet, but rather a series of coevolutionary processes in which different writing systems followed their own transformations".

195 Cf. also the absolute statement that "[o]verall, it is argued that morphographic systems are inferior to phonographic ones" (cf. Jones and Mooney 2017: 13).

Even though it should have become clear by now that writing systems do not follow the exact same path(s) in their development, a general notion that has remained firmly at the centre of diachronic research on writing is the idea of an 'evolution' of writing (systems).[196] As Dehaene's (2009: 150, emphasis added) quote cited in the previous section stated, "writing *evolved* to fit the cortex" because writing as an invention is too young to have prompted evolutionary changes in humans. To reiterate, this is precisely why the history of writing and universal tendencies found in it are so inseparably associated: changes, unless they are 'historical accidents' (see above), are driven by underlying motivations, and if these are widespread – because they are, for example, of fundamental cognitive nature –, they lead to commonalities in the development of writing that can result in universals (which is also why and how this historical section fits into this chapter). Interestingly, although they are frequently relegated to the background in grapholinguistics, graphetic features come to the forefront in the question of how cognition, diachronic development, and universals are connected (cf., for example, Salomon 2012 for the description of some patterns in the change of scripts). The reason for this is rather trivial: because graphetic features are not bound to specific languages, factors other than human capacities (such as the type or even the specific structure of a given language) usually do not interfere in their development (see below for exceptions).

In this respect, a riveting study was published by Miton and Morin (2021), whose aim was to investigate certain questions surrounding the graphic complexity of scripts used for writing systems: "(1) What determines character complexity? (2) Can we find traces of evolutionary change in character complexity? (3) Is complexity distributed in a way that makes character recognition easier?" (Miton and Morin 2021: abstract). They found that the size of a script (i.e., the number of basic shapes it includes) – which is associated with the type of the writing system the script is used for – is related to the complexity of basic shapes. This is a relatively expected finding, since basic shapes logically must become more complex in large scripts in order to stay distinctive. A more important finding in the context of this historical section is that no decrease of graphic complexity over the long-term history of scripts was found. Two possible explanations are provided for this, the first of which is that differences in the actual use of scripts (or writing systems employing those scripts) create statistical noise. This

196 Cf. Pettersson (1991) and a review thereof in Watt (1994) for a critical view of evolutionary accounts of writing. Also noteworthy not only for using the notion of 'evolution' in its title but also for underlining the contemporary grapholinguistic interest in the diachronic development of writing systems is a special issue of the *Zeitschrift für Sprachwissenschaft* titled *The evolution of writing systems* (cf. Hartmann, Nowak, and Szczepaniak 2021).

is the point at which one must concede that the role of cognition, regardless of how important it may be, should not be absolutised at the expense of social, cultural, political, material, etc. factors, which may intervene or even dominate in certain cases (see below). The second explanation holds that the reduction of complexity could occur "early and rapidly in the history of scripts" (Miton and Morin 2021: sec. 4.2., para. 3). This possibility is supported by both experimental settings in which the effects of transmission on cultural evolution are studied (cf., for example, Garrod 2007; Caldwell and Smith 2012; Tamariz and Kirby 2015 and Meletis 2020a: 308–315 for an overview) and a case study of the reduction of complexity in the history of the young writing system of Vai (cf. Kelly et al. 2020). Since the latter system was developed only in the 19th century, the simplification that could be observed had to have occurred during a relatively short span of time. This highlights the importance of considering so-called *emergent writing systems*, the results of modern grammatogenies, as these can help uncover developmental trends in the history of writing (see below).

As has already been mentioned, due to the cultural 'nature' of writing, cognition cannot be the sole decisive factor in its history, and in the section dealing with universals above, cultural differences were indeed stressed as an important explanation for diversity in the world's writing systems. For this reason, Downey (2014: 306) cautions against a "strong form of [. . .] neurological determinism" as propagated, in his opinion, by Dehaene, who mentions diversity throughout his work but cannot explain it (completely) satisfactorily on the basis of only neurocognition. The bottom line, Downey notes, is that myriad more factors must be taken into consideration in studying the evolution of writing. He illustrates this with an example:

> To account for the neuro-cultural emergence of mass literacy in the West with its own peculiar history, for example, we would have to consider theological upheaval, changing class structure, the invention of moveable type, pedagogical innovations, and the democratization of primary education, but we must also recognize how recalcitrantly conservative writing systems can be. (Downey 2014: 311)

This leads Downey to the conclusion that the framework most suited for a study of the 'evolution' of writing is anthropological co-evolutionary theory, "in which theorists recognize the interaction of socially-transmitted information or behavior with the underlying genetic endowment of a species, given sufficient time" (Downey 2014: 311–312). Finally, a crucial point raised by him is that we might be focusing on the wrong tendencies and that the "question of universality could be turned on its head" (Downey 2014: 313). Accordingly, the apparent and most reasonable question to ask may not be how cognition and additional factors have led to universals in the many systems that have ultimately sprung from the few independently conceived original systems but instead how (and why) the observed diversity could arise from these shared origins in the first place (cf. also Sampson 2016a; Trigger 1998).

After these important general considerations about the evolution of writing and the inadequacy of teleologies, more concrete questions concerning the history of writing shall be foregrounded. The most global are *when*, *where*, *why*, and *how* writing was invented (cf. Houston 2004a for a collection of contributions addressing, among others, these questions). None of them is simple or straightforward to answer, but for the first two, which are descriptive rather than explanatory in nature, there exists more tangible evidence, so the focus here will be on them. The question of a monogenesis vs. a polygenesis of writing is usually answered in favour of the latter, although this is sometimes still questioned (cf. Damerow 2006: 2–3). Even if some scholars deem it possible that writing in Mesopotamia and China was connected through stimulus diffusion, the decisive criterion pointing towards polygenesis is writing in Mesoamerica, which for several reasons has to have emerged independently of the literate tradition in the Middle East (cf., for example, Downey 2014 for this position). Thus, the dominant contemporary view is that assuming a monogenesis of writing is untenable as "[e]verything in present knowledge points to the fact that writing was engendered independently by several relatively advanced sedentary civilizations characterized by urbanization, division of labour, and a surplus economy" (Coulmas 2003: 192; cf. also Senner 2001). As for the specifics of polygenesis, contemporary consensus is that writing was 'invented' at least[197] three times: what Daniels (2013: 56) calls ancient grammatogenies, i.e., initial creations of writing, occurred in Mesopotamia, China, and Mesoamerica (for the writing systems that sprung from these creations ⟶ Section 6.3).

While the assumption of inherently evaluative and absolute teleologies is inadequate, from a purely descriptive point of view, it is undeniable that in the first, originally purely morphographic writing systems, striking commonalities can be observed in the development of phonography. These shared changes have been noted by many scholars (cf., exemplarily, Trigger 1998: 46–49; cf. also Robertson

197 Several authors (for example, Handel 2019; Voogt 2021) mention Egypt as a fourth place where writing was invented independently (cf. Daniels 2013: 58, 2017: 86 for a different view), while others also do not rule out the possibility that writing was also independently devised in Oceania (cf. Downey 2014; Rogers 2005), although it is still heatedly debated whether Rongorongo, discovered on Easter Island, counts as writing. It is also noteworthy that Harald Haarmann (e.g., Haarmann 2010) holds that writing was first invented in Southeastern Europe in the form of the so-called Vinča symbols (also known as *Danube script*). However, most scholars of writing disagree with this view (cf. Dürscheid 2016a: 106–108).

2004 for a theoretical modelling of the strategies involved). For example, the *rebus principle* allows using morphographic graphemes for their phonographic value only. What is nowadays largely accepted as an incentive for its development is “the desire to record personal names and names of places and names of things” (Powell 2009: 246). What the users of these ancient writing systems discovered in writing, thus, was double articulation. To this day, the strategy of desemanticising graphemes to write names, among other foreign linguistic material, is practiced in morphographic Chinese (⟶ Section 5.2).

Important ‘phonetic’ developments such as the rebus principle as well as semantic developments in the first, independently devised writing systems are summed up by Handel:

> [. . .] the mechanisms of extension are both simple and universal, and must therefore be intuitively obvious to human beings once the crucial breakthrough of associating signs with words has been achieved. The two most basic mechanisms are phonetic extension and semantic extension. These mechanisms are powerful, providing the flexibility and combinatorial power needed to represent spoken language. They carry with them, however, an inevitable disadvantage: they lead to polyvalency in graphic representation, increasing the possibility for ambiguity and confusion, and thus increasing the cognitive load on the process of reading. Techniques of disambiguation naturally follow, including semantic determination, phonetic determination, and graphic modification.
>
> (Handel 2019: 309–310)

The strategies of phonetic or semantic extension and determination will not be elaborated here (for details, cf., for example, Boltz 1994: Chapter 3), but what Handel’s conclusion clearly emphasises, again, is that the reason for common “developmental pathways” (Handel 2019: 312) is to be found in cognition. Indeed, these commonalities are so striking that they were apparently not affected by the fact that the writing systems in which they occurred were engendered in vastly different cultures.

Since this section aims to present open issues with respect to the history of writing to foster discussion, an interesting hypothesis should be mentioned at this point – interesting because it runs counter to the idea that in their evolution, writing systems ‘usually’ develop from morphography towards (at least the partial inclusion of) phonography. It was proposed by Sampson, who claims that writing systems “evolve from being phonetically-based when they are young, towards being lexically-distinctive as they mature” (Sampson 2018: 10). Of course, the systems that Sampson refers to are ones that were primarily phonographic from the outset. Even more so, the systems in question were/are also phonographically transparent, i.e., “tend to hug the phonetic ground quite closely” (Sampson 2018: 12). Lexical distinctiveness, according to Sampson, combines two components: (1) assigning “a constant written shape to each lexical element – each morpheme, or at least each root", a shape that is (2) "distinctive in the sense of having few near neighbours" (Sampson 2018: 10). The second aspect captures that in 'lexically distinct' graphematic words, substituting one grapheme for another will not result in the graphematic representation of a different existing word but rather produces a nonword (or pseudoword). In a nutshell, in the development assumed by Sampson, phonographic writing systems introduce secondary morphography by gradually giving priority to the uniform graphematic representation of morphemes rather than phonemes, and thus come to ignore, for example, morphophonemic variation. This tendency reflects the changing functions of writing in literate societies as well as a shift in the prioritisation of groups of readers (and to a lesser degree, writers): in early stages of a community's literacy, most members are learners, and phonographic transparency is commonly argued to be more beneficial for literacy acquisition (cf. the orthographic depth hypothesis, Katz and Frost 1992). At a later point in both sociogenetic and ontogenetic development, however, the needs of "mature, skilled readers" (Sampson 2018: 21) are foregrounded – and they read for meaning, not for sound.

In his contribution, Sampson also includes what he calls a 'reductio ad absurdum', a thought experiment in which the writing system of English exhibits an extreme degree of lexical distinctiveness as words are assigned "completely random letter-strings" (Sampson 2018: 18). Examples include the spelling <pfg> for *cat* and <wxxq> for *dog*. While this may baffle readers familiar with the actual English alphabet, Sampson (2018: 19) mentions that one such system is in use and "works very well": Chinese. Of course, a crucial difference ignored by this line of argument is that Chinese started out precisely that way, which means that comparing English and Chinese here is comparing apples and oranges. In sum, Sampson claims phonographic writing systems exhibit the tendency to increase lexical distinctiveness. However, when the main question is rephrased or reduced to the question of whether primarily phonographic writing systems let go of their phonography *completely* (so that <cat> is written <pfg>), as hypothesised in Sampson's thought experiment, the answer is, most likely, no. Thus, the actually existing tendency that Sampson describes in his paper is the increase of *secondary* morphography in phonographic systems. Crucially, as was argued in ⟶ Section 6.1, primary morphography as found in systems such as Chinese and secondary morphography as found in phonographic writing systems (including English) may not be conflated. In other words, a primarily phonographic writing system such as the English alphabet will not be superseded by a writing system in which the graphemes are completely rid of their phonographic correspondence.

In fact, a recent study by Berg and Aronoff (2021) provides (partial) evidence against the lexical distinctiveness hypothesis, at least with respect to English, which, however, Sampson himself treats as an outlier (cf. Sampson 2018: 14). The authors investigated how homophonous stems are spelled in English, specifically whether they are predominantly written heterographically as in <pair> vs. <pare> vs. <pear>, which would point to the 'principle of heterography' being an important feature of the English writing system. Their data contradicts this as there does not appear to be a diachronic trend for stems to be graphematically differentiated. The actual reason for spellings such as <pair> and <pare> is, according to the authors, sound change: at an earlier developmental stage of English, these words were written differently because they had different corresponding pronunciations (cf. Berg and Aronoff 2021: 326). Thus, the conclusion is that there is no systematicity behind distinguishing homophonous monomorphemic stems and heterogeneous spellings such as <pair> and <pare> are mere historical accidents (cf. Berg and Aronoff 2021: 327). It should be noted, however, that the situation differs significantly for derivational suffixes, for which Berg and Aronoff (2018) *did* find processes of differentiation. Thus, one can thus sum up that "[w]hile English writers have no problem with stem homonymy, they prefer their affixes distinct" (Berg and Aronoff 2021: 327). Sampson, thus, appears to be wrong in assuming a process of *lexical* differentiation when what can actually be observed – at least in English – is a process of *grammatical* differentiation. Notably, Sampson also provides examples from other writing systems such as Korean (cf. Sampson 2018: 14–15) to support his hypothesis, examples which cannot be explained by retaining spelling despite sound change.

As for English, examples such as the distinct spellings <pair> and <pare> for stems that are synchronically homophonous highlight the conservatism of the written modality. It is arguably related to one of the forces of change (or in this case non-change) mentioned by Watt (1983), namely inertia (cf. the preceding section), and affects all three modules of writing systems: graphetics,[198] graphematics, and particularly orthography. The major points in the history of writing at which changes and innovations *do* occur despite this prevalent conservatism involve the adoption and adaptation of writing systems for languages they were not originally devised for (and often did not fit). Given that writing was invented only a few times, the majority of the world's writing systems were conceived through such adaptation processes. These, crucially, also represented driving forces behind developments from morphography towards phonography. Trigger describes how adaptation may have overcome conservatism:

> These conservative values may explain why major shifts towards phonographic writing occurred mainly when scripts were adopted by foreign peoples who were not yet bound by firmly established cultural traditions or by social and political interests relating to literacy. (Trigger 1998: 57)

198 For conservatism concerning basic shapes, cf. Treiman and Kessler (2014: 159).

Notably, writing system adaptation is by no means a homogeneous process as there are multiple ways writing can be transmitted, adopted, and adapted. Daniels (2007, 2013, 2017) has described several major ways these processes took place: through (1) misunderstanding, (2) tradition, or (3) scholarship. Misunderstanding is by far the most important, and the instance that is arguably most discussed is the addition of vowel letters to the Phoenician variety of Greek. Daniels reconstructs how this misunderstanding could have occurred:

> A Greek merchant (who did not speak Phoenician well) might have observed a Phoenician keeping accounts and, realizing what a boon that was for business, asked how it was done. Phoenician has several consonants absent from Greek, and when the Phoenician pronounced the letter names beginning with those consonants, the Greek heard not the consonants, but the vowels that followed them – and used those letters for a, e, i, o, u instead: segmental phonology had been fully grasped. (Daniels 2013: 59)

For transmission by tradition (which amounts to adoption without any/much modification of the borrowed system) and transmission by scholarship (which amounts to different degrees of adapting the borrowed system), Daniels provides examples of how writing was diffused across Asia. For tradition, he mentions the West Semitic abjad and the transmission sequence Imperial Aramaic > Syriac > Manichaean > Sogdian > Uyghur > Mongolian > Manchu. He adds that "[f]rom early in the first millennium BCE almost to the third millennium BCE [. . .] the orthographic principles, and hence the skeleton of the writing system remained essentially the same" (Daniels 2018: 140) as it was 'merely' passed on from one "scribal school" to the next. As for transmission by scholarship, on the other hand, which involves the modification of writing systems and is thus the only type that "involves *deliberate* change, by people who have given deep attention to the nature of their writing system" (Daniels 2007: 61, emphasis in original), a significant example is the design of Korean Han'gŭl. It is commonly attributed to fifteenth-century monarch King Sejong, although it is likely, as Daniels goes on to mention, that a commission was instructed to develop it instead. Major influences on Han'gŭl that the creator(s) likely had to have been aware of are the writing system of 'Phags-pa, whose script may have served as a visual model for the basic shapes of Han'gŭl, and Chinese phonological theory. As for the latter, the fact that the Korean scholar(s) working on Han'gŭl transcended the Chinese classification of initial (the onset of a syllable) vs. final (its rime) by providing graphemes for all vowels and consonants is a sign of their sophistication and "deep study" (Daniels 2017: 86).

What must be mentioned at the end of this section has already been briefly alluded to above in the context of the Vai writing system: for a diachronic grapholinguistic perspective, not only the ancient history but also the recent history of writing is paramount. This brings to the forefront recent creations of writing systems (cf. Schmitt 1980) – what Daniels refers to as modern grammatogenies – and their relatively short development. Studying them can illuminate the ancient history of writing since some of the same (types of) developments are found in them – but in a much shorter span of time. Crucially, this also means that in many such cases, data or evidence for all stages of the development from the very beginnings of the system up until its recent form are available (cf. Kelly et al. 2020), which is not the case (to the same degree) for ancient writing systems.

The most important of these recently developed systems are so-called emergent writing systems, "*secondary* inventions of writing generated via stimulus diffusion" that were "created in near isolation by non-literate inventors who borrowed the idea of writing but did not directly acquire its principles [. . .] from literate teachers" (Kelly et. al 2020: sec. 'Emergent writing systems and what they might tell us', para. 2., emphasis in original). Prominent examples mentioned above include the writing systems of Cherokee and Vai. At one point, Daniels referred to these inventions of writing as 'unsophisticated' grammatogenies, a designation that was meant to highlight that the creators in such inventions had not been literate. By contrast, creations such as Cree were 'sophisticated' given that "the inventor of Cree Syllabics was English-literate and familiar with the phonetic science of his day" (Daniels 2013: 55). The difference between the two types, thus, is the inventors' literacy background. Arguably, the investigation of both is revelatory in its own right: unsophisticated grammatogenies may to a larger degree echo how writing was devised the very first times thousands of years ago, whereas sophisticated grammatogenies may share more features with adaptations of writing systems (such as Japanese adapting Chinese, Akkadian adapting Sumerian, etc.). Note, however, that it has been called into question whether such a differentiation is reasonable or necessary (cf. Houston 2004b; Voogt 2021), and the choice of terminology can also be scrutinised. In any case, it is vital to keep in mind that the history of writing is not restricted to developments from long ago but also subsumes recent changes and, crucially, is still unfolding before our eyes. New impetus for both ongoing and future change comes from modern technologies that affect the way we write (cf. Dürscheid and Frick 2016) and thus how writing may look in the future. That being said, a chapter on the history of writing may already look decidedly different a thousand years in the future.

7 Conclusion and outlook

Writing is an engrossing object of investigation so vast and multi-layered that it cannot be studied comprehensively with only linguistic methods and theories. Thus, this book – as advertised in the description of *Trends in Linguistics*, the series in which it is published – strives to open up new perspectives in our understanding of the subject and provides insights by adopting an interdisciplinary approach. As its title suggests, our book focuses not exclusively on *writing systems* themselves, i.e., their structures and the functions they assume, but also on their *use*, i.e., how people write and read to communicate or obtain information, to name just two of many purposes. Accordingly, the book's main chapters are foremost devoted to a formal and functional description of writing: how it relates to language in general and to speech in particular (⟶ Chapter 2), how its material manifestation and the social functions it assumes can be described (which is studied by *graphetics* ⟶ Chapter 3), which written units assume linguistic functions (*graphematics* ⟶ Chapter 4), how writing is standardised and regulated (*orthography* ⟶ Chapter 5), as well as the different major ways in which it can relate to language(s) (*writing system typology* ⟶ Chapter 6). To account for use, these chapters also include dedicated sections introducing vital usage-based perspectives from other disciplines. The issues addressed in this context stem from anthropology, typography research, semiotics and communication science, psychology and cognitive science, as well as sociolinguistics, and range from an investigation of units that play a role in (cognitive models of) reading processes to heated reactions in the context of orthography reforms. Importantly, these usage-related questions were not merely appended to the respective chapters but were thematically linked to them. This – as well as the brief discussion of changes to writing systems that shall follow below – underlines that in grapholinguistics, diverse disciplinary perspectives on writing should best not be juxtaposed but interrelated to reveal the 'bigger picture' and to comprehensively explain how writing functions.

As a modality serving as the basis for so many different purposes, writing has gradually cemented itself as an indispensable part of our everyday lives and is now arguably more widely used than ever before. Against this background, it is important to highlight that as the study of all aspects of writing, grapholinguistics is by no means invested only in a theoretical treatment of writing systems, it is interested also in these realities of how writing and literacy assume important functions in our lives. Indeed, precisely such 'real-life situations' centred around issues of writing emphasise that theoretical and applied questions are intimately interconnected, as has been shown in the preceding chapters. This shall now be elaborated a little further in the final chapter of this book.

https://doi.org/10.1515/9783110757835-007

Take as illustrative examples four modifications of writing systems in the 20th and 21st centuries: (1) the simplification as well as the discarded plans of a Romanisation of Chinese characters, (2) the switch from Arabic to Roman script for Turkish, (3) the many script changes for Azeri in a relatively short span of time (from Arabic to Roman to Cyrillic and back to Roman, cf. Hatcher 2008), or, just in 2021, (4) the transition from Cyrillic to Roman for Kazakh. Such changes to the status quo generally reveal the necessity for an interdisciplinary approach in grapholinguistics given that they affect multifaceted aspects of both the structure and the use of writing. In the following, we will explain this in more detail with reference to these examples.

When the script used in a writing system is switched, as was the case for Turkish in 1928–1929, the system's entire appearance is altered – which is where the theoretical study of *graphetics* merges with complex *sociolinguistic* questions. These issues are delicate as it is often precisely a system's visuality that members of a literate community associate most with writing. This is not surprising since, much like language itself, writing is an essential common good in their lives. In most cases, such script changes are motivated politically. Thus, Kazakh's recent switch from Cyrillic to Roman is intended, among other things, to weaken ties with Russia. Of course, this political motivation only makes sense on the basis that Cyrillic is associated with Russia(n) in the first place, circling back to the crucial observation that a writing system's appearance has symbolic value.

Practical reasons underlying script changes can be of technological nature: certain scripts (especially Roman) may be more suitable to the use of (digital) technology, which itself becomes increasingly important as large parts of communication are relegated to the digital realm. Simultaneously, one must bear in mind that any prospective gain in technological efficiency may be counterbalanced by the cost of transitioning from the old script to the new one. For example, in 2018, the cost of switching from Cyrillic to Roman for Kazakh was estimated at $664 million.[199] Changing a script in such a manner is an incisive act also because people must acquire a new script to remain literate in their own language. Inversely, children who learn only this new script in school are cut off from literature printed in the old one, losing access to (part of) their cultural heritage – which is the case in Azerbaijan and, in the future, Kazakhstan. Note that on the other hand, depending on the new script in question, the switch may also facilitate the acquisition of other writing systems using the same script (such as the globally important English for Roman script).

---

199 Cf. https://www.bbc.com/worklife/article/20180424-the-cost-of-changing-an-entire-countrys-alphabet (accessed October 30th, 2021).

In any case, such script changes create a complex situation of biscriptality (⟶ Section 5.5.3.1), especially during the time of transition in which both scripts are in use. The mentioned aspects of such a shift can be described using theoretical perspectives from *graphematics* (for instance, how the old and new basic shapes relate to the units of the language) and applied ones from *psycholinguistics* (regarding, for example, literacy acquisition or reading and writing processes in general). Since regardless of the structural level of a writing system they concern, external changes are acts of regulation, they are always *orthographic* in nature. Indeed, they are often decided on by specialised commissions but affect everyone who is literate. As such, they can be welcomed (such as the above-mentioned switch from Cyrillic to Roman in Kazakhstan) or met with fervent criticism or even rejection (such as the German orthography reform of 1996 ⟶ Section 5.5.3.4).

While changes of script, as described, can complicate matters of literacy, reforms of orthography – which are also largely politically driven – often have the opposite goal. This was also shown in the course of ⟶ Chapter 5. Simplifying (the use of) a writing system has as one desired outcome an increase of literacy rates. Such was the case for the simplification of Chinese characters, a process that itself bundles various questions addressed by different branches of grapholinguistics. For example, since changes (specifically, stroke reductions) of Chinese characters were inconsistent, they disrupted the internal systematics of the writing system and effectively reduced graphematic transparency (⟶ Section 6.4), which in turn can have effects on reading and writing. A different issue concerns the fact that while the simplified versions of characters are used in Mainland China, the traditional ones were retained in Hong Kong and Taiwan (⟶ Section 4.6.4). This orthographic distinction perpetuates a political and sociocultural boundary, one that for many users is also tied to identity. Notably, the changes to the Chinese writing system were not as drastic as they could have been, as there also existed proposals to Romanise Chinese (cf. DeFrancis 1943). This would have changed not only the visual appearance of the writing system but the entire way it functions.

In the context of such considerations, the graphematic aspects of *writing system typology* come to the forefront, which in this case highlight that switching to an alphabet may not be beneficial or even feasible in a language for which a morpho(syllabo)graphic writing system is suited (⟶ Section 6.3). Further complicating matters is the fact that the Chinese writing system is the oldest one still in use today, which means altering it so drastically would equal a massive departure from the cultural history and memory it carries with/in it. This also underlines that changes are not enforced in a (synchronic) vacuum but are embedded in contexts enriched by diachrony, which was discussed in ⟶ Section 6.5. And not only Chinese but all writing systems have a history that is often very long and ties them to cultures and users, thus factoring heavily into any decisions that result in their modification.

In changes of writing systems, the relation between speech, i.e., the spoken modality of a language, and writing, its written modality, is relevant, e.g., because spoken language develops dynamically and the written norms lag behind it. However, this relationship is nowhere as central as in literacy development (⟶ Section 5.5.3.2). More accurately, it is the interaction and intermeshing of established oral practices and emerging literacy practices in a newly literate culture – practices best described under the lens of *anthropology* (⟶ Section 2.5) – that rests at the core of such a complex introduction of literacy. Additionally, most of the issues described above – including the choice of a script, the implementation of orthographic norms, etc. – also apply to the process of creating a new writing system from scratch. In a nutshell, a comprehensive investigation of all aspects relevant in literacy development reveals the true breadth as well as the academic and real-life relevance of grapholinguistics.

Against this background, it is all the more surprising that writing was long discarded by linguistics as a secondary manifestation of language, as being subordinate to speech. In our treatment of graphetics, to underline the neglect of questions concerning the materiality of writing, we mentioned the fitting metaphor of the window pane (⟶ Section 3.1.1). In its original formulation (cf. Krämer 1998), it expresses the assumption that when we study writing, but also when we encounter written texts in our everyday lives, we commonly look right through their appearance without noticing it (= the window pane) to see directly the linguistic information that it 'shows' us (= what is behind the window). This metaphor, in our opinion, can be extended to writing as a whole, capturing the scripticist written language bias: for a long time, linguistic research looked through all aspects of writing and focused only on the language (or even just speech) 'behind' it. The window itself was either treated as secondary or entirely ignored. However, it is precisely the investigation of how this window works (including the graphetics, graphematics, and orthography of writing systems) that can enrich our understanding of not only how it shows us what is behind it but also the way it shapes or frames our view of what is behind it. Fortunately, the recent establishment of grapholinguistics reflects a moment of refocusing on precisely these questions and the impact that writing has on languages that are not only spoken and heard but also written and read. To sum up, the question whether we need a study of writing has been replaced by the question of what exactly this study should look like.

The focus of this conclusion until now has been on different disciplinary perspectives. However, it is also paramount to mention the diversity of writing systems. In our perception, individual writing systems have thus far been studied predominantly in isolation rather than having been compared. For instance, alphabets such as English or German, which the majority of grapholinguistic research has been devoted to, have seldom been examined in the same context as morphographic systems such as Chinese. One reason for this is the lack of a unified framework that would make possible cross-grapholinguistic description. Providing such a framework was a main aim of this book, resulting in, among other things, the proposal of broader definitions of such concepts as *grapheme*, *allography*, or *orthography*. Nevertheless, with respect to the examples that were provided and discussed throughout the book as well as the literature that was consulted, a certain residual alphabetocentric bias (which grapholinguistic research should strive to get rid of) can still be identified. This is in part because much of the work in the field originates in the German-language area. Thus, another goal of our book was not only making this research available to an international readership to show its potential despite a narrow focus on German but also combining it with work from other regions as well as different disciplines.

At the end, we proceed to an outlook: Stating that the future of grapholinguistics depends on the future of its subject is trivial. But that is precisely the fundamental question: what does the future hold for writing? While many languages of the world – some of them endangered – remain unwritten to this day, others employ writing systems whose scripts are not yet encoded in Unicode and thus not available digitally.[200] At the other end of the spectrum, in many literate cultures, the omnipresence of digital communication gradually blurs the line between orality on the one hand and literacy on the other. Indeed, while Walter Ong had already described a secondary orality that arises in literate cultures, an orality "of telephones, radio, and television, which depends on writing for its existence" (Ong 2012: 3; ⟶ Section 2.5.1), in highly technologised cultures, we may have now reached the next stage of so-called "tertiary orality" (cf. Heyd 2021). It is characterised by the "destabilization of the boundary" between orality and literacy which "touches upon many practices of digital communication" (Heyd 2021: 137) – both spoken and written. This is highlighted, for example, by text functions which are included in almost all applications centring on spoken digital communication (such as video conferences or livestreams) but also by multimodal elements such as animated GIFs. Not only do the latter often include text, but while they are devoid of audio, an "auditory quality" is also "firmly implied by their very origin, and sometimes spoken words can be inferred from the mouth-

200 At http://www.worldswritingsystems.org (accessed October 5th, 2021), the category 'Unicode' distinguishes scripts encoded in Unicode from those that are not (yet); the latter group includes scripts such as Maya hieroglyphs or Hieratic script.

ing of the characters on display" (Heyd 2021: 137). Furthermore, with the rise of digital assistants (such as Siri or Alexa) and human-machine communication in general (such as with social robots), orality affects another crucial boundary, that between human and nonhuman agency in (oral) communication. For example, machines sometimes speak to humans in a way that makes it impossible to recognise that a machine is speaking (cf. Brommer and Dürscheid 2021). And probably the most important observation in the context of tertiary orality concerns the production of utterances in general, where speech that automatically derives from written texts and written texts originating from spoken utterances have ceased to be exceptions.

Notably, these few remarks concern only the present and the near future while the distant future of writing remains a big question mark, not least because writing is embedded in societies and cultures and thus generally dependent on how we humans develop. Yet, interesting but speculative research has attempted to ask how we could communicate with humans in millions of years (e.g., to caution them against dangerous final disposal sites for nuclear waste; cf. Posner 1990 for some proposals). While it is obvious that there can be no answer to such a question, its very existence – and indeed importance – shows us that communication systems, among them writing, will always be needed, as will be disciplines that study them.

With these considerations, we reach the end of our book. In the preceding chapters we have covered many important facets of the topic of writing. However, it also became clear that further in-depth studies of both theoretical and empirical nature are needed to explore the large field of grapholinguistics. Indeed, as the chapter on writing system typology exemplarily showcased, there remain a myriad of open questions to be studied. Nevertheless, we hope to have succeeded in presenting a variety of perspectives on the field and condensing them to a coherent framework of studying writing. In the best case, these reflections will continue to spread and will stimulate discussion and further grapholinguistic research.

References

AbiFarès, Huda Smitshuijzen. 2019. Working bi-Scriptual: Multiscriptual typographic design and typesetting. In Ben Wittner, Sascha Thoma & Timm Hartmann (eds.), *Bi-Scriptual: Typography and graphic design with multiple script systems*, 12–23. Salenstein: Niggli.

Ágel, Vilmos. 2003. Prinzipien der Grammatik. In Anja Lobenstein-Reichmann & Oskar Reichmann (eds.), *Neue historische Grammatiken. Zum Stand der Grammatikschreibung historischer Sprachstufen des Deutschen und anderer Sprachen*, 1–46. (Reihe Germanistische Linguistik 243). Tübingen: Niemeyer. https://doi.org/10.1515/9783110913194.1

Ágel, Vilmos & Roland Kehrein. 2002. Das Wort – Sprech- und/oder Schreibzeichen? Ein empirischer Beitrag zum latenten Gegenstand der Linguistik. In Vilmos Ágel, Andreas Gardt, Ulrike Haß-Zumkehr & Thorsten Roelcke (eds.), *Das Wort. Seine strukturelle und kulturelle Dimension. Festschrift für Oskar Reichmann zum 65. Geburtstag*, 3–28. Tübingen: Niemeyer. https://doi.org/10.1515/9783110937596.3

Akinnaso, F. Niyi. 1982. On the differences between spoken and written language. *Language and Speech* 25(2). 97–125. https://doi.org/10.1177/002383098202500201

Akinnaso, F. Niyi. 1983. *The structure of divinatory speech: A sociolinguistic analysis of Yoruba 'Sixteen-Cowry' divination*. Berkeley: University of California dissertation.

Akinnaso, F. Niyi. 1985. On the similarities between spoken and written language. *Language and Speech* 28(4). 323–359. https://doi.org/10.1177/002383098502800401

Albrow, Kenneth H. 1972. *The English writing system: Notes towards a description*. London: Longman.

Almog, Guy. 2019. Getting out of hand? Examining the discourse of 'character amnesia'. *Modern Asian Studies* 53(2). 690–717. https://doi.org/10.1017/S0026749X1700035X

Althaus, Hans Peter. [1973] 1980. Graphetik. In Hans Peter Althaus, Helmut Henne & Herbert Ernst Wiegand (eds.), *Lexikon der germanistischen Linguistik*, 2nd edn., 138–142. Tübingen: Niemeyer. https://doi.org/10.1515/9783110960846.138

Altmann, Gabriel. 2004. Script complexity. *Glottometrics* 8. 64–74.

Amtliche Regelung. 2018. „Regeln und Wörterverzeichnis. Aktualisierte Fassung des amtlichen Regelwerks entsprechend den Empfehlungen des Rats für deutsche Rechtschreibung 2016. Redigierte Fassung vom Januar 2018“. Mannheim: Rat für deutsche Rechtschreibung. http://www.rechtschreibrat.com/DOX/rfdr_Regeln_2016_redigiert_2018.pdf (accessed 25 September 2021)

Anbar, Ada. 1986. Reading acquisition of preschool children without systematic instruction. *Early Childhood Research Quarterly* 1(1). 69–83. https://doi.org/10.1016/0885-2006(86)90007-4

Anbar, Ada. 2004. *The secret of natural readers: How preschool children learn to read*. Westport: Praeger.

Anderson, Stephen R. 1992. *A-morphous morphology*. (Cambridge Studies in Linguistics 62). Cambridge: Cambridge University Press. https://doi.org/10.1017/CBO9780511586262

Androutsopoulos, Jannis. 2000. Non-standard spellings in media texts: The case of German fanzines. *Journal of Sociolinguistics* 4(4). 514–533. https://doi.org/10.1111/1467-9481.00128

Androutsopoulos, Jannis. 2004. Typography as a resource of media style: Cases from music youth culture. In Klimis Mastoridis (ed.), *Proceedings of the 1st International Conference on Typography and Visual Communication*, 381–392. Thessaloniki: University of Macedonia Press.

https://doi.org/10.1515/9783110757835-008

Anthony, Jason L. & David J. Francis. 2005. Development of phonological awareness. *Current Directions in Psychological Science* 14(5). 255–259. https://doi.org/10.1111/j.0963-7214.2005.00376.x

Antos, Gerd. 2001. Sprachdesign als Stil? Lifting oder: Sie werden die Welt mit anderen Augen sehen. In Eva-Maria Jakobs & Annely Rothkegel (eds.), *Perspektiven auf Stil*, 55–76. Tübingen: Niemeyer. https://doi.org/10.1515/9783110941524.55

APCEIU (The Asia-Pacific Centre of Education for International Understanding) (ed.). 2015. *The story of nine Asian alphabets*. Seoul: Hollym.

Asfaha, Yonas Mesfun, Jeanner Kurvers & Sjaak Kroon. 2009. Grain size in script and teaching: Literacy acquisition in Ge'ez and Latin. *Applied Psycholinguistics* 30(4). 709–724. https://doi.org/10.1017/S0142716409990087

Aşıcıoğlu, Faruk & Nurten Turan. 2003. Handwriting changes under the effect of alcohol. *Forensic Science International* 132. 201–210. https://doi.org/10.1016/s0379-0738(03)00020-3

Assmann, Jan. 1988. Im Schatten junger Medienblüte. Ägypten und die Materialität des Zeichens. In Hans Gumbrecht & Karl Ludwig Pfeiffer (eds.), *Materialität der Kommunikation*, 141–160. Frankfurt a. M.: Suhrkamp.

Assmann, Jan. 2018. *Das kulturelle Gedächtnis: Schrift, Erinnerung und politische Identität in frühen Hochkulturen*, 8th edn. München: C. H. Beck.

Auberlen, Wieland. 1990. Der Einfluss makrotypographischer Markierungen auf die Textverarbeitung in Abhängigkeit von der Leseintention. In Gerd Kegel, Thomas Arnhold, Klaus Dahlmeier, Gerhard Schmid & Bernd Tischer (eds.), *Sprechwissenschaft und Psycholinguistik. Beiträge aus Forschung und Praxis*, vol. 4, 99–150. Wiesbaden: Westdeutscher Verlag.

Baddeley, Susan & Anja Voeste (eds.). 2012. *Orthographies in early modern Europe*. Berlin/Boston: De Gruyter. https://doi.org/10.1515/9783110288179

Balestra, Miriam B. 2017. *Vokalschreibungen im Deutschen: Eine graphotaktische Analyse einsilbiger Nomen*. Frankfurt a. M.: Peter Lang. https://doi.org/10.3726/b11532

Bartlett, Lesley, Diana López, Lalitha Vasudevan & Doris Warriner. 2011. The anthropology of literacy. In Bradley A. U. Levinson & Mica Pollock (eds.), *A companion to the anthropology of education*, 154–176. Malden/Oxford: Wiley-Blackwell. https://doi.org/10.1002/9781444396713.ch10

Baur, Ruedi & Ulrike Felsing (eds.). 2020. *Visual coexistence: Informationdesign and typography in the intercultural field*. Baden: Lars Müller Publishers.

Behaghel, Otto. 1927. *Von deutscher Sprache. Aufsätze, Vorträge und Plaudereien*. Lahr: Moritz Schauenburg.

Behrens, Ulrike. 1989. *Wenn nicht alle Zeichen trügen. Interpunktion als Markierung syntaktischer Konstruktionen*. (Arbeiten zur Sprachanalyse 9). Frankfurt a. M.: Peter Lang.

Berg, Kristian. 2016a. Graphemic analysis and the spoken language bias. *Frontiers in Psychology* 7. 388. https://doi.org/10.3389/fpsyg.2016.00388

Berg, Kristian. 2016b. Graphematische Variation. In Birgit Mesch & Christina Noack (eds.), *System, Norm und Gebrauch – drei Seiten derselben Medaille? Orthographische Kompetenz und Performanz zwischen System, Norm und Empirie*, 9–23. Baltmannsweiler: Schneider Hohengehren.

Berg, Kristian. 2019. *Die Graphematik der Morpheme im Deutschen und Englischen*. Berlin/Boston: De Gruyter. https://doi.org/10.1515/9783110604856

Berg, Kristian & Mark Aronoff. 2017. Self-organization in the spelling of English suffixes: The emergence of culture out of anarchy. *Language* 93(1). 37–64. https://doi.org/10.1353/lan.2017.0000

Berg, Kristian & Mark Aronoff. 2018. Further evidence for self-organization in English spelling. *Language* 94(1). e48–e53. https://doi.org/10.1353/lan.2018.0013

Berg, Kristian & Mark Aronoff. 2021. Is the English writing system phonographic or lexical/morphological? A new look at the spelling of stems. *Morphology* 31(3). 315–328. https://doi.org/10.1007/s11525-021-09379-5

Berg, Kristian & Martin Evertz. 2018. Graphematik – die Beziehung zwischen Sprache und Schrift. In Stefanie Dipper, Ralf Klabunde & Wiltrud Mihatsch (eds.), *Linguistik – Eine Einführung (nicht nur) für Germanisten, Romanisten und Anglisten*, 187–195. Berlin: Springer. https://doi.org/10.1007/978-3-662-55589-7_10

Berg, Kristian, Beatrice Primus & Lutz Wagner. 2016. Buchstabenmerkmal, Buchstabe, Graphem. In Ulrike Domahs & Beatrice Primus (eds.), *Handbuch Laut, Gebärde, Buchstabe*, 337–355. (Handbooks of Linguistic Knowledge 2). Berlin/Boston: De Gruyter. https://doi.org/10.1515/9783110295993-019

Besnier, Niko. 2000. Literacy. *Journal of Linguistic Anthropology* 9(1–2). 141–143.

Bi'lak, Peter. 2019. Expanding possibilities of type design today. In Ben Wittner, Sascha Thoma & Timm Hartmann (eds.), *Bi-Scriptual: Typography and graphic design with multiple script systems*, 10–11. Salenstein: Niggli.

Biber, Douglas. 1988. *Variation across speech and writing*. Cambridge: Cambridge University Press. https://doi.org/10.1017/CBO9780511621024

Biber, Douglas & Edward Finegan. 1989. Styles of stance in English: Lexical and grammatical marking of evidentiality and affect. *Text* 9(1). 93–124. https://doi.org/10.1515/text.1.1989.9.1.93

Birk, Elisabeth & Sonja Häffner. 2005. Was ist phonologische Bewusstheit? Schrifttheoretische Analyse einer psychologischen Fragestellung. In Hans-Werner Huneke (ed.), *Geschriebene Sprache: Strukturen, Erwerb, didaktische Modellbildungen*, 53–72. (Schriftenreihe der Pädagogischen Hochschule Heidelberg 45). Heidelberg: Mattes.

Blachman, Benita A. 2000. Phonological awareness. In Michael L. Kamil, Peter B. Mosenthal, P. David Pearson & Rebecca Barr (eds.), *Handbook of reading research*, vol. 3, 483–502. Hillsdale: Lawrence Erlbaum Associates Publishers.

Bloomfield, Leonard. 1933. *Language*. New York: Henry Holt and Co.

Böhm, Manuela & Olaf Gätje. 2014. Handschreiben – Handschriften – Handschriftlichkeit: Zu Praktik, Materialität und Theorie des Schreibens mit der Hand. *OBST* 85. 7–21.

Boland, Julie E. & Robin Queen. 2016. If you're house is still available, send me an email: Personality influences reactions to written errors in email messages. *PLoS One* 11(3). e0149885. https://doi.org/10.1371/journal.pone.0149885

Boltz, William G. 1994. *The origin and early development of the Chinese writing system*. (American Oriental Series 78). New Haven: American Oriental Society.

Bosshard, Hans R. 1996. *Sechs Essays zu Typografie, Schrift, Lesbarkeit*. Teufen: Niggli.

Boudelaa, Sami, Manuel Perea & Manuel Carreiras. 2020. Matrices of the frequency and similarity of Arabic letters and allographs. *Behavior Research Methods* 52. 1893–1905. https://doi.org/10.3758/s13428-020-01353-z

Bow, Catherine. 2013. Community-based orthography development in four Western Zambian languages. *Writing Systems Research* 5(1). 73–87. https://doi.org/10.1080/17586801.2012.747427

Bredel, Ursula. 2008. *Die Interpunktion des Deutschen: Ein kompositionelles System zur Online-Steuerung des Lesens*. (Linguistische Arbeiten 522). Tübingen: Niemeyer. https://doi.org/10.1515/9783484970502

Bredel, Ursula. 2009. Das Interpunktionssystem des Deutschen. In Angelika Linke & Helmuth Feilke (eds.), *Oberfläche und Performanz*, 117–136. (Reihe Germanistische Linguistik 283). Tübingen: Niemeyer. https://doi.org/10.1515/9783484971240.2.117

Bredel, Ursula. 2011. *Interpunktion*. (Kurze Einführungen in die germanistische Linguistik 11). Heidelberg: Winter.

Brekle, Herbert E. 1971. Einige Bemerkungen zur Graphematik-Diskussion. *Linguistische Berichte* 16. 53–59.

Brekle, Herbert E. 1981. Zur Integration eines speziellen Typs ikonischer Elemente in primär schriftsprachlichen Wortbildungen einiger europäischer Sprachen. In Wolfgang Pöckel (ed.), *Europäische Mehrsprachigkeit. Festschrift zum 70. Geburtstag von Mario Wandruszka*, 197–207. Tübingen: Niemeyer.

Brekle, Herbert E. 1994a. Die Buchstabenformen westlicher Alphabetschriften in ihrer historischen Entwicklung. In Hartmut Günther & Otto Ludwig (eds.), *Schrift und Schriftlichkeit/Writing and its use*, vol. 1, 171–204. (Handbooks of Linguistics and Communication Science 10.1). Berlin/Boston: De Gruyter. https://doi.org/10.1515/9783110111293.1.2.171

Brekle, Herbert E. 1994b. Typographie. In Hartmut Günther & Otto Ludwig (eds.), *Schrift und Schriftlichkeit/Writing and its use*, vol. 1, 204–227. (Handbooks of Linguistics and Communication Science 10.1). Berlin/Boston: De Gruyter. https://doi.org/10.1515/9783110111293.1.2.204

Brekle, Herbert E. 1995. Neues über Groß- und Kleinbuchstaben. Theoretische Begründung der Entwicklung der römischen Majuskelformen zur Minuskelschrift. *Linguistische Berichte* 155. 3–21.

Brenneman, Kimberly, Christine Massey, Steven F. Machado & Rochel Gelman. 1996. Young children's plans differ for writing and drawing. *Cognitive Development* 11(3). 397–419. https://doi.org/10.1016/S0885-2014(96)90011-8

Brentari, Diane. 2002. Modality differences in sign language phonology and morphophonemics. In Richard P. Meier, Kearsy Cormier & David Quinto-Pozos (eds.), *Modality and structure in signed and spoken languages*, 35–64. Cambridge: Cambridge University Press. https://doi.org/10.1017/CBO9780511486777.003

Bright, William. 2000. A matter of typology: Alphasyllabaries and abugidas. *Studies in the Linguistic Sciences* 30(1). 63–71.

Brommer, Sarah & Christa Dürscheid (eds.). 2021. *Mensch. Maschine. Kommunikation. Beiträge zur Medienlinguistik*. Tübingen: Narr.

Brown, Adam. 1988. *Homophones and homographs in Thai, and their implications*. (Forum Phoneticum 43). Hamburg: Helmut Buske.

Buchmann, Franziska. 2015. *Die Wortzeichen im Deutschen*. (Germanistische Bibliothek 56). Heidelberg: Winter.

Buckley, Eugene. 2018. Core syllables vs. moraic writing. *Written Language & Literacy* 21(1). 26–51. https://doi.org/10.1075/wll.00009.buc

Bugarski, Ranko. 1993. Graphic relativity and linguistic constructs. In Robert J. Scholes (ed.), *Literacy and language analysis*, 5–18. Hillsdale: Erlbaum.

Bunčić, Daniel. 2016. A heuristic model for typology. In Daniel Bunčić, Sandra L. Lippert & Achim Rabus (eds.), *Biscriptality: A sociolinguistic typology*, 51–71. (Akademiekonferenzen 24). Heidelberg: Winter.

Bunčić, Daniel, Sandra L. Lippert & Achim Rabus (eds.). 2016. *Biscriptality: A sociolinguistic typology*. (Akademiekonferenzen 24). Heidelberg: Winter.

Burger, Harald & Martin Luginbühl. 2014. *Mediensprache. Eine Einführung in Sprache und Kommunikationsformen der Massenmedien*, 4th rev. edn. (De Gruyter Studienbuch). Berlin/Boston: De Gruyter. https://doi.org/10.1515/9783110285925

Busch, Florian. 2021. *Digitale Schreibregister. Kontexte, Formen und metapragmatische Reflexionen*. (Linguistik – Impulse & Tendenzen 92). Berlin/Boston: De Gruyter. https://doi.org/10.1515/9783110728835

Butt, Matthias & Peter Eisenberg. 1990. Schreibsilbe und Sprechsilbe. In Christian Stetter (ed.), *Zu einer Theorie der Orthographie: Interdisziplinäre Aspekte gegenwärtiger Schrift- und Orthographieforschung*, 34–64. (Reihe Germanistische Linguistik 99). Tübingen: Niemeyer. https://doi.org/10.1515/9783111372280.34

Cahill, Michael. 2014. Non-linguistic factors in orthographies. In Michael Cahill & Keren Rice (eds.), *Developing orthographies for unwritten languages*, 9–25. Dallas: SIL International.

Cahill, Michael & Keren Rice (eds.). 2014. *Developing orthographies for unwritten languages*. Dallas: SIL International.

Caldwell, Christine A. & Kenny Smith. 2012. Cultural evolution and perpetuation of arbitrary communicative conventions in experimental microsocieties. *PLoS ONE* 7(8). e43807. https://doi.org/10.1371/journal.pone.0043807

Caligiuri, Michael P. & Linton A. Mohammed. 2012. *The neuroscience of handwriting: Applications for forensic document examination*. Boca Raton: CRC Press.

Carlisle, Joanne F. 2010. Effects of instruction in morphological awareness on literacy achievement: An integrative review. *Reading Research Quarterly* 45(4). 464–487. https://doi.org/10.1598/RRQ.45.4.5

Carney, Edward. 1994. *A survey of English spelling*. London: Routledge.

Carreiras, Manuel & Cathy J. Price. 2008. Brain activation for consonants and vowels. *Cerebral Cortex* 18(7). 1727–1735. https://doi.org/10.1093/cercor/bhm202

Carreiras, Manuel, Manuel Perea, Cristina Gil-Lopez, Reem Abu Mallouh & Elena Salillas. 2013. Neural correlates of visual versus abstract letter processing in Roman and Arabic scripts. *Journal of Cognitive Neuroscience* 25(11). 1975–1985. https://doi.org/10.1162/jocn_a_00438

Carter, Ronald & Michael McCarthy. 2006. *Cambridge grammar of English: A comprehensive guide to spoken and written grammar and usage*. Cambridge: Cambridge University Press.

Catach, Nina. 2001. Graphetik/Graphétique. In Günter Holtus, Michael Metzeltin & Christian Schmitt (eds.), *Lexikon der Romanistischen Linguistik (LRL): Band I/1 Geschichte des Faches Romanistik. Methodologie (Das Sprachsystem)*, 725–735. Tübingen: Niemeyer. https://doi.org/10.1515/9783110938388-029

Cattell, James McK. 1885. Über die Zeit der Erkennung und Benennung von Schriftzeichen, Bildern und Farben. *Philosophische Studien* 2. 635–650.

Chafe, Wallace. 1982. Integration and involvement in speaking, writing, and oral literature. In Deborah Tannen (ed.), *Spoken and written language: Exploring orality and literacy*, 35–53. Norwood, NJ: Praeger.

Chandler, Daniel. 1994. "Biases of the ear and the eye". http://visual-memory.co.uk/daniel/Documents/litoral/litoral1.html (accessed 12 October 2021).

Chang, Li-Yun, Yen-Chi Chen & Charles A. Perfetti. 2018. GraphCom: A multidimensional measure of graphic complexity applied to 131 written languages. *Behavior Research Methods* 50(1). 427–449. https://doi.org/10.3758/s13428-017-0881-y

Changizi, Mark A. & Shinsuke Shimojo. 2005. Character complexity and redundancy in writing systems over human history. *Proceedings of the Royal Society B* 272. 267–275. https://doi.org/10.1098/rspb.2004.2942

Changizi, Mark A., Qiong Zhang, Hao Ye & Shinsuke Shimojo. 2006. The structures of letters and symbols throughout human history are selected to match those found in objects in natural scenes. *The American Naturalist* 167(5). E117–E139. https://doi.org/10.1086/502806

Chomsky, Noam & Morris Halle. 1968. *The sound pattern of English*. New York: Harper & Row.

Cocq, Coppélie & Kirk Sullivan (eds.). 2018. *Perspectives on Indigenous writing and literacies* (Studies in Writing 37). Leiden: Brill. https://doi.org/10.1163/9789004298507

Cohen, Marcel. 1958. *La grande invention de l'écriture et son évolution*. Paris: Imprimerie nationale.

Collins, James. 1995. Literacy and literacies. *Annual Review of Anthropology* 24. 75–93. https://doi.org/10.1146/annurev.an.24.100195.000451

Coltheart, Max. 1981. Disorders of reading and their implications for models of normal reading. *Visible Language* 15(3). 245–286.

Coltheart, Max, Kathleen Rastle, Conrad Perry, Robyn Langdon & Johannes Ziegler. 2001. DRC: A dual route cascaded model of visual word recognition and reading aloud. *Psychological Review* 108(1). 204–256. https://doi.org/10.1037/0033-295X.108.1.204

Cook, Vivian & Des Ryan (eds.). 2016. *The Routledge handbook of the English writing system*. London/New York: Routledge.

Corder, Stephen P. 1967. The significance of learner's errors. *International Review of Applied Linguistics* 5(4). 161–170. https://doi.org/10.1515/iral.1967.5.1-4.161

Coulmas, Florian. 1981. *Über Schrift*. (Suhrkamp-Taschenbuch Wissenschaft 378). Frankfurt a. M.: Suhrkamp.

Coulmas, Florian. 1989. *The writing systems of the world*. (The Language Library). Oxford: Wiley-Blackwell.

Coulmas, Florian. 1996a. *The Blackwell encyclopedia of writing systems*. Oxford: Wiley-Blackwell. https://doi.org/10.1002/9781118932667

Coulmas, Florian. 1996b. Typology of writing systems. In Hartmut Günther & Otto Ludwig (eds.), *Schrift und Schriftlichkeit/Writing and its use*, vol. 2, 1380–1387. (Handbooks of Linguistics and Communication Science 10.2). Berlin/Boston: De Gruyter. https://doi.org/10.1515/9783110147445.2.9.1380

Coulmas, Florian. 2003. *Writing systems: An introduction to their linguistic analysis*. (Cambridge Textbooks in Linguistics). Cambridge: Cambridge University Press. https://doi.org/10.1017/CBO9781139164597

Coulmas, Florian. 2014. *Writing and society: An introduction*. Cambridge: Cambridge University Press. https://doi.org/10.1017/CBO9781139061063

Coulmas, Florian. 2016. Prescriptivism and writing systems. In Ingrid Tieken-Boon van Ostade & Carol Percy (eds.), *Prescription and tradition in language: Establishing standards across time and space*, 39–56. Bristol: Multilingual Matters. https://doi.org/10.21832/9781783096510-005

Crystal, David. 1997. Toward a typographical linguistics. *Type* 2(1). 7–23.

Crystal, David. 2008. *A dictionary of linguistics and phonetics*. Oxford: Blackwell.

Crystal, David & Derek Davy. 1979. *Investigating English style*. London: Longman.

Damerow, Peter. 2006. The origins of writing as a problem of historical epistemology. *Cuneiform Digital Library Journal* 2006(1). https://cdli.ucla.edu/pubs/cdlj/2006/cdlj2006_001.html (accessed 3 October 2021)

Daniels, Peter T. 1990. Fundamentals of grammatology. *Journal of the American Oriental Society* 110(4). 727–731. https://doi.org/10.2307/602899
Daniels, Peter T. 1991. Is a structural graphemics possible? *LACUS Forum* 18. 528–537.
Daniels, Peter T. 1992. The syllabic origin of writing and the segmental origin of the alphabet. In Pamela Downing, Susan D. Lima & Michael Noonan (eds.), *The linguistics of literacy*, 83–110. (Typological Studies in Language 21). Amsterdam/Philadelphia: John Benjamins. https://doi.org/10.1075/tsl.21.10dan
Daniels, Peter T. 1996. The study of writing systems. In Peter T. Daniels & William Bright (eds.), *The world's writing systems*, 3–17. Oxford: Oxford University Press.
Daniels, Peter T. 2001. Writing systems. In Mark Aronoff & Janie Rees-Miller (eds.), *The handbook of linguistics*, 43–80. Oxford/Malden: Wiley-Blackwell.
Daniels, Peter T. 2006. On beyond alphabets. *Written Language & Literacy* 9(1). 7–24. https://doi.org/10.1075/wll.9.1.03dan
Daniels, Peter T. 2007. Littera ex occidente: Toward a functional history of writing. In Cynthia L. Miller & Charles E. Jones (eds.), *Studies in Semitic and Afro-Asiatic linguistics presented to Gene B. Gragg*, 53–68. (Studies in Ancient Oriental Civilization 60). Chicago: Oriental Institute of the University of Chicago.
Daniels, Peter T. 2009. Grammatology. In David R. Olson & Nancy Torrance (eds.), *The Cambridge handbook of literacy*, 25–45. Cambridge: Cambridge University Press.
Daniels, Peter T. 2013. The history of writing as the history of linguistics. In Keith Allan (ed.), *The Oxford handbook of the history of linguistics*, 53–69. Oxford: Oxford University Press. https://doi.org/10.1093/oxfordhb/9780199585847.013.0003
Daniels, Peter T. 2017. Writing systems. In Mark Aronoff & Janie Rees-Miller (eds.), *The handbook of linguistics*, 2nd edn., 75–94. Oxford/Malden: Wiley-Blackwell. https://doi.org/10.1002/9781119072256.ch5
Daniels, Peter T. 2018. *An exploration of writing*. Bristol: Equinox.
Daniels, Peter T. & David L. Share. 2018. Writing system variation and its consequences for reading and dyslexia. *Scientific Studies of Reading* 22(1). 101–116. https://doi.org/10.1080/10888438.2017.1379082
Daniels, Peter T. & William Bright (eds.). 1996. *The world's writing systems*. Oxford: Oxford University Press.
Davidson, Andrew. 2019. Writing: The re-construction of language. *Language Sciences* 72. 134–149. https://doi.org/10.1016/j.langsci.2018.09.004
Davis, Colin J. 2010. The spatial coding model of visual word identification. *Psychological Review* 117(3). 713–758. https://doi.org/10.1037/a0019738
DeFrancis, John. 1943. The alphabetization of Chinese. *Journal of the American Oriental Society* 63(4). 225–240.
DeFrancis, John. 1989. *Visible speech: The diverse oneness of writing systems*. Honolulu: University of Hawaii Press.
Dehaene, Stanislas. 2009. *Reading in the brain: The new science of how we read*. New York: Penguin.
Derrida, Jacques. 1997. *Of grammatology*. Baltimore/London: Johns Hopkins University Press.
Diringer, David. 1948. *The alphabet: A key to the history of humankind*. London: Hutchinson.
Diringer, David. 1962. *Writing*. (Ancient Peoples and Places 25). New York: Praeger.
Domahs, Ulrike & Beatrice Primus. 2015. Laut – Gebärde – Buchstabe. In Ekkehard Felder & Andreas Gardt (eds.), *Handbuch Sprache und Wissen*, 125–142. (Handbooks of Linguistic Knowledge 1). Berlin/Boston: De Gruyter. https://doi.org/10.1515/9783110295979.125

Donzelli, Aurora & Alexandra Powell Budgen. 2019. The 'Tiny Hand' of Donald Trump and the metapragmatics of typographic parody. *Signs and Society* 7(2). 217–244. https://doi.org/10.1086/702567

Downey, Greg. 2014. All Forms of Writing. *Mind & Language* 29(3). 304–319. https://doi.org/10.1111/mila.12052

Driver, Russel W., Ronald M. Buckley & Dwight D. Frink. 1996. Should we write off graphology? *International Journal of Selection and Assessment* 4(2). 78–86. https://doi.org/10.1111/j.1468-2389.1996.tb00062.x

Dürscheid, Christa. 2006. Äußerungsformen im Kontinuum von Mündlichkeit und Schriftlichkeit. Sprachwissenschaftliche und sprachdidaktische Aspekte. In Eva Neuland (ed.), *Variation im heutigen Deutsch: Perspektiven für den Sprachunterricht*, 375–388. (Sprache – Kommunikation – Kultur 4). Frankfurt a. M.: Lang.

Dürscheid, Christa. 2016a. *Einführung in die Schriftlinguistik*, 5th edn. (UTB 3740). Göttingen: Vandenhoeck & Ruprecht.

Dürscheid, Christa. 2016b. Graphematische Mikrovariation. In Ulrike Domahs & Beatrice Primus (eds.), *Handbuch Laut, Gebärde, Buchstabe*, 492–510. (Handbooks of Linguistic Knowledge 2). Berlin/Boston: De Gruyter. https://doi.org/10.1515/9783110295993-027

Dürscheid, Christa. 2020. Zeichen setzen im digitalen Schreiben. In Jannis Androutsopoulos & Florian Busch (eds.), *Register des Graphischen: Variation, Interaktion und Reflexion in der digitalen Schriftlichkeit*, 31–52. Berlin/Boston: De Gruyter. https://doi.org/10.1515/9783110673241-002

Dürscheid, Christa & Karina Frick. 2016. *Schreiben digital: Wie das Internet unsere Alltagskommunikation verändert*. (Einsichten 3). Stuttgart: Kröner.

Dürscheid, Christa & Dimitrios Meletis. 2019. Emojis: A grapholinguistic approach. In Yannis Haralambous (ed.), *Graphemics in the 21st Century*, 167–183. (Grapholinguistics and Its Applications 1). Brest: Fluxus Éditions. https://doi.org/10.36824/2018-graf-duer

Dürscheid, Christa & Jürgen Spitzmüller. 2006. Jugendlicher Sprachgebrauch in der Deutschschweiz: Eine Zwischenbilanz. In Christa Dürscheid & Jürgen Spitzmüller (eds.), *Zwischentöne. Zur Sprache der Jugend in der Deutschschweiz*, 13–48. Zürich: Verlag Neue Zürcher Zeitung.

Ehlich, Konrad. 1981. Text, Mündlichkeit, Schriftlichkeit. In Hartmut Günther (ed.), *Geschriebene Sprache – Funktion und Gebrauch, Struktur und Geschichte*, 23–51. (Forschungsberichte des Instituts für Phonetik und sprachliche Kommunikation der Universität München 14). München: Institut für Phonetik und sprachliche Kommunikation der Universität München.

Ehlich, Konrad. 2007. *Sprache und sprachliches Handeln*. Berlin/Boston: De Gruyter. https://doi.org/10.1515/9783110922721

Ehlich, Konrad, Florian Coulmas & Gabriele Graefen (eds.). 1996. *A bibliography on writing and written language*. (Trends in Linguistics 89). Berlin/Boston: De Gruyter. https://doi.org/10.1515/9783110889352

Eira, Christina. 1998. Authority and discourse: Towards a model for orthography selection. *Written Language & Literacy* 1(2). 171–224. https://doi.org/10.1075/wll.1.2.03eir

Eisenberg, Peter. 1983. Writing system and morphology. Some orthographic regularities of German. In Florian Coulmas & Konrad Ehlich (eds.), *Writing in focus*, 63–80. (Trends in Linguistics 24). Berlin/Boston: De Gruyter. https://doi.org/10.1515/9783110822830.63

Eisenberg, Peter. 1989. Die Schreibsilbe im Deutschen. In Peter Eisenberg & Hartmut Günther (eds.), *Schriftsystem und Orthographie*, 57–84. (Reihe Germanistische Linguistik 97). Tübingen: Niemeyer. https://doi.org/10.1515/9783111372266.57

Eisenberg, Peter. 2020. *Grundriss der deutschen Grammatik. Bd. 1: Das Wort*, 5th rev. edn. Stuttgart: Metzler. https://doi.org/10.1007/978-3-476-05096-0

Elmentaler, Michael. 2018. *Historische Graphematik des Deutschen: Eine Einführung*. (Narr Studienbücher). Tübingen: Narr.

Erfurt, Jürgen. 1996. Sprachwandel und Schriftlichkeit. In Hartmut Günther & Otto Ludwig (eds.), *Schrift und Schriftlichkeit/Writing and its use*, vol. 2, 1387–1404. (Handbooks of Linguistics and Communication Science 10.2). Berlin/Boston: De Gruyter. https://doi.org/10.1515/9783110147445.2.9.1387

Evertz, Martin. 2016. Graphematischer Fuß und graphematisches Wort. In Ulrike Domahs & Beatrice Primus (eds.), *Handbuch Laut, Gebärde, Buchstabe*, 377–397. (Handbooks of Linguistic Knowledge 2). Berlin/Boston: De Gruyter. https://doi.org/10.1515/9783110295993-021

Evertz, Martin. 2018. *Visual prosody: The graphematic foot in English and German*. Berlin/Boston: De Gruyter. https://doi.org/10.1515/9783110583441

Evertz, Martin & Beatrice Primus. 2013. The graphematic foot in English and German. *Writing Systems Research* 5(1). 1–23. https://doi.org/10.1080/17586801.2013.765356

Ewald, Petra. 2007. Zur orthographischen Regel. In Dieter Nerius (ed.), *Deutsche Orthographie*, 4th edn., 40–54. Hildesheim: Olms.

Eysenck, Michael W. & Mark T. Keane. 2020. *Cognitive psychology: A student's handbook*, 8th edn. London/New York: Psychology Press.

Faber, Alice. 1992. Phonemic segmentation as epiphenomenon: Evidence from the history of alphabetic writing. In Pamela Downing, Susan D. Lima & Michael Noonan (eds.), *The linguistics of literacy*, 111–134. (Typological Studies in Language 21). Amsterdam/Philadelphia: John Benjamins. https://doi.org/10.1075/tsl.21.11fab

Février, James-Germain. 1948. *Histoire de l'écriture*. Paris: Payot.

Fiehler, Reinhard. 2000. Gesprochene Sprache – gibt's die? *Jahrbuch der ungarischen Germanistik* 2000. 93–104.

Fiehler, Reinhard. 2009. Gesprochene Sprache. In *Duden. Die Grammatik*, 8th rev. edn., 1165–1244. Mannheim/Leipzig/Wien/Zürich: Dudenverlag.

Figueredo, Lauren & Connie K. Varnhagen. 2005. Didn't you run the spell checker? Effects of type and spelling error and use of a spell checker on perceptions of the author. *Reading Psychology* 24(4–5). 441–458. https://doi.org/10.1080/02702710500400495

Filek, Jan. 2013. *Read/ability – Typografie und Lesbarkeit*. Sulgen: Niggli.

Finkbeiner, Matthew & Max Coltheart. 2009. Letter recognition: From perception to representation. *Cognitive Neuropsychology* 26(1). 1–6. https://doi.org/10.1080/02643290902905294

Finnegan, Ruth. 1990. What is orality – if anything? *Byzantine and Modern Greek Studies* 14. 130–150. https://doi.org/10.1179/byz.1990.14.1.130

Fiset, Daniel, Caroline Blais, Martin Arguin, Karine Tadros, Catherine Éthier-Majcher, Daniel Bub & Frédéric Gosselin. 2009. The spatio-temporal dynamics of visual letter recognition. *Cognitive Neuropsychology* 26(1). 23–35. https://doi.org/10.1080/02643290802421160

Frangou, Satu-Maarit, Heli Ruokamo, Riina Parviainen & Jan Wikgren. 2018. Can you put your finger on it? The effects of writing modality on Finnish students' recollection. *Writing Systems Research* 10(2). 82–94. https://doi.org/10.1080/17586801.2018.1536015

French, M. A. 1976. Observations on the Chinese script and the classification of writing systems. In William Haas (ed.), *Writing without letters*, 101–129. (Mont Follick Series 4). Manchester: Manchester University Press.

Friedman, Rhonda B. 1980. Identity without form: Abstract representations of letters. *Perception & Psychophysics* 28(1). 53–60. https://doi.org/10.3758/BF03204315
Friedrich, Johannes. 1966. *Geschichte der Schrift unter besonderer Berücksichtigung ihrer geistigen Entwicklung*. Heidelberg: Winter.
Frost, Ram. 2012. Towards a universal model of reading. *Behavioral and Brain Sciences* 35(5). 263–279. https://doi.org/10.1017/S0140525X11001841
Fuhrhop, Nanna. 2008. Das graphematische Wort (im Deutschen): Eine erste Annäherung. *Zeitschrift für Sprachwissenschaft* 27(2). 189–228. https://doi.org/10.1515/zfsw.2008.010
Fuhrhop, Nanna. 2015. *Orthografie*, 4th edn. (Kurze Einführungen in die germanistische Linguistik 1). Heidelberg: Winter.
Fuhrhop, Nanna. 2018. Graphematik des Deutschen im europäischen Vergleich. In Angelika Wöllstein, Peter Gallmann, Mechthild Habermann & Manfred Krifka (eds.), *Grammatiktheorie und Empirie in der germanistischen Linguistik*, 587–616. (Germanistische Sprachwissenschaft um 2020 1). Berlin/Boston: De Gruyter. https://doi.org/10.1515/9783110490992-020
Fuhrhop, Nanna & Franziska Buchmann. 2009. Die Längenhierarchie: Zum Bau der graphematischen Silbe. *Linguistische Berichte* 218. 127–155.
Fuhrhop, Nanna & Franziska Buchmann. 2016. Graphematische Silbe. In Ulrike Domahs & Beatrice Primus (eds.), *Handbuch Laut, Gebärde, Buchstabe*, 356–376. (Handbooks of Linguistic Knowledge 2). Berlin/Boston: De Gruyter. https://doi.org/10.1515/9783110295993-020
Fuhrhop, Nanna, Franziska Buchmann & Kristian Berg. 2011. The length hierarchy and the graphematic syllable: Evidence from German and English. *Written Language & Literacy* 14(2). 275–292. https://doi.org/10.1075/wll.14.2.05fuh
Fuhrhop, Nanna & Jörg Peters. 2013. *Einführung in die Phonologie und Graphematik*. Stuttgart: Metzler. https://doi.org/10.1007/978-3-476-00597-7
Fuhrhop, Nanna & Karsten Schmidt. 2014. Die zunehmende Profilierung der Schreibsilbe in der Geschichte des Deutschen. *Beiträge zur Geschichte der deutschen Sprache und Literatur* 136(4). 538–568. https://doi.org/10.1515/bgsl-2014-0047
Gadamer, Hans-Georg. 1998. Unterwegs zur Schrift? In Aleida Assmann, Jan Assmann & Christof Hardmeier (eds.), *Schrift und Gedächtnis. Archäologie der literarischen Kommunikation I*, 3rd edn., 10–19. München: Fink.
Galambos, Imre. 2015. Variant characters. In Rint Sybesma (ed.), *Encyclopedia of Chinese language and linguistics*. Leiden: Brill. https://doi.org/10.1163/2210-7363_ecll_COM_00000438
Gallmann, Peter. 1986. The graphic elements of German written language. In Gerhard Augst (ed.), *New trends in graphemics and orthography*, 43–79. Berlin/Boston: De Gruyter. https://doi.org/10.1515/9783110867329.43
Ganopole, Selina J. 1987. The development of word consciousness prior to first grade. *Journal of Reading Behavior* 19(4). 415–436. https://doi.org/10.1080/10862968709547614
Garbe, Burckhard. 1985. Graphemtheorien und mögliche strukturmodelle zur beschreibung der orthographie. In Gerhard Augst (ed.), *Graphematik und Orthographie. Neuere Forschungen der Linguistik, Psychologie und Didaktik in der Bundesrepublik Deutschland*, 1–21. Frankfurt a. M.: Peter Lang.
Garrod, Simon, Nicolas Fay, John Lee, Jon Oberlander & Tracy McLeod. 2007. Foundations of representation: Where might graphical symbol systems come from? *Cognitive Science* 31(6). 961–987. https://doi.org/10.1080/03640210701703659
Gaur, Albertine. 1984. *A history of writing*. New York: Scribner's.

Gee, James. 2007. *Social linguistics and literacies: Ideology in discourses*, 3rd edn. London/New York: Routledge.
Gelb, Ignace J. [1952] 1963. *A study of writing*, 2nd edn. Chicago: University of Chicago Press.
Gerth, Sabrina, Thomas Dolk, Annegret Klassert, Michael Fliesser, Martin H. Fischer, Guido Nottbusch & Julia Festman. 2016. Adapting to the surface: A comparison of handwriting measures when writing on a tablet computer and on paper. *Human Movement Science* 48. 62–73. https://doi.org/10.1016/j.humov.2016.04.006
Giampietro, Rob. 2004. "New Black Face: Neuland and Lithos as stereotypography". https://linedandunlined.com/archive/new-black-face/ (accessed 18 October 2021)
Gillon, Gail T. 2018. *Phonological awareness. From research to practice*, 2nd edn. New York: The Guilford Press.
Glück, Helmut. 1987. *Schrift und Schriftlichkeit. Eine sprach- und kulturwissenschaftliche Studie*. Stuttgart: Metzler. https://doi.org/10.1007/978-3-476-03235-5
Glück, Helmut. 2016a. Graphetik. In Helmut Glück & Michael Rödel (eds.), *Metzler Lexikon Sprache*, 5th edn., 253. Stuttgart: Metzler.
Glück, Helmut. 2016b. Interdependenzhypothese. In Helmut Glück & Michael Rödel (eds.), *Metzler Lexikon Sprache*, 5th edn., 301–302. Stuttgart: Metzler.
Glück, Helmut. 2016c. Schriftlichkeit. In Helmut Glück & Michael Rödel (eds.), *Metzler Lexikon Sprache*, 5th ed., 595–596. Stuttgart: Metzler.
Glück, Helmut. 2016d. Schriftlinguistik. In Helmut Glück & Michael Rödel (eds.), *Metzler Lexikon Sprache*, 5th edn., 596. Stuttgart: Metzler.
Glück, Helmut & Michael Rödel (eds.). 2016. *Metzler Lexikon Sprache*, 5th edn. Stuttgart: Metzler. https://doi.org/10.1007/978-3-476-05486-9
Gnanadesikan, Amalia E. 2009. *The writing revolution: Cuneiform to the internet*. (The Language Library). Oxford/Malden: Wiley-Blackwell. https://doi.org/10.1002/9781444304671
Gnanadesikan, Amalia E. 2012. Maldivian Thaana, Japanese kana, and the representation of moras in writing. *Writing Systems Research* 4(1). 91–102. https://doi.org/10.1080/17586801.2012.693459
Gnanadesikan, Amalia E. 2017. Towards a typology of phonemic scripts. *Writing Systems Research* 9(1). 14–35. https://doi.org/10.1080/17586801.2017.1308239
Gombert, Jean E. & Michel Fayol. 1992. Writing in preliterate children. *Learning and Instruction* 2(1). 23–41. https://doi.org/10.1016/0959-4752(92)90003-5
Gomez, Pablo, Roger Ratcliff & Manuel Perea. 2008. The overlap model: A model of letter position coding. *Psychological Review* 115(3). 577–600. https://doi.org/10.1037/a0012667
Gong, Yushu. 2006. Graph typology of ancient Chinese and Sumerian writing systems: A comparative perspective. *Oriental Studies* 6. [Special Issue]. 39–108.
Gong, Yushu, Haiying Yan & Yinghui Ge. 2009. The accounts of the origin of writing from Sumer, Egypt and China: A comparative perspective. *Wiener Zeitschrift für die Kunde des Morgenlandes* 99. 137–158.
Goodnow, Jacqueline J. & Rochelle A. Levine. 1973. "The grammar of action": Sequence and syntax in children's copying. *Cognitive Psychology* 4(1). 82–98. https://doi.org/10.1016/0010-0285(73)90005-4
Goody, Jack. 1977. *The domestication of the savage mind*. (Themes in the Social Sciences). Cambridge: Cambridge University Press.
Goody, Jack & Ian P. Watt. 1963. The consequences of literacy. *Comparative Studies in History and Society* 5(3). 304–345. https://doi.org/10.1017/S0010417500001730

Graff, Harvey J. 1986. The legacies of literacy: Continuities and contradictions in Western society. In Suzanne de Castell, Allan Luke & Kieran Egan (eds.), *Literacy, society, and schooling: A reader*, 61–86. Cambridge: Cambridge University Press.

Graham, Steve. 2018. Handwriting instruction: A commentary on five studies. *Reading and Writing* 31(6). 1367–1377. https://doi.org/10.1007/s11145-018-9854-5

Grainger, Jonathan & Walter J. B. Van Heuven. 2004. Modeling letter position coding in printed word perception. In Patrick Bonin (ed.), *Mental lexicon: "Some words to talk about words"*, 1–24. New York: Nova Science.

Gredig, Andi. 2021. *Schreiben mit der Hand: Begriffe – Diskurs – Praktiken*. Berlin: Frank & Timme. https://doi.org/10.26530/20.500.12657/46049

Guilbert, Jessica, Denis Alamargot & Marie-France Morin. 2019. Handwriting on a tablet screen: Role of visual and proprioceptive feedback in the control of movement by children and adults. *Human Movement Science* 65. 30–41. https://doi.org/10.1016/j.humov.2018.09.001

Gumperz, John J. 1957. Language problems in the rural development of North India. *The Journal of Asian Studies* 16(2). 251–259. https://doi.org/10.2307/2941382

Günther, Hartmut. 1981. Das Prinzip der Alphabetschrift begreifen lernen – einige Thesen zu einem fragwürdigen Konzept. In Hartmut Günther (ed.), *Geschriebene Sprache – Funktion und Gebrauch, Struktur und Geschichte*, 53–68. (Forschungsberichte des Instituts für Phonetik und sprachliche Kommunikation der Universität München 14). München: Institut für Phonetik und sprachliche Kommunikation der Universität München.

Günther, Hartmut. 1983. Charakteristika von schriftlicher Sprache und Kommunikation. In Hartmut Günther & Klaus-B. Günther (eds.), *Schrift – Schreiben – Schriftlichkeit. Arbeiten zur Struktur, Funktion und Entwicklung schriftlicher Sprache*, 17–39. (Reihe Germanistische Linguistik 49). Tübingen: Niemeyer. https://doi.org/10.1515/9783111375687-004

Günther, Hartmut. 1988. *Schriftliche Sprache: Strukturen geschriebener Wörter und ihre Verarbeitung beim Lesen* (Konzepte der Sprach- und Literaturwissenschaft 40). Berlin/Boston: De Gruyter. https://doi.org/10.1515/9783110935851

Günther, Hartmut. 1990a. Typographie, Orthographie, Graphetik. Überlegungen zu einem Buch von Otl Aicher. In Christian Stetter (ed.), *Zu einer Theorie der Orthographie. Interdisziplinäre Aspekte gegenwärtiger Schrift- und Orthographieforschung*, 90–103. (Reihe Germanistische Linguistik 99). Tübingen: Niemeyer. https://doi.org/10.1515/9783111372280.90

Günther, Hartmut. 1990b. Zur neueren Schriftlichkeitsforschung. *Beiträge zur Geschichte der deutschen Sprache* 112. 349–370. https://doi.org/10.1515/bgsl.1990.1990.112.349

Günther, Hartmut. 1993a. Graphetik – Ein Entwurf. In Jürgen Baurmann, Hartmut Günther & Ulrich Knoop (eds.), *Homo scribens. Perspektiven der Schriftlichkeitsforschung*, 29–42. (Reihe Germanistische Linguistik 134). Tübingen: Niemeyer. https://doi.org/10.1515/9783111377087.29

Günther, Hartmut. 1993b. Die Studiengruppe ‚Geschriebene Sprache' bei der Werner Reimers Stiftung, Bad Homburg. In Jürgen Baurmann, Hartmut Günther & Ulrich Knoop (eds.), *Homo scribens. Perspektiven der Schriftlichkeitsforschung*, 371–378. (Reihe Germanistische Linguistik 134). Tübingen: Niemeyer. https://doi.org/10.1515/9783111377087.371

Günther, Hartmut & Otto Ludwig (eds.). 1994/1996. *Schrift und Schriftlichkeit/Writing and its use*. (Handbooks of Linguistics and Communication Science 10.1 & 10.2). Berlin/Boston: De Gruyter. https://doi.org/10.1515/9783110111293.1, https://doi.org/10.1515/9783110147445.2

Haarmann, Harald. 1991. *Universalgeschichte der Schrift*, 2nd edn. Frankfurt a. M.: Campus-Verlag.

Haarmann, Harald. 2010. *Einführung in die Donauschrift*. Hamburg: Buske.

Haas, William. 1976. Writing: The basic options. In William Haas (ed.), *Writing without letters*, 133–208. (Mont Follick Series 4). Manchester: Manchester University Press.

Häcki Buhofer, Annelies. 1985. *Schriftlichkeit im Alltag. Theoretische und empirische Aspekte – am Beispiel eines Schweizer Industriebetriebs*. (Zürcher Germanistische Studien 2). Bern/Frankfurt a. M./New York: Lang.

Hagemann, Jörg. 2003. Typographische Kommunikation. In Jörg Hagemann & Sven F. Sager (eds.), *Mündliche und schriftliche Kommunikation. Begriffe, Methoden, Analysen. Festschrift für Klaus Brinker zum 65. Geburtstag*, 101–115. Tübingen: Stauffenburg.

Hahn, Reinhard F. 1991. *Spoken Uyghur*. Seattle: University of Washington Press.

Halverson, John. 1992. Goody and the implosion of the literacy thesis. *Man* 27(2). 301–317. https://doi.org/10.2307/2804055

Handel, Zev. 2013. Can a logographic script be simplified? Lessons from the 20th century Chinese writing reform informed by recent psycholinguistic research. *Scripta* 5. 21–66.

Handel, Zev. 2019. *Sinography: The borrowing and adaptation of the Chinese script*. Leiden: Brill. https://doi.org/10.1163/9789004352223

Hannas, William C. 1997. *Asia's orthographic dilemma*. Honolulu: University of Hawai'i Press.

Hannas, William C. 2003. *The writing on the wall: How Asian orthography curbs creativity*. (Encounters with Asia). Philadelphia: University of Pennsylvania Press.

Harley, Trevor A. 2017. *Talking the talk: Language, psychology and science*, 2nd edn. London/New York: Routledge.

Harris, Roy. 1980. *The language-makers*. London: Duckworth.

Harris, Roy. 2005. Schrift und linguistische Theorie. In Gernot Grube, Werner Kogge & Sybille Krämer (eds.), *Schrift: Kulturtechnik zwischen Auge, Hand und Maschine*, 61–80. (Kulturtechnik). München: Wilhelm Fink.

Harrison, Michael. n. d. "Logocentrism". https://lucian.uchicago.edu/blogs/mediatheory/keywords/logocentrism/ (accessed 30 October 2021)

Hartmann, Reinhard R. K. & Gregory James. 1998. *Dictionary of lexicography*. London/New York: Routledge.

Hartmann, Stefan, Jessica Nowak & Renata Szczepaniak (eds.). 2021. The evolution of writing systems. [Special Issue]. *Zeitschrift für Sprachwissenschaft* 40(3).

Hatcher, Lynley. 2008. Script change in Azerbaijan: Acts of identity. *International Journal of the Sociology of Language* 192. 105–116. https://doi.org/10.1515/IJSL.2008.038

Havelock, Eric A. 1963. *Preface to Plato*. Cambridge: Harvard University Press.

Heilmann, Till A. 2014. Handschrift im digitalen Umfeld. *OBST* 85. 169–192.

Heller, Klaus & Dieter Nerius. 2007. Zur Stellung der geschriebenen Sprache und Orthographie in der neueren Linguistik. In Dieter Nerius (ed.), *Deutsche Orthographie*, 4th edn., 55–72. Hildesheim: Olms.

Henderson, Leslie. 1985. On the use of the term 'grapheme'. *Language and Cognitive Processes* 1(2). 135–148. https://doi.org/10.1080/01690968508402075

Hennig, Mathilde. 2000. Können gesprochene und geschriebene Sprache überhaupt verglichen werden? *Jahrbuch der ungarischen Germanistik* 2000. 105–125.

Heyd, Theresa. 2021. Tertiary orality? New approaches to spoken CMC. *Anglistik* 32(2). 131–147. https://doi.org/10.33675/ANGL/2021/2/10

Hill, Archibald A. 1967. The typology of writing systems. In William M. Austin (ed.), *Papers in linguistics in honor of Léon Dostert*, 92–99. (Janua Linguarum. Series Maior 25). Berlin/Boston: De Gruyter. https://doi.org/10.1515/9783111675886-008

Hillburger, Christina. 2016. Character amnesia: An overview. *Sino-Platonic Papers* 264. 51–70.

Ho, Connie S.-H., Ting-Ting Ng & Wing-Kin Ng. 2003. A 'radical' approach to reading development in Chinese: The role of semantic radicals and phonetic radicals. *Journal of Literacy Research* 35(3). 849–878. https://doi.org/10.1207/s15548430jlr3503_3

Hockett, Charles F. 1960. The origin of speech. *Scientific American* 203(3). 88–96. https://doi.org/10.1038/scientificamerican0960-88

Hoffman, Paul, Matthew A. Lambon Ralph & Anna M. Woollams. 2015. Triangulation of the neurocomputational architecture underpinning reading aloud. *Proceedings of the National Academy of Sciences of the United States of America* 112(28). E3719–E3728. https://doi.org/10.1073/pnas.1502032112

Høien, Torleiv, Ingvar Lundberg, Keith E. Stanovich & Inger-Kristin Bjaalid. 1995. Components of phonological awareness. *Reading and Writing* 7(2). 171–188. https://doi.org/10.1007/BF01027184

Holisky, Dee Ann. 1996. The Georgian alphabet. In Peter T. Daniels & William Bright (eds.), *The world's writing systems*, 364–369. Oxford: Oxford University Press.

Horobin, Simon. 2013. *Does spelling matter?* Oxford: Oxford University Press.

Houston, Stephen D. (ed.). 2004a. *The first writing: Script invention as history and process.* Cambridge: Cambridge University Press.

Houston, Stephen D. 2004b. Overture to the first writing. In Stephen D. Houston (ed.), *The first writing: Script invention as history and process*, 3–15. Cambridge: Cambridge University Press.

Hsieh, Feng-fan. 2015. Transcribing foreign names. In Rint Sybesma (ed.), *Encyclopedia of Chinese language and linguistics.* Leiden: Brill. https://doi.org/10.1163/2210-7363_ecll_COM_00000182

Hu, Zhuanglin. 2015. The standardization of Chinese characters. *Chinese Semiotic Studies* 11(2). 123–133. https://doi.org/10.1515/css-2015-0007

Huang, Shuting, Yacong Zhou, Menglin Du, Ruiming Wang & Zhenguang G. Cai. 2021. Character amnesia in Chinese handwriting: A mega-study analysis. *Language Sciences* 85. 101383. https://doi.org/10.1016/j.langsci.2021.101383

Inkelas, Sharon, Keith Johnson, Charles Lee, Emil Minas, George Mulcaire, Gek Yong Keng & Tomomi Yuasa. 2013. Testing the learnability of writing systems. In Matthew Faytak, Matthew Goss, Nicholas Baier, John Merrill, Kelsey Neely, Erin Donnelly & Jevon Heath (eds.), *Proceedings of the 39th Annual Meeting of the Berkeley Linguistics Society, Berkeley, USA, 2013*, 75–89. Berkeley: Berkeley Linguistics Society. https://doi.org/10.3765/bls.v39i1.3871

Jaffe, Alexandra M., Jannis Androutsopoulos, Mark Sebba & Sally Johnson (eds.). 2012. *Orthography as social action.* (Language and Social Processes 3). Berlin/Boston: De Gruyter. https://doi.org/10.1515/9781614511038

Jäger, Ludwig. 2018. Mythos *Cours*. Saussures Sprachidee und die Gründungslegende des Strukturalismus. In Martin Endres & Leonhard Herrmann (eds.), *Strukturalismus, heute: Brüche, Spuren, Kontinuitäten*, 11–28. Stuttgart: Metzler. https://doi.org/10.1007/978-3-476-04551-5_2

James, Karin H. & Laura Engelhardt. 2012. The effects of handwriting experience on functional brain development in pre-literate children. *Trends in Neuroscience and Education* 1(1). 32–42. https://doi.org/10.1016/j.tine.2012.08.001

Jensen, Hans. 1969. *Sign, symbol and script.* Translated by George Unwin. 3rd edn. London: George Allen & Unwin.

Johnson, Sally. 2002. On the origin of linguistic norms: Orthography, ideology and the first constitutional challenge to the 1996 reform of German. *Language in Society* 31. 549–576. https://doi.org/10.1017/S0047404502314039

Jones, Edward A. & Chisato Aoki. 1988. The processing of Japanese kana and kanji characters. In Derrick de Kerckhove & Charles J. Lumsden (eds.), *The alphabet and the brain: The lateralization of writing*, 301–320. Berlin/Heidelberg: Springer. https://doi.org/10.1007/978-3-662-01093-8_17

Jones, Mari C. & Damien Mooney. 2017. Creating orthographies for endangered languages. In Mari C. Jones & Damien Mooney (eds.), *Creating orthographies for endangered languages*, 1–35. Cambridge: Cambridge University Press. https://doi.org/10.1017/9781316562949.001

Joyce, Terry. 2011. The significance of the morphographic principle for the classification of writing systems. *Written Language & Literacy* 14(1). [Special issue]. 58–81. https://doi.org/10.1075/wll.14.1.04joy

Joyce, Terry & Susanne R. Borgwaldt. 2011. Typology of writing systems: Special issue introduction. *Written Language & Literacy* 14(1). [Special issue]. 1–11. https://doi.org/10.1075/wll.14.1.01joy

Joyce, Terry & Hisashi Masuda. 2019. On the notions of orthography and graphematic representation from the perspective of the Japanese writing system. *Written Language & Literacy* 22(2). 247–279. https://doi.org/10.1075/wll.00028.joy

Joyce, Terry & Dimitrios Meletis. 2021. Alternative criteria for writing system typology. Cross-linguistic observations from the German and Japanese writing systems. *Zeitschrift für Sprachwissenschaft* 40(3). 257–277. https://doi.org/10.1515/zfs-2021-2030

Justeson, John S. 1976. Universals of language and universals of writing. In Alphonse Juilland, Andrew M. Devine, & Laurence D. Stephens (eds.), *Linguistic studies offered to Joseph Greenberg on the occasion of his 60th birthday*, vol. 1, 57–94. (Studia linguistica et phonologia 4). Saratoga: Amna Libri.

Justeson, John S. 1978. *Mayan scribal practice in the classical period: A test-case of an explanatory approach to the study of writing systems*. Stanford: Stanford University dissertation.

Karan, Elke. 2014. Standardization: What's the hurry? In Michael Cahill & Keren Rice (eds.), *Developing orthographies for unwritten languages*, 107–138. Dallas: SIL International.

Karavanidou, Eleni. 2017. Is handwriting relevant in the digital era? *Antistasis* 7(1). 153–167.

Karg, Ina. 2015. *Orthographie: Öffentlichkeit, Wissenschaft und Erwerb*. (Germanistische Arbeitshefte 46). Berlin/Boston: De Gruyter. https://doi.org/10.1515/9783110366679

Katz, Leonard & Ram Frost. 1992. The reading process is different for different orthographies: The orthographic depth hypothesis. In Ram Frost & Leonard Katz (eds.), *Orthography, phonology, morphology, and meaning*, 67–84. Amsterdam: Elsevier. https://doi.org/10.1016/S0166-4115(08)62789-2

Katzen, May. 1977. *The visual impact of scholarly journal articles*. Leicester: University of Leicester, Primary Communications Research Centre.

Kay, Paul. 1977. Language evolution and speech style. In Mary Sanches & Ben G. Blount (eds.), *Sociocultural dimensions of language use*, 21–33. (Language, Thought and Culture: Advances in the Study of Cognition). New York: Academic Press.

Kaye, Alan S. 1996. Adaptations of Arabic script. In Peter T. Daniels & William Bright (eds.), *The world's writing systems*, 743–762. Oxford: Oxford University Press.

Keage, Hannah A. D., Scott Coussens, Mark Kohler, Myra Thiessen & Owen F. Churches. 2014. Investigating letter recognition in the brain by varying typeface: An event-related potential study. *Brain and Cognition* 88. 83–89. https://doi.org/10.1016/j.bandc.2014.05.001

Kelly, Piers, James Winters, Helena Miton & Olivier Morin. 2020. The predictable evolution of letter shapes: An emergent script of West Africa recapitulates historical change in writing systems. *Current Anthropology*. 1–38.

Kenner, Charmian. 2004. *Becoming biliterate: Young children learning different writing systems*. Stoke on Trent, UK/Sterling: Trentham Books.

Kim, Sung-Do. 2011. Iconicity of Korean writing: A media semiotic approach. In Antonio Loprieno, Carsten Knigge Salis & Birgit Mersmann (eds.), *Bild, Macht, Schrift: Schriftkulturen in bildkritischer Perspektive*, 171–199. Weilerswist: Velbrück Wissenschaft.

Kirchhoff, Frank. 2016. Interpunktion und Intonation. In Ulrike Domahs & Beatrice Primus (eds.), *Handbuch Laut, Gebärde, Buchstabe*, 398–417. (Handbooks of Linguistic Knowledge 2). Berlin/Boston: De Gruyter. https://doi.org/10.1515/9783110295993-022

Kirchhoff, Frank & Beatrice Primus. 2016. Punctuation. In Vivian Cook & Des Ryan (eds.), *The Routledge handbook of the English writing system*, 95–111. (Routledge Handbooks in Linguistics). London: Routledge.

Klinkenberg, Jean-Marie & Stéphane Polis. 2018. On scripturology. *Signata: Annals of Semiotics* 9. 57–102. https://doi.org/10.4000/signata.1885

Koch, Peter & Wulf Oesterreicher. 1985. Sprache der Nähe – Sprache der Distanz. Mündlichkeit und Schriftlichkeit im Spannungsfeld von Sprachtheorie und Sprachgeschichte. *Romanistisches Jahrbuch* 36(1). 15–43. https://doi.org/10.1515/9783110244922.15

Koch, Peter & Wulf Oesterreicher. 1994. Schriftlichkeit und Sprache. In Hartmut Günther & Otto Ludwig (eds.), *Schrift und Schriftlichkeit/Writing and its use*, vol. 1, 587–604. (Handbooks of Linguistics and Communication Science 10.1). Berlin/Boston: De Gruyter. https://doi.org/10.1515/9783110111293.1.5.587

Koch, Peter & Wulf Oesterreicher. 2012. Language of immediacy – language of distance: Orality and literacy from the perspective of language theory and linguistic history. In Claudia Lange, Beatrix Weber & Göran Wolf (eds.), *Communicative spaces: Variation, contact, and change – Papers in honour of Ursula Schaefer*, 441–473. Frankfurt a. M.: Peter Lang.

Kohrt, Manfred. 1985. *Problemgeschichte des Graphembegriffs und des frühen Phonembegriffs*. (Reihe Germanistische Linguistik 61). Tübingen: Niemeyer. https://doi.org/10.1515/9783111371207

Kohrt, Manfred. 1986. The term 'grapheme' in the history and theory of linguistics. In Gerhard Augst (ed.), *New trends in graphemics and orthography*, 80–96. Berlin/Boston: De Gruyter. https://doi.org/10.1515/9783110867329.80

Kohrt, Manfred. 1990. Die 'doppelte Kodifikation' der deutschen Orthographie. In Christian Stetter (ed.), *Zu einer Theorie der Orthographie: Interdisziplinäre Aspekte gegenwärtiger Schrift- und Orthographieforschung*, 104–144. (Reihe Germanistische Linguistik 99). Tübingen: Niemeyer. https://doi.org/10.1515/9783111372280.104

Köller, Wilhelm. 1988. *Philosophie der Grammatik. Vom Sinn grammatischen Wissens*. Stuttgart: Metzler. https://doi.org/10.1007/978-3-476-03252-2

König, Anne R. 2004. *Lesbarkeit als Leitprinzip der Buchtypographie. Eine Untersuchung zum Forschungsstand und zur historischen Entwicklung des Konzeptes „Lesbarkeit"*. (Alles Buch. Studien der Erlanger Buchwissenschaft VII). Universität Erlangen-Nürnberg. http://alles-buch.uni-erlangen.de/Koenig.pdf (accessed 18 October 2021)

Krämer, Sybille. 1998. Das Medium als Spur und als Apparat. In Sybille Krämer (ed.), *Medien, Computer, Realität. Wirklichkeitsvorstellungen und Neue Medien*, 73–94. (Suhrkamp-Taschenbuch Wissenschaft 1379). Frankfurt a. M.: Suhrkamp.

Krämer, Sybille. 2014. Über die Handschrift: Gedankenfacetten. *OBST* 85. 23–34.

Kreiner, David S., Summer D. Schnakenberg, Angela G. Green, Michael J. Costello, Anis F. McClin. 2002. Effects of spelling errors on the perception of writers. *Journal of General Psychology* 129(1). 5–17. https://doi.org/10.1080/00221300209602029

Lavine, Linda O. 1977. Differentiation of letterlike forms in prereading children. *Developmental Psychology* 13(2). 89–94. https://doi.org/10.1037/0012-1649.13.2.89

Lévi-Strauss, Claude. 1966. *The savage mind*. Chicago: University of Chicago Press.

Li, Chris W.-C. 2007. Foreign names into native tongues: How to transfer sound between languages – transliteration, phonological translation, nativization, and implications for translation theory. *Target* 19(1). 45–68. https://doi.org/10.1075/target.19.1.04li

Li, Julia X. & Karin H. James. 2016. Handwriting generates variable visual input to facilitate symbol learning. *Journal of Experimental Psychology: General* 145(3). 298–313. https://doi.org/10.1037/xge0000134

Li, Shi Pui Donald, Sam-Po Law, Kai-Yan Dustin Lau & Brenda Rapp. 2021. Functional orthographic units in Chinese character reading: Are there abstract radical identities? *Psychonomic Bulletin & Review* 28. 610–623. https://doi.org/10.3758/s13423-020-01828-2

Lillis, Theresa & Carolyn McKinney. 2013. The sociolinguistics of writing in a global context: Objects, lenses, consequences. *Journal of Sociolinguistics* 17(4). 415–439. https://doi.org/10.1111/josl.12046

Lindqvist, Christer. 2001. *Skandinavische Schriftsysteme im Vergleich*. (Linguistische Arbeiten 430). Tübingen: Niemeyer. https://doi.org/10.1515/9783110927085

Linell, Per. 2005. *The written language bias in linguistics. Its nature, origins and transformations*. (Routledge Advances in Communication and Linguistic Theory). London: Routledge. https://doi.org/10.4324/9780203342763

Lockwood, David G. 2001. Phoneme and grapheme: How parallel can they be? *LACUS Forum* 27. 307–316.

Logan, Robert K. [1986] 2004. *The alphabet effect: A media ecology understanding of the making of Western civilization*. New York: Hampton Press.

Longcamp, Marieke, Marie-Thérèse Zerbato-Poudou & Jean-Luc Velay. 2005. The influence of writing practice on letter recognition in preschool children: A comparison between handwriting and typing. *Acta Psychologica* 119(1). 67–79. https://doi.org/10.1016/j.actpsy.2004.10.019

Longcamp, Marieke, Yevhen Hlushchuk & Riita Hari. 2011. What differs in visual recognition of handwritten vs. printed letters? An fMRI study. *Human Brain Mapping* 32(8). 1250–1259. https://doi.org/10.1002/hbm.21105

Ludwig, Otto. 2007. Skripte. Konturen einer Konzeption. *Zeitschrift für germanistische Linguistik* 35(3). 376–396. https://doi.org/10.1515/zgl.2007.025

Lund, Ole. 1999. *Knowledge construction in typography: The case of legibility research and the legibility of sans serif typefaces*. Reading: University of Reading dissertation.

Lüpke, Friederike. 2011. Orthography development. In Peter Austoin & Julia Sallabank (eds.), *Handbook of endangered languages*, 312–336. Cambridge: Cambridge University Press. https://doi.org/10.1017/CBO9780511975981.016

Lurija, Aleksandr R. 1976. *Cognitive development: Its cultural and social foundations*. Cambridge: Havard University Press.

Lurija, Aleksandr R. 1977. The development of writing in the child. *Soviet Psychology* 16(2). 65–114. https://doi.org/10.2753/RPO1061-0405160265
Lyons, John. [1981] 1992. *Die Sprache*, 4th rev. edn. München: Beck.
Maas, Utz. 1992. *Grundzüge der deutschen Orthographie*. (Reihe Germanistische Linguistik 120). Tübingen: Niemeyer. https://doi.org/10.1515/9783111376974
Maas, Utz. 2010. Literat und orat. Grundbegriffe der Analyse geschriebener und gesprochener Sprache. *Grazer Linguistische Studien* 73. 21–150.
Maas, Utz. 2015. Vom Sinn der Rechtschreibung. *Networx* 68. http://www.mediensprache.net/networx/networx-68.pdf (accessed 25 September 2021)
Mangen, Anne & Jean-Luc Velay. 2010. Digitizing literacy: Reflections on the haptics of writing. In Mehrdad Hosseini Zadeh (ed.), *Advances in haptics*, 385–401. Rijeka: InTech. https://doi.org/10.5772/8710
Manolitsis, George, George K. Georgiou, Tomohiro Inoue & Rauno Parrila. 2019. Are morphological awareness and literacy skills reciprocally related? Evidence from a cross-linguistic study. *Journal of Educational Psychology* 111(8). 1362–1381. https://doi.org/10.1037/edu0000354
Martinet, André. 1962. *A functional view of language*. London: Clarendon Press.
Masayuki, Tsukimoto. 2009. The development of Japanese kana. *Scripta* 1. 45–59.
McCarthy, Suzanne. 1995. The Cree syllabary and the writing system riddle: A paradigm in crisis. In Insup Taylor & David R. Olson (eds.), *Scripts and literacy: Reading and learning to read alphabets, syllabaries and characters*, 59–75. (Neuropsychology and Cognition 7). Dordrecht: Springer. https://doi.org/10.1007/978-94-011-1162-1_5
McCawley, James D. 1994. Some graphotactic constraints. In William C. Watt (ed.), *Writing systems and cognition*, 115–127. (Neuropsychology and Cognition 6). Dordrecht: Springer. https://doi.org/10.1007/978-94-015-8285-8_7
McClelland, James L. & David E. Rumelhart. 1981. An Interactive Activation Model of context effects in letter perception: Part 1. An account of basic findings. *Psychological Review* 88(5). 375–407. https://doi.org/10.1037/0033-295X.88.5.375
McLuhan, Marshall. 1962. *The Gutenberg galaxy: The making of typographic man*. Toronto: University of Toronto Press.
McLuhan, Marshall. 1964. *Understanding media: The extensions of man*. New York: McGraw-Hill.
Medwell, Jane & David Wray. 2008. Handwriting – A forgotten language skill? *Language and Education* 22(1). 34–47. https://doi.org/10.2167/le722.0
Meier, Thomas, Michael R. Ott & Rebecca Sauer. 2015. *Materiale Textkulturen: Konzepte – Materialien – Praktiken*. (Materiale Textkulturen 1). Berlin/Boston: De Gruyter. https://doi.org/10.1515/9783110371291
Meisenburg, Trudel. 1996. *Romanische Schriftsysteme im Vergleich: Eine diachrone Studie* (ScriptOralia 82). Tübingen: Narr.
Meletis, Dimitrios. 2015. *Graphetik: Form und Materialität von Schrift*. (Typo|Druck). Glückstadt: Verlag Werner Hülsbusch. https://resolver.obvsg.at/urn:nbn:at:at-ubg:3-6661
Meletis, Dimitrios. 2017. Review of U. Domahs & B. Primus (eds.). 2016. Handbuch Laut, Gebärde, Buchstabe. *Zeitschrift für Rezensionen zur germanistischen Sprachwissenschaft* 9(1–2). 109–115. https://doi.org/10.1515/zrs-2017-0019
Meletis, Dimitrios. 2018. What is natural in writing? Prolegomena to a Natural Grapholinguistics. *Written Language & Literacy* 21(1). 52–88. https://doi.org/10.1075/wll.00010.mel

Meletis, Dimitrios. 2019. The grapheme as a universal basic unit of writing. *Writing Systems Research* 11(1). 26–49. https://doi.org/10.1080/17586801.2019.1697412

Meletis, Dimitrios. 2020a. *The nature of writing. A theory of grapholinguistics.* (Grapholinguistics and Its Applications 3). Brest: Fluxus Éditions. https://doi.org/10.36824/2020-meletis

Meletis, Dimitrios. 2020b. Types of allography. *Open Linguistics* 6. 249–266. https://doi.org/10.1515/opli-2020-0006

Meletis, Dimitrios. 2020c. Warum hassen alle Comic Sans? Metapragmatische Onlinediskurse zu einer typographischen Hassliebe. In Jannis Androutsopoulos & Florian Busch (eds.), *Register des Graphischen: Variation, Interaktion und Reflexion in der digitalen Schriftlichkeit*, 253–284. Boston/Berlin: De Gruyter. https://doi.org/10.1515/9783110673241-010

Meletis, Dimitrios. 2020d. Reintroducing graphetics: The study of the materiality of writing. *Scripta* 11. 91–132.

Meletis, Dimitrios. 2021a. On being a grapholinguist. In Yannis Haralambous (ed.), *Grapholinguistics in the 21st Century, Proceedings, Part I, Paris, France, 2020*, 47–62. (Grapholinguistics and Its Applications 4). Brest: Fluxus Éditions. https://doi.org/10.36824/2020-graf-mele

Meletis, Dimitrios. 2021b. 'Is your font racist?' – Metapragmatic online discourses on the use of typographic mimicry and its appropriateness. *Social Semiotics*. https://doi.org/10.1080/10350330.2021.1989296

Meletis, Dimitrios. In press. Universality and diversity in writing systems. *LACUS Forum* 46.

Mesch, Birgit & Christina Noack. 2016. System, Norm und Gebrauch – drei Seiten derselben Medaille? In Birgit Mesch & Christina Noack (eds.), *System, Norm und Gebrauch – drei Seiten derselben Medaille? Orthographische Kompetenz und Performanz zwischen System, Norm und Empirie*, 1–8. Baltmannsweiler: Schneider Hohengehren.

Mignolo, Walter. 1989. Literacy and colonization: The new world experience. In René Jara & Nicholas Spadaccini (eds.), *1492–1992: Re/Discovering colonial writing*, 51–96. (Hispanic Issues 4). Minneapolis: Prisma Institute.

Mihm, Arend. 2016. Zur Theorie der vormodernen Orthographien: Straßburger Schreibsysteme als Erkenntnisgrundlage. *Sprachwissenschaft* 41(3–4). 271–309.

Miton, Helena & Olivier Morin. 2021. Graphic complexity in writing systems. *Cognition* 214. https://doi.org/10.1016/j.cognition.2021.104771

Morais, José. 2021. The phoneme: A conceptual heritage from alphabetic literacy. *Cognition* 213. https://doi.org/10.1016/j.cognition.2021.104740

Morford, Jill P., Erin Wilkinson, Agnes Villwock, Pilar Piñar & Judith F. Kroll. 2011. When deaf signers read English: Do written words activate their sign translations? *Cognition* 118(2). 286–292. https://doi.org/10.1016/j.cognition.2010.11.006

Morin, Olivier. 2018. Spontaneous emergence of legibility in writing systems: The case of orientation anisotropy. *Cognitive Science* 42(2). 664–677. https://doi.org/10.1111/cogs.12550

Mueller, Pam A., & Daniel M. Oppenheimer. 2014. The pen is mightier than the keyboard: Advantages of longhand over laptop note taking. *Psychological Science* 25(6). 1159–1168. https://doi.org/10.1177/0956797614524581

Murphy, Keith M. 2017. Fontroversy! Or, How to care about the shape of language. In Jillian R. Cavanaugh & Shalini Shankbar (eds.), *Language and materiality. Ethnographic and theoretical explorations*, 63–86. Cambridge: Cambridge University Press. https://doi.org/10.1017/9781316848418.004

Myers, James. 2019. *The grammar of Chinese characters: Productive knowledge of formal patterns in an orthographic system*. London: Routledge.
Naumann, Carl L. 1989. *Gesprochenes Deutsch und Orthographie. Linguistische und didaktische Studien zur Rolle der gesprochenen Sprache im System und Erwerb der Rechtschreibung*. (Theorie und Vermittlung der Sprache 8). Frankfurt a. M.: Peter Lang.
Nawar, Haytham. 2020. *Language of tomorrow: Towards a transcultural visual communication system in a posthuman condition*. Bristol/Chicago: Intellect.
Neef, Martin. 2005. *Die Graphematik des Deutschen*. (Linguistische Arbeiten 500). Berlin/Boston: De Gruyter. https://doi.org/10.1515/9783110914856
Neef, Martin. 2015. Writing systems as modular objects: Proposals for theory design in grapholinguistics. *Open Linguistics* 1. 708–721. https://doi.org/10.1515/opli-2015-0026
Neef, Martin & Beatrice Primus. 2001. Stumme Zeugen der Autonomie – Eine Replik auf Ossner. *Linguistische Berichte* 187. 353–378.
Neef, Sonja. 2008. *Abdruck und Spur. Handschrift im Zeitalter ihrer technischen Reproduzierbarkeit*. Berlin: Kulturverlag Kadmos.
Neef, Sonja. 2011. *Imprint and trace. Handwriting in the age of technology*. Translated by Anthony Mathews. London: Reaktion Books.
Nerius, Dieter. 2007. Begriff und Merkmale der Orthographie. In Dieter Nerius (ed.), *Deutsche Orthographie*, 4th edn., 30–40. Hildesheim: Olms.
Nerius, Dieter. 2020. Kodifikation der Schreibung. In Thomas Niehr, Jörg Kilian & Jürgen Schiewe (eds.), *Handbuch Sprachkritik*, 368–375. Stuttgart: Metzler. https://doi.org/10.1007/978-3-476-04852-3_46
Nerius, Dieter & Gerhard Augst (eds.). 1988. *Probleme der geschriebenen Sprache. Beiträge zur Schriftlinguistik auf dem XIV. internationalen Linguistenkongreß 1987 in Berlin*. (Linguistische Studien, A 173). Berlin: Akademie der Wissenschaften der DDR.
Nöth, Winfried. 1990. *Handbook of semiotics*. (Advances in Semiotics). Indiana: Indiana University Press.
Nottbusch, Guido. 2008. *Handschriftliche Sprachproduktion: Sprachstrukturelle und ontogenetische Aspekte*. (Linguistische Arbeiten 524). Tübingen: Niemeyer. https://doi.org/10.1515/9783484970717
Nunberg, Geoffrey, Ted Briscoe & Rodney Huddleston. 2002. Punctuation. In Rodney Huddleston & Geoffrey Pullum (eds.), *The Cambridge grammar of the English language*, 1723–1764. Cambridge: Cambridge University Press. https://doi.org/10.1017/9781316423530.021
Nunberg, Geoffrey. 1990. *The linguistics of punctuation*. Stanford: CSLI Publications.
Ochs, Elinor. 1979. Planned and unplanned discourse. In Talmy Givon (ed.), *Discourse and syntax*, 51–80. Leiden: Brill. https://doi.org/10.1163/9789004368897_004
Olson, David R. 1977. Oral and written language and the cognitive processes of children. *Journal of Communication* 27(3). 10–26. https://doi.org/10.1111/j.1460-2466.1977.tb02119.x
Olson, David R. 1994. *The world on paper: The conceptual and cognitive implications of reading and writing*. Cambridge: Cambridge University Press.
Olson, David R. 2002. What writing does to the mind. In Eric Amsel & James P. Byrnes (eds.), *Language, literacy, and cognitive development: The development and consequences of symbolic communication*, 159–171. Mahwah, NJ: Lawrence Erlbaum Associates.
Olson, David R. 2016. *The mind on paper: Reading, consciousness and rationality*. Cambridge: Cambridge University Press. https://doi.org/10.1017/CBO9781316678466
Ong, Walter J. [1982] 2012. *Orality and literacy: The technologizing of the word*, 30th anniversary edn., with additional chapters by John Hartley. London/New York: Routledge.

Osterkamp, Sven & Gordian Schreiber. 2021. Challenging the dichotomy between phonography and morphography: Transitions and gray areas. In Yannis Haralambous (ed.), *Grapholinguistics in the 21st Century, Proceedings, Part I, Paris, France, 2020*, 47–82. (Grapholinguistics and Its Applications 4). Brest: Fluxus Éditions. https://doi.org/10.36824/2020-graf-oste

Otake, Shoko, Rebecca Treiman & Li Yin. 2017. Differentiation of writing and drawing by U.S. two- to five-year-olds. *Cognitive Development* 43. 119–128. https://doi.org/10.1016/j.cogdev.2017.03.004

Pacton, Sébastien, Amélie Sobaco, Michel Fayol & Rebecca Treiman. 2013. How does graphotactic knowledge influence children's learning of new spellings? *Frontiers in Psychology* 4. 701. https://doi.org/10.3389/fpsyg.2013.00701

Pae, Hye K. 2011. Is Korean a syllabic alphabet or an alphabetic syllabary. *Writing Systems Research* 3(2). 103–115. https://doi.org/10.1093/wsr/wsr002

Pae, Hye K., Sungbong Bae & Kwangoh Yi. 2019. Is the consonant primacy script-universal or script-specific? Evidence from non-Roman script Korean Hangul. *Reading and Writing* 32. 1085–1106. https://doi.org/10.1007/s11145-018-9896-8

Page, Christina J. 2013. A new orthography in an unfamiliar script: A case study in participatory engagement strategies. *Journal of Multilingual and Multicultural Development* 34(5). 459–474. https://doi.org/10.1080/01434632.2013.783035

Parush, Shula, Vered Pindak, Jeri Hahn-Markowitz & Tal Mazor-Karsenty. 1998. Does fatigue influence children's handwriting performance? *Work* 11(3). 307–313. https://doi.org/10.3233/WOR-1998-11307

Patel, Purushottam G. 2010. *The Brahmi writing system: Cross-fertilizing epigraphy, archaeology and linguistics*. New Delhi: Black & White.

Patel, Purushottam G., Pramod Pandey, & Dilip Rajgor (eds.). 2007. *The Indic scripts: Palaeographic and linguistic perspectives*. New Delhi: D. K. Printworld.

Paul, Hermann. 1891. *Principles of the history of language*. London: Longmans, Green and Co.

Pelli, Denis G., Catherine W. Burns, Bart Farell & Deborah C. Moore-Page. 2006. Feature detection and letter identification. *Vision Research* 46(28). 4646–4674. https://doi.org/10.1016/j.visres.2006.04.023

Petit, Jean-Philippe, Katherine J. Midgley, Philipp J. Holcomb & Janathan Grainger. 2006. On the time course of letter perception: A masked priming ERP investigation. *Psychonomic Bulletin & Review* 13(4). 674–681. https://doi.org/10.3758/BF03193980

Petitto, Laura A., Clifton Langdon, Adam Stone, Diana Andriola, Geo Kartheiser & Casey Cochran. 2016. Visual sign phonology: Insights into human reading and language from a natural soundless phonology. *WIREs Cognitive Science* 7. 366–381. https://doi.org/10.1002/wcs.1404

Pettersson, John Sören. 1991. *Critique of evolutionary accounts of writing*. (Reports from Uppsala University Linguistics 21). Uppsala: Department of Linguistics, Uppsala University.

Plaut, David C., James L. McClelland, Mark S. Seidenberg & Karalyn Patterson. 1996. Understanding normal and impaired word reading: Computational principles in quasi-regular domains. *Psychological Review* 103(1). 56–115. https://doi.org/10.1037/0033-295X.103.1.56

Poser, William J. 1992. The structural typology of phonological writing. Paper presented at the annual meeting of the Linguistic Society of America, Philadelphia, 12 January, 1992.

Posner, Roland (ed.). 1990. *Warnungen an die ferne Zukunft: Atommüll als Kommunikationsproblem*. (Raben Streifzüge). München: Raben.

Powell, Barry B. 2009. *Writing: Theory and history of the technology of civilization*. Oxford/Malden: Wiley-Blackwell. https://doi.org/10.1002/9781118293515

Primus, Beatrice. 2003. Zum Silbenbegriff in der Schrift-, Laut- und Gebärdensprache – Versuch einer mediumübergreifenden Fundierung. *Zeitschrift für Sprachwissenschaft* 23(1). 3–55. https://doi.org/10.1515/zfsw.2003.22.1.3

Primus, Beatrice. 2004. A featural analysis of the Modern Roman Alphabet. *Written Language & Literacy* 7(2). 235–274. https://doi.org/10.1075/wll.7.2.06pri

Primus, Beatrice. 2006. Buchstabenkomponenten und ihre Grammatik. In Ursula Bredel & Hartmut Günther (eds.), *Orthographietheorie und Rechtschreibunterricht*, 5–43. (Linguistische Arbeiten 509). Tübingen: Niemeyer. https://doi.org/10.1515/9783110921199.5

Primus, Beatrice. 2007. The typological and historical variation of punctuation systems: Comma constraints. *Written Language & Literacy* 10(2). 103–128. https://doi.org/10.1075/wll.10.2.07pri

Primus, Beatrice. 2010. Strukturelle Grundlagen des deutschen Schriftsystems. In Ursula Bredel, Astrid Müller & Gabriele Hinney (eds.), *Schriftsystem und Schrifterwerb: linguistisch – didaktisch – empirisch*, 9–46. (Reihe Germanistische Linguistik 289). Berlin/Boston: De Gruyter. https://doi.org/10.1515/9783110232257.9

Ratcliffe, Robert R. 2001. What do "phonemic" writing systems represent? Arabic Huruuf, Japanese Kana, and the moraic principle. *Written Language & Literacy* 4(1). 1–14. https://doi.org/10.1075/wll.4.1.02rat

Rayner, Keith & Erik D. Reichle. 2010. Models of the reading process. *WIREs Cognitive Science* 1(6). 787–799. https://doi.org/10.1002/wcs.68

Reinken, Niklas. 2018. Die Längenhierarchie in Hand- und Unterschriften. *Deutsche Sprache* 18(4). 336–365. https://doi.org/10.37307/j.1868-775X.2018.04.04

Reißig, Tilo. 2015. *Typographie und Grammatik: Untersuchung zum Verhältnis von Syntax und Raum*. (Stauffenburg Linguistik 84). Tübingen: Stauffenburg.

Rey, Arnaud, Stéphane Dufau, Stéphanie Massol & Jonathan Grainger. 2009. Testing computational models of letter perception with item-level event-related potentials. *Cognitive Neuropsychology* 26(1). 7–22. https://doi.org/10.1080/09541440802176300

Rezec, Oliver. 2009. *Zur Struktur des deutschen Schriftsystems: Warum das Graphem nicht drei Funktionen gleichzeitig haben kann, warum ein* <a> *kein* <ɑ> *ist und andere Konstruktionsfehler des etablierten Beschreibungsmodells. Ein Verbesserungsvorschlag*. München: Ludwig-Maximilians-Universität dissertation. https://doi.org/10.5282/edoc.10730

Rezec, Oliver. 2010. Der vermeintliche Zusammenhang zwischen Buchstabenformen und Lautwerten. Erwiderung auf einige Thesen von B. Primus. *Linguistische Berichte* 223. 343–366.

Rezec, Oliver. 2011. Der vermeintliche Zusammenhang zwischen Buchstabenformen und Lautwerten. Zweite Erwiderung. *Linguistische Berichte* 225. 89–100.

Rezec, Oliver. 2013. Ein differenzierteres Strukturmodell des deutschen Schriftsystems. *Linguistische Berichte* 234. 227–254.

Rimzhim, Anurag, Leonard Katz & Carol A. Fowler. 2014. Brāhmī-derived orthographies are typologically Āksharik but functionally predominantly alphabetic. *Writing Systems Research* 6(1). 41–53. https://doi.org/10.1080/17586801.2013.855618

Rjeily, Rana. 2011. *Cultural connectives: Bridging the Latin and Arabic alphabets*. New York: Mark Batty Publishers.

Roberts, David. 2011. A tone orthography typology. *Written Language & Literacy* 14(1). 82–108. https://doi.org/10.1075/wll.14.1.05rob
Robertson, John S. 2004. The possibility and actuality of writing. In Stephen D. Houston (ed.), *The first writing: Script invention as history and process*, 16–38. Cambridge: Cambridge University Press.
Robins, Sarah, Rebecca Treiman, Nicole Rosales & Shoko Otake. 2012. Parent-child conversations about letters and pictures. *Reading and Writing* 25(8). 2039–2059. https://doi.org/10.1007/s11145-011-9344-5
Rogers, Henry. 2005. *Writing systems: A linguistic approach*. Oxford: Wiley-Blackwell.
Rosa, Eva, Manuel Perea & Peter Enneson. 2016. The role of letter features in visual-word recognition: Evidence from a delayed segment technique. *Acta Psychologica* 169. 133–142. https://doi.org/10.1016/j.actpsy.2016.05.016
Rumelhart, David E. & Patricia Siple. 1974. Process of recognizing tachistoscopically presented words. *Psychological Review* 81. 99–118. https://doi.org/10.1037/h0036117
Safadi, Yasin H. 1978. *Islamic calligraphy*. London: Thames & Hudson.
Sakamoto, T. & Kiyoshi Makita. 1973. Japan. In John Downing (ed.), *Comparative reading: Cross-national studies of behavior in reading and writing*, 440–465. New York: Macmillan.
Salomon, Richard G. 2000. Typological observations on the Indic script group and its relationship to other alphasyllabaries. *Studies in the Linguistic Sciences* 30(1). 87–104.
Salomon, Richard. 2012. Some principles and patterns of script change. In Stephen D. Houston (ed.), *The shape of script: How and why writing systems change*, 119–133. Santa Fe: School for Advanced Research Press.
Sampson, Geoffrey. 1994. Chinese script and the diversity of writing systems. *Linguistics* 32. 117–132. https://doi.org/10.1515/ling.1994.32.1.117
Sampson, Geoffrey. [1985] 2015. *Writing systems. A linguistic introduction*, 2nd edn. Sheffield/Bristol: Equinox.
Sampson, Geoffrey. 2016a. Typology and the study of writing systems. *Linguistic Typology* 20(3). 561–567. https://doi.org/10.1515/lingty-2016-0027
Sampson, Geoffrey. 2016b. Writing systems: Methods for recording language. In Keith Allan (ed.), *The Routledge handbook of linguistics*, 47–61. London/New York: Routledge.
Sampson, Geoffrey. 2018. From phonemic spelling to distinctive spelling. *Written Language & Literacy* 21(1). 3–25. https://doi.org/10.1075/wll.00008.sam
Sandler, Wendy & Diane Lillo-Martin. 2006. *Sign language and linguistic universals*. Cambridge: Cambridge University Press. https://doi.org/10.1017/CBO9781139163910
Sato, Hitomi. 2015. Do different orthographies share the same mechanisms of reading? A review of research on and models for Japanese acquired dyslexia. *Aphasiology* 29(10). 1189–1218. https://doi.org/10.1080/02687038.2015.1034084
Saussure, Ferdinand de. 1916. *Cours de linguistique générale*. Lausanne/Paris: Payot.
Scancarelli, Janine. 1996. Cherokee writing. In Peter T. Daniels & William Bright (eds.), *The world's writing systems*, 587–592. Oxford: Oxford University Press.
Scharnhorst, Jürgen. 1988. Die graphische Ebene im Modell des Sprachsystems. In Dieter Nerius & Gerhard Augst (eds.), *Probleme der geschriebenen Sprache. Beiträge zur Schriftlinguistik auf dem XIV. internationalen Linguistenkongreß 1987 in Berlin*, 87–102. (Linguistische Studien, A 173). Berlin: Akademie der Wissenschaften der DDR.

Scheerer, Eckart. 1993. Mündlichkeit und Schriftlichkeit – Implikationen für die Modellierung kognitiver Prozesse. In Jürgen Baurmann, Hartmut Günther & Ulrich Knoop (eds.), *homo scribens. Perspektiven der Schriftlichkeitsforschung*, 141–176. (Reihe Germanistische Linguistik 134). Tübingen: Niemeyer. https://doi.org/10.1515/9783111377087.141

Scheffler, Christian. 1994. Kalligraphie. In Hartmut Günther & Otto Ludwig (eds.), *Schrift und Schriftlichkeit/Writing and its use*, vol. 1, 228–255. (Handbooks of Linguistics and Communication Science 10.1). Berlin/Boston: De Gruyter. https://doi.org/10.1515/9783110111293.1.2.228

Schimmel-Fijalkowytsch, Nadine. 2018. *Diskurse zur Normierung und Reform der deutschen Rechtschreibung. Eine Analyse von Diskursen zur Rechtschreibreform unter soziolinguistischer und textlinguistischer Perspektive.* (Studien zur deutschen Sprache 75). Tübingen: Narr.

Schmidt, Karsten. 2016. <Der graphematische Satz.> Vom Schreibsatz zur allgemeinen Satzvorstellung. *Zeitschrift für germanistische Linguistik* 44(2). 215–256. https://doi.org/10.1515/zgl-2016-0011

Schmidt, Karsten. 2018. *Phonographie und Morphographie im Deutschen. Grundzüge einer wortbasierten Graphematik.* (Stauffenburg Linguistik 107). Tübingen: Stauffenburg.

Schmitt, Alfred. 1980. *Entstehung und Entwicklung von Schriften*, ed. by Claus Haebler. Köln/Wien: Böhlau.

Schreiber, Gordian. Submitted. Visual politeness: Remarks on cursivization as found in pre-modern Japanese handbooks on letter writing. In *The idea of writing*, vol. 4. Leiden: Brill.

Schroeder, Klaus-Henning. 1981. Schrifttheorie und Konnotation der Schriftzeichen. In Thomas Kotschi (ed.), *Beiträge zur Linguistik des Französischen*, 123–140. (Tübinger Beiträge zur Linguistik 154). Tübingen: Narr.

Schwellnus, Heidi, Debra Cameron & Heather Carnahan. 2012. Which to choose: Manuscript or cursive handwriting? A review of the literature. *Journal of Occupational Therapy, Schools, & Early Intervention* 5(3–4). 248–258. https://doi.org/10.1080/19411243.2012.744651

Scott, Graham G., Jason Sinclair, Emma Short & Gillian Bruce. 2014. It's not what you say, it's how you say it: Language use on Facebook impacts employability but not attractiveness. *Cyberpsychology, Behavior, and Social Networking* 17(8). 1–5. https://doi.org/10.1089/cyber.2013.0584

Scribner, Sylvia & Michael Cole. 1981. *The psychology of literacy.* Cambridge: Harvard University Press.

Sebba, Mark. 2007. *Spelling and society: The culture and politics of orthography around the world.* Cambridge: Cambridge University Press. https://doi.org/10.1017/CBO9780511486739

Sebba, Mark. 2009. Sociolinguistic approaches to writing systems research. *Writing Systems Research* 1(1). 35–49. https://doi.org/10.1093/wsr/wsp002

Selkirk, Elisabeth O. 1984. *Phonology and syntax: The relation between sound and structure.* (Current Studies in Linguistics 10). Cambridge: MIT Press.

Senner, Wayne M. (ed.). 1991. *The origins of writing*. Lincoln: University of Nebraska Press.

Share, David L. 2008. On the Anglocentricities of current reading research and practice: The perils of overreliance on an "outlier" orthography. *Psychological Bulletin* 134(4). 584–615. https://doi.org/10.1037/0033-2909.134.4.584

Share, David L. 2014. Alphabetism in reading science. *Frontiers in Psychology* 5. 752. https://doi.org/10.3389/fpsyg.2014.00752

Share, David L. & Peter T. Daniels. 2016. Aksharas, alphasyllabaries, abugidas, alphabets and orthographic depth: Reflections on Rimzhim, Katz and Fowler (2014). *Writing Systems Research* 8(1). 17–31. https://doi.org/10.1080/17586801.2015.1016395
Shepherd, Margaret. 2011. *Learn world calligraphy*. New York: Watson-Guptill.
Shu, Hua & Richard C. Anderson. 1999. Learning to read Chinese: The development of metalinguistic awareness. In Jian Wang, Albrecht W. Inhoff & Hsuan-Chih Chen (eds.), *Reading Chinese script: A cognitive analysis*, 1–18. Mahwah: Lawrence Erlbaum.
Sirat, Colette. 1994. Handwriting and the writing hand. In William C. Watt (ed.), *Writing systems and cognition*, 375–460. (Neuropsychology and Cognition 6). Dordrecht: Springer. https://doi.org/10.1007/978-94-015-8285-8_18
Smith, Janet S. (Shibamoto). 1996. Japanese writing. In Peter T. Daniels & William Bright (eds.), *The world's writing systems*, 209–217. Oxford: Oxford University Press.
Spitzmüller, Jürgen. 2013. *Graphische Variation als soziale Praxis. Eine soziolinguistische Theorie skripturaler ‚Sichtbarkeit'*. (Linguistik – Impulse & Tendenzen 56). Berlin/Boston: De Gruyter. https://doi.org/10.1515/9783110334241
Spitzmüller, Jürgen. 2015. Graphic variation and graphic ideologies: A metapragmatic approach. *Social Semiotics* 25(2). 126–141. https://doi.org/10.1080/10350330.2015.1010323
Spitzmüller, Jürgen. 2016a. Typographie. In Christa Dürscheid, *Einführung in die Schriftlinguistik*, 5th edn., 209–241. (UTB 3740). Göttingen: Vandenhoeck & Ruprecht.
Spitzmüller, Jürgen. 2016b. Schrift als materielles, soziales und ideologisches Phänomen. In Jürgen Schiewe (ed.), *Angemessenheit. Einsichten in Sprachgebräuche*, 97–110. Göttingen: Wallstein.
Sproat, Richard. 2000. *A computational theory of writing systems*. (Studies in Natural Language Processing). Cambridge: Cambridge University Press.
Stetter, Christian. 1994. Orthographie als Normierung des Schriftsystems. In Hartmut Günther & Otto Ludwig (eds.), *Schrift und Schriftlichkeit/Writing and its use*, vol. 1, 687–697. (Handbooks of Linguistics and Communication Science 10.1). Berlin/Boston: De Gruyter. https://doi.org/10.1515/9783110111293.1.6.687
Stjernfelt, Frederik. 1993. Buchstabenformen, Kategorien und die Apriori-Position. Ein Essay in angewandter Grammatologie. In Hans U. Gumbrecht & K. Ludwig Pfeiffer (eds.), *Schrift*, 289–310. (Materialität der Zeichen A 12). München: Wilhelm Fink.
Stöckl, Hartmut. 2004. Typographie: Körper und Gewand des Textes. Linguistische Überlegungen zu typographischer Gestaltung. *Zeitschrift für Angewandte Linguistik* 41. 5–48.
Stöckl, Hartmut. 2005. Typography: Body and dress of a text – A signing mode between language and image. *Visual Communication* 4(2). 204–214. https://doi.org/10.1177/1470357205053403
Stokoe, William C. 1960. *Sign language structure: An outline of the visual communication systems of the American Deaf*. Buffalo: Dept. of Anthropology and Linguistics, University of Buffalo.
Stötzner, Andreas. 2003. Signography as a subject in its own right. *Visual Communication* 2(3). 285–302. https://doi.org/10.1177/14703572030023003
Strätling, Susanne & Georg Witte. 2006. Die Sichtbarkeit der Schrift zwischen Evidenz, Phänomenalität und Ikonizität. Zur Einführung in diesen Band. In Susanne Strätling & Georg Witte (eds.), *Die Sichtbarkeit der Schrift*, 7–20. (Kulturtechnik). München: Wilhelm Fink.
Street, Brian V. 1984. *Literacy in theory and practice*. New York: Cambridge University Press.
Street, Brian V. 1993. The new literacy studies. *Journal of Research in Reading* 16(2). 81–97. https://doi.org/10.1111/j.1467-9817.1993.tb00039.x

Street, Brian V. 1995. *Social literacies: Critical approaches to literacy in development, ethnography and education*. London/New York: Routledge.

Street, Brian V. & Adam Lefstein. 2007. *Literacy: An advanced research book for students*. London/New York: Routledge.

Sülzenbrück, Sandra, Mathias Hegele, Gerhard Rinkenauer & Herbert Heuer. 2011. The death of handwriting: Secondary effects of frequent computer use on basic motor skills. *Journal of Motor Behavior* 43(3). 247–251. https://doi.org/10.1080/00222895.2011.571727

Taft, Marcus, Xiaoping Zhu & Danling Peng. 1999. Positional specificity of radicals in Chinese character recognition. *Journal of Memory and Language* 40(4). 498–519. https://doi.org/10.1006/jmla.1998.2625

Takagi, Mariko. 2014. *Hanzi graphy: A typographic translation between Latin letters and Chinese characters*. Berlin: form+zweck.

Takagi, Mariko. 2016. *Kanji Graphy: Typographische Begegnungen zwischen Japan und dem Westen*. Berlin: form+zweck.

Tamariz, Mónica & Simon Kirby. 2015. Culture: Copying, compression, and conventionality. *Cognitive Science* 39. 171–183. https://doi.org/10.1111/cogs.12144

Tannen, Deborah (ed.). 1982. *Spoken and written language: Exploring orality and literacy*. Norwood, NJ: Ablex Publishing Corporation.

Taverna Livia, Tremolada Marta, Sabattini Francesca. 2020. Drawing and writing. Learning of graphical representational systems in early childhood. In Enrico Cicalò (ed.), *Proceedings of the 2nd International and Interdisciplinary Conference on Image and Imagination. IMG 2019*, 216–229. Cham: Springer. https://doi.org/10.1007/978-3-030-41018-6_20

Taylor, Insup & Martin M. Taylor. 2014. *Writing and literacy in Chinese, Korean and Japanese*, revised edn. Amsterdam/Philadelphia: John Benjamins. https://doi.org/10.1075/swll.14

Taylor, Isaac. 1883. *The alphabet: An account of the origin and development of letters*, vol. 1: Semitic alphabet, vol. 2: *Aryan alphabets*. London: Kegan Paul, Trench.

Thiessen, Myra, Marl Kohler, Owen Churches, Scott Coussens & Hannah Keage. 2015. Brainy type: A look at how the brain processes typographic information. *Visible Language* 49(1–2). 175–189.

Thomassen, Arnold J. W. M. & Hein J. C. M. Tibosch. 1991. A quantitative model of graphic production. In Jean Requin & George E. Stelmach (eds.), *Tutorials in motor neuroscience*, 269–281. (NATO ASI Series, Behavioural and Social Sciences 62). Dordrecht: Springer. https://doi.org/10.1007/978-94-011-3626-6_22

Tillmann, Hans Günther & Hartmut Günther. 1986. Zum Zusammenhang von natur- und geisteswissenschaftlicher Sprachforschung – Phonetik und Phonologie. *Zeitschrift für Sprachwissenschaft* 5(2). 187–208. https://doi.org/10.1515/zfsw.1986.5.2.187

Tinker, Miles A. 1963. *The legibility of print*. Ames: Iowa State University Press.

Tokovinine, Alexandre. 2017. "Beginner's visual catalog of Maya hieroglyphs". https://www.mesoweb.com/resources/catalog/Tokovinine_Catalog.pdf (accessed 8 September 2021)

Tolchinsky, Liliana. 2003. *The cradle of culture and what children know about writing and numbers before being taught*. New York/London: Psychology Press.

Tolchinsky Landsmann, Liliana & Iris Levin. 1985. Writing in preschoolers: An age-related analysis. *Applied Psycholinguistics* 6(3). 319–339. https://doi.org/10.1017/S0142716400006238

Tong, Xiuli, Catherine McBride-Chang, Hua Shu & Anita M-Y. Wong. 2009. Morphological awareness, orthographic knowledge, and spelling errors: Keys to understanding early

Chinese literacy acquisition. *Scientific Studies of Reading* 13(5). 426–452. https://doi.org/10.1080/10888430903162910
Tranter, Nicolas. 2013. Logography and layering: A functional cross-linguistic analysis. *Written Language & Literacy* 16(1). 1–31. https://doi.org/10.1075/wll.16.1.01tra
Treiman, Rebecca & Brett Kessler. 2014. *How children learn to write words*. Oxford: Oxford University Press. https://doi.org/10.1093/acprof:oso/9780199907977.001.0001
Treiman, Rebecca, Kristina Decker & Brett Kessler. 2019. Adults' sensitivity to graphotactic differences within the English vocabulary. *Applied Psycholinguistics* 40(1). 167–182. https://doi.org/10.1017/S0142716418000516
Treiman, Rebecca, Kevin Mulqueeny & Brett Kessler. 2015. Young children's knowledge about the spatial layout of writing. *Writing Systems Research* 7(2). 235–244. https://doi.org/10.1080/17586801.2014.924386
Trigger, Bruce G. 1998. Writing systems: A case study in cultural evolution. *Norwegian Archaeological Review* 31(1). 39–62. https://doi.org/10.1080/00293652.1998.9965618
Unger, Gerard. 2018. *Theory of type design*. Rotterdam: nai010.
Unger, J. Marshall & John DeFrancis. 1995. Logographic and semasiographic writing systems: A critique of Sampson's classification. In Insup Taylor & David R. Olson (eds.), *Scripts and literacy: Reading and learning to read alphabets, syllabaries and characters*, 45–58. (Neuropsychology and Cognition 7). Dordrecht: Springer. https://doi.org/10.1007/978-94-011-1162-1_4
Unseth, Peter. 2005. Sociolinguistic parallels between choosing scripts and languages. *Written Language & Literacy* 8(1). 19–42. https://doi.org/10.1075/wll.8.1.02uns
Vachek, Josef. 1939. Zum Problem der geschriebenen Sprache. *Travaux du Cercle Linguistique de Prague* 8. 94–104.
Vachek, Josef. 1989. *Written language revisited*. Amsterdam/Philadelphia: John Benjamins. https://doi.org/10.1075/z.41
Vater, Heinz. 2001. *Einführung in die Textlinguistik*, 3rd rev. edn. (UTB 1660). München: Fink.
Velan, Hadas & Ram Frost. 2007. Cambridge University versus Hebrew University: The impact of letter transposition on reading English and Hebrew. *Psychonomic Bulletin & Review* 14(5). 913–918. https://doi.org/10.3758/BF03194121
Verhoeven, Ludo & Charles A. Perfetti. 2022. Universals in learning to read across languages and writing systems. *Scientific Studies of Reading* 26(2). 150–164. https://doi.org/10.1080/10888438.2021.1938575
Verhoeven, Ludo & Charles A. Perfetti (eds.). 2017. *Learning to read across Languages and writing systems*. Cambridge: Cambridge University Press. https://doi.org/10.1017/9781316155752
Virl, Hermann. 1949. *Die Entstehung und die Entwicklung der Schrift*. Stuttgart: Blersch.
Voogt, Alex de. 2021. The evolution of writing systems: An introduction. In Nathalie Gontier, Andy Lock & Chris Sinha (eds.), *The Oxford handbook of human symbolic evolution*. Cambridge: Cambridge University Press. https://doi.org/10.1093/oxfordhb/9780198813781.013.35
Voß, Viola. 2003. *Schrifttypologie und das japanische Schriftsystem*. (Berliner Beiträge zur Linguistik 2). Berlin: Weißensee Verlag.
Wajda, Shirley T. 1999. Inscribing the self. *American Quarterly* 51(2). 461–471.
Walker, Sue. 2001. *Typography and language in everyday life: Prescriptions and practices*. (Language in Social Life Series). London: Longman.

Waller, Robert H. W. 1980. Graphic aspects of complex texts: Typography as macropunctuation. In Paul A. Kolers, Merald E. Wrolstad & Herman Bouma (eds.), *Processing of visible language*, vol. 2, 241–253. (Nato Conference Series 13). Boston: Springer. https://doi.org/10.1007/978-1-4684-1068-6_17

Waller, Robert H. W. 1987. Typography and reading strategy. In Bruce K. Britton & Shawn M. Glynn (eds.), *Executive control processes in reading*, 81–106. Hillsdale: Lawrence Erlbaum Associates.

Wang, Li-Chih & Hsien-Ming Yang. 2014. Classifying Chinese children with dyslexia by dual-route and triangle models of Chinese reading. *Research in Developmental Disabilities* 35(11). 2702–2713. https://doi.org/10.1016/j.ridd.2014.07.001

Wang, Ruiming, Shuting Huang, Yacong Zhou & Zhenguang G. Cai. 2020. Chinese character handwriting: A large-scale behavioral study and a database. *Behavioral Research Methods* 52. 82–96. https://doi.org/10.3758/s13428-019-01206-4

Warde, Beatrice. [1932] 1991. Printing should be invisible. In Paul A. Bennett (ed.), *Books and printing: A treasury for typophiles*, 109–114. Savannah: Frederic C. Beil.

Waterfield, Robin. 2002. Translation of Plato's *Phaedrus*. (Oxford World's Classics). Oxford/New York: Oxford University Press.

Watt, William C. 1975. What is the proper characterization of the alphabet? I: Desiderata. *Visible Language* 9(4). 293–327.

Watt, William C. 1980. What is the proper characterization of the alphabet? – II: Composition. *Ars Semeiotica* 3(1). 3–46.

Watt, William C. 1981. What is the proper characterization of the alphabet? – III: Appearance. *Ars Semeiotica* 4(3). 269–313.

Watt, William C. 1983. Mode, modality, and iconic evolution. In Tasso Borbé (ed.), *Semiotics unfolding. Proceedings of the second Congress of the International Association for Semiotic Studies, Vienna, Austria, 1979*, vol. 3, 1543–1550. (Approaches to Semiotics 68). Berlin/Boston: De Gruyter. https://doi.org/10.1515/9783110869897-185

Watt, William C. 1988. What is the proper characterization of the alphabet? IV: Union. *Semiotica* 70(3–4). 199–241. https://doi.org/10.1515/semi.1988.70.3-4.199

Watt, William C. 1994. Evolution, atavism, and plain reasoning. *Semiotica* 98(1–2). 207–218. https://doi.org/10.1515/semi-1994-981-213

Watt, William C. 1999. How to recognize extraterrestrial symbols, when and if. *Semiotica* 125(1–3). 75–82. https://doi.org/10.1515/semi.1999.125.1-3.75

Watt, William C. 2002. What is the proper characterization of the alphabet? V: Transcendence. *Semiotica* 138. 131–178. https://doi.org/10.1515/semi.2002.001

Watt, William C. 2012. What is the proper characterization of the alphabet? VI: Three-finger exercises. *Semiotica* 190. 177–209. https://doi.org/10.1515/sem-2012-0046

Watt, William C. 2015. What is the proper characterization of the alphabet? VII: Sleight of hand. *Semiotica* 207. 65–88. https://doi.org/10.1515/sem-2015-0064

Wehde, Susanne. 2000. *Typographische Kultur. Eine zeichentheoretische und kulturgeschichtliche Studie zur Typographie und ihrer Entwicklung*. (Studien und Texte zur Sozialgeschichte der Literatur 69). Tübingen: Niemeyer. https://doi.org/10.1515/9783110945799

Weingarten, Rüdiger. 2011. Comparative graphematics. *Written Language & Literacy* 14(1). 12–38. https://doi.org/10.1075/wll.14.1.02wei

Wendt, Dirk. 2000. Lesbarkeit von Druckschriften. In Rudolf P. Gorbach (ed.), *Lesen Erkennen. Ein Symposium der Typographischen Gesellschaft München*, 9–63. München: Typographische Gesellschaft München.

Werner, Valentin. 2021. Text-linguistic analysis of performed language: Revisiting and re-modeling Koch and Oesterreicher. *Linguistics* 59(3). 541–575. https://doi.org/10.1515/ling-2021-0036

Whitney, Carol. 2001. How the brain encodes the order of letters in a printed word: The SERIOL model and selective literature review. *Psychonomic Bulletin & Review* 8(2). 221–243. https://doi.org/10.3758/BF03196158

Wickberg, Adam. 2020. New materialism and the intimacy of post-digital handwriting. *Trace* 4. http://tracejournal.net/trace-issues/issue4/05-wickberg.html (accessed 17 October 2021)

Willberg, Hans Peter & Friedrich Forssman. 2010. *Lesetypografie*, 5th edn. Mainz: Hermann Schmidt.

Willberg, Hans Peter & Friedrich Forssman. 2013. *Erste Hilfe in Typographie. Ratgeber für Gestaltung mit Schrift*, 7th edn. Mainz: Hermann Schmidt.

Wilson, Anita. 2000. There's no escape from third-space theory: Borderland discourse and the in-between literacies of prison. In David Barton, Mary Hamilton & Roz Ivanič (eds.), *Situated literacies*, 54–69. London: Routledge.

Winskel, Heather. 2009. Reading in Thai: The case of misaligned vowels. *Reading and Writing* 22(1). 1–24. https://doi.org/10.1007/s11145-007-9100-z

Wittner, Ben, Sascha Thoma & Timm Hartmann (eds.). 2019. *Bi-Scriptual: Typography and graphic design with multiple script systems*. Salenstein: Niggli.

Wittner, Ben. 2019. Script is language is communication. In Ben Wittner, Sascha Thoma & Timm Hartmann (eds.), Bi-*Scriptual: Typography and graphic design with multiple script systems*, 6–8. Salenstein: Niggli.

Wong, Kimberly, Frempongma Wadee, Gali Ellenblum & Michael McCloskey. 2018. The devil's in the g-tails: Deficient letter-shape knowledge and awareness despite massive visual experience. *Journal of Experimental Psychology: Human Perception and Performance* 44(9). 1324–1335. https://doi.org/10.1037/xhp0000532

Wu, Xiaoying, Richard C. Anderson, Wenling Li, Xinchun Wu, Hong Li, Jie Zhang, Qiu Zheng, Jin Zhu, Hua Shu, Wei Jiang, Xi Chen, Qiuying Wang, Li Yin, Yeqin He, Jerome Packard & Janet S. Gaffney. 2009. Morphological awareness and Chinese children's literacy development: An intervention study. *Scientific Studies of Reading* 13(1). 26–52. https://doi.org/10.1080/10888430802631734

Xiao, Wen & Rebecca Treiman. 2012. Iconicity of simple Chinese characters. *Behavior Research Methods* 44(4). 954–960. https://doi.org/10.3758/s13428-012-0191-3

Yagelski, Robert P. n. d. "The oral vs. the literate". https://www.albany.edu/faculty/rpy95/webtext/critique.htm (accessed 12 October 2021)

Yen, Miao-Hsuan, Ralph Radach, Ovid J.-L. Tzeng & Jie-Li Tsai. 2012. Usage of statistical cues for word boundary in reading Chinese. *Reading and Writing* 25(5). 1007–1029. https://doi.org/10.1007/s11145-011-9321-z

Yen, Yuehping. 2005. *Calligraphy and power in contemporary Chinese society*. Oxon: Routledge Curzon.

Yu, Lili & Erik D. Reichle. 2017. Chinese versus English: Insights on cognition during reading. *Trends in Cognitive Sciences* 21(10). 721–724. http://dx.doi.org/10.1016/j.tics.2017.06.004

Zachrisson, Bror. 1965. *Studies in the legibility of printed text*. (Acta Universitatis Stockholmiensis: Stockholm Studies in Educational Psychology 11). Stockholm: Almqvist & Wiksell.

Zepter, Alexandra L. 2014. Zur Körperlichkeit der Schreibhandlung. *OBST* 85. 151–168.

Zhang, Haiwai. 2014. A review of stroke order in hanzi handwriting. *Journal of the European Confederation of Language Centres in Higher Education* (CercleS) 4(2). 423–440. https://doi.org/10.1515/cercles-2014-0022

Zhao, Shouhui & Richard B. Baldauf. 2007. *Planning Chinese characters: Reaction, evolution or revolution?* New York/London: Springer. https://doi.org/10.1007/978-0-387-48576-8

Subject index

https://doi.org/10.1515/9783110757835-009

Name index

https://doi.org/10.1515/9783110757835-010

www.ingramcontent.com/pod-product-compliance
Lightning Source LLC
Chambersburg PA
CBHW050514170426
43201CB00013B/1957

* 9 7 8 3 1 1 1 6 3 1 7 6 9 *